# Shifting Sites of Practice

## Field Education in Canada

**Julie Drolet** | **Natalie Clark** | **Helen Allen**
Thompson Rivers University     Thompson Rivers University     Vancouver Community College

# Shifting Sites of Practice

## Field Education in Canada

**Pearson Canada**
Toronto

**Library and Archives Canada Cataloguing in Publication**

Drolet, Julie, 1971–
    Shifting sites of practice : field education in
Canada / Julie Drolet, Natalie Clark, Helen Allen.

Includes index.
ISBN 978-0-13-701341-8

    1. Social service—Fieldwork—Canada. 2. Social work
education—Canada. I. Clark, Natalie, 1968– II. Allen,
Helen, 1950– III. Title.

HV11.8.C3D76 2012          361.3'20971          C2010-905923-9

ISBN 978-0-13-701341-8

Vice President, Editorial Director: Gary Bennett
Editor-in-Chief: Ky Pruesse
Editor, Humanities and Social Sciences: Joel Gladstone
Marketing Manager: Lisa Gillis
Developmental Editor: Rema Celio
Project Manager: Cheryl Noseworthy
Production Editor: Raj Singh/MPS
Copy Editor: Deborah Cooper-Bullock
Proofreader: Sally Grover
Composition: MPS Limited, a Macmillan Company
Art Director: Julia Hall
Cover Design: Anthony Leung
Cover Image: PhotoDisc


1 2 3 4 5     15 14 13 12 11


Printed and bound in United States of America.

*This book is dedicated to all field agencies and their staff who welcome students and create the possibility for learning without whom the next generation would not have the opportunity to learn the art of practice.*

# Brief Contents

# Contents

## 11   Distance Field Education: New Technologies and Tools for Learning

### Jessica Ayala, Myra Baynton, and Ellen Perrault   209

## 12   Rural and Remote Field Education: Practice Dynamics in Smaller Communities

### Joanna Pierce and Glen Schmidt   233

# Preface

## PURPOSE AND AUDIENCE FOR THE BOOK

This book offers current theoretical concepts and perspectives that shape field education programs in social work, human service, and child and youth care, and provides examples of practice in the Canadian context. Critical reflection on preparing students for field practice is accompanied by content on strategies and methods that mitigate oppression in practice and educational settings, and promote social justice.

This text is needed for Canadian students to develop understanding about field education issues. Building critical knowledge and practical skills is necessary in social work, human service, child and youth care, and allied health and social service diploma and undergraduate programs, where often studies are focused on the preparation for field education placements. Without an awareness or knowledge of the Canadian field education context, there can be little appreciation for the importance of field education in social work, human service, child and youth care, social service, and allied professional educational programs.

Many professional programs have long recognized the importance of field education as a means for integrating knowledge with practice skills. As professionals in the making, students attend classes to learn practice principles, values and ethical behaviours, a body of specialized knowledge, and the scientific basis for practice. In field instruction, students apply, under supervision, what they have been learning in the classroom to real situations. Thus, the preparation to become a social work or human service professional is composed of formal learning as well as practical experience, sometimes known as field instruction, field placement, field work, a practicum, or an internship. Field education remains an integral and valuable component of the social work, human service, and child and youth care curriculum. It is in the field that material covered in the curriculum gets a real-life examination outside the classroom by providing students with experiential learning.

Professional programs in social work, human service, and child and youth care employ a variety of approaches to nurture integration of theoretical content and field instruction. Field education programs bring together students, faculty, field instructors, and practitioners, and with this book we hope that a central tenant will be reflexivity in promoting dialogue across and between the chapters and ideas. Many programs encourage reflective learning about how our own life experiences contribute to our ability to recognize, appreciate, and affirm clients and their efforts and strengths. In this book, we utilize the concept of reflexivity, which encourages students to question not only their own values and assumptions but also those of their profession.

This is the first Canadian field education textbook for social work, human service, child and youth care, and social service students at the diploma program and undergraduate level. It is both timely and much-needed.

We chose to do an edited text to capture different theoretical, geographic, and sites of learning. Our contributing authors wrote from their diverse locations, practices and perceptions based on their field experiences, and as such provide a rich overview of the many contexts in which students' learning and field education take place.

We also recognize that just as students experience a variety of sites of learning, the practices, policies, and procedures also vary across educational programs.

## STRUCTURE OF THE BOOK

The book is divided into 14 chapters. The first seven chapters cover key theoretical and critical foundations of field education and provide the tools to assist students in their learning and practice. Chapters 1 and 2 outline the history of field education, explore our current context, and provide practical guidance to assist students in getting started. Chapters 3 and 4 ground us in important ethical, legal, and theoretical contexts to guide our learning and practice. Chapters 5, 6, and 7 provide learners with the tools for change, including reflexivity, social justice, human rights, advocacy, and community-based research.

Chapters 8 to 12 provide important and critical sites of learning for field education, including Indigenous field education, diversity in field education, international field placements, rural and remote sites of practice, and the use of technology to facilitate distance field education.

The last two chapters of the book assist students with their transition from students to professionals. Chapter 13 considers the issues of inter-professional practice and reciprocity, while Chapter 14 covers the development of students' future careers and life-long learning.

## DEFINITION OF FIELD EDUCATION TERMS

The human service field, encompassing social work, social service, and child and youth care, utilizes a variety of terms to express the roles and responsibilities for engaging in learning about practice. Each professional area or each program will have its preferred nomenclature. In this book, the terms are used interchangeably. The following is a compilation of the different terms that may be used to represent a particular role in relation to the student's experience.

*Field placement, field practicum,* or *field experience:* These terms are used to identify the setting or location where practice will be learned. The sites for practice are diverse, and may include large government agencies, not-for-profit organizations, or residential facilities, or be carried out through a project with a number of organizations. Each setting will be structured with staff members who have a distinct mandate to provide service.

*Field instructor, field mentor,* or *supervisor:* These terms refer to the person at the field site who is primarily responsible for providing students with assignments, providing feedback, and ensuring there is accountability for the work that is expected of students.

*Field coordinator* or *field director:* These terms identify the person at the educational institution who is responsible for ensuring that students find a field placement. This may be a specifically designated individual whose only responsibility is organizing all of the field placements or it may be a faculty member or program coordinator who teaches, conducts research, and finds placements for students.

*Faculty liaison, field advisor,* or *field visitor:* Each program will have a person from the educational institution who is available to support the student in the field setting and the agency-based supervisor to ensure that the expectations of the program are being fulfilled. The faculty liaison or field visitor normally visits the field setting several times throughout the field placement experience to provide guidance and feedback and to create a link between the educational program and the field experience.

## FEATURES

The book includes a number of features in each chapter to appeal to many different learner styles.

Each chapter begins with chapter objectives in a short bulleted list.

"Voices from the Field" describe students' or field instructors' real experiences set in diverse contexts that aim to bring to life field education experiences.

"Case Scenarios" provide narratives of hypothetical situations or cases followed by one or two questions. The case scenarios are drawn from social work, child and youth care, and human service practice realities.

Discussion questions are used to emphasize important sections of each chapter that instructors might want to highlight or spend more time on in their classes or integrative field seminars.

Exercises are directive in nature. This feature outlines various topics for students to engage with or to write about in their journals.

A chapter summary is provided at the end of each chapter with a brief review of the key points.

Several critical-thinking questions—"big picture" or "synthesis" questions—follow the chapter summary to stimulate reflection and encourage students to locate themselves before they enter into practica.

A list of suggested readings and websites are also provided for further reference.

References include all works cited in each chapter and are featured at the end of the book.

Some of the chapters include checklists or tips to summarize key elements. A checklist is used to set apart important information from the body of the text. Tips are used to provide suggestions or recommendations.

## COURSESMART FOR INSTRUCTORS

CourseSmart goes beyond traditional expectations to provide instant, online access to the textbooks and course materials you need at a lower cost for students. And even as students save money, you can save time and hassle with a digital eTextbook that allows you to search for the most relevant content at the very moment you need it. Whether it's evaluating textbooks or creating lecture notes to help students with difficult concepts, CourseSmart can make your life a little easier. See how when you visit www.coursesmart.com/instructors.

## COURSESMART FOR STUDENTS

CourseSmart goes beyond traditional expectations to provide instant, online access to the textbooks and course materials you need at an average savings of 60 percent. With instant access from any computer and the ability to search your text, you'll find the content you need quickly, no matter where you are. And with online tools such as highlighting and note-taking, you can save time and study efficiently. See all the benefits at www.coursesmart.com/students.

## ACKNOWLEDGMENTS

Our thanks go to the team at Pearson Canada who have seen this book through from manuscript to finished product, including Joel Gladstone, Acquisitions Editor; Rema Celio, Developmental Editor; Richard Di Santo and Cheryl Noseworthy, Project Managers; Deborah Cooper-Bullock, Copy Editor; and Sally Glover, Proofreader. We would also like to thank Raj Singh and his team at MPS.

We would like to thank many students and field instructors who shared their voices and experiences in the book. With thanks to: Linda Danson, Nona Moscovitz, Chris Van Deen, Nadine Mathews, Kathy McKinnon, Kristin Zegers, Mark Darcy, Paula K. Smith, Kim Kidder, Francisca Hamilton, Miriam Samuel, Jenny Turco, Joanna Pierce, Jennifer Tkachuk, Beverly Van Dern Weide, Twyla Russell and all those who wish to remain anonymous.

In addition, we thank the many anonymous contributors and external peer reviewers from across Canada who read through earlier drafts of chapters and provided valuable feedback and comments. These include the following:

Katrina McDonald, *St. Lawrence College*
Shelley Styles, *Algonquin College*
David Hannis, *Grant MacEwan College*
Tammy Kerr, *Loyalist College*
Elaine Spencer, *Red Deer College*

Elizabeth Jones, *University of British Columbia*
Patrick Konkin, *Vancouver Island University*
Tammy Stubley, *University of Northern British Columbia*
Walt Goffin, *Niagara College*
Jane Jones, *Algonquin College*
Jennifer Clarke, *Ryerson University*

## ABOUT THE EDITORS

### JULIE DROLET, PhD, MSW

Julie Drolet is Assistant Professor and Field Education Coordinator in the BSW program at Thompson Rivers University in Kamloops, British Columbia. Julie is a member of the Field Education Committee of the Canadian Association for Social Work Education (CASWE) and a member of the Task Force on International Exchanges and Research of the International Association of Schools of Social Work (IASSW). She is the inaugural Director of the Centre for International Social Work and Research at TRU, and engaged in research on international field education, international social work, and Indigenous field education funded by SSHRC and CIHR.

### NATALIE CLARK, MSW, PhD (cand.)

Natalie Clark is Faculty and Field Education Coordinator for the Human Service Program at Thompson Rivers University in Kamloops, British Columbia. She has extensive experience as a field instructor in the community and as a faculty liaison, in addition to her role as Field Education Coordinator. Natalie is a strong proponent of research and field education. Together with Julie Drolet and other colleagues, she currently holds a SSHRC project grant for Indigenous field education and cultural safety; she is also partnering on research regarding rural and remote field education and intra-professional practice.

### HELEN SZEWELLO ALLEN, MSW

Helen Allen is Vice-President Education at Vancouver Community College. Helen has extensive experience in field education in Canada, having been the Director of Field Education at the McGill School of Social Work and Field Education Coordinator for the School of Social Work at the University of British Columbia. She has developed field education manuals for students, field evaluation tools, reflective practice tools, and training for field instructors in the community. Helen conducted a research project on field education in child welfare in British Columbia in 2000, surveying students and field instructors to identify best practices in preparation for the development of the child welfare specialization in social work and child and youth care degree programs in British Columbia.

# ABOUT THE CONTRIBUTORS

**Marion Bogo** is Professor at the Factor-Inwentash Faculty of Social Work, University of Toronto, and is recognized as a national and international leader in field education in social work. Her research focuses on the development and testing of field education models and innovative approaches to assessment of student competence.

**Glen Schmidt** practiced social work for 15 years in the isolated single-industry towns and First Nations communities of northern Manitoba. He worked in the areas of child welfare and community mental health as a front-line worker, supervisor, and manager. He has been a faculty member at University of Northern British Columbia since 1994, and he served as Field Director for six of those years.

**Joanna Pierce**, prior to joining the School of Social Work Faculty at the University of Northern British Columbia (UNBC), practiced social work for eight years in the remote communities of northern British Columbia. Her research interests are in northern and remote practice, mental health, community development, child welfare, and cross-cultural communications. As part of her UNBC faculty position, Joanna has been Field Director for the past three years and is currently serving as the National Field Education Representative on the board of the Canadian Association for Social Work Education.

**Shelly Johnson** is from Keeseekoose First Nation, a Saulteaux community in Saskatchewan. For 25 years she has practiced in British Columbia as a social worker, Aboriginal child welfare policy analyst, and Chief Executive Officer of a delegated First Nations child welfare agency. Currently, she is completing her doctorate in education and is an assistant professor at the School of Social Work at Thompson Rivers University.

**Paul René Tamburro,** PhD, MSW, MA, "Môjassadop Spiwi Pakholigan" (*Began with a Drum* in Abenaki). Paul is enrolled with the Piqua Shawnee (Alabama) and Abenaki (Vermont) tribes, and is a grandfather. He has taught and been a field instructor in social work programs in Canada and the United States since 1990. Currently, he teaches at Thompson Rivers University in British Columbia. His doctoral work focuses on cultural revival, and his master's studies focused on Aboriginal child welfare.

**Duane Seibel**, Diploma CYC, BA (CYC), MA. Duane is currently the coordinator of the Human Service Diploma at Thompson Rivers University (TRU) in Kamloops, British Columbia. He has been involved in child and youth care education for the past 20 years in the post-secondary system in British Columbia at the University of Victoria, Fraser Valley University, Vancouver Island University, Selkirk College, and now TRU.

**Mary Harber-Iles** is currently an assistant professor in the School of Social Work and Human Service at Thompson Rivers University. She has been a social worker for 24 years and has practiced in a variety of contexts, including child welfare, addictions, youth, sexuality, and disability and is focused on FASD and creative engagement in her current research.

**Sandra deVink-Leblanc** is a retired full-time faculty member from St. Thomas University, where she was the field education coordinator for 18 years and was instrumental in establishing the social action component of the field education program. She is currently Director of the St. Thomas Labrador BSW program.

**Linda Turner** is an associate professor in the School of Health at University of New England in Armidale, Australia. In her former role as a faculty member of the St. Thomas Social Work Department, she served as Field Education Coordinator for six years.

**Brian Carty** is an assistant professor in the Department of Social Work at St. Thomas University. He is currently coordinating the social action field placements for the post-degree BSW program.

**Ransford Danso**, PhD, is a regional editor of *Current Research Journal of Social Sciences*. He holds an MA degree and an MSW degree from the University of Calgary and the University of Toronto, respectively, and currently teaches at Sheridan College Institute of Technology and Advanced Learning.

**Dr. Jessica Ayala** is Assistant Professor and Director of Field Education in the Faculty of Social Work at the University of Calgary. Her teaching and research interests include distance education and e-leaning in social work, field education, and human sexuality. She won the University of Calgary Students' Union Teaching Excellence Award in 2008.

**Myra Baynton** has an academic background in psychology and sociology, a master's degree in social work, and a PhD in Adult Education (Distance Learning). She has worked in a variety of contexts, including social services, education, health care, and municipal government, and has worked overseas in Saudi Arabia and Ireland. Since 2004, she has been the Field Coordinator for the MSW Leadership in Human Services Distance Program for the Faculty of Social Work at the University of Calgary.

**Dr. Ellen Perrault** is an instructor and field coordinator in the Faculty of Social Work at the University of Calgary. She has more than 20 years of experience in social work practice in the areas of community development, clinical work, field education, and collaborative practice. She is particularly interested in how people work together successfully during inter-organizational collaboration and social work education.

**Dr. Jeanette Robertson** has been a faculty member at Thompson Rivers University (TRU) in the School of Social Work and Human Services since 1998. In addition to teaching and fulfilling a faculty field liaison role, she also coordinated field education in the BSW program at TRU for five years and at the University of British Columbia's distance MSW program for three years. She recently completed a national study of field education coordinators' experience and approach of addressing professional suitability.

**Saara Greene** is an assistant professor in the School of Social Work at McMaster University. Saara does HIV/AIDS community-based research on housing and homelessness, pregnancy, and motherhood. In all of her HIV research, Saara is committed to the Greater Involvement of People Living with HIV (GIPA) through ensuring community involvement and leadership in all stages of the research process.

**Grant Larson**, PhD, is an associate professor in the School of Social Work and Human Service at Thompson Rivers University, where he was the dean of the school for many years, and Vice-President of the Canadian Association for Social Work Education. Primary research interests include mental health, social work education, international social work, and disaster rehabilitation. Grant teaches social work theory, mental health and social work, family practice, and field practice, and utilizes a modern critical theory perspective in teaching and research.

**Grant Charles** MSW, PhD is Associate Professor and Chair of Field Education in the School of Social Work at the University of British Columbia. He is currently conducting research in the areas of young caregivers, children of parents with mental illnesses, interprofessional education, practice education and international service learning.

**Dr. Shafik Dharamsi** is Assistant Professor, Department of Family Medicine, and Faculty Lead of the Global Health Network with the Liu Institute for Global Issues at the University of British Columbia. His research is in the areas of medical education, social responsibility, ethics, global health, and service-learning.

**Carla Alexander** MSW, PhD (Cand.) works as a consultant and educator in community development and relational practice. She is a sessional instructor at Douglas College.

# Chapter 1

## Importance of Field Education: Current Trends and Historical Context

Marion Bogo

## Chapter Objectives

- Learn about the history of and current trends in field education for social work and human service.
- Understand the research in field education for social work and human service and its implications for field instruction.
- Use a model — the integration of theory and practice (ITP) loop — to guide teaching and learning about field education for social work and human service.

## Voices from the Field[1]

When I thought about beginning the field practicum, I was really excited. I thought that at last I'd have a chance to learn what I came here for: how to work with people. But then I started wondering what the people at the agency would think of me. Would they see me as a kid, someone who doesn't know anything, and a nuisance? (Anonymous, student)

## Voices from the Field

Some students like to be thrown in and start seeing clients on their own right away. And some need to start more slowly. I try to get a sense of that through talking with them. Everyone goes at his or her own pace, but the main thing about learning here is that students learn through doing social work. (Anonymous, field instructor)

---

[1] All student and field instructor reflections in this chapter are adapted from Litvack, A. (2003). *Critical issues in field education: Developing field instructor competence* [Educational videotape and teaching guide]. Toronto, ON: University of Toronto Press.

# FIELD EDUCATION FOR SOCIAL WORK AND HUMAN SERVICE PRACTICE

Social workers and professionals in health and human service occupations are generally unanimous in crediting their field education or practicum experiences as essential to their development into competent practitioners (Kadushin, 1991; Lager & Robbins, 2004). It is in these real-life settings — working with clients, service users, community members, and agency committees and projects — that students develop the wide range of skills and competencies that will enable them to practice their professions. In the field, the knowledge taught in a college or university program comes to life — providing clear and often poignant examples of the struggles and challenges, as well as the strengths and resilience, of individuals, families, and communities. As students engage in practice, they often find their values challenged; ethical dilemmas are no longer just interesting case examples for critical discussion but are highly relevant to everyday life. The personal self of the student is very much engaged as he or she confronts individuals and communities faced with such challenges as poverty, homelessness, abuse and neglect, violence, and oppression. Students often find themselves reacting strongly to such circumstances, wishing they could do something to alleviate pain and suffering but also questioning whether their choice of career is a good fit.

One of the most influential effects of learning in field education comes from students actually observing experienced practitioners. In classroom courses, knowledge and information is often presented sequentially, with specific topics covered in separate sections. Human service work, however, involves practitioners in complex situations and problems presented in unclear ways. Effective practice consists of making sense of these situations through applying knowledge learned; working in collaboration with clients, community members, and colleagues; and employing competencies and complex sets of practice behaviours. Over time, each practitioner evolves her or his own approach to practice — that is, each practitioner develops a unique personal style. Students witness these personal styles when they observe experienced professionals at work. With opportunities to reflect on, discuss, and debrief, through observation students learn how theory and practice are linked, how values are integrated into work practice, and how skills come together to facilitate effective service. Students learn from these role models and are inspired by the commitment of mentors. And field instructors help students develop their own unique integration of knowledge, values, and skills (Bogo, 2010).

In this chapter, we will review trends in the development and current status of field education. This review will address how the roles of student learner-practitioner and field instructor-supervisor-practitioner have been defined over time. A brief discussion of some key research findings will contribute to building an evidence base for field teaching. As well, a model — the integration of theory and practice (ITP) loop — developed by Bogo and Vayda (1998), is provided as a guide for teaching and learning. This framework offers students, field instructors, and faculty members a set of ideas about the various components and processes that contribute to a quality learning experience. A good understanding of the purpose of field education can help students play as active a role as possible in their current and ongoing professional development.

## HISTORY AND DEVELOPMENT

A brief review of some key developments in the history of field education provides some clarification about the range of terms used for various roles in the field. Changes in terminology reflect changes in thinking about how learning evolves from practice. From the inception of university-based courses in social work in the early part of the twentieth century, programs included academic courses and an agency- or community-based field component. For example, in the United States, students were required to receive what was known as "supervision" in an agency from a member of the American Association of Social Workers. Since Canadian schools of social work were highly influenced by developments in the United States, we assume that the same model was used. At this time, field education was referred to as "field work." This term captured the idea that learning was a product of providing a service to clients and communities in the real world of agency settings.

By the mid-1950s, researchers identified the primary focus of the field as educational; hence, the terminology changed to *field instruction*, *field education*, or *practicum*. Human service uses additional terms, such as *internship* or *residency*. Historically, the term given to the agency practitioner who organized the experience was the *student supervisor*. This title was consistent with agency practices, where social workers and human service workers were supervised by senior and experienced practitioners. Over time, two distinct bodies of research evolved in recognition of the differences between supervision and field education. *Supervision* now refers to overseeing, providing professional development for, and supporting staff employed by agencies to carry out a mandate. In contrast, *field instruction* refers to the professional education of social work and human service students in a field agency or setting (Bogo & McKnight, 2005; Kadushin & Harkness, 2002). While some concepts, processes, and techniques may be similar and used interchangeably in both domains, the difference in context and purpose of the supervision of staff and the field education of students supports this division in the literature. Supervision of staff is fundamentally an agency-based administrative function that ensures accountability for service delivery. Education and support are used to promote workers' development and increased competence in the interest of meeting this goal. Field education's fundamental purpose is educating students to become competent and effective practitioners. Since education takes place in an organizational context, instructors are accountable for the service students provide and so must oversee their work in some manner. The primary role of instructors, however, is to educate, with the goal that students will develop into professional practitioners. It is important to remember that students' learning occurs through delivering a service and providing professional interventions (through working with clients, communities, and projects), and that this service is in the interest of students learning their future profession.

Confusion about terminology persists, since the original terminology of supervision, which reflects its agency-based context, often continues to be used in informal discussion, in some schools' manuals and correspondence, and even in some research literature. It is not uncommon for the terms *supervisor*, *supervision*, and *field work* to be used to describe an activity whose objective is education. As you will see throughout this book, a range of terms are still used to identify field education in social work and human service.

## Voices from the Field

Once I started, I couldn't believe how lucky I was.... The field instructor said that the most important thing was my learning ... that soon enough I'd be a worker and this was a precious time for me ... I could watch, I could become involved, but most important, I was in the agency as a student. (Anonymous, student)

The Canadian Association for Social Work Education (CASWE), through its educational policy statements and accreditation function (CASWE, 2009), sets standards for social work education in Canada. The field education component must be part of the core curriculum, is required of all students, and provides supervised social work practice experience (CASWE, 2009, p. 6.) (Surprisingly, this educational document still uses the term "supervision" to refer to an educational role.) The policy emphasizes the primacy of the educational mission and requires that students have direct responsibilities, receive instruction, conduct field practice teaching, and undergo professional development and practice performance evaluation. Education programs are also responsible for providing field instructors with educational development and evaluation. The educational purpose must also be ensured through administrative agreements between schools and field settings. These requirements aim to ensure that students are not seen as quasi-workers, present in the agency to lend an extra pair of hands. Schools must have sufficient resources to provide practica that meet these missions and standards.

A distinctive feature of Canadian educational policy is its commitment to equity with "particular attention to those experiencing systemic discrimination on the basis of gender, ethnic origin, skin colour, language, religious beliefs, class, sexual orientation, disability, age, culture or any other characteristic (CASWE, 2009, p. 3). Furthermore, the policy requires content that "provide opportunities for analysis of the dynamics and consequences of oppression as these relate to populations at risk, particularly those relevant to the programme's mission or geographical location, and for competent practice deriving from that analysis" (CASWE, 2009, p. 6).

In contrast, the educational policy frameworks for accreditation of schools of social work outside Canada focus more particularly on developing students' competence for professional practice. For example, the Council on Social Work Education (CSWE) in the United States recently adopted a competency-based educational framework that views competencies as measurable, complex practice behaviours comprised of knowledge, values, and skills (CSWE, 2008). Ten core competencies are identified, which programs are expected to use to guide curriculum development and to assess student learning and programs' achievement of their mission and goals. These competencies include social work values, such as equity, diversity, and the advancement of human rights and social and economic justice. Field education is recognized as the *signature pedagogy* of social work, a term introduced by Lee Shulman (2005), an educational theorist and former president of the Carnegie Foundation for the Advancement of Teaching. It refers to the central form of instruction and learning in which a profession socializes its students to think, act, and behave as they would in a professional role. Through signature pedagogy, students learn to connect, integrate, and apply theory and values into their practice. "It is a basic precept of social work education that the two interrelated components of curriculum — classroom and field — are of equal importance within the curriculum, and each contributes to the development of the requisite competencies of professional practice" (CSWE, 2008, p. 8).

In England, in part as a result of increased demands for public accountability regarding front-line social work practice, the central government established a task force to conduct a comprehensive review of social work. The task force recommended reforms to social work education and emphasized the importance of preparing a professional workforce distinguished by high-quality, professional knowledge, skills, and judgment in order to benefit both individuals who use services and society as a whole (Social Work Task Force, 2010). Recognizing the importance of field education, the task force highlighted the importance of creating new, high-quality practice placements for all social work and human service students with expert field education and assessment of student learning. The report also emphasized the importance of providing funding to field practicum agencies and setting national standards and benchmarks for practicums field instructors. In this regard, the English school system intends to develop a new career designation (*practice educator*), and will designate *advanced teaching organizations* that demonstrate best practices in field teaching.

## BEST PRACTICES: PRINCIPLES BASED ON FIELD EDUCATION RESEARCH

A rich body of empirical studies conducted over the past two decades provides useful information for students, field instructors, and faculty members as they participate in the practicum experience. A review of recent studies (Bogo, 2010) found that students report moderately high to high satisfaction with their field practica when the field instructor–student relationship was perceived of as high quality. Furthermore, the following four key components emerge in association with quality field instruction: (1) available and supportive field instruction, (2) a balance between structure and autonomy, (3) opportunities for observing others and being observed with constructive feedback, and (4) opportunities for reflection and linkage to a knowledge base. The first two dimensions relate to the field instructor–student relationship, and the last two relate to educational activities.

## The Field Instructor–Student Relationship

**Supportive Field Instruction**  A number of studies reveal that many students experience high anxiety when learning to practice (Ellison, 1994). Such anxiety is in part related to their perception that they are expected to be helpful and effective in providing service. All students in field settings and internships are confronted with a dilemma: They are expected to offer service while still learning how to competently perform that service. While much social work education literature discusses ways of decreasing anxiety, educational theorist Lee Shulman (2005) observes that anxiety enhances motivation for learning and can be mediated through routine educational practices that structure learning. When the roles and expectations of students and the field instructor are clarified regularly, an optimal balance between the students' concerns and excitement can be achieved. The foundation for such a structure appears to relate to the perception that students' field instructors are accessible. Accessibility requires the presence of weekly structured meetings in which the student and field instructor collaboratively address both educational and service needs. In addition to benefiting from these regular sessions, students feel supported when they know who to turn to in the face of immediate practice issues. An easily accessible field instructor or a designated agency person helps to undercut students' normal apprehension about not knowing what to do in challenging or crisis situations.

## Voices from the Field

I really think it's important to make the student feel comfortable right from the start. And that's the responsibility of everyone on the team. Since we're a small agency I like to have everyone get to know the student and welcome them here. We are all in this together, and students need to feel they can approach me and all the team members when they need help. (Anonymous, field instructor)

A cluster of valued field instructor characteristics emerge from the empirical literature associated with a supportive climate. Field instructors are valued when they are seen as warm, honest, likable, sociable, trustworthy, and sincere. Students can expect support from reliable, prepared, skillful, and expert instructors (Strozier, Barnett-Queen & Bennett, 2000). Students also feel supported when the field education setting has a socio-emotional climate that takes their feelings into account (Fortune & Abramson, 1993). Such a climate is distinguished by instructors who recognize and respond to students' emotional reactions to situations in the field — those situations related to their practice settings, to professional and organizational issues, and to tensions inherent in the field instructor–student relationship. Encountering new and challenging individual and social problems can make some students feel overwhelmed, helpless, and demoralized. For example, Sun (1999) found that some undergraduate students feel that they cannot be of help to clients because of their perceived lack of knowledge, skills, or related experience for effectively dealing with situations and issues. Students often report feeling great sympathy for clients' predicaments, wanting to rescue clients, and feeling responsible for clients' well-being. Moreover, when students indicated that when they develop strong relationships with clients, ending the relationship is difficult. Supportive instructors can help students in these situations. Since self-esteem is connected to practice, supportive instructors are able to assist students through the phases of learning so that they might develop necessary knowledge and skills without loss of personal and professional confidence. Effective field instructors can normalize students' feelings, provide support, and help students recognize that learning involves making mistakes and recovering from these errors.

**A Balance between Structure and Autonomy**   When students are provided with structure in field education, their learning is guided and focused. It can, however, diminish students' initiative and autonomy. The field instructor must strive to create and balance guidance and direction, on the one hand, and, on the other, opportunities for student autonomy and self-direction. Structure appears to be important in the early stage of field learning. Field instructors must take the lead in orienting students to the setting, to the nature of the population served, to the specific practice models used, and to agency procedures. With respect to the student–field instructor relationship, Shulman (1993) recommends a learning contract as a means to clarify structure, roles, and expectations. Four interrelated processes consist of the field instructor (1) sharing his or her sense of purpose, (2) describing his or her role, (3) requesting feedback from the student about the student's perceptions of the teaching and learning relationship and educational activities, and (4) discussing the mutual obligations and expectations about the authority of the field instructor. The field instructor's discussion of purpose and their respective role includes attention to the methods that can be used in teaching and learning. Providing some concrete examples of teaching style will clarify what the field instructor and student's work together will entail. Such a discussion should also include attention to the student's preferred learning style.

Autonomy and self-direction can be initially fostered through collaboration between the field instructor and the student. Collaboration is framed as involving students as partners in their own learning. Students are asked to identify their practice strengths and areas for development. It is likely that students have some background in social work or human services from volunteer activities and classroom activities. As students prepare for professional careers, they will need the skills to become lifelong learners, and participating in self-assessment of their knowledge and skills is the basis for continuing professional development.

Initially, as part of providing structure, students receive practice assignments and feedback from the primary designated field instructor. Students engage in the setting and see the work of other professionals. Self-direction can be encouraged by inviting students to identify learning experiences and staff members from whom they would like to learn and receive additional assignments. Students can also observe others' practice and participate in debriefing. Initiative in choosing others to learn from encourages autonomy in field education, which is consistent with study reports that students wish for more independence as their learning progresses (Fortune et al., 1985; Urbanowski & Dwyer, 1988). In a study of students' development of practice competence over the course of their programs, Deal (2002) noted that student progress is not constant. It ebbs and flows, and students' feelings about how much independence they want or need at various points throughout the practicum will also fluctuate. Variations along this dimension depend on the issues presented by new practice assignments, and whether students perceive that they have the knowledge, experience, and skills needed to be effective.

Developmental stage models for training counselling psychologists identify three developmental levels students progress through as they move from the beginner to the expert stage (Stoltenberg, 2005; Stoltenberg, McNeill, & Delworth, 1998). The description of changes in three areas may be similar for other human service professionals. These areas include (1) awareness of self and other, (2) student's motivation, and (3) student's autonomy. While beginners are motivated in this model, they tend to have high anxiety with a focus on learning skills and doing the right things in practice. They are more focused on self, depend on their instructor to provide teaching, and prefer structure and positive feedback rather than critical feedback.

At the intermediate stage, similar to what Deal (2002) observed, students' feelings about their competence vacillate between confidence and confusion, wanting more autonomy at times and more dependency at others. When interested in self-development and awareness, students focus more on the client, or "other," in the helping encounter. At this stage, students supplement their skills by learning how to conceptualize their practice in order to develop relevant interventions.

In the advanced stage of development, students' confidence about their effectiveness has developed and their work with their instructor becomes more collegial. More complex understandings of self and other emerge, as does a more in-depth understanding of advanced concepts and parallel processes. Only one small study in social work supports these development stage notions (Deal, 2000). Nevertheless, these developmental models are theoretically interesting and may guide students and field instructors as they balance the degree of structure and autonomy throughout the field learning experience.

Before leaving the topic of the field instructor–student relationship, it is a significant, repetitive finding that a field instructor–student relationship can positively or negatively affect learning. In small, qualitative studies, students have discussed these dynamics at length (Barlow & Hall, 2007), and similar findings emerge from a national sample of social workers in the United States who were asked to recall critical incidents in field learning (Giddings, Vodde & Cleveland, 2003). For example, Litvack, Bogo, and

Mishna (in press) found that relationships that students perceived as positive assisted them greatly in coping with challenging client situations and organizational stressors. In contrast, students found that negative relationships did not provide the support seen as necessary to handle difficult client, professional, and organizational issues, and instead they create additional sources of strain and stress. Negative factors were reported by field instructors who conveyed that they did not have the interest or time for field instruction and had taken on the responsibility because of agency pressure. Instructors who largely focused on students' weaknesses when providing feedback also were seen negatively. As were instructors who had a harsh, rigid, and overly challenging style that lacked empathy and sensitivity to students' needs (Giddings et al., 2003). Boundary crossing was also important; students felt negatively about instructors who revealed too much information about their personal and professional lives or probed aggressively into students' personal lives.

From this brief review of studies, we can recognize the importance of developing and maintaining a positive and collaborative learning and teaching relationship. Students and their field instructors must commit to clearly communicating with each other about what is expected, what works, and what can be added — on the part of each participant — to make the field experience a positive one. Field instructors need to take the lead and introduce their expectation of collaboration in all aspects of teaching and learning in field education. In this respect, instructors are modelling good social work practice, and the student learns from the experience of participating in a process that is somewhat parallel to the collaborative work done with clients, committees, and communities.

## Voices from the Field

Early on the field instructor asked me what my expectations were and then told me what hers were and that we would negotiate the learning plan so that both of our goals would be met. She asked me how that was for me. I was so impressed. I thought, "she's practising with me what she does with clients — setting the stage, checking it out, asking for feedback." She also asked me how I felt things were going and when I said they were great she said, "That is good, and I hope that when things are not so great you will feel that you can tell me that also." (Anonymous, student)

Field instructors, by virtue of their role in the setting, their knowledge and experience, and their position as evaluators, have greater power in the field instructor–student relationship — a fact that some students report is of considerable concern to them (Barlow & Hall, 2007). Field instructors need to be attuned to ways in which they can use this power productively in their work with students. Transparency, clear communication, attention to students' verbal and non-verbal cues about relationship issues, and non-defensive encouragement when students express opinions that differ from the instructor's can demonstrate a commitment to greater collaboration.

Students also have power and the ability to affect the relationship process. Feedback can be expressed in a clear and specific manner, identifying what facilitates learning and suggesting other useful approaches that the student believes would have a positive impact (Power & Bogo, 2002). It is important in the early stages of the contracting phase to discuss power dynamics, evaluation issues, expectations about giving and receiving feedback, and how disagreements and conflict may be resolved. An interesting study examined students' initial reactions to the field agency and the field instructor, including whether students thought their learning goals could be met (Fortune, 2001). The researcher found that initial impressions were correlated with student satisfaction at the end of the field experience. That is, initial impressions were not changed through the learning and teaching activities of the particular field setting and field instructor. This finding further supports the importance of explicit discussion of learning goals and teaching and learning needs and styles at the beginning of and throughout the field practicum.

## Educational Activities

**Opportunities for Observing Others and Being Observed with Constructive Feedback** In a significant program of research on factors contributing to effective learning in the field, Fortune and colleagues (2001) identified a range of teaching activities. For students in the first and second years of master's programs, valued learning activities included working with instructors; observing other practitioners, including the field instructor; and receiving feedback on students' own practice. Studies have found that students and field instructors perceive that direct observation of practice with debriefing and feedback is viewed as a highly effective approach. Observation can occur directly through watching an experienced worker's practice or having the student's practice observed directly, through working collaboratively, using a one-way mirror, or reviewing an audio- or video-recording. The observation methods used in the reported studies were most frequently verbal or written records rather than the three methods just mentioned (Maidment, 2000; Rogers & McDonald, 1995). Observation of student practice with clients, activity in the community, and participation in committees and projects provides the actual material for use by students and their instructors in teaching and learning. It is very difficult for instructors to give accurate feedback on performances they can only imagine from verbal or written reports. In community settings and agencies, students have many opportunities to observe other practitioners and the field instructor. More challenging for time-strapped instructors is managing to observe students' practice. Since it is not feasible to observe all of students, instructors must decide how to select samples of students' performances for review, for teaching feedback and evaluation of performance.

A collection of studies about feedback is useful in identifying conditions and principles for giving and receiving information that can be incorporated into learning. Students value feedback that is based on observation of their practice, is offered in specific terms, is close in time to the practice situation, and suggests alternate ways of interacting or intervening (Fortune & Abramson, 1993; Freeman, 1985). Feedback is also more easily used when it is offered within the context of a positive relationship, when it balances negative and positive comments, when it invites collaborative brainstorming about alternative ways of behaving, and when it encourages student self-critique (Abbott & Lyter, 1998). In a study of students' perceptions of feedback, some objectionable styles were described as demeaning, harsh, or not geared toward promoting growth.

Finally, a study by Fortune, Lee, & Cavazos (2007) revealed that students' learning is enhanced by their practice of professional skills. When students were able to practice, they reported higher self-evaluation of the skills they had practised than for those they did not, and they also gave their field performance and satisfaction with their field a higher overall evaluation. Associated with this finding are the higher ratings that field instructors give these students. Aware of these findings, field instructors should ensure that students are provided with enough practice assignments to give them the chance to learn, gain feedback on, and reuse the skills necessary to become competent practitioners.

**Opportunities for Reflection and Linkage to a Knowledge Base**  Emanating from the research studies of Fortune and her colleagues about educational activities in the field is the finding that among those most valued by students are explanations of practice situations provided by field instructors (Fortune, McCarthy, & Abramson, 2001). This finding was true of first-year and second-year students in master's programs. Second-year students also valued instructors who made connections between the practice situations students encountered and the theories they were studying in school or learning about in the agency. Similarly, in a study conducted in Hong Kong, Choy, Leung, Tam, and Chu (1998) found that students highly rated field instructors who could integrate theory and practice and who were knowledgeable about what students were learning in their classroom courses. These data provide support for the importance of field instructors in assisting students to make linkages between the two domains of education — the college or university and the community practice setting. In fact, the ability to teach students how to use knowledge to understand and guide practice is the hallmark of an educational practicum. In contrast, an apprenticeship teaches students only how to perform a task.

In the following section, a model is provided that integrates the various educational activities we have discussed: observation, reflection and discussion, linkage of theory and practice, and feedback and practice.

# INTEGRATION OF THEORY AND PRACTICE (ITP) LOOP

## Voices from the Field

Students like the experience of shadowing me. The important thing about shadowing is what you want students to observe and then what sense you and the student will make of it after the session. So, I structure it; depending on what we're working on, I tell them to watch for certain things — from the clients and from my interventions. And after the session I ask them to write up some reflections on those topics and to include their questions and their thoughts. Then, when we meet to discuss their log, they have something to start off with. I encourage them to think about what they've seen and to discuss it through ideas they are learning in school. (Anonymous, field instructor)

Social work and human service professional education is carried out in two domains: classroom courses and field practica. Learning is facilitated when educational approaches bridge these two domains. Bogo and Vayda (1987; 1998) developed a model to integrate theory and practice to guide field instructors and students (called *the integration of theory and practice* (ITP) *loop model*). Four phases in an ITP loop model show how thinking, feeling, and doing in practice are a cumulative process that moves forward and backward. Each phase of the loop affects the next in a repetitive way. The phases are (1) retrieve and recall the practice situation and relevant facts and experiences, (2) reflect on the practitioner's personal reactions and associations to parts of or the total experience, (3) link the experience and reactions to concepts discussed in courses, readings, and the field, and (4) plan for the next professional response, taking into account the insights gained from reflection and linkage.

Social work's enduring focus on the person in context or the ecosystemic framework provides the basis for addressing specific content areas in each phase. This includes notions of power and structural oppression, as well as a consideration of the individual, the social context, and the transactions among these various domains. Psychosocial, interactive, organizational, and contextual-societal factors can be added to key concepts taught in a school's program to facilitate stronger links between learning and teaching in the classroom and the field.

The first factor, psychosocial, refers to the thoughts, feelings, and behaviours of the participants in a situation and could include individual and family development and dynamics, stress and trauma, and unique adaptations to crisis and to life challenges, needs, and difficulties. Social identity characteristics relate to a range of diverse individual and cultural features. The second factor, interactive, refers to the relationship and interactions between the worker and a client, a committee, or community members. The impact of the practitioner's values, attitudes and personality on the nature of the working relationship is included, along with the recognition that views of reality and the self are co-constructed through interactions with the social environment and are affected by language, culture, and power. Similarities, issues of diversity, and the social location of each participant are taken into account. The third factor, organizational, refers to agency policies, programs, and practices that affect what services are offered and what the student will learn. In interprofessional settings, the assigned roles, work, and communication styles of the team are also examined. The fourth and final factor is contextual-societal. This factor refers to societal attitudes, values, beliefs, and structural issues that systematically oppress individuals and serve as impediments to their maximal social functioning. Obviously, school programs cannot cover all factors and levels in great depth for every situation; however, through varied practice experiences in the practicum, over time, students will likely address all the issues.

In the process of the loop, in the first phase of retrieval and recall, students and their field instructors use a range of methods to observe or report on what transpires in a practice situation. Students are then encouraged to reflect, to "identify their feelings, thoughts, and assumptions regarding the practice data" (Bogo & Vayda, 1998, p. 111), and to recognize the impact of their behaviour and actions on the evolving interviews or meetings. These reflections can be examined in relation to students' own experiences and the issues in the practice situation, in identifying similarities and differences in psychosocial and organizational factors, and in societal contexts of the student's and the client's or community's experiences. Such recognition of similarity and difference can help students tease out instances where their assessment of practice situations is overly interpreted through a lens of personal experience rather than professional knowledge (Bogo, in press).

In the linkage phase, students and instructors review the knowledge and concepts students are learning in classroom courses and in discussions in the field setting and use them as explanatory frameworks to help answer the question: "Why does this problem exist in this situation?" Theory guides our awareness of what types of information are important to collect and what is not necessary. Hence, concepts taught in the program reflect its view of what is important for understanding human well-being and social justice. Practice theory or models are also considered in this phase, as they offer direction about how to intervene to support or bring about change. These models present principles, techniques, and tasks to accomplish at various phases. They also provide structure for practitioners as they assess, plan, and intervene. Some models are derived from research studies about what is effective, and others are more general and based on years of practice wisdom and experience.

The final phase of taking action through a professional response is the culmination of thinking through the previous phases. This phase can be seen as the student's preparation for the next meeting. New insights and new knowledge are considered, and thought is given to choose next steps for the student's meeting with the client or community members. Since collaboration and partnership is a social work value and practice principle, students must also give thought to how they will share new insights and recognize that clients must be involved in decisions about next steps.

The following exercises will help students learn how to use the ITP loop model.

## Exercise

If you are new to social work and do not have practice experience at your field setting, ask your field instructor to work with you on this exercise.

1. Observe your field instructor in practice with the understanding that you will both use the ITP loop model to reflect on and analyze this shared experience.

2. Write an analysis of what you observed by using the following guidelines:

   - **Retrieval.** What are the relevant facts of the situation?

   - **Reflection.** What are your personal reactions to the situation? What effect did the social worker's or human service worker's interventions have on the situation?

   - **Linkage.** How can you explain the situation you observed? What ideas or readings from course work help you understand it?

   - **Professional response.** Given your analysis, what should happen next?

## Exercise

This exercise will help you understand your own practice. You can complete it on your own, with a colleague, or with your field instructor. The instructions are provided as if you will be reflecting on it alone. If you use the exercise with another individual, take turns sharing a practice situation with a client, community member, committee member, or colleague in a project and lead your partner through the reflective questions.

### Retrieval
Recall a recent practice experience where you felt positively about your work. Or, choose a situation you feel negatively about that is troubling you.

### Reflection
Recall your thoughts and feelings about this situation.

- What beliefs and attitudes were operating on your part? Did this reflect aspects of your personality, world view, or particular life experiences? How were these issues apparent in your thoughts, judgments, and behaviour?
- How is the work progressing? Are there signs of progress? Are your efforts making a difference?

### Linkage

- What were some of the things you did? Why?
- How did you decide to do what you did?
- Were your actions based on concepts or ideas from your readings, your classes, or ideas you heard in the setting? Try to put into words these underlying influences.
- Do the explanations you have about this situation come from one or many sources? If they come from many sources, do the explanations support or contradict one another?

**Professional Response**

- In retrospect, were your responses selected through deliberate reflection, linkage, and planning? If not, how did they arise?
- Having completed this exercise, what might you do differently at the next encounter?
- Do you need more information, knowledge, or advice to make this decision? Where will you find it: in the literature, from a colleague, or from your field instructor? (Adapted from Bogo, 2006)

## CHAPTER SUMMARY

A review of field education demonstrates that it endures as a valued component of social work education. This value is underscored in studies of students' reactions to their education and is highlighted in the policy statements for accreditation of schools of social work in three countries: Canada, the United States, and England. Students and field instructors can now follow the guidelines created from a growing and robust body of research to fashion learning contracts or plans and to carry out their respective roles and responsibilities in teaching and learning.

Similar to helping traditions in human services, valued field instruction arises in the context of a positive educational environment — an environment based on an available, accessible, and supportive relationship between student and field instructor. In such an environment, a balance is provided between structure and autonomy, and this balance fluctuates based on students' developmental stage and needs. Students report that they can receive and use critical feedback about their practice in such an environment.

Students benefit significantly from the opportunity to observe practitioners at work and to debrief with these professionals about the reasons for their actions and directions. Students' observations of practitioners are valuable because these role models demonstrate concrete examples of using theory in practice. In addition, students appreciate being observed themselves, as they carry out practice assignments and use the skills and competencies they have learned. Observations of students by field instructors, with opportunities for immediate feedback and discussion, provide immediacy as well as rich examples from which to draw the links between theory and practice. Conceptual frameworks and literature covered in classroom courses are linked to assessments and inform decisions about subsequent actions. A conceptual base for one's practice builds toward thoughtful, independent graduates. To learn a professional practice, students need multiple opportunities to practice or take action, followed by guided reflection that involves awareness of personal perspectives, analysis of situations, and feedback about performance. Out of these continuous and repetitive sequences of doing, feeling, and thinking, new ideas and interventions are formulated and then put into practice in subsequent encounters with the practice situation. This process has been referred to as the integration of theory and practice (ITP) loop.

## Critical-Thinking Questions

1. The purpose of field education is to further students' learning to become professional practitioners. When students find themselves in small, community-based settings that have limited resources, they may be asked to take on a range of activities, some of which may be clerical or housekeeping in nature. Think through the issues arising from such requests and how students might respond.

2. Students learn about the populations they will serve and practice models and principles in their college or university courses. Think of a set of concepts studied in these courses that are challenging for you. Provide examples of when these concepts "come to life" for you in the field and instances where you think the theories do not illuminate the situations you are encountering in your practice. In the latter instance, analyze why this disconnect may be occurring.

## Suggested Readings

Birkenmaier, J., & Berg-Weger, M. (2006). *The practicum companion for social work: Integrating class and field work* (2nd ed.). Boston, MA: Allyn and Bacon.

Bogo, M. (in press). *Achieving competence in social work through field education*. Toronto, ON: University of Toronto Press.

Bogo, M., & Vayda, E. (1998). *The practice of field instruction in social work: Theory and process*. Toronto, ON: University of Toronto Press.

Hendricks, C. O., Finch, J. B., & Franks, C. (2005). *Learning to teach: Teaching to learn*. Washington, D.C.: Council on Social Work Education.

## Relevant Websites

### Canadian Association for Social Work Education
www.caswe-acfts.ca/en
The website provides the standards of accreditation for all social work programs in Canada, including the requirements for field education components within both baccalaureate and master's-level education programs.

### Competency for Professional Practice Initiative, University of Toronto
www.socialwork.utoronto.ca/research/initiatives/competency.htm
This section of the University of Toronto website, sponsored by the Factor-Inwentash Faculty of Social Work, presents the ongoing research currently underway on enhancing professional competence, particularly in field education. Within the Knowledge Building section of the website (located on the left-hand side

of the page), there are an extensive number of citations and many full-text articles regarding field educa-tion, summaries of projects with implications for field teaching, and a number of empirically developed evaluation tools.

**North American Network of Field Educators and Directors (NANFED)**
www.nanfed.org
This organization promotes the interests of field education in the United States and Canada through networking, encouraging publications, hosting symposiums and business meetings, and mentoring new field directors.

# Chapter 2

## Getting Started: Preparing to Learn in the Field

Helen Szewello Allen

## Chapter Objectives

- Develop a self-assessment of current skills, knowledge, and values.
- Explore a variety of learning goals for practice in the field.
- Prepare for an interview with an agency.
- Prepare to begin the field placement.
- Understand the expectations of professional behaviour in practice.

Embarking on a practice experience in the community is life-changing. No matter how much students have learned in the classroom or experienced in the past, this new professional field experience will provide hands-on training and a feel for what it is really like to work in their chosen field. Students will learn about people who have a variety of needs for support and intervention in their lives. They will also learn more about themselves and the engagement that occurs in the process of caring and helping than they will have imagined. The best way to enter any new experience is to be well prepared for it. This chapter will get the preparation process started.

In the classroom, faculty members prepare students for the field experience in many ways. They provide important knowledge about the many contexts in which human services are carried out, the legal and policy frameworks that govern service delivery, and the methods that are used in providing service. Classroom courses also ground students' understanding about the needs of individuals who will welcome the support of a professional person, such as a practicum student. All the knowledge gained in the classroom and from readings and research serve as important preparation for the field experience. The field placement is an opportunity to shift the method of learning; it is about learning by doing. We will discuss a number of activities to help prepare students to step out of the classroom and become involved in a field placement agency.

# SETTING LEARNING GOALS

Every educational program will have a list of agencies and organizations that are ready to offer students a field placement. These agencies can be quite varied, providing services to everyone from children to older adults, including people with disabilities; people who have just arrived in Canada or who are indigenous to this country; people who are facing challenges of poverty, unemployment, or relationship stress; people who have broken the law; or people who struggle with addiction. Further, there are agencies that offer a multitude of services and some that provide only one specialized service. Agencies may also vary in their service delivery approach. On the one hand, some agencies can be very structured and bureaucratic, where clients are only seen after they have been assessed, screened, and referred to a particular program. On the other hand, some agencies offer informal drop-in centres, where people can come in off the street to socialize, attend an activity, or have a meal. All these components add to the complexity of the learning environment. Knowing where to fit in best and learn the most is important. The question of fit depends on individual goals and learning needs at this point in a student's career. Students will be expected to locate their interests within specific learning goals. Recognizing that one already has knowledge and skills is an important step in the process.

By choosing a program, students have begun a learning journey that will prepare them for a new professional career. They are often very excited to begin the field placement component of their program and want to make it a meaningful experience. The following exercise will identify students' strengths, values, beliefs, knowledge, and skills. This self-assessment process isolates the foundational experience that each student brings to the field placement. It establishes a jumping-off point from which they can formulate sharper and clearer learning goals, leading to a better match with an agency, client group, and/or social issue and structure, which will facilitate placement in the best setting for this point in their careers.

## Exercise

Your program will expect you to meet some specific learning goals and program objectives in your field placement. Your program faculty member will share these with you. However, you will also want to prepare yourself for your own unique and personal goals. This exercise will assist you in their developing and allow you reflect on your learning style.

To complete this exercise, you will need about an hour of quiet time. Think of this hour as a special time to focus on yourself at this point in your life's journey and to reflect on the past, present, and future. Get yourself a notebook and begin by answering each section. The best way to do this exercise is to free write — that is, just write whatever comes to mind. Don't worry about sentence structure or coming up with the right words. You can write in point form or in whatever way is the easiest for you to name the thoughts that enter your mind after each prompt. These questions serve only as a guide. If you wish to explore other themes for each area, these extra themes will only enrich your understanding of yourself and your learning style. Let's begin:

1.  Think about your early schooling. What did you enjoy about elementary school? What did you learn from your teachers? Is there a teacher that stands out who had a real impact on you? What was that impact? What kind of student were you?

2.  Think about your high school years. What was enjoyable about these years? What was challenging? What did you learn from your teachers? What did you learn from your friends and peer group? What kind of student were you? What did you discover about the way you learned — that is, your learning style? What do you think was the most important thing you learned in high school?

3.  Think about your family. What have you learned from your parents, siblings, grandparents, caregivers, and extended family of uncles and aunts? What values did your family share? What were the most important events in your family, and why were they important? What were the patterns of daily living in your family? What did you learn from the way your family organized its daily activities? What were some challenges your family faced? How were these handled and what did you learn as you observed your family manage challenges? What beliefs did your family hold dear? What was the most important thing you learned about yourself from your family?

4.  Think about your neighbourhood. What kind of community did you grow up in? What community values did you observe? What were your neighbours like? What type of community do you live in now? How would you describe your relationships with your neighbours and community? What community events do you enjoy? Why are these community activities important to you? What have you contributed to the communities and neighbourhoods you have lived in?

5.  Think about your friends. Who are they? Why are they your friends? What are the characteristics of your friends that you enjoy the most? What do you contribute to these friendships? What have you learned about yourself from your friends? What values do you and your friends share in common?

6.  Think about your volunteer work or jobs that you have held (even babysitting counts). How would you describe your work habits? What have you enjoyed about volunteer work and/or your jobs? List the skills you have gained through your work situations. What are your expectations of a work environment? How do you expect to be treated by the people you work with? What do you enjoy most about your work situations?

7.  Think about your significant others: your partner, spouse, and special friends. What have you learned about yourself from the intimate relationships that you have been involved in or are currently involved in? What are the unique qualities that you bring to your relationships? What values are shared in your intimate relationships? How have these values been expressed in the decisions you have made together with someone?

8.  If you have children, what have they taught you about yourself and your values? Describe your parenting skills. What are your children learning from you? Have you become like your mother/father? What goals do you have for your children?

Some of these questions may not be relevant to you. This is not important. But it is necessary that you reflect on those situations that are relevant. For some, this exercise may bring a considerable amount of pain, and you may wish to speak to someone who can assist you in your reflections and the learning that your experiences have provided. All our life experiences teach us something. We can move forward when we are able to understand their impact on us and what we have gained from them.

Now, go back over what you have written and identify all the values and beliefs that are important to you and the skills that you have attained. This step will allow you to see that you are entering your field experience with a wealth of knowledge about yourself and what you will be able to contribute.

Take this exercise further and identify what you think you need to learn next. The field placement will provide you with the next stepping stone in your life's learning journey. You may wish to share the learning you have gained from this exercise with your field supervisor, who may be able to select specific experiences in your field placement that will help you achieve your personal goals. This holistic way of viewing your learning goals will help you establish your learning contract.

## USING THE LEARNING CONTRACT AS A LEARNING TOOL

A learning contract is a document that is normally developed between a student and his or her field instructor during the first few weeks of a field placement by using an outline prepared by the program. This document reflects the expectations of the program and includes some set learning objectives that a student must meet at the field setting. Specific field settings may also include additional expectations for their particular agency. Contracts also provide students with an opportunity to express their learning interests and needs (Bogo & Vayda, 1998). The learning contract may be a simple or complex document, depending on the professional area of study and the specific program. The contract lays out the expectations for what will take place in the field placement. It provides students with a detailed description of the skills, knowledge, and values that they will learn throughout the duration of the placement, the specific assignments that will provide the context for the learning, and an explanation of how the student will be evaluated. The purpose of the learning contract is to link classroom learning (theory) and field experience (practice) within an organized and thoughtful process.

Every social work and human service program has identified learning goals that all students are required to accomplish in their field setting as an expectation of completion of the program. These learning goals arise from the theoretical frameworks that are taught in the program. Goals may be identified as program objectives or specific practice competencies. Further, the learning goals are linked to the field evaluation tool that will be used to evaluate students' practice in the field setting.

1.  Locate the learning contract outline for your program. Review your program learning goals for the field placement and reflect on your personal goals. Review the expectations that are laid out and think about what your contribution will be to establishing the learning contract with your field instructor.

2.  Use what you learned about yourself in the exercise above to identify learning goals that match what is expected in the learning contract outline. Remember that not all your learning goals will be met in your first field experience.

3.  Your learning goals will change as you begin your field placement, and you may need to revise your learning contract from time to time. Find out what the process for doing this is in your program.

4.  Find the field evaluation tool that will evaluate your field practice. Reflect on the expectations of the field evaluation and what learning experiences you wish to include in your learning contract to ensure that you will be evaluated successfully in your field placement.

To become effective practitioners, it is vital that students know themselves well, as noted by Bob Shebib (2007): "Knowledge of self, including consciousness of one's values and beliefs and the impact of one's behaviour on others, is a prerequisite for effective counseling.... Competent professionals know themselves.... They accept that exploring and reflecting on one's competence and the limits of one's role and expertise are fundamental to professional practice" (p. vii). Shebib adds that this process continues throughout one's career and will be an ongoing part of their professional lives.

## FINDING THE BEST FIELD PLACEMENT AND PRESENTING YOURSELF AT THE AGENCY

The specific process for choosing and identifying a field placement is quite varied. Some programs offer their students an opportunity to express interest in particular settings or client populations (e.g., students may indicate that they wish to work in child welfare or in a drop-in centre for the homeless). The process may be self-directed, where a student finds the field placement from a list of agencies provided by the program. In contrast, other programs may match students with placements without student input. In yet other instances, students will be required to interview at several agencies to see which agency will accept them. Each program has a faculty member or field coordinator who provides information on the process for matching students with field placements in the community. Even when the program has identified the specific agency where a student may carry out a placement, the process will usually involve an interview with the prospective agency to complete the match. Some programs may have unique challenges in finding field placements for students who have particular language and travel requirements. It is also important to note that not all agencies are able to take students. Changes in their staffing or funding may preclude them from being able to offer a field placement opportunity at a particular time.

Students need to work closely with the program field coordinator and within the process identified by their program for selecting a field placement. They will want to ensure that their learning goals will be met, but they need to understand that some agencies may not provide the best setting for an initial placement. Agencies welcome students if they can see that they will be open to learning and will make a contribution to the services they provide. Both the student and the agency have to agree that they are a good match. The interview at a prospective agency will allow both the student and the agency to assess the right fit for learning about practice.

## CASE SCENARIO

Janet is a single mother who has returned to school to study social work. She has had many challenges in her life and feels that she is ready to learn and wants to use her life experiences to help other single mothers. She has been poor and has experienced abuse from the father of her children. She wants to do her field placement at a women's shelter because she understands the cycle of violence and the challenges of starting all over with no money. She has a keen interest in women's issues and has been very excited to learn about feminist approaches to practice in her classes and her readings. She is now keen to apply her new feminist understanding by doing a field placement at a women's shelter. She wonders if her background and theoretical approach would be acceptable at many of the other agencies that take students.

### Questions

1. What do you think are the advantages of Janet doing her field placement at a women's shelter?

2. What potential challenges can you see Janet having if she does her placement at a women's shelter?

3. How might the women's shelter view Janet's background and theoretical perspective?

## Preparing for an Interview with an Agency

To prepare for negotiating a field placement, students need to have a detailed résumé ready to present to the program field coordinator. This résumé may also need to be presented to a prospective field placement agency. Even if a "hiring" interview is not part of a particular program's process, it is still a good idea to take a résumé to the first student–agency meeting because it summarizes a student's background and experiences for the prospective field instructor.

A résumé should summarize academic knowledge, work and volunteer experience, and particular skills. In the social work and human service field, all experience and education is important. If one already has a business certificate or has coached floor hockey, these experiences should be included on the résumé, as they reflect a diversity of knowledge and skills. In the domain of human service, all experience reflects an ability to form relationships and understand different social systems and contexts. For example, a business certificate will be very useful if an agency asks a student to attend a board of directors meeting at which a budget is discussed. A business background will enable the student to quickly understand the financial management of an organization. Sports skills provide useful points of connection when trying to build relationships with children and youth. A résumé should clearly state the education and experience achieved to date and additional comments on community activities, hobbies, and languages spoken. It is very important that the résumé's presentation is professional; students should ensure that there are no spelling errors and no acronyms or short forms, and that it is well structured and easy to read. Once résumés are prepared for the first time, students can easily update them as they progress through their program; they can add field placement experiences, any workshops or conferences they attend, and presentations or special research projects they carry out. Upon graduation, the résumé is ready for job interviews and a first professional position.

## Preparing for a First Interview

**Setting Up the Interview**  Students should make sure they have the name of the person they are calling and know his or her title and something about his or her work. The program field coordinator should provide students with this information. When contacting an agency by phone, students should ensure that they speak clearly, identifying themselves and their program of study. If students must leave a message, as will often be the case, they should make sure they speak slowly and clearly, and leave a number where they can be reached. If they have not heard from the person they are trying to reach after a few days, call again. If students are asked to contact the agency supervisor by email, they should use a formal style of letter writing. Students should not use slang or shortened words common in texting, and should make sure their message contains no spelling or grammatical errors.

**Arriving at the Agency**  Once students have an appointment set, they should arrive at the agency early. They should take time to look around the waiting room and observe the people entering and leaving the agency. Students can glance at brochures and posters and take note of the messages the agency is communicating at this point of entry. By doing these things, students will be making their first assessment about this agency. The waiting room is also what students' prospective clients will view when they walk in. Students' observations may provide a conversation starter when they begin their interview.

**Presenting Oneself** Students should dress professionally for their first interview. They should make sure their clothes are clean and neat. Once they are at the agency, students should observe what others are wearing and use this information as a clue as to what is expected of them once they are working at their placement there. There may be times when students will be expected to dress more formally, as when they attend a board meeting, an interagency case conference, or court. It is appropriate for students to ask their supervisor about how they should dress for such meetings. Students will want to ensure that their appearance does not detract from the assistance they will be providing to clients. Rather, how students dress can play a role in their ability to establish positive, professional relationships with them.

**Disclosing Personal Information** When students completed the earlier exercise, they may have had to grapple with the implications of some challenges they have faced in their lives. Should students share these challenges with their field supervisor? After disclosing this information to their field coordinator, they should develop a strategy for how to disclose or not to disclose information, as appropriate. Some agencies specifically look for students who have had life experiences similar to their clients' experiences, and they will welcome this information and be interested in knowing how students have handled their experiences. Some agencies will ask students about their healing journey. Again, students should discuss this with their program faculty so that they can anticipate the conversation and feel comfortable with how they approach it.

**Presenting Knowledge, Skills, and Interests** Students should bring their résumé with them. They may also wish to bring some course outlines from their program or a paper they have written related to the client population at this agency to demonstrate to their prospective field supervisor their interest in being accepted. Students will likely be asked what they are hoping to learn and why they wish to learn at this particular agency. They should have their answers ready.

Some questions that may be asked include the following:

- Tell me about yourself and your background.
- What led you to consider this area of professional study?
- What talents and skills can you bring to this agency?
- What do you think will be most difficult for you at this agency?
- What courses have you taken and what theories will you be using?
- Why should we consider you for field work at this agency?

Students' detailed self-assessments will assist them in preparing for the interview. If they have summarized the earlier exercise, they will have with them a list of their skills, knowledge, experiences, and learning style. Students should review this information before they go for the interview and be able to share this background information. Students' life stories can also assist in explaining their unique backgrounds, their strengths, and the things they now need to learn to move forward in their career.

**Preparing Oneself to Be Surprised**  The agency director may decide to attend the interview without students' prior knowledge, or students may be interviewed by the whole team they will be working with. Students may be approached by clients who want to talk to them and find out who they are. These encounters are the beginning of your practice experience: Coping with the unexpected will be a daily part of your field placement.

**Ensuring Learning Goals Will Be Met**  Both the field supervisor and the student must agree that they are a good match. To assist in determining how they will fit into this agency, students should have a list of questions that they want to ask to determine whether it will in fact meet their learning goals.

Here are some questions students may want to include on their list:

- With whom does this agency work? What unique services does it provide?
- What does a typical day look like at this setting?
- Will I be working with other staff, and what will they expect of me?
- How will I receive feedback on my work?
- How much room will I be given to define my work within the framework of the expectations of the agency?
- Will I be expected to write a journal, process recordings, or a reflective log?
- What other writing will be expected of me at the agency?
- Will I have to learn the agency computer system?
- How often will I be formally supervised?
- Do you require a criminal record check?
- Do you require any specific immunizations?

These additional questions are very practical:

- What do people at this agency do for lunch or coffee?
- Am I expected to have lunch with the staff?
- What will my scheduled hours be at the agency?
- Will there be specific times for meetings or special events outside of my normal field placements that I will be expected to attend?
- Am I expected to purchase supplies, drive clients, or incur any other costs? If so, how will I be reimbursed?
- Who do I call if I am sick and can't come to work?
- Is there staff parking?
- Are there things I can read before I begin my placement to prepare for it?

These questions will allow the prospective field supervisors to see that students have put some careful thought into preparing for their field placement experience and that they are genuinely interested in the learning in which they will be engaging at this agency. The key characteristics that field supervisors look for when they interview students are curiosity, openness, and flexibility. Students' questions will assist the supervisor in assessing them.

This section has shown how complex planning for a field placement can be. There are many practical matters to consider. A shifting schedule may be an issue, and students will need to think about how they will manage this. For example, the agency may have a board meeting on Tuesday nights, a Saturday family event, or an important staff meeting on Monday mornings. Class schedules, part-time employment, and/or family responsibilities may conflict with these expectations. These concerns should be identified right away to see whether the agency can be flexible or whether a student can make arrangements to accommodate the expectations of the agency. In some instances, accommodation will not be possible and students will need to find another placement. Working closely with the program field coordinator to seek a solution will allow students to plan for and manage the various demands of their competing responsibilities.

## CASE SCENARIO

David is a recent immigrant to Canada. He has been working in a factory and has decided that he wants to improve his job opportunities. He was a teacher in Africa before coming to Canada and loved working with students. He is now enrolled in a child and youth worker program. He has seen the challenges youth face in Canada and believes he can make a difference. He is very motivated to attend college, but needs to work 30 hours a week at his factory job to have enough money for his living and school expenses. David had an interview at a group home for teenagers and really wants to do his placement there. The placement will take place from 1:00 p.m. to 9:00 p.m. three days per week. He has classes on the other two days. He has his reading and assignments to complete, as well.

### Questions

1. How would you suggest David manage his time?

2. What decisions might David have to make to accomplish all that he needs to do?

## Preparing to Start a Field Placement

Once a field placement setting has been secured and an interview has taken place, students are ready to think about next steps. Many students are both excited and anxious at this point. The reality of working with people with serious challenges in their lives can feel overwhelming and daunting. The interview experience may have revealed that the staff of the prospective agency is very skilled and competent, and the student may suddenly feel unsure of their skills and knowledge for the particular setting. Feeling this way is normal. It is helpful to remember that the agency has offered a field placement and is willing to teach students. Planning and preparing before beginning at the agency will assist in ensuring a successful start to the placement. Students can prepare in a number of ways so they can walk into an agency with confidence and feel excited about the new learning about to begin. The following list of advice will ensure that students are as prepared as possible for their field placements:

- Make sure your criminal record check is done and at the agency before your placement starts. You may be prevented from beginning your placement if it is not completed.
- Make sure you have obtained any immunizations the agency requires.
- Contact your agency supervisor and ask for material that you can read before you start your placement, if this information was not provided at your interview. This initiative will greatly impress your supervisor. He or she can provide you with agency annual reports, articles about the client population with whom you will be working, and pamphlets describing the agency's services.
- Conduct a web search on your agency. If the agency has a website, read as much as you can about the agency there. Look for news articles that have been written about the agency or the people at the agency. Take note of significant events and people.
- Do a community walk. Spend a few hours exploring the area where your agency is located. This outing will provide you with some practical knowledge, such as which bus to take to get there or where to park, so you don't have to figure that out on your first day. But, more importantly, experience what the neighbourhood feels like. What do the buildings in the area tell you about the community? Have a cup of coffee and people watch for a while. What do you notice? Are there other service agencies in the area? Take notes on what you see.
- Find the offices of the federal Member of Parliament (MP) and the provincial Member of the Legislative Assembly. Visit these offices and find out what information they have about the community where you will be doing your placement. These offices have extensive information about government programs and services and will be able to give you important information about the issues facing the community. You may even meet your MP and be able to tell him or her about what you will be doing. You can follow this up later by writing a letter to her or him expressing your views on what you have learned and what issues still need to be addressed in the community.
- Start reviewing your local newspaper for articles about community issues, activities, and services. Clip these and start keeping a file. You can learn a great deal about your community from local media. You may also see events advertised that you may wish to attend to gain a better knowledge of how your community addresses concerns. Forums are particularly helpful.
- Visit your local library and ask the reference librarian for information about the community. The library may have an annual report on your agency or other agencies in the area. Your librarian can also provide you with community profiles that can inform you about the its unique characteristics.

- Go to your own college or university library website and find a few articles about the specific population or social issue you will be working with and read them as a way of immersing yourself in the professional literature in this specific field.
- Refer to the following checklists for specific suggestions.

---

## Getting Ready for Your Field Placement

The following checklists will guide you through specific activities that will greatly assist you in getting started and gaining legitimacy at your field placement agency.

### CHECKLIST FOR ADVANCE PREPARATION

☑ Review the field placement course outline and field manual.

☑ Write down questions for your first meetings with the field instructor.

☑ Do you have any questions about the agency's services as a whole? Have these ready for your field instructor.

☑ Think about what you really want to learn and how you will benefit from your practicum experience. Make a list of your goals, being as specific as possible. This list will provide you with a good start in formulating your learning contract.

☑ Collect course material — course outlines, reading lists, and handouts — and share what you are learning in the classroom with your field instructor.

☑ Review your notes from your community walk, your visit to your MP's offices, your readings, and your "community file."

### CHECKLIST FOR THE FIRST DAY

☑ In your first meeting with your agency supervisor:

    ☑ Find out what the plans are for your orientation and introduction to the agency and how you will begin your work there; offer ideas from your list, and review the questions you prepared.

    ☑ Discuss your résumé and share learning interests with your field instructor (if you haven't already done so).

    ☑ Establish supervision times — these should be scheduled weekly.

    ☑ Establish work hours.

    ☑ Seek to learn your supervisor's and agency's most pressing service problems and priorities.

☑ Make a list of all staff and their jobs.

☑ Learn where the policy and procedure manuals are kept.

☑ Observe the office norms in dress, breaks for coffee and lunch, making and cleaning up coffee, and socializing.

## CHECKLIST FOR THE FIRST WEEK

☑ Have your notebook with you and add questions, issues, and other information to it for your field instructor.

☑ Learn office routines for obtaining files, using phones (e.g., making long–distance calls), advising the receptionist of your schedule, using government cars or mileage, keeping work/caseload statistics, giving work to thes receptionist, obtaining office supplies, and completing forms.

☑ Find out from your field instructor who will be the "backup supervisor" when she or he is absent.

☑ Schedule time to talk with other staff members individually.

☑ Begin a list of resources that the agency uses most frequently.

☑ Plan your time by using a daily log. The first priority will be your field instructor's orientation program, but anticipate "blank spots" by having ideas for how to advance your own learning. Check your ideas with your field instructor.

☑ Review policy or other manuals.

☑ Read up on typical problems presented by clients. The staff of your agency library will have such material.

☑ Propose to your field instructor that you visit the local resources (formal and informal) — for example, police, community centres, neighbouring service agencies, or employment counsellors. Talk with the staff at these locations and develop a list of advice. Use this information to begin your own resources file.

☑ Ask if you can read some client files.

☑ Review legislation related to the work of your agency.

☑ Ask other staff members whether you can observe their work.

☑ Attend relevant community meetings or activities.

☑ Plan some pleasurable and relaxing after-work activity — this is going to feel like a tough week.

☑ Don't forget to pay for your coffee!

(Used and adapted with permission from the School of Social Work, University of British Columbia.)

# Becoming a Professional

From the moment you first contact an agency, you are entering into a professional relationship. How you conduct and present yourself will form an important first impression.

Yes, you are still a student, taking a required course that provides a learning experience. However, you must now adhere to the expectations of an agency in a professional practice context. It is not unlike walking into a stranger's house and feeling like a guest. You should be on your best behaviour and look for clues that will help you understand the context you have entered.

It is expected that students will be nervous when they begin a field placement. Research has noted that field instructors are equally nervous as they start working with a new student (Royse, 2010). The field instructor may be new to working with students or may have had many students over their professional career.

## Voices from the Field

There's a whole issue for students I think about being a professional, what that means. For many that means putting on a hat or putting on a facade or not getting too involved and not getting too close. Helping them to find their comfort level. You know, mine may be closer than some in terms of my personal space or my boundaries. But trying to figure out with them what feels comfortable and appropriate for them and how they can identify where there should be a boundary. What are the limits of the work that they do? What does it mean to be a professional and what's conflict of interest and what's too close and what's too far. Trying to help them to measure those kinds of things. They're subtle. It's hard to talk about. It's something that is just ongoing and our discussing how they experience a client. So that's in the back of my mind and we talk about [those things and that] we're going to work on those things....

So, if they're starting off afraid to speak with a client, then I need to start with the basics — go through interviewing skills, their concerns and worries. The first thing I tell all the students is that I don't want them to get any kind of job done. That if they see a client my first concern is that they're kind and caring to the client. If the client is rude and angry, they need to leave. Say, "You know, it's not a good day, it's not a good phone call, I'll speak to you later" and then come and talk to me. But if the client is asking them about something and they really don't have a clue, they don't have to worry about saying that they're not sure. They can say, "Let me make a list of the things that we're going to work on and I'll go find out and get back to you." If they leave and nothing happened, that's fine. They still had the experience. They still have the connection and that they need to find something they like about the client. Something they have in common, some quality that they can say, that's okay. So that would be ... the beginning. (Linda Danson, field instructor)

Every field placement will be a unique learning experience. Whatever the students' starting point, it is the right place to start. As noted earlier, feelings of anxiety can be overcome with preparation, reflection, and planning. Understanding the importance of professionalism will be the key to success in a field placement. Although students will discuss professionalism and ethical behaviour in their classes, the following checklist is an excellent prompt for thinking about how this behaviour will specifically relate to field placements:

## Checklist for Behaving Professionally

At your field placement you will be expected to behave professionally at all times. To do so, do the following:

- ☑ Always be punctual.
- ☑ Return phone calls as soon as possible and meet all work deadlines.
- ☑ Dress appropriately for your setting and change your dress as needed for specific functions or events.
- ☑ Use appropriate language; never swear or use overly familiar language.
- ☑ Be truthful about actions and information, even when you make a mistake.
- ☑ Maintain confidentiality.
- ☑ Be aware of your own limitations, and ask for help when you need to.
- ☑ Be open to feedback.
- ☑ Be sensitive to all you encounter — clients, staff members, and other professionals.
- ☑ Engage actively in your own learning; seek out learning opportunities.
- ☑ Volunteer to take on assignments and engage in activities.
- ☑ When you are part of a team, participate, contributing as required.
- ☑ Demonstrate your leadership by bringing forward your ideas.
- ☑ Be respectful of diversity.
- ☑ Be respectful of opinions and attitudes different from your own.
- ☑ Ensure that your environment is safe for you and others.
- ☑ Ensure that your practice is grounded in theory and evidence-based research.

The Checklist for Behaving Professionally reflects important aspects of professional behaviour that may be new and different. If students are unsure as to exactly how to fulfill these expectations, they should raise them in the classroom when field placements are discussed. Most programs also will have a faculty member assigned to function as a field liaison who will visit students at the agency and meet with the student and the field instructor. This person may be a faculty member the student has already encountered in the program or may be someone specifically hired to do the agency visiting for the program. This person is vital to the success of the field placement, assisting students with thinking about and developing the required professional practice in the specific agency. For example, if a student is trying to establish relationships in a setting in which teenagers use slang and swear all the time, a student may question the type of language that is appropriate to use. He or she could raise this excellent example of a professional issue in class or with the field liaison.

Engaging in practice at a field placement agency allows students to learn about individuals asking for support and assistance. This work is carried out under the guidance and direction of what will be a new professional relationship with a field supervisor. This is a crucial relationship, as this person will be witness to the student's anxieties and successes. Field supervisors enjoy working with students and want you to succeed.

## Voices from the Field

We take [students] because we need them ... it's come to the point where we really rely on the students for a lot of the work that we do. I also really enjoy supervising students. I find they bring new ideas, new blood. I always look forward to September because there's a whole new dynamic that starts. They come in with energy, and they add a lot the agency. (Nona Moscovitz, field instructor)

Not only are students in a learning process, but the field supervisor is also learning from students. Students bring new knowledge from the literature they review that is based in current research. They also bring their unique background of cultural experiences and talents.

Each party in the student–supervisor relationship has unique knowledge and each may be lacking knowledge. Figure 2.1 represents a way of examining this knowledge framework:

---

**Figure 2.1** Varieties of Knowledge

Supervisor's Knowledge
- assessment and intervention strategies in working with clients
- social services available for this client population
- relevant legislation
- problem-solving approaches
- unique cultural background and repertoire of experience

Student's Knowledge
- most recent research learned in class
- exposure to a variety of theoretical approaches taught in the program
- particular cultural background, language spoken, and life experiences
- openness to learning, curiosity

Supervisor and Student's Shared Knowledge
- cultural group experiences
- language
- workshop or conference experience
- community life
- personal interests

Knowledge that Supervisor and Student Both Need to Attain
- background information about a client from a cultural group that neither has worked with before
- background information about a social problem that neither has experienced before
- knowledge about a new legal framework just presented that needs to be incorporated into practice

---

# Thinking about Beginning Practice

The activities suggested in this chapter have focused on knowing one's strengths and knowledge and being well prepared. The reality of the field placement, however, may present unanticipated circumstances. Agencies are always experiencing change. Students enter the agency at various stages of this change. Sometimes this can create a confusing environment, even for the most prepared student. Some examples of agency change include the following: funding has been cut and the agency needs to lay off several staff members; a new project has been approved and new staff members are being hired; a tragic client death has greatly affected the staff; or the government has announced new legislation that will change the services of the agency. Change is a constant in social work and human service work. Learning to understand and cope with change will be a key competency of the practicum experience. While the variety of changes cannot be anticipated, some occur with greater frequency. The following exercise identifies changes that practicum students have encountered. Thinking about these scenarios will help students develop management skills, which are important for a career in the helping profession.

## Exercise

You walk into your agency and something unanticipated happens. What will you do? The following quotations show some potential realities of agency life and field supervisor workload responsibilities. Pretend that each of the comments below is made to you by an agency employee and consider the following questions:

1. What potential strengths could I gain from this situation?
2. What are the potential difficulties of this situation?
3. What steps do I need to take to ensure that this situation will result in a positive learning experience for me?

   A. "We don't like to be too formal and structured in this agency—why don't you just join in wherever you want or do whatever you find interesting."
   B. "I think the best way for you to start is by observing other workers. So just do that for a while, and we can talk later about you picking up some work for yourself."
   C. "I have a project that has just been approved. It would be good experience for you, I think. It involves searching our files and collecting data on who uses the service of our agency. I know it doesn't exactly fit your program's learning contract, but it sure would help me out. Could you work on this project during your placement?"
   D. "Our receptionist will be away next week. It would be good experience for you to do that job as you'd get to know the kind of calls that come into this agency. I know it isn't really social work but we are really stuck and it would be great if you could help us out."

E.  "One of our groups is without a leader. Could you start by taking this group on for us? They meet on Wednesday nights."

F.  "I have one client I am going to assign to you. You will be co-interviewing with a staff member. You will stay with that client for January. If all goes well, I will assign a second client in February."

G.  "Before we can assign you any responsibilities, you must be very familiar with our policies. I would like you to take these manuals and spend the next few days reading them so that you are aware of the legislation, policies, and procedures that we work under."

H.  "Look, you've arrived at a very busy time. I have to get a report ready for the government and I don't have any time to spend with you right now. How about visiting some of the agencies in the neighbourhood and making yourself familiar with what's happening in the community?"

I.  "I want you to spend some time in the drop-in centre getting to know the people we work with. So I'd like you to spend the next few weeks talking to people, having coffee with them, and getting to know about their lives."

J.  "I've just had a case transferred to me by the intake worker. It's a teenager who is First Nations. Since you're a First Nations student, I think this would be a good case for you to work with." (Replace with any other client that is self-identified in the same way as you.)

K.  "I have been working with a group of clients from our agency, getting their feedback about our services. I'm having a really tough time with the leader of this group as she continually challenges my authority. Could you sit in on this group for a while and see if you could develop a better rapport with her?"

L.  "Did you know I graduated from your program 10 years ago? Are a couple of my old faculty members still there [they are named]? They were out of touch with the realities of practice then, and I'll bet they're still teaching you the same old useless stuff."

# USING HELPFUL TOOLS FOR YOUR FIELD PLACEMENT

## Using a Reflective Journal or Log

Begin writing about what you are observing, doing, and learning. The practice of writing will assist you in thinking through your experiences, reactions, and plans for further action. It can also be thought of as a process of self-supervision. Students who use a reflective journal or log often come to their supervision meetings prepared to discuss the issues they are encountering and what they plan to do next.

You can use the following outline:

- Activities I carried out (what action I took) ...
- What I learned (information, attitudes, skills I tested) ...

- Difficulties I encountered …
- My reactions, feelings, and interpretations …
- Based on my reflection, what I need to learn …
- Based on my reflection, what I will do next …
- What I need to discuss with my supervisor …

Find some time each day to write in your journal or log. Writing down all your ideas, thoughts, and questions will help you let go of them until you meet with your supervisor to discuss them. You will find that this will help you to relax and enjoy your field placement, and it will allow you to see how your learning is progressing.

## Voices from the Field

There's no structure to it. There's no goal. It's not like, answer that question type thing. They're just asked to reflect about their own thoughts. Some of them have difficulty putting their thoughts on paper … I want them to learn to do that. I think when you write things down and five weeks later when you look back at it, it's a helpful process. It's a process you want to look at. When you're talking and learning … it's different, it's still learning, but it's not cyclical. You haven't been able to analyze it…. It gives me an opportunity to see their writing…. It gives me an opportunity for me to see how they think…. I want to see what they're thinking about. (Kim Kidder, field instructor)

## CHAPTER SUMMARY

This chapter focused on field placement preparation. Students have completed personal self-assessments to identify the strengths and experience they bring to their program and their field placement. This self-assessment has allowed students to clarify the learning goals they will achieve in the practice experience. Various exercises have provided methods for students to research prospective agencies, prepare and participate in exploratory interviews, prepare for a field placement, and develop strategies for success at the field placement agency. Students have learned that preparing by anticipating expectations at a field placement allows them to be confident and ready for practice. Students have also learned how to work with the program faculty, field coordinator, and faculty liaison to identify the location of the field placement, prepare for their first encounter with their supervisor, prepare for their field placement, and start on the path to be coming a competent professional. This chapter has provided a thorough understanding of the professional behaviour that is expected in the helping professions. It includes exercises that will strengthen students' confidence in preparing for unanticipated changes that may occur in the agency setting. Successfully getting started in a field placement begins the process of learning in a new professional arena.

## Critical-Thinking Questions

1. What do you anticipate will be the most challenging learning situation for you at your field placement?
2. What are you most curious to learn as you anticipate your field placement?
3. What personal support systems will you need to have in place to balance your classroom work and your field placement expectations?
4. What is your theoretical framework for your practice at your field placement?

## Suggested Readings

Rath, T. (2007). *StrengthsFinder 2.0: A new and upgraded edition of the online test from Gallup's Now, discover your strengths.* New York, NY: Gallup Press.

Buckingham, M., & Clifton, D. (2001). *Now, discover your strengths.* Riversisde, NJ: Simon & Schuster Publishers.

# Chapter 3

## Ethical and Legal Issues: Roles, Rights, and Responsibilities

Mary Harber-Iles and Duane Seibel

## Chapter Objectives

- Identify general aspects of the Canadian legal system.
- Describe professional liability and how it applies to student placements.
- Recognize ethical issues that students may encounter.
- Describe the limits and responsibility of various ethical and legal concepts, such as confidentiality, duty to warn and protect, informed consent, and exceeding one's level of professional expertise.

What roles do students play in their practice settings in terms of understanding legal issues as learning professionals and employees? Students in practica are often seen as quasi-employees — not fully hired agency employees, yet working within agency practice and protocol. In addition, students work under the support and guidance of a third party: their college or university. In this context, who is responsible for what and what roles do students take on in terms of legal issues and concerns in practice? This chapter will explore some of the basic legal and ethical concepts essential for students moving into practicum settings. Although this chapter will cover a variety of legal and ethical issues, it is by no means exhaustive in terms of the breadth of legal and ethical issues relating to various practice areas.

## THE CANADIAN LEGAL SYSTEM AND ITS IMPACT ON PRACTICE

Canadian law affects all social work and human service practice. We acknowledge that only lawyers should provide legal advice, and yet social workers, child and youth care workers, and human service workers can best assist clients through gaining an understanding of applicable laws and legal processes. The laws that students will need to become familiar with will vary by setting and client group. Horejsi & Garthwait (2002) describe three broad categories in which social work and human service agencies and their staff are guided, directed, or mandated by law: (1) laws regulating services or actions related to a specific client, (2) laws regulating a field of practice or type of human service program, and (3) laws regulating the professional practice of social workers or other human service professionals (p. 181). In gaining understanding of the laws associated with their specific field of practice, students will be better able to anticipate client challenges and refer clients to relevant services or resources when necessary.

It would be impossible to go into great detail in this chapter about all the laws that may have an impact on social work and human service practice. Instead, this chapter will acknowledge broader categories that affect service areas. Regehr and Kanani (2006) classify provincial and federal laws affecting work with clients in the following nine categories:

1. Family law — encompassing marriage, divorce, and child custody.

2. Child protection — including the obligation of all citizens to report suspected abuse and neglect and the responsibility of the state to protect children from harm.

3. Consent and capacity — highlighting the need to determine, at times, the ability of individuals to make decisions regarding their own treatment, care, and management of their financial affairs because of illness or infirmity.

4. Mental illness — highlighting the need to determine, at times, the ability of individuals to make decisions regarding their own treatment, care, and management of their financial affairs because of mental illness. Also, the determination of whether someone may be held criminally responsible for their actions because of mental illness. Guidance may be provided to those within the social work or human service fields regarding their responsibility to warn others if they believe they may be at risk of harm because of mental illness.

5. Youth criminal justice — defining the special consideration and treatment given to youth and their families once they come into conflict with the law.

6. Victims of violence — providing mechanisms and steps for support and services to both the perpetrators and the victims of crime.

7. Aboriginal rights and status of First Nations communities — providing guidance on (i) how the rights to services for those identified as Aboriginal or First Nations differ from people in the general public, (ii) who has the responsibility to deliver this service; and (iii) the manner in which these services are delivered.

8. Human rights — including the protection of people from discrimination based on protected grounds, such as race, gender, religion, and sexual orientation, in employment, goods, services, and accommodation.

9.  Immigrants and refugees — encompassing the support of those people attempting to gain entry into Canada, including through adoption, and addressing the challenges faced by immigrants after entry.

In some of these categories, both federal and provincial laws come into play, while others are wholly under the jurisdiction of one or the other. In situations where only the provincial government is responsible for a particular piece of legislation, such as mental health and child protection, there may be differences among jurisdictions in the overall legislation and thus in the procedures associated with the laws (see Table 3.1). Therefore, the knowledge students gain at their practica about the applicable laws governing practice is not necessarily transferable to another province or territory. Even in cases where a law is federally created, such as the *Youth Criminal Justice Act* (2002), the implementation and administration of services will differ from province to province.

**Table 3.1** Differences in Mental Health and Child Protection Legislation by Province

| Province | Mental Health Legislation | Child Protection Legislation |
| --- | --- | --- |
| British Columbia | *Mental Health Act*, R.S.B.C. 1996 | *Child, Family and Community Services Act*, 1986 |
| Alberta | *Mental Health Act*, S.A. 1988 | *Child Welfare Act*, 2000 |
| Saskatchewan | *Mental Health Services Act*, S.S. 1984–85–86 | *Child and Family Services Act*, 1989–90 |
| Manitoba | *Mental Health and Consequential Amendments Act*, S.M. 1998 | *Child and Family Services Act*, 1985 |
| Ontario | *Mental Health Act*, R.S.O. 1990 | *Child and Family Services Act*, RSO 1990 |
| Quebec | *An Act Respecting the Protection of Persons Whose Mental State Presents a Danger to Themselves and Others*, S.Q. 1997 | *Youth Protection Act*, 2003 |
| New Brunswick | *Mental Health Act*, R.S.N.B. 1973 | *Family Services Act*, 1983 |
| Nova Scotia | *Hospitals Act*, S.N.S. 1989 | *Child and Family Services Act*, 2002 |
| Prince Edward Island | *Mental Health Act*, S.P.E.I. 1994 | *Child Protection Act*, 2003 |
| Newfoundland and Labrador | *Mental Health Act*, R.S.N. 1990 | *Child, Youth and Family Services Act*, 1998 |
| Northwest Territories | *Mental Health Act*, R.S.N.W.T. 1988 | *Child and Family Services Act*, 1997 |
| Nunavut | | *Child and Family Services Act*, 1997 |
| Yukon | *Mental Health Act*, S.Y.T. 1989–90 | *Children's Act*, 2002 |

Identify the legislation that will most likely have an impact on those receiving service from your practicum agency. Are there several areas of legislation that you may need to consider? How might this legislation overlap?

# LEGAL CONSIDERATIONS AND PROFESSIONAL LIABILITY

In the field, judgments and decisions are made based on individual practitioner knowledge, experience, and values. As developing professionals, students are expected to make sound decisions and are accountable for decisions that will have an impact on people's lives. Therefore, it is important to understand the possible effect of a decision. Students are often excited to be provided with the opportunity to apply what they have learned within their classes to the practice setting and may wish to make decisions contrary to agency policy or professional practice norms. The practicum provides most students with their first experience in the field that they have been preparing for — an experience that often makes students anxious and afraid about the unknown. This anxiety may be compounded as students reflect on the possibility that they may make mistakes. Mistakes no doubt will happen and are an important part of the learning process! Thus, it is important for students to understand that in practice, when they make decisions, they must be aware of a great deal; one of their most important considerations should be their legal and professional responsibilities. It is through a practicum, supported by those practising within the profession, that students experience some of their most meaningful learning as "a result of having to deal with frustration and unexpected events" (Horejsi & Garthwait, 2002, p. 2).

## Understanding Liability

The term *liability* in its broadest definition is simply an obligation an individual has to either do something or refrain from doing something (Yogis & Cotter, 2009, p. 160). In professional practice, we refer to liability as an acknowledgment of responsibility to the legal obligation that social workers and human service practitioners accept when they enter into practice. Claims for liability by clients or others against social workers or human service workers and other professionals may be based on such issues as inaccurate record keeping, breach of confidentiality, lack of informed consent, conflict of interest, and professional misrepresentation.

Liability is not often an issue dealt with by an individual, unless a practitioner works in a private practice. In these situations, it is important that the private practitioner has practice insurance and is linked to professional bodies, such as associations for social workers or human service workers, to access additional support and safeguards. Across disciplines, there are several bodies to which professionals can attach themselves to acquire support and liability insurance. For example, the Canadian Association of Social Workers is a federation of nine provincial and one territorial social work organizations, which provides a national leadership role in strengthening and advancing the social work profession in Canada (*www.casw-acts.ca*). This organization provides information about liability issues and addresses key issues in the field. Child and youth care associations across Canada provide similar guidance.

## Students and Liability

Practice and professional liability is an important issue for consideration as a practicum student and, although most situations will not involve legal recourse, it is prudent for students to understand the legal ramifications of their actions. Students have a unique role: They are not an employee typically covered by the agency in terms of liability, and yet they are doing work that requires adherence to the policy and practice rules outlined by agency standards and legal or contractual obligations. Although students are held to the same standards, they have the benefit of being in a learning atmosphere in which supervisors assist them in working through accountability issues. Despite their special status, students are still obligated to be aware of and to understand how work with others is guided, directed, and sometimes mandated by law. Students may have to learn about laws directed at providing service with a specific client (e.g., involuntary hospitalization, consent forms), or they may have to learn about laws that regulate a specific area of practice (e.g., youth agencies, child protection, professional regulations about various codes such as ethics, licensing, and duties to clients) (Horejsi & Garthwait, 2002).

While the supervisor of the agency and the educational institution often maintain legal responsibility for students' actions, it is still critical that students establish a clear set of boundaries about their practice with their supervisors, because they are expected to understand the limitations of their skills and knowledge and to seek supervision when they are unsure about a practice decision. A review of the literature reveals that there is little case law involving malpractice suits against social workers (Besharov & Besharov, 1987, as cited in Bogo & Vauda, 1998). Although the risk is limited, it still exists, making it important to understand potential risk and how to manage this risk proactively. The following sections discuss student–client situations that could be causes for criminal or civil action.

**Failing to Inform Client of Student Status**   Students must always let their clients know that they are students in a learning position. This declaration lets clients know not that they are receiving substandard support, but that the student's role has limits and that students will receive additional supervision to ensure that clients are receiving the best possible service. Sharing student status also serves to further develop a transparent and honest relationship.

**Providing Treatment without Proper Consent** Receiving consent is critical in all working relationships. Again, facilitating relationship transparency is important to ensure that students are not violating a client's rights and are supporting the ethic of self-determination.

**Keeping Inaccurate or Inadequate Records** Record keeping and paperwork may not be a favourite part of social work or human services work, but it is necessary and important. Students must understand that their records and information may be subpoenaed in a court of law and that the accuracy of their records is critical. It is good practice for supervisors to review all students' written records to ensure accuracy and clarity regarding fact versus opinion. Clients also have a right to their paperwork and records, which is another reason why accurate, objective, and honest recording is an important part of practice.

**Failing to Seek Proper Supervision** Because they will be evaluated, students may be tempted to showcase their skills and knowledge without the aid of supervision to highlight their learning and practice potential. There comes a point in the practicum at which it is important for students to take initiative and show some independence; however, it is dangerous for students to make practice decisions that will affect clients and the course of their lives without the support of supervision. It's important for students to remember that even seasoned practitioners seek and use supervision to ensure that their decisions are sound. When starting a practicum, students should not only review agency policy and practice procedures, but also clarify their student roles and be sure to address practice issues such as the following:

- decision-making power
- client interviews (whether a supervisor should be present)
- transportation expectations (students are not typically permitted to transport clients)
- supervised visits by students with individuals or family service clients
- youth and children work
- supervisor availability during difficult situations

Although students are expected to take on more independent work as the placement progresses, supervision is an integral part of the practicum experience.

In summary, liability issues are a concern, and the best way to address them is to be proactive and to thoroughly understand the legal context of the practice setting, the context of the profession, and how the agency deals with various issues within the parameters of its own policy. While it is important to understand the limits of a student's role in a practice setting, it is also true that "a client who consents to service from a practicum student has not agreed to receive inferior or harmful service" (Bonosky, as cited by Bogo & Vauda, 1998). In light of these types of supervisory issues, it is important for students and field instructors to review all legal aspects of a practicum and discuss these with field education or agency supervisors when assessing potential placements.

Sandy was working at a practicum in a deferred custody program for youth on court-ordered addictions counselling. As a part of every participant's court order, clients were required to refrain from consuming alcohol and nonprescription drugs. Sandy was approached by Ted, who was 17 years old, with whom she had developed a strong working relationship. Ted was an active participant, always showed up for meetings, and was seen as a leader and a positive influence on the group. Ted disclosed to Sandy that he had "slipped" and had smoked marijuana on the weekend. He felt bad about this and stated that this was a one-time-only slip and he was committed to not using again. Sandy knew that if she reported Ted's drug use to the supervisor, Ted would likely be breached and could be removed from the program.

### Questions

1. What is Sandy's justification for choosing to
   a. report the information?
   b. not report the information?
2. If Sandy does not report this incident, what are the potential liabilities and consequences?

Professionals in the fields of social work, child and youth care, and human service are not only responsible for carrying out legal policy and contractual obligations and for meeting legal requirements according to specific areas of practice, but they are also responsible for framing their practice around their disciplines' code of ethics. For example, human service workers must follow provincial legislation regulating child welfare practice along with professional ethics and practice guidelines. Legal obligations related to practice are often identified within legislation and, as Regehr and Kanani (2006) acknowledge, each province has legislation that specifies who can identify as a social worker, and in many cases as a social service worker, and provides guidance on which body may provide oversight of this practice (p. 196).

A common expectation of all professionals is the responsibility to adhere to codes of ethics and to maintain legal understanding within practice. Professional liability is in place to ensure that helping professionals maintain a standard of practice that will ensure the safety of those they are entrusted to work with, which in most cases is with people who are most vulnerable.

## CODES OF ETHICS

Disciplines develop codes of ethics based on accepted values. Codes exist to provide guidance in ethical situations (Merrill Education, 2005, p. 2). Membership in a professional body requires the adherence to that body's code of ethics. Although each distinct discipline has its own code of ethics, great similarities exist between the ethics guidelines of different counselling and helping professions (Cottone & Tarvydas, 2003, p. 77).

Established codes of ethics have the following purposes:

- Because they act autonomously and regulate those within the profession, they protect professional bodies from government regulation (Merrill Education, 2005).
- They provide the opportunity to proactively address and control the internal conflicts within a professional body (Merrill Education, 2005).
- They provide some level of safety from the public for those within the profession; namely, if professionals act within their professional ethical guidelines and standards, they are less likely to experience public scrutiny or litigation (Merrill Education, 2005; Regehr & Kanani, 2006).

Students within a helping professional program are required to become familiar with and adhere to an identified code of ethics while in the program, within a practicum, and in future professional practice. Moreover, educational institutions have additional codes of conduct that highlight personal and professional expectations and performance for students while they are in the classroom or the practice setting. Codes of ethics and conduct are not recipe books for practice; instead, they "… provide guidelines, based on the experiences and values, of how professionals should behave. In many ways ethical standards represent the collected wisdom of a profession at a particular time but nothing else" (Merrill Education, 2005, p. 3).

Codes of ethics are not law, but they do provide professional bodies with the ability to support their members and, in situations where the members have not adhered to the code, to discipline or sanction practising members. Although codes of ethics clearly highlight that any illegal activity is in contravention of the code, it is possible to make a decision that might contravene a legal responsibility, such as choosing not to breach a youth for using an illegal substance. Professionals who are in breach of the code of ethics may be restricted for a period or banned completely from practising within their field. Students who breach the code of ethics or an educational institution's code of conduct could be removed from their practicum, program of study, or, ultimately, their college or university. Thus, students' familiarity and adherence to their program's expectations for appropriate behaviour is vitally important.

## Exercise

Identify what ethical guidelines your program expects you to abide by while in practicum and then answer the following questions.

1. Are there specific institutional policies that will guide your practice?
2. Are you expected to adhere to professional codes of ethics?

# Ethical Decision Making

This book examines various areas of practice in the context of a practicum setting and often
mentions that we are guided by ethical practice. But what does *ethical* really mean? Ethics,
although sounding ominous, are merely values in action. In other words, ethical decision
making is about what is valued in terms of our professional and personal practice mandate
and how professionals enact that in their work. For example, if one values honesty, then
transparency in practice could be a way to bring that value to life, and the way he or she
works with individuals, groups, and communities would reflect this value. Although ethical
decision making can be difficult, examining a situation from many different perspectives
can make a decision more clear. An ethical dilemma stems from the idea that a variety of
decisions could have merit, and deciding how to select the "best" course of action could be
thought of as working with the "grey area" of decision making. Decisions must be considered in light of practice codes of ethics and personal values and beliefs.

**Ethical Decision-Making Models**  Ethical decision making is not an inherent skill
and requires that practitioners identify situations in which they may not act responsibly
because of conflicts between their personal and professional values. Additionally, a professional must consider the clients' values, culture, and religious beliefs while making
ethical decisions. Many models assist professionals in working through dilemmas. Corey,
Schneider Corey, & Callanan's (2007) model provides an eight-step decision-making
approach to working through ethical problems: (1) identify the problem or dilemma,
(2) identify the potential issues involved, (3) review the relevant ethical codes, (4) know
the applicable laws and regulations, (5) obtain consultation, (6) consider possible and
probable courses of action, (7) enumerate the consequences of various decisions, and
(8) decide on the best course of action. This model is not necessarily linear, as some steps
may be skipped or the order in which they are applied may differ among situations. We
explore some of the activities that could occur at each of these steps below:

**Step 1.**  In this step, it is important to access as much information as possible, including
the determination of whether the issue is ethical, legal, clinical, professional, or
moral (or a combination). Ethical dilemmas are complex; therefore, it is important to look at the situation from various perspectives, including from the
perspectives of those involved in the dilemma.

**Step 2.**  This step requires that an assessment is made of what information is relevant
and what information is not. Also considered are the rights, responsibilities,

and welfare of those involved, and context issues such as culture and power differentials.

**Step 3.** Earlier in the chapter, students were asked to identify the applicable code(s) of ethics in their practice setting. They should consider whether this code provides clarity or guidance. If the code does provide guidance, yet you find your own personal values in conflict, can you identify a rationale for your position? It is important that you document this part of the process to demonstrate your commitment to solving the dilemma.

**Step 4.** Earlier in the chapter, students were also asked to identify those laws and regulations that guide practice in their practicum agency. Students should consider whether any of these laws or regulations provide help in understanding what to do. At times, a professional association can assist students in identifying their legal obligations in certain situations.

**Step 5.** For many students, obtaining consultation is likely the first step to take when confronted with a challenging decision. Students can consult with colleagues, a practicum supervisor, or a faculty member. A professional with legal questions will likely seek legal advice. Students can consult anybody who has expertise they lack — for example, people from a different culture or with a different world view. It is wise for students to document their consultation.

**Step 6.** After they have gathered a great deal of information, students are in a position to brainstorm various solutions to the dilemma. A list of possible actions should always include the possibility of no action at all.

**Step 7.** Once they have identified possible actions, students should consider the possible impact of each. They can identify the various benefits and possible drawbacks.

**Step 8.** Based on the above information, students can select the best course of action. They can answer the following questions as a final test:

- Does this decision fit with my code of ethics?

- Does this decision fit with the cultural values and experiences of my client?

- How have my own values been affirmed or challenged?

- How might others assess my action?

Students may also find that the outcome of their decision takes the situation in a new direction. As a result, they may want to revisit this process for the new situation or in light of revised information. This process is helpful when decisions in practice seem complicated or multilayered.

These steps do not guarantee the prefect outcome; however, when the above components are considered, good decision making will result. Using such an ethical decision-making process provides for a reflective process that ensures that all aspects of a situation are explored and understood to determine the best outcome at a particular time. Thoughtful decisions explore alternatives and their impacts. For students, this process is a great opportunity for self-reflection and ongoing learning.

Arjun is a youth worker with a local recreational program in a faith-based organization. He knows that one of the youth he is supporting, Aaron, is questioning his sexual orientation. He also knows that if he suggests that Aaron attend an information session with the local gay, lesbian, two-spirited, transgendered, and questioning (GLBTQ) organization, this youth would be resistant and embarrassed. Arjun also knows that Aaron would find the group useful, and it could diminish Aaron's feelings of isolation regarding his sexuality. Arjun brings this issue to his team, and his team generates the following possible courses of action:

- Don't mention the meeting but leave pamphlets out for Aaron to see and possibly pick up.

- On an outing, arrange to "accidentally" run into a member of the GLBTQ organization.

- Have a GLBTQ representative come and do a session with all the group members.

- Use faith-based information to point Arjun in the "right" direction.

### Questions

1. Which course of action may be appropriate and why?

2. Which course of action would you choose? If you do not care for any of these, create your own response. Discuss this response with other students.

# CONFIDENTIALITY

Confidentiality is one of the first concepts learned in social work and human service practice. Students must respect people's right to share information with whomever they choose and not share clients' information unless clients give their permission. Confidentiality of information is standard practice in various codes of ethics and helps to preserve the integrity of the helping relationship. Because confidentiality makes those sharing personal information feel safe, it helps to build a relationship between clients and practitioners and ensures that the practitioner honours and respects the relationship.

The CASW Code of Ethics (2005a) clearly describes the embedded value of confidentiality:

A cornerstone of professional social work relationships is confidentiality with respect to all matters associated with professional services to clients. Social workers demonstrate respect for the trust and confidence placed in them by clients, communities and other professionals by protecting the privacy of client information and respecting the client's right to control when or whether this information will be shared with third parties. Social workers only disclose confidential information to other parties (including family members) with the informed consent of clients, clients' legally authorized representatives or when required by law or court order. The general expectation that social workers will keep information confidential does not apply when disclosure is necessary to prevent serious, foreseeable and imminent harm to a client or others. In all instances, social workers disclose the least amount of confidential information necessary to achieve the desired purpose. (p. 7)

As evidenced by this strong statement, confidentiality is critical to practice, and yet despite this, there are times when we cannot and must not maintain confidentiality for the safety of our client or others.

It is important that clients understand that there are limits to the rules of confidentiality and that social workers and human service workers do not have privilege, which is a different concept than confidentiality. *Privilege* refers to information that a client shares with a professional that the professional does not have to disclose. In Canadian law, privilege extends only to lawyers. Therefore, social workers and other helping professionals may be compelled by law to share or report information. For example, in the following circumstances, social workers and human service workers may have to share information and break the rule of confidentiality:

- Testifying in court. If helping professionals are asked to testify in court, individuals cannot be held liable for what they say — although they can be held liable for failing to inform their clients that their information may be used in court proceedings.
- Concerns about child abuse or neglect. By law, helping professionals must share these concerns with the provincial child protection service agency (i.e., *duty to protect*).
- A clear risk to the health or safety of a third party. In these cases, there may be a *duty to warn and protect* (see "Duty to Warn and Protect" below for more information).
- A high risk of suicide. Helping professionals have the responsibility to call treatment resources and share this information
- A subpoena, warrant, or court order mandating disclosure of information. If records are used in court, individuals cannot be held liable for what they say in the records they kept — although they can be held liable for failing to inform their clients that their information may be used in court proceedings.
- A complaint being investigated by a professional regulatory body
- A duty to share information is identified within legislation, guiding professionals to share information with others
- A legal responsibility to cooperate with police or a child intervention investigation

It is critical to share with clients the limit of confidentiality at the very outset of the relationship. Students often fear that they will damage the potential for a supportive relationship when disclosing this to clients. Although the potential exists, if rapport is established, then typically clients do not leave the relationship and work continues. Failure to warn clients about the limitations of confidentiality constitutes negligent practice and will damage the relationship even more. In their guidance regarding information sharing to Human Service Workers in Alberta, the partnering ministries of the Alberta Children and Youth Initiative (2007) suggest that practitioners need to be clear that information should be shared only on a need-to-know basis. They provide the following guiding questions to assist in this decision making:

1) Think About It (What information do you need to know or disclose to best serve the child, youth, adult or family?); 2) Talk About It (Sometimes people disagree on what needs to be shared. Discuss why you need the information and what you hope to accomplish for the child, youth, adult or family.); 3) Try to Understand and Reach Agreement (Reaching an agreement on what information should be shared will require ongoing communication, patience, and trust.) (p. 2)

## CASE SCENARIO

Patsy is a child and youth care counsellor in a local community agency. She is working with a 16-year-old and 14-year-old brother and sister, who are currently in foster care. The 16-year-old mentioned that his younger sister often talks about committing suicide when they are together. She has never mentioned suicide to you. The brother is worried about his sister and wants to know how to handle this kind of conversation but asks you not to mention it to his sister, as this betrayal would break their confidence as siblings.

### Questions

1. What would you say to the brother about addressing confidentiality?
2. In this situation, what are the key points to consider when making a decision about breaking confidentiality?
3. How would you address the issue of suicide with the sister? What ethical guidelines would you follow when you decide to break confidentiality?

Students may have to consider some additional situations specific to their particular agency or community that may have an impact on confidentiality. Because students are in training and need to seek supervision and support while working with individual clients, clients should know that they are working with a student and that, as a part of the training, case consultation and supervision will occur. Therefore, it is always a good idea to get consent from the client about sharing information with colleagues in the same agency. Students may also be asked to present case studies as assignments in their classrooms. In these situations, it is important to remember that confidentiality must be maintained by changing names and any other potentially identifying information.

A small community presents various challenges for confidentiality. For example, what happens if a child and youth care worker is in the community with a youth and runs into his or her friends while they are out? Students must consider these things before they happen and discuss these either in the classroom setting or with their field instructors.

## Voices from the Field

I was working with a very high profile youth in a small community and as a child and youth support worker my job included taking this youth out in the community. I was out at the local mall and I ran into a couple of friends that I hang out with socially. I didn't want to ignore them but I also didn't want to break confidentiality. I casually said hello and moved on — they asked me later who that was and I couldn't talk about it since it related to my work — I felt awkward and unsure about how to maintain confidentiality. (Anonymous, student)

## Duty to Warn and Protect

Several situations have been mentioned in the chapter in which the worker may need to breach the confidentiality contract. When a professional must make an ethical decision about safety before confidentiality, it is referred to as a duty to warn and protect. This condition occurs when the practitioner believes that a third party may be hurt or a person may hurt themselves or others. A duty to warn and protect ethic must be adhered to both professionally and legally. A famous California case from the 1970s highlights the importance of the legal issues of the duty to warn and protect. In the Tarasoff case, a clinician failed to warn a third party about potential violence and was sued because the violence occurred (Bryce, 2005). In Canada, more and more professionals, such as physicians, psychologists, psychiatrists, and counsellors, are ensuring that issues related to the duty to warn and protect are adhered to in practice. Bryce (2005) points out that counsellors in Canada have a duty to warn and protect in situations where they know a person has human immunodeficiency virus (HIV) or has acquired immune deficiency syndrome (AIDS) and is not taking precautions in order to not infect others through unprotected sex or through sharing drug paraphernalia. Even though the right to privacy is very clear for those with HIV/AIDS, the need to protect others from contracting the virus supersedes the privacy of the individual.

## Informed Consent

Informed consent is integral to practice and speaks to ethical standards, legal issues, and upholding the ethic of honest and transparent self-determined service. It is important for students to understand the policies and procedures around informed consent, which can be verbal, written, or implied. Social service agencies may act on the assumption that if people seek service, they are giving consent to treatment. Although assumed, it may not always be the case. Clarity and understanding about consent to service is an important step in practice.

# HARASSMENT AND DISCRIMINATION

Whether in the classroom, the workplace, or the community, human rights laws protect individuals from harassment and discrimination. *Discrimination* can be defined as differential treatment of an individual or group based on membership in a social group (Whitley & Kite, 2010). This differential treatment is considered discriminatory if it places burdens or disadvantages or withholds opportunities for members of those groups identified as having special protection, or "the protected grounds." Federally, as well as in each province and territory, legislation has been created to identify protected grounds, such as gender, sexual orientation, family status, marital status, religion, political beliefs, physical or mental disability, age, race, colour, ancestry, place of origin, and unrelated criminal convictions. *Harassment* is often tied directly to these protected grounds and can be defined as any unwelcome conduct or comment that adversely affects those that they target. Ultimately, people who experience discrimination or harassment in the educational or work environment are being denied their basic right to dignity and respect.

Students should understand their rights in terms of discrimination and harassment by becoming familiar with both agency and college or university policies. Dealing with and reporting harassment or discrimination can be difficult for students, who are not in a position of power and who may feel that their practicum and/or education may be jeopardized. Post-secondary institutions have harassment and discrimination policies, which extend to students while they are on practicum. If students believe they are experiencing discrimination or harassment, it is critical that they contact the educational field liaison and discuss these issues before they grow and become litigious.

## Exercise

Examine the following list of issues and choose three that may cause you the greatest anxiety in practice.

- informed consent
- practice liability
- confidentiality
- abuse or neglect
- duty to warn and protect
- harassment

1. Create a chart like Figure 3.1.

2. List the issue and write out a "what if" scenario. Then list your knowledge about that particular issue and write out what you may ask in consultation with your supervisor to gain clarity.

---

**Figure 3.1** What If ... Practice Activity

| Issue | Fear (What if ...) | Knowledge | Use of Supervision |
|-------|---------------------|-----------|--------------------|
| _____ | _____ | _____ | _____ |
| _____ | _____ | _____ | _____ |
| _____ | _____ | _____ | _____ |
| _____ | _____ | _____ | _____ |

---

# RECORD KEEPING AND DOCUMENTATION

Agencies have clear policies on what data employees should collect about clients and what form record keeping should take. Becoming familiar with these guidelines is a necessary part of the practicum experience. Records are an important aspect of most client care and treatment. Information needs to be presented in a professional manner and the storage and maintenance of this information must ensure client and agency safety. Specifically, you must ensure that only those that should have access to client information are provided access. All clients are entitled to having their personal information secured.

The manner in which records are kept and who has access to these records varies considerably from agency to agency. It is always important to remember that regardless of the intended audience of the record, clients, through freedom of information legislation in each province, can gain access to any of their own information that is collected and recorded. This includes all formal documentation, as well as less formal records such as handwritten notes for personal reference. Additionally, these documents may also be subpoenaed by a court and become part of legal processes.

Moline, Williams, and Austin (1998) highlight numerous reasons that records should be kept, including the fact that most professional organizations have this rule as a "standard of care" that provides clinicians with greater ability to assist their clients through documenting their condition at differing times. For agencies, this documentation both provides evidence that service has been provided to clients and provides valuable information should a client be transferred to another resource or service. For the clinician, clinical records provide professional protection against possible legal action or in cases where their ethical conduct may be reviewed. Often, as in child protection work, it is a legislated expectation that records be kept (as cited in Corey et al., 2007).

Agencies will normally expect that no client files will leave the building without permission. There should be no reason for students to remove client records. Cottone and

Tarvydas (2002) suggest that the removal of files from clinical sites is a dangerous practice as "a file in a briefcase can be stolen, files may be left in an unsecured automobile, and a counsellor's family may have access to files in the home setting" (p. 133).

Students are often required to keep a journal of their field experience and should treat this with the same care they give agency files. They should ensure that the journal notes are free of identifying client information and that only their supervisor or classroom instructor has access.

## COMPUTER-MEDIATED COMMUNICATION (CMC) AND PROFESSIONAL PRACTICE

The manner in which people in Canada communicate continues to evolve with the advent of new technology. Literature is now identifying those born after the year 1980 as "digital natives." This term refers to those who, since their earliest memories, have had access to digital technologies and have developed the skills to use them (Palfrey & Gasser, 2008). With this familiarity comes the added risk that these modes of communication can create issues in professional practice. Today, most "digital natives" find it second nature to use cellphone text messaging, email, social networking sites (e.g., Facebook, MySpace), and instant messaging and tweets (e.g., MSN Messenger, Twitter) to keep in touch with one another and to share information. It is important to remember that none of these technologies can be considered confidential and, in many situations, are far more public than most users understand. There have been situations around the world where individuals have been terminated from their jobs for sharing too much information about their work through these mediums. It is important to use caution with any information that is posted online or sent to others electronically.

Comments made via modern technology have wide audiences and can easily transfer among people. For example, Twitter is a newer form of instant information sharing in which a person may share a short statement regarding their day, thoughts, and so on. Others can follow these threaded statements, and if students make disparaging comments about a practicum site or clients, these comments may reach an unintended audience. Moreover, an email sent to a person who is allowed access to client information could eventually be forwarded to someone who should not have access. Dolgoff, Loewenberg, and Harrington (2009) acknowledge that many professional associations are now warning members to take great care when using technology to either record or share client information and progress (p. 81).

## CHAPTER SUMMARY

Legal issues relate to personal practice ethics, professional practice ethics, specific types of practice, and agency policy and protocol. Students must be aware of all levels of responsibility in practice and become familiar with agency protocol regarding specific legal requirements of practice. Key issues include confidentiality, duty to warn and protect, informed consent, and duty to report. Issues relating to liability and ethical decision making require the development of a reflective practice framework and ethical decision making skills. Students, after reviewing this chapter, are better equipped to identify general aspects of the Canadian legal system and to understand how liability issues in the field relate not only to professionals, but also to students in a practicum setting. When learning about legal issues, it is imperative that students understand the parameters of ethical issues and decision making, and identify frameworks used in the field. This discussion explores areas related to the limits of responsibility and legal and ethical concepts, including the legal aspects of workplace harassment and discrimination and the use of technology.

## Critical-Thinking Questions

1. Thinking about legal issues both as a practitioner and in relation to a specific area of your field, what do you feel are the most important ethical issues that may drive your decision making?
2. When does the law interfere with ethical practice? Can you give an example?
3. What do you think the following quote by an anonymous author means in practice? *"An ethical person ought to do more than he/she is required to do and less than he/she is allowed to do."*

## Suggested Readings

Bjorkquist, B. (2002). *The principles of ethical reasoning: Ethics and policing in a civil society.* Toronto, ON: Prentice Hall.

Cressy Wells, C., & Masch, K. M. (1991). *Social work ethics day to day.* Prospect Heights, IL: Waveland Press.

Swain, P. A., & Rice, S. (Eds.). (2009). *In the shadow of the law the legal context of social work practice* (3rd ed.). Annandale, Australia: Federation Press.

Turner, D., & Uhlemann, M. (Eds.). (2007). *Legal skills for helping professionals* (3rd ed.). Victoria, BC: University of Victoria.

## Relevant Websites

**BC Association of Clinical Counsellors**
www.bc-counsellors.org/requests.aspx
This website contains information on professional ethics and guidelines.

## Canadian Association of Social Workers

www.casw-acts.ca

The Canadian Association of Social Workers website contains information about codes of ethics and provincial bodies governing social work practice.

## Council of Canadian Child and Youth Care Associations

www.cyccanada.ca

This website contains information regarding child and youth care codes of ethics and provincial bodies for child and youth care practitioners.

## Journal of Social Work Values and Ethics

www.socialworker.com/jswve

This journal's website includes current information on ethical and professional issues affecting social work practice.

# Chapter 4
## Theories and Values in Action
### Grant Larson

## Chapter Objectives

- Describe what the term *theory* means and why it is important for social work and human service practice.
- Understand the relationship of values to theory and practice.
- Describe a range of theoretical approaches used in social work and human service practice.
- Describe the importance of critical thinking and reflection.
- Identify the barriers to integrating theory and practice, and describe how academic and human service organizations might work together to overcome these barriers.
- Formulate a framework for practice that is informed by theory.

This chapter will assist students as they prepare for the practicum experience by encouraging the development of an open mind and a critical attitude toward theoretical frameworks and an understanding of how theories inform the nature and effectiveness of social and human service work. Some students may initially indicate that they are more interested in skills, practice, and "doing the work" than in theory, formal knowledge, or "thinking about" practice. This chapter aims to make students interested in and passionate about *why* they do what they do to assist clients. The *why* is explained by theory. Throughout the chapter, students are encouraged to evaluate how they can best integrate theory into practice to enhance the quality of their professional work.

## CRITICAL THINKING AND THEORY ORIENTATION

It is important that readers have a clear understanding of the major theoretical approaches used in the field, as well as the ability to evaluate (i.e., *think critically* about) these approaches and their assumptions for particular practice settings. Critical thinking refers to the process of becoming aware of the ideas and beliefs that frame an understanding of the nature of work and their influence on practice (Oko, 2008).

> When we become critical thinkers, we develop an awareness of the assumptions under which we, and others, think and act. We learn to pay attention to the context in which our actions and ideas are generated. We become skeptical of quick-fix solutions, of single answers to problems, and of claims to universal truth. We also become open to alternative ways of looking at, and behaving in the world. (Brookfield, quoted in Oko, 2008, p. 11)

Critical thinking and reflection require that students have knowledge of the biases and preferences of authors and practitioners so that they can establish their own viewpoints. The theoretical approach of this chapter, then, can be described as anti-oppressive, structural, and strength-based. Anti-oppressive and structural theory is concerned with inequality and oppression, and focuses largely on understanding that the cause of social problems is related to larger societal factors outside the control of individuals. A strengths perspective recasts problems as possibilities and focuses on the resilience and abilities of individuals, groups, and communities in responding to negative circumstances. Additional information on these theoretical approaches and others, will be summarized and explained later in the chapter. It will become evident, however, that it is important to respect and value all theoretical approaches. Often, a consideration of a range of theories is most effective in assisting clients to reach their goals in specific circumstances. As well, the particular strategies and techniques used with clients are best determined by collaborative discussions with them about how to make change in their lives feasible and meaningful.

# VALUES AND PURPOSE OF PROFESSIONAL PRACTICE

Values and purpose lie at the very centre of professional social work and human service practice. *Values* are a set of beliefs about what is right or good that forms the basis for deciding what kinds of behaviour or activities should be used in a particular practice situation. *Purpose* refers to the general aim, objective, or reason for engaging in a set of activities. Practitioners have both personal and professional values and purposes, and both are important. Personal values are a key component of an individual's motivation for choosing a human service career and are crucial in determining his or her specific preferences for practice interventions, techniques, and strategies. It is critical that students become aware of their personal values so that they do not unconsciously direct their clients to particular courses of action that fit with their own rather than their clients' values. For example, if a student highly values post-secondary education, he or she might direct a client to enrol in university or college classes when this is not what the client actually wants or needs. Or a student who personally ascribes to "pro-life" beliefs may generate only "pro-life" options for an unplanned pregnancy situation.

Some professional values and purposes become formal bases for practice. These are generally accepted and expressed values that guide practice in all settings and are often codified in professional codes of ethics or conduct (Oko, 2008). Heinonen and Spearman (2001) suggest that "the way clients are viewed and social policies are conceptualized, developed and implemented" is shaped by the ideology, values, and purposes of the profession (p. 35). It is important that students understand the core values behind all social work and human service professions so that they can determine if their own values agree with those of the profession they are entering. Although there has been considerable debate in the literature about the values and purposes for human service and social work practice (McKay, 1999), it is generally agreed that social work is based on humanitarian and egalitarian values. Humanitarianism refers to a "fundamental respect for the worth, dignity and inherent rights of all people" (Heinonen & Spearman, 2001, p. 35). Egalitarianism is the belief that "all people are equal and should have the same rights and privileges despite differences in race, culture, spiritual beliefs, sexual orientation, ability, gender and other characteristics" (Heninonen & Spearman, 2001, p. 35). If students do not believe that same-sex couples should have the right to marry, then they will find their personal values in conflict with the values of professional social work. Other, secondary values, such as self-determination, respect, and acceptance, follow from these core values (Mullaly, 2007).

Personal and professional values and purposes are also related to theories of practice and help shape the specific theoretical orientation of the practitioner. Students are encouraged to consider how the fundamental assumptions and beliefs of a specific theory fit with their own and with their profession's values and purposes. For example, consider how a medical model approach — an approach often used in mental health settings that ascribes power to professionals as experts who diagnose pathology (Larson, 2008) — fits with the profession's values of egalitarianism, self-determination, positive worth, and acceptance.

McKay (1999) articulates three goals of the social work profession: "to support and strengthen people's natural abilities and capacities for handling their own affairs; to improve environments to ensure the conditions are present to maximize social well-being and provide care where needed; and to work toward transforming the conditions and social structures that create an inequitable social order" (pp. 15–16). Although McKay was referring specifically to social work, these three goals are applicable to all human service practice. In the pages that follow, students are asked to think about how their own objectives for entering the profession fit with these purposes. Before developing theoretical frameworks for practice, they must also consider how specific theoretical frameworks fit with the profession's purposes.

## CASE SCENARIO

A 15-year-old Indo-Canadian male student has recently become a resident in a youth emergency shelter in a mid-sized Canadian city. The student acknowledges that he has significant difficulties but reports that the reason he needs emergency shelter is because his parents "kicked him out of the house." He reports using marijuana daily, is on probation for a break-and-enter conviction, has difficulty in school, and is in constant conflict with his parents over curfew, choice of friends, school attendance, and vulgar language. You are a social worker at the emergency centre, and you have been asked to develop a positive relationship with this youth to try to understand the nature of his difficulties and how the centre might be of assistance to him and his family.

### Question

1. Recognizing that there is limited information in this scenario, brainstorm all the factors or explanations that might be related to why this young man and his family are experiencing difficulty.

## THEORY, PRACTICE, AND PRAXIS

The case scenario above demonstrates that there are many ways to perceive and understand a situation. The varied approaches are neither right nor wrong; they are simply different explanations for the same phenomena. As the social worker, you might have focused on the 15-year-old's individual characteristics and behaviours, such as his self-esteem, intellectual ability, or substance misuse, which appear to be causing conflict with his family, school, and community. Or you might have focused on the student's relationship with his family and friends, communication patterns and skills, or his family's ability to resolve conflicts. Or you might have understood this situation as a result of larger structural issues, such as the racism he has experienced as an Indo-Canadian youth in a predominantly white community. Your list of explanations and factors will be more exhaustive and specific than the three options just mentioned, but these examples help demonstrate that there are many ways to understand what is happening in any situation and to decide what potential courses of action might be.

A theory "can be described as representing a set of related ideas and assumptions that are drawn upon to help explain a particular phenomenon. A theory represents, therefore, an explanatory framework which attempts to help us make sense of the phenomenon in question ... and help us answer the question of what is going on, what can be done to help and why" (Oko, 2008, p. 6). Some authors and practitioners might draw a distinction between a framework, an approach, a perspective, and a theory. For the purpose of this chapter, these terms are considered interchangeable and are a means of determining what can be done to improve difficult or challenging circumstances.

In most professional fields, including social work and human service, theories become formalized in the sense that they are systematic, rationalized, written down, taught in educational institutions, and understood by many people working in the field. Theories used in social work and human service, such as cognitive-behavioural theory, ecological systems theory, and feminist theory, are examples of formal theory. Other "theories" or knowledge that explain phenomenon remain less formalized and outside of academic and professional practice discourse. Oral traditions, intuition, agency-specific strategies, and common sense approaches represent less formal theoretical frameworks, but they nonetheless explain beheviour and provide direction for how to proceed.

People use theory in their everyday lives when trying to understand events and determine how to proceed with a course of action; however, this guidance is not always regarded as theory (Healy, 2005; Mullaly, 1997). For example, a parent who is having difficulty getting his two-year-old daughter to stay in bed after bedtime may believe the child's actions are related to her insecurity and fear of the dark, and thus may provide a night light and extra reassurance at bedtime. The father has used a "theory" about what caused his daughter's behaviour. It is important that students recognize that everyone, including themselves and their clients, has some idea about what created their problem-atic situations and what might be done to alleviate them. This understanding may not be organized, systematic, and articulated as formal theory, or even well understood, but it does form the basis for deciding why the problem exists and what the next steps might be (Mullaly, 1997). Karen Healy (2005) writes, "Each of us constructs understandings that guide us in identifying who and what should be the focus of our practice and how we should proceed" (p. xii). Informal theories are often based on myth, tradition, common sense, and dominant beliefs passed down through families, schools, churches, and other institutions of socialization. These theories may be inadequate and at times dangerous in assisting clients, as they may reinforce the very ideas and beliefs that have kept people from moving toward change. It is important that practitioners and clients understand and make explicit these explanations so that they do not inadvertently direct relationships or work in negative and unhelpful ways.

## CASE SCENARIO

A student doing a practicum at a substance misuse agency indicates that he believes that alcoholics need to "go to the bottom" before they are ready for treatment and motivated to change. Although this belief is not uncommon in some self-help substance misuse groups, it does represent a negative and limiting theory of change. The student who believes this is restricted to waiting until clients have experienced even more destructive consequences of their substance misuse rather than working from a positive, strength-based approach that helps clients understand that they can make changes to their lives whenever they choose.

## Questions

1.  Do you know people who hold the belief that things must get worse before they get better?
2.  How would you respond to someone who held this belief?

Practice can be described as the particular behaviours and skills that social work and human service practitioners use in assisting clients with identified problems. Mullaly (1997) states that "practice is viewed as common sense, concrete and occurring in the real world, and that social work is a pragmatic profession that carries out practical tasks" (p. 99). Practice, then, involves doing the work and includes activities such as providing community education, supervising youth in a child care organization, providing assessment and intervention for mental health problems, implementing statutory laws (e.g., in child protection or probation cases ), assessing and managing risk situations, or doing research and policy analysis.

*Praxis* is a term used to describe the meeting place of theory and practice (i.e., how explanations for behaviour translate into actions that improve social and human conditions). Payne (2005) suggests that the concept of praxis means

> that we must implement theories in practice, so that practice reflects on and alters the theory.... Theory must come partly from ideas outside daily practice, otherwise it would be a simple reflection of that practice, but it must not be totally outside recognizable practice. (p. 230)

It is important to understand the definition of praxis because it is at the very root of the integration of theory and practice. Students must not think of theory as separate from practice, but understand that it is only when theory is put into practice that it becomes useful and practical. Social work and human service students sometimes think that theory is irrelevant to practice or that practice is devoid of theory. Both are incorrect. As discussed earlier, all practitioners use formal and informal theories to help them explain phenomena and direct their actions, whether they recognize the theories as theories or not. Informed practitioners understand why they decide to embark on particular courses of action with their clients. This is praxis.

Informed practitioners also benefit from being *reflective practitioners.* Oko (2008) describes *reflection* as "an engaging process that involves asking questions about our practice and its influences … which allows us to think critically about the knowledge, skills, and beliefs that inform our practice and thus evaluate their impact" (p. 12). Payne

(2005) indicates that reflective practice "implies a structural system for thinking things through either as we are taking in the situation or as a learning or review technique after the event" (p. 33). Thus, reflective practitioners think about their theories of understanding phenomenon and about how these theories help them make sense of their practice. Such practitioners consider multiple explanations and alternative methods and evaluate them within the context of the organization where they work, what has worked in the past, what fits with their own and client understandings, and what is feasible. The concept of the reflective practitioner is discussed in more detail later in Chapter 5.

### Exercise

As you read "Major Practice Theories," which describes eight types of theoretical approaches, revisit your list of reasons for why the 15-year-old in the first case scenario might be having difficulty. Try to match each of your explanations with a theoretical framework category.

# MAJOR PRACTICE THEORIES

This section will briefly highlight some of the major theories used in general social work and human service practice. Before summarizing categories of theoretical approaches, it is important to understand that there are different kinds and levels of theory. Mullaly (1997) and Lehmann and Coady (2001) classify theories as grand, mid-range, and practice.

Grand theories are frameworks such as Aboriginal or Indigenous theories and feminist theory. These theories are grand in the sense that they describe phenomenon at a high level of abstraction and provide general understandings of the nature of the human condition. Aboriginal or Indigenous theories, for example, focus on First Peoples' world views, beliefs, and values; the relationship and unity of the environment and universe; concepts of harmony, balance, healing, and spirituality; and the good nature of humans (Hart, 2002). Aboriginal perspectives also understand Indigenous peoples' circumstances as related to a long history of oppression and domination. Feminist theory, which began with a primary focus on women and their concerns but may be applied to many oppressed populations, explains social conditions as a result of patriarchy (institutionalized male privilege) and classism. It includes principles such as linking the personal to the political, reducing power differences, raising consciousness, and celebrating diversity (Heinonen & Spearman, 2001). Feminist theory is considered a grand theory because it represents a large grouping of ideas and concepts that explain the domination of women and marginalized people. There are, in fact, many specific feminist theories that differ from one another in many ways (Lehmann & Coady, 2001, p. 36). Some would argue that grand theories are less helpful in explaining the specific conditions of individuals, families, or communities, and provide little direction for practitioners. However, as grand theories evolve, they tend to develop more concrete ideas about how practitioners can intervene to resolve difficulties.

Mid-range theories, such as ecological systems theory, strengths perspective, and attachment theory, explain particular phenomenon or issues and identify general courses of action. The problems or issues they address and the intervention strategies they describe are more specific than those of grand theories. However, mid-range theories remain at a higher level of abstraction and generalizability than practice theories or models. Ecological systems theory and strengths perspective will be described later in the chapter, as they are two of the major social work and human service practice theories. Another example, attachment theory, is a specific theory that understands psychological problems as arising from deficits or distortions in relationships that stem from the need to be close to another person, such as a parent (Stalker, 2001). Thus, if infants or young children do not develop a secure, consistent, and loving relationship with a parent or caregiver, they may develop a range of behavioural and emotional difficulties with forming meaningful, intimate relationships with others throughout their lives. Although specific explanatory constructs are part of mid-range theories, general frameworks and processes for helping are provided rather than specific techniques. As with grand theories, mid-range theories are sometimes criticized for their lack of specific directive techniques for face-to-face relationships with clients.

Practice theories, sometimes called *models of practice*, go one step further than mid-range theories and describe specific principles of action with prescribed and often structured techniques and strategies (Mullaly, 2007). They do not, however, usually emphasize theoretical explanations for behaviour; instead, they borrow these explanations from other theories (Lehmann & Coady, 2001, p. 30). Practice theories focus on providing specific strategies, steps, and processes that a practitioner might engage in to bring about a desired change. Thus, the theories have a low level of abstraction. Crisis intervention theory, for example, includes major concepts for understanding what happens to individuals in crisis situations and delineates specific steps and intervention strategies that practitioners might use to work through various stages of crisis (Knox & Roberts, 2001). Wraparound process, another practice model, focuses on a specific approach to working with high-risk children and families by emphasizing strengths, individualized plans, community resources, and a collaboration of multiple systems (Brown, 2001). This process focuses on action that promotes resolution rather than explanations of the origin of the child's and the family's problems. Models of practice are specific practice theories that are less concerned about explaining why phenomena occur and more interested in techniques, processes of intervention, and skills.

Another way to categorize theories of helping is based on their scope and field of practice. This includes considering how broad or narrow the theory and its application is, and the specific populations, problems, or contexts to which the theory applies. Payne (2005) classifies theories into three groups based on these criteria: (1) those related to work with individuals and families, (2) those related to group work, and (3) those related to community work, macro-social work, and administration. These groupings are a helpful way to categorize theories because they allow practitioners to study and select approaches that are relevant to their specific fields of practice.

While all levels and types of theory are important and play a valuable role in understanding human phenomena and how to proceed with social and human service work, it is beyond the scope of this chapter to describe them in full detail. Rather, a summary of eight major categories of contemporary theories used in general social work and human service practice is presented. The brief summaries that follow do not do justice to the diversity, complexity, and comprehensiveness of the identified theories. For more information on specific theories, please refer to the resources in "Suggested Readings" and "Relevant Websites" at the end of the chapter.

1.  **Individual change theories:** Included in this category are theories such as attachment theory, interpersonal therapy, self psychology, cognitive-behavioural theory, and several human development theories (Lehmann & Coady, 2001). Essentially, these theories hold that emotional, behavioural, and cognitive difficulties stem from intrapersonal processes, interpersonal processes, and a person's inability to successfully master stages of human development. They tend to focus on explaining difficulties in terms of the individual. Treatment strategies involve acquiring insight; exploring beliefs, feelings, and behaviour; and teaching techniques that influence how individuals perceive themselves and interact with their surroundings. A critique of individual change theories is that they may pathologize individuals and families, and do not consider larger explanations for problems.

2.  **Ecological system theory:** This framework examines individuals within their environments and suggests that all people share a reciprocal relationship with one another and a need for a "goodness of fit" with their environment (Lehmann & Coady, 2001). Ecological systems theory has been a major and consistent framework used in social and human service work since the early 1970s (Payne, 2005). Using concepts borrowed from the biological sciences, this theory explores the social whole and the relationship of individuals to their social environment to maintain balance and equilibrium in functioning. The theory suggests that when a problem arises in one part of the system, this problem affects other parts of the system. For example, if a parent is under considerable stress at work, this stress may affect a marital relationship or a parent–child relationship. The target of change, then, is the system rather than the individual. Ecological systems theory has been criticized as an expository and descriptive theory in that it provides a way of analyzing phenomenon but no specific explanation for, or prescription about, how to affect change (Payne, 2005). Specific adaptations of ecological systems theory, such as the life model of social work practice and the eco-social approach, however, provide specific tools (e.g., ecomaps and genograms) for working from these perspectives (Payne, 2005).

3.  **Critical theories:** Theories in this broad category postulate that social and human service work should strive to change how the larger society has created social problems. Anti-oppressive structural social work and feminist, radical, antiracist, and

antidiscriminatory theories all state that "the problems of a person, group, family or community are not all their own fault, but are caused largely by factors outside their control" (Ife, 2005, p. 4). As such, critical theories generally reject capitalism, economic liberalism, racism, patriarchy, sexism, heterosexism, ableism, ageism, and other forms of structural oppression, and focus on the emancipation of oppressed groups from the existing social order. The core of critical theories, then, is structural rather than personal explanations for social problems and concern about inequality and oppression (Payne, 2005). Critical theorists tend to reject the current social order and focus on strategies that challenge existing institutional structures in political and transformational ways. Opponents of critical theories suggest that these approaches tend to concentrate primarily on collective social action and neglect the immediate personal needs of clients. As well, they suggest that critical theories are, in fact, ideologies based on political philosophy rather than theories that can be tested empirically (Payne, 2005, p. 248).

4. **Strengths perspective:** Unlike many of the theories described in this chapter, the strengths perspective shifts work with clients from a focus on problems to a focus on strengths. Dennis Saleebey (1997), the first to clearly articulate the strengths perspective, describes the approach as "predicated on helping to discover and embellish, explore and exploit clients' strengths and resources in the service of assisting them to achieve their goals, realize their dreams, and shed the irons of their own inhibitions and misgivings" (p. 3) The positive focus of this perspective is on empowerment, resilience, membership in groups, healing and wholeness, collaboration and suspension of beliefs (Saleebey, 1997). Instead of concentrating on what is wrong, pathological, or deficient with clients, the strengths perspective encourages thinking about possibility and hope. Some authors (e.g., Heinonen & Spearman, 2001) suggest that a focus on strengths is not new to social work and human service practice, and that it is not a unified theory or even a specific model of practice. Instead, they suggest that it is a collection of concepts, ideas, and values that might be included in other theoretical frameworks. Nevertheless, a focus on strengths is viewed here as a critical component to social work and human service practice, and it must become part of every practitioner's attitude and process for working with clients.

5. **Aboriginal and Indigenous perspectives:** Michael Hart (2002) provides a comprehensive description of Aboriginal philosophy, world views, and approaches for engagement in decolonizing and resistance work with Canadian First Nations peoples. While his description may not be an organized theory or a singular Indigenous perspective (i.e., it does not represent the diversity of Aboriginal thought), it does provide an interesting and compelling approach to working with First Nations peoples in culturally safe and relevant ways. Indigenous perspectives, as described by Hart (2002), focus on wholeness, balance, harmony, healing, and community. These perspectives are incredibly important for those working in social work and human services because many clients of social service agencies are Aboriginal (Hart, 2001). Culturally sensitive

practice must be an essential component of practice in order that workers from the dominant culture do not explicitly or implicitly impose dominant values, treatments, or processes on First Nations people who have been victims of domination for centuries. An understanding of their history of oppression is essential so that "helping and healing can take place in the context of First Nations Peoples' community and culture" (Hart, 2001, p. 232).

6. **Problem-solving approaches:** Problem-solving approaches have for many years been the basis of social and human service work. They are characterized by "collaborative, highly structured, time-limited and problem-focused approaches to practice" (Healy, 2005, p. 108). Perlman's social casework, Reid and Epstein's task-centred practice, and Parad's crisis intervention are all examples of problem-solving approaches. In many ways, social work and human service work has traditionally been about problem solving: A practitioner assists a client in identifying a specific problem; fully assesses and analyzes the nature and context of the problem; sets realistic and measurable goals; engages the client in concrete tasks, actions, or strategies; and evaluates progress toward the goals in time-limited relationships (Heinonen & Spearman, 2001). Problem solving is considered a practice theory or model in that it involves little theoretical explanation for the cause of problems but focuses rather a specific structured course of action or process for responding to identified problems. Critics of problem-solving approaches suggest that they are negatively focused and do not generally take into account larger systems, the environment, or structural factors that create problems.

7. **Community development theories:** Community development work is a form of social work and human service work that engages people with shared interests in specific localities, regions, or cultures to identify common concerns and work together to develop common solutions (Payne, 2005). The focus of the work is generally on providing locally responsive and determined solutions to local issues. There are different definitions of community development work; however, they are based on particular ideological and theoretical foundations. The ideological bases for community theories often arise from the discipline of sociology. Brown and Hannis (2008) distinguish community development practices by suggesting that some are based on a "top-down versus a bottom-up approach" (p. 9) Ife and Tesoriero (2006) indicate that two foundational theories for community development work include an ecological perspective and a social justice and human rights perspective. Historically, Rothman (1970) presented one of the first descriptions of community development approaches by distinguishing among those focused on locality development, social action, and social planning. And more recently, with the prominence of environmental concerns, Zapf (2009) presented a case for including the physical environment along with the social environment when conceptualizing community development work. Finally, Payne (2005, p. 49) presents a typology of models of

community development and macro-work that is helpful for students trying to understand its theoretical bases.

8. **Group work theories:** Social work and human service work often engage groups of individuals for therapy, education, self-help activities, or collective action on identified needs. Students may be familiar with group work examples such as self-help groups for substance misusers (e.g., Alcoholics Anonymous); group therapy for specific mental health and social problems, such as sex offending or grief and loss; psycho-educational groups, such as anger management groups; and advocacy groups for issues such as poverty or human rights. Theory regarding group work includes concepts such as "group development, tasks and goals, process, growth, interaction, cohesion, roles, skills and strengths, power, conflict, norms and values" (Heinonen & Spearman, 2001, p. 197). Douglas (1993), among others, suggests that group work theory is largely based on existing theoretical foundations, such as humanism and feminism. Payne (2005) presents an interesting and helpful classification of group work theories based largely on an evaluation of group work literature.

## Exercise

1.  Identify a social service agency that you are familiar with and describe what you believe are the dominant theoretical frameworks used in this organization.
2.  Contact a worker in this organization and interview him or her about the specific theoretical perspectives the organization uses in practice.
3.  Compare your ideas about what you thought were the dominant theories with what the worker actually reported.

## WHY IS THEORY IMPORTANT?

To be effective, social work and human service practitioners need to base their work on a variety of theories and approaches that are applicable at the individual, family, community, and societal levels. It is important to ground practice in theory for the following reasons:

- Theory guides practice and gives practitioners a basis for deciding what the focus of an assessment and an intervention should be (Healy, 2005). Without a theory to guide and direct, social workers and human service practitioners would need to begin anew with each and every client with a comprehensive and detailed analysis of each situation. Although it is important to acknowledge that each individual's circumstances are different, a theoretical framework provides a starting point for deciding what to focus on or how to move forward with strategies for change. Formalized theories provide practitioners with existing and relevant knowledge, enabling them to move forward in efficient and timely ways.

- Theories help practitioners see elements of clients' situations they may otherwise miss. For example, if practitioners do not use a strengths perspective, it is unlikely that they will focus on the resiliency aspects and strengths of a client's situation rather than the pathological issues and problems presented.
- Theories provide a means for holding practitioners and agencies accountable for the work they do and the resources and funds they expend for social services. It is important that practitioners be able to explain why they engage in the strategies they use and why they need particular resources to support these strategies. Most social services provided by social work and human service practitioners are supported and funded by public and not-for-profit organizations. Evaluation and evidence-based practice are becoming increasingly important as organizations aim to use resources in ethical and effective ways.
- Theories provide a basis for improving practice and building on the effectiveness of past experience. Practitioners have the opportunity to revise and alter theories with input from practice (i.e., praxis).

## THEORY IN PRACTICE: THE ISSUES

Theories are essential for good practice, but there are some barriers and limitations to using theory in practice. For example, practitioners may report that large caseloads and heavy recording requirements limit their ability to use particular kinds of theory because they simply do not have the time to implement the theory well. Others report that it is difficult to stay abreast of new theory development or to examine theory in light of new programs or initiatives; it is easier to rely on older, more established ways of thinking and acting. And finally, practitioners may report that the particular organizations they work for subscribe to, or encourage, only certain kinds of theoretical and practice approaches, and that this limits their ability to engage in reflection and to apply new theories.

### Exercise

List all the factors that you think influence, inform, or determine the specific approach a social worker or human service practitioner uses when working at a specific agency. Brainstorm as many factors as you can. Do not limit your list to what you think should influence the worker; include all the influences on his or her selection of a practice approach.

The point of this exercise is to illustrate that many factors (in addition to theory) determine how workers practice. Lists likely include factors such as the specific type of problem the agency works with, the particular theoretical and ideological framework of the agency, the funding base of the organization, practice wisdom, traditions, common sense, the policy and legal framework, the personal beliefs and values of the practitioner, and the approaches taught in social work and human service educational programs. The challenge for practitioners, then, becomes how to balance these diverse influences and still engage in thoughtful, reflective practice that is guided by professional values, a critical assessment, and the use of appropriate theoretical frameworks.

# THE ORGANIZATIONAL CONTEXT OF PRACTICE

Healy (2005) presents a convincing case that the purpose, ideological standpoint, and tasks of different agencies vary considerably by institutional context. The context for work as a child protection worker in a government setting is considerably different than work as a poverty advocate in a community-based agency. One might assume that the particular theories used by practitioners are to some extent influenced by the power and funding base of their employing organization and its stated organizational goals and purposes. Complicating the issue further is the fact that social work and human service work does not have a single institutional base; instead, the work takes place in a wide range of public, non-profit, and private organizations. When discussing the application of theory, educators and academic institutions often refer to the institutional context as "minimally relevant, or even something to overcome" (Healy, 2005, p. 2). Some theorists also indicate that particular theoretical frameworks (e.g., radical and critical approaches) are difficult to use in organizations that are unsupportive of such views (Mullaly, 2007).

Organizational context is significant, and students, educators, and employers must understand how practice theory both informs and is informed by it. If workers primarily enact theories, methods, and approaches that are inconsistent with the dominant values, purposes, and tasks required of them in their organizations, they are more likely to burn out quickly, experience conflict with their employers, and be inadequate at their jobs. For example, a child welfare worker who decides to use time-intensive individual interpersonal therapy with the depressed parents of a child in care (i.e., under the protection of a child and family service organization) may learn that the purpose, context, and theoretical orientation of the organization is unsupportive. The pragmatics of what is required to do a specific job in a particular organization is important, and, if it is not attended to, social work and human service practitioners run the risk of giving up fields of practice to other disciplines.

Then again, organizational context must not solely determine which practice theories and methods are used. Organizational change is often created or initiated through ideas that originate outside the organization. Students and new practitioners have a valuable role to play in challenging organizations on the frameworks they have traditionally used. It is important to recognize that organizational context does matter and should be considered integral to any discussion of theory, but also that a healthy tension should exist between working within a context and actually trying to change the context of practice.

# THE EDUCATIONAL CONTEXT

Do faculty members set students up for discouragement when the theories and approaches they teach are not accepted in the agencies where they work? This is one of the great paradoxes of the academy (Larson, 2008). Students often leave school convinced that particular ideologies and practices are superior. However, when they begin work, they discover that their employers, agencies, and even other practitioners do not necessarily adhere to or support these approaches. Mullaly (1997) states that social work and human services students often come into contact with practising practitioners who are skeptical of the theory taught and instead emphasize the value of experience. For example, the predominance of the teaching of critical approaches (e.g., feminist, anti-oppressive, structural, and radical) in post-secondary institutions is often met with disdain or even hostility in practice organizations. New practitioners are encouraged to adopt more conservative, traditional approaches used in community organizations. Bright, strong students may withstand the tendency to abandon "ivory tower" theory, but many practitioners soon become socialized to the dominant understandings and perspectives that their employing organizations use. Thus it is extremely important that college and university professors teach students not only the basic concepts of theoretical approaches, but also how to use them in practice. This teaching is best accomplished by collaborating with practising social workers, human service practitioners, and child and youth care workers.

## Transfer of Learning from Classroom to Practice

One of the most difficult aspects of professional social work and human service education is the transfer and evaluation of learning from the classroom to the field. Although course assignments and practicum evaluations attempt to measure learning, there is no way to ensure that what students learn in their courses will transfer to actual work in the community after they graduate. Mullaly (1997) thinks that curricula are often ordered in such a way as to create anti-theoretical bias in that students learn theory first, in university, and then go out into the field to learn practice. It becomes complicated to measure whether what students do in agencies is related or correlated with what they learned in school. Role plays, case scenarios, and experiential learning are all tools used by faculty member in the hopes that students will be able to bridge the gap between the "ivory tower" and real life.

The key to successful learning transfer lies not in the ability of the instructor to teach good theory, or in the capacity of the field instructor to model good intervention skills, but in the relationship between faculty members and practitioners, which should include a healthy, ongoing dialogue about how to work together to create the most effective learning experience for students. All too often, faculty members stay in the university and practitioners in their agencies, rather than working together in collaborative teaching.

## THE CLIENT'S PERSPECTIVE

A factor not often considered when thinking about the theory and practice approaches is the client's understanding of, and orientation toward, those approaches. One might even suggest that at the end of the day, the practitioner's appreciation for and use of a particular theoretical approach is not as important as the client's understanding of his or her situation. For example, if a client understands his or her problem as emanating from a particular cause or factor, the extent of the practitioner's skill in a particular approach's techniques will not matter if the approach does not fit with the client's understanding. The work then becomes more complicated than a practitioner simply becoming a good worker within a particular approach.

How do practitioners take their clients' understandings and viewpoints into consideration? Good practitioners always work in collaboration with their clients by seeking to understand how the clients perceive why they are experiencing the particular issues that brought them to the agency. Practitioners must work within clients' views, cultures, and understandings. They may, however, introduce clients to new frameworks and new explanations to assist them in creating change. Remember the earlier example of a belief that a substance misuser must "go to the bottom" before being ready for change? If a client held this belief, which is in essence a theory, and practitioners ignored it, they would run the risk of investing time, energy, and resources in activities that would not create change. Rather, practitioners must acknowledge the beliefs and theories of clients, and then encourage them to think in new ways about their situations if they wish to move toward change.

## COMMON SENSE AS A THEORY FOR PRACTICE

### Voices from the Field

My third year practicum setting was at a Regional Correctional Centre Classroom where I quickly realized that my ethics as a social worker, and the theories of criminality I had been learning in the academy, were not consistent with the views espoused by guards and other colleagues in the classroom. Most often these tensions would accumulate in the lunch room when I would try to engage guards and teachers in discussions about the justice system....

It is not uncommon to hear practitioners and students advocate for the notion of a common sense approach to practice. However, when asked to clarify what this phrase actually means, the concept becomes vague and fuzzy. Still, it seems to imply very practical, immediate, and commonly known responses to behaviour. Rather than trying to understand a situation from a theoretical perspective, students and practitioners using common sense just do what they "know is right."

Most issues that bring clients to social work and human service practitioners or child and youth care workers are complex. Explanations are rarely straightforward, and many factors contribute to the buildup of a problematic situation. Although immediate and practical responses are often needed, they should not be solely founded on "common sense," tradition, or myth. If they could be (while still being effective), then there would be little need for educational and training programs for social work and human service practitioners. Professional responses should be grounded in both theoretical and practical knowledge about what has created the problem and what must be done to ameliorate the conditions.

## DEVELOPMENT OF A THEORETICAL FRAMEWORK FOR PRACTICE

After studying a range of theoretical frameworks, students may be puzzled about how they are to choose which theories to use in practice. Some students may ask whether they can select any theoretical approach as long as they have engaged in a critical reflective process to determine what works for them. Others might suggest that academic institutions and professional associations have a responsibility to ensure that the practice theories they choose to teach respect the cardinal values and ethics of the profession, have strong evidence of their effectiveness (i.e., evidence-based practice), and fit with the purpose and objectives of social work and human service organizations. Payne (2005) argues for a careful selection of theories and for a cautious, coordinated, and planned approach to eclecticism, which involves selecting concepts or ideas from a number of theories. Healy (2005) presents a useful framework for assessing how theories of practice are relevant and useful in particular practice settings.

Answering the following questions will help students develop their particular theoretical frameworks for practice.

- What are your most important social, economic, and political beliefs or values? Rank them in order of importance.

- Which theoretical frameworks are congruent with your personal and professional values?
- What is the specific context for your practice? What kind of organization will or do you work in? What are its mission and objectives? What are its dominant values?
- Which theoretical frameworks are congruent with your practice context? (You are not limited to using only the frameworks used within the organizational context; as a practitioner, you will have a role in changing the dominant values and approaches of your organization. You must do this, however, with full knowledge of the potential for conflict.)
- As you reflect on your practice experience, which theoretical frameworks fit best with that experience?
- What populations and kinds of issues are most prominent in your work organization, and what theories specifically address those issues?
- What research or empirical evidence exists that supports the use of the identified theories?
- What do others think of your chosen theoretical framework(s)? Test out your ideas on other practitioners, both on a casual and formal basis.
- Write out a statement of your chosen theoretical frameworks with a full rationale for why and how this works for you in your particular practice setting.

It is important that beginning social work and human service practitioners develop a meaningful understanding of theoretical approaches that will work for them in enhancing the work they do with clients. This process is not easy or rapid; it will evolve as students begin to integrate theory with their practice experiences. Students must take sufficient time when selecting theories and approaches that work for them. All too often students migrate toward and affirm quickly the frameworks and theories preferred by their professors, and then, as they enter the workforce, they abandon these approaches for those espoused by practitioners. Teachers of educational programs for social work and human service practice must strive to work with practitioners to teach students about practice theories. This collaboration should involve practitioner speaking engagements in theory and practice courses; discussions of theory at field placements among students, field instructors, and university liaisons; orientation and training of field instructors regarding the importance and value of practice theory; and professional development opportunities that focus on practice theory for professors, students, and agency practitioners.

## Voices from the Field

I have learned over my degree that it is irresponsible to take residence in the far extremes of any theoretical camp. If we are to build practices that are theoretically sound, and also responsive to the complex problems facing our clients, these approaches must take a structural approach in analyzing social problems and oppression; however, they must also respect that there are immediate needs that clients have (access to medical care, housing, food, and support services). (Chris Van Veen, student)

# CHAPTER SUMMARY

In this chapter, we explored theories for social work and human service practice. The aim was to emphasize that sound theory is essential for effective social work and human service practice, and that regardless of their awareness of it, all practitioners use theory. The differences between formal and informal theory were discussed, as were the barriers presented by academic institutions and practice organizations in assisting students with integrating theory and practice.

Eight categories of helping theories were described, and students were encouraged to engage in critical thinking and reflective practice in determining which practice theories are relevant and appropriate for their work. In addition, students were encouraged to begin thinking about their preferred practice theory while in school, as well as to engage in a process of praxis, whereby their experience in work settings informs their theoretical perspective. Once students engage in this process, theory will guide and influence their work, creating dynamic practice that is in the best interests of their clients. A sound theoretical basis for practice involves understanding why social work and human service practitioners do what they do in assisting clients. This is essential for both practitioners and clients, so that all who are involved in the change process understand why particular courses of action are being taken.

## Critical-Thinking Questions

1. Review "Major Practice Theories," which provides summaries of the eight categories of major theoretical frameworks. Explain how each category is similar or dissimilar to every other category in terms of its view of and response to social problems.

2. Identify theories summarized in this chapter that use a problem-oriented approach to social work and human service practice. Identify theories that focus on a community, environmental, and structural approach to practice.

3. Based on your past and current educational and practice experience, identify your preferred theoretical framework at this point in your professional development.

## Suggested Readings

Hart, M. (2002). *Seeking mino-pimatisiwin: An Aboriginal approach to helping.* Halifax, NS: Fernwood Publishing.

Healy, K. (2005). *Social work theories in context: Creating frameworks for practice*. New York, NY: Palgrave MacMillan.

Heinonen, T., & Spearman, L. (2010). *Social work practice: Problem solving and beyond*. Toronto, ON: Nelson Education.

Lehmann, P., & Coady, N. (Eds.). (2001). *Theoretical perspectives for direct social work practice*. New York: Springer Publishing Company.

Mullaly, B. (2007). *The new structural social work* (3rd ed.) Don Mills, ON: Oxford University Press.

Oko, J. (2008). *Understanding and using theory in social work*. Exeter, England: Learning Matters.

Payne, M. (2005). *Modern social work theory* (3rd ed.) Chicago, IL: Lyceum Book.

Saleebey, D. (Ed.). (2008). *The strengths perspective in social work practice* (5th ed.) New York, NY: Longman.

## Relevant Websites

### International Federation of Social Workers

www.ifsw.org/home

The International Federation of Social Workers is a global social work organization related to social justice, human rights and social development. The website contains many up-to-date resources for global human service work related to theory, policy and practice.

### Journal of Social Work Theory and Practice

www.bemidjistate.edu/sw_journal

This is the online version of the Journal of Social Work Theory and Practice, available through the Inter-University Centre based in Dubronik, Croatia.

### Canadian Centre for Policy Alternatives

www.policyalternatives.ca

Canadian website of progressive policy ideas rooted in social justice and environmental sustainability.

# Chapter 5

## Beyond the Reflective Practitioner

Natalie Clark

## Chapter Objectives

- Define reflective practice and its links to social work and human service professions.
- Understand the difference between reflective practice and reflexivity.
- Identify strategies and tools for engaging in reflexive practice.
- Understand the importance of reflexivity to the future of human service and social work practice.

## REFLECTIVE PRACTICE TO REFLEXIVE PRACTICE: A HISTORY

Reflection has been an essential part of social work and human service education and practice since the inception of these fields in the early 1900s. This section will consider the movement from reflective practice, or reflection on one's self and profession, to the emergence of reflexive practice. Reflexivity and reflective practice are very similar in many ways and are often used interchangeably. However, there are some distinct differences that are important to understand.

## Reflective Practice: A Definition

*Reflective practice*, or *reflection*, is an activity all humans engage in as a result of their interactions with others. It is the process whereby individuals think critically about their words or actions. For some, this is an internal dialogue or individual act, while for others it involves storytelling or sharing an experience that leads to reflection. Each approach is valid and important.

Depending on the context, the word *reflection* has a number of meanings. However, within the fields of social work and human service, it can be understood as both an internal state of mediation and rumination and as a process whereby thoughts, actions, and processes are reflected back from other sources, such as supervisors, instructors, and peers. Reflective practice is viewed as an essential foundational skill that facilitates the linking of theory with practice toward the goals of improving competence and promoting new learning. In contrast to reflexive practice, which focuses on the profession itself and how knowledge is constructed within it, reflective practice is concerned with the self of the student or practitioner.

---

## Discussion Questions

1. Identify three values that led you to choose a career in social work or human service.

2. Identify one personal belief or value that has been brought into question since you have learned about your professional role.

3. List three beliefs that you hold about the role of a social worker or human service practitioner.

4. Which aspect of your practicum do you think will most clearly reflect your values?

5. In which aspect of your work do you think your values will be most at odds with your working environment?

---

**Reflective Practice and the Change Process**   Reflective practice is the process by which thoughts and actions are linked to reflection in a feedback loop. It involves thinking about one's thoughts and actions with the goals of improving your professional practice, that of others, and your profession. A key element in this process is an exploration of the values and assumptions that underlie the profession itself. The theory of reflective practice can be traced back to educational theorists such as John Dewey (1933), Donald Schön (1987), and D. A. Kolb (1984). These theorists identified that a key element in learning is the ability to integrate experience with reflection and theory with practice. In fact, they argued that learning cannot take place without this reflection. Reflection is described in these theories as the process of moving from an intuitive sense that there is a problem to exploration and identification of the problem, application of knowledge from professional training and supervision, and finally resolution, thereby informing one's actions in the present or the future.

## A Model for Reflection in Field Education: The ITP Loop

As introduced in Chapter 1, the ITP loop, or integration of theory and practice, was developed by Canadian social workers (Bogo and Vayda, 1998). It is one of the most well-known field education models for engaging in reflective practice. This ITP loop helps students identify the assumptions, values, thoughts, and beliefs that underpin the actions they take in professional situations. Its purpose is to uncover and reflect on the ideas that inform interventions in specific situations. The four steps suggested in the model include (1) recollecting the experience, (2) reflecting on the experience, (3) relating the experience to theory and knowledge, and (4) responding to the situation (Bogo & Vayda, 1998). Review Chapter 1 for practice in applying the steps of the ITP loop in practice.

## Field Education and Reflective Practice

Practicum and field education seminars are the primary sites where students learn about the concept and practice of reflection, and as such these seminars function like the mirror to which students and practitioners hold up their thoughts and actions. Practicum is often the place in students' educations when they begin to apply the theory and practice learned in the classroom — and in doing so begin to question it. Field seminars and discussions between students and their field instructors are two avenues through which students begin to develop their skills in using reflective practice. The voices and experience of others, including fellow students, field instructors, and faculty, are key elements of a reflective practice (Schön, 1987).

## The Move to Reflexive Practice

Reflective practice, although historically linked to the artistry of decision making alongside the scientific process (Schön 1987), has been critiqued as being an individualistic and superficial model that is overly focused on the present and how things *should* be (West, 2009; Fook, 2002). Karban and Smith (2009) assess reflective practice as uniprofessional; they say "an emphasis on self reflection frequently fails to broaden the lens to take into account wider issues of power and inequality, to move beyond technical rationalism and remains at the individual level rather than being embedded within relational notions of dialogue both within teams and across professions" (Karban & Smith, 2009, p. 1). In other words, reflective practice, through its focus on the individuals, fails to adequately address issues of power or promote learning from across disciplines outside of social work and human service.

The shift toward reflexivity in social work and human service education emerged in many ways as a response to a movement in the field in the 1970s and 1980s that focused on objectivity, accountability, procedures, and evidence-based practice. As Parton (2000) argues, "In recent years, social work has become legalised and proceduralised and there have been increasing efforts to scientize and rationalize practice and emphasize empiricism, outcomes and the 'evidence-based' approach" (p. 450). Influenced by critical social theories such as feminism and postmodernism, there has been growing recognition in the field of social work and human service of the need to move beyond reflective practice and its focus on the individual toward a relational and critical approach — that of reflexivity (see D'Cruz, Gillingham, & Melendez, 2007b). Feminist theory and other critical social theories, often called *postmodern theories*, centralized the role of power in practice and challenged the construction of "truth" in theory that informs practice.

> In postmodernism there is a willingness to live with uncertainty and contingency. There is no univalence, no single theoretical discourse. There is no meaning out there in the world; meaning is embedded in language and language changes over time and across cultures. (Howe, 1994, pp. 520–521)

## Critical Reflection and Reflexivity

With roots both in the social sciences in disciplines such as sociology and in social science research, the terms *critical reflection* and *reflexivity* are often used interchangeably in the literature. Definitions for *critical reflection* and *reflexivity* often share the key element of critical engagement with how knowledge is created and its relationships to systems and structures of power, in contrast to reflective practice, which focuses on the professional self. This diversity of meanings is indicative of the evolution of these concepts and their growing application within the fields of social work and human service (D'Cruz, Gillingham, & Melendez, 2007b).

**Critical Reflection and Reflexivity: The Same But Different**  The emergence of the term *critical reflection* in the literature signalled a movement away from viewing the social work and human service practitioner as an objective helper. Rather, critical reflection envisions the practitioner's role as more dynamic and embedded in a relationship with the service user or client. In this view, the practitioner's previous experiences inform his or her practice and ultimately contribute to the creation of knowledge. Thus the focus of change in critical reflection is the individual practitioner.

In contrast, reflexivity focuses on change in the profession and in society (Sheppard et al., 2002, as cited in D'Cruz et al., 2007a). Reflexivity acknowledges and considers the importance of power not only at the micro level of self and in a practitioner's relationships with others, but also at the macro level, as it considers the role of power within society and the history of social work. It has been described as a process of looking outward at the formation of knowledge in our practice as well as inward to challenge our own understanding of objectivity and meaning making (White, 2001). More recently, theorists have expanded the definition of *reflexivity* to include the emotions of the practitioner, and, in doing so, they continue to challenge the movement toward "evidence-based practice" and risk assessment, which imply objectivity in practice (D'Cruz & Jones, 2004).

In terms of social and human service work, this approach demonstrates a commitment to questioning the theory and practice that these professions are founded on. Reflexive practice calls for the possibility of multiple truths (as opposed to one objective "truth") and the inclusion of a diversity of perspectives — in fact, it privileges voices from the margins or those excluded from the "expert" role (Bolzan, Heycox, & Hughes,

2001). In other words, it moves beyond reflective practice — which acts as a bridge between theory and practice, as evidenced by the ITP loop model — to question who built the bridge, whether we need a bridge at all, and what other alternatives exist.

---

### Discussion Questions

1. What challenges have you experienced in applying the theory and practice you learned in the classroom in the field?

2. What theories or practices from your program have you questioned? Which ones have you not questioned, and why?

3. How did you arrive at this questioning? How can you facilitate more questioning of theory and the profession?

4. How would you describe the difference between reflective and reflexive practice?

---

## Looking in the Mirror: The Importance of Reflexivity in the Human Service and Social Work Fields

The imperative to engage in reflexive practice is found in the well-meaning but predominantly unexamined roots of social work and human service. Many students identify their reason for choosing social work as "I just want to help people," but they have no awareness or insight of the history of the profession and how it connects with oppression. Cindy Blackstock, in her article "The Occasional Evil of Angels" (2005), draws attention to the fact that social work as a profession believes so strongly in its ability to do good in society that it does not examine, or reflect, on the "potential to do harm" (p. 1). She argues that the social work and helping professions have created a "white noise barrier" that has prevented them from seeing their own reflection and the harm it can create. In many ways, the reflection taught in many social work and human service programs is this barrier: It is a reflection that is overly focused on the student and the self, and does not examine the key role of power in the creation of knowledge.

## Voices from the Field

Many unique opportunities arose during my practicum placement to facilitate this deepening of self and learning. These occurred and were processed in a relationship with (my field instructor) that was safe and significant. She has a highly developed anti-oppressive practice and way of living that is inspiring. One goal I set was to develop a more self-reflexive practice that includes but is not limited to a deeper understanding of my relational location in the community, where I am (the descendent) of colonizers on Shuswap territory, and how my privilege and location within the 'dominant' group impacts on cross cultural work with Aboriginal people. (Nadine Mathews, student)

The student experience described above is a great example of reflexive practice and the call for social work to "look in the professional mirror to see its history — not just from its own perspective — but from the multiple perspectives of those who experienced the harm" (Blackstock, pp. 40–41).

## TOOLS TO SUPPORT REFLEXIVITY IN PRACTICE

A number of tools can support students engaging in reflexive practice, such as grounding in personal experience, reflexive journal writing; counter-storytelling, and intersectional frameworks.

### Grounding in Your Own Experience: Self-Awareness, Values, and Ethics

When learning the process of reflexive practice, it is important that students start with themselves. They should reflect on their prejudices, judgments, and stereotypes, as the absence of these is unlikely at this stage in their learning. They must acknowledge their limitations and be willing to reflect on them to ensure they do not get in the way of their work, learning, and relationships. However, we have discussed, staying at this level of reflection on the self is not enough — it is only the starting point of good critical reflexivity. Students' willingness to question their own power and privilege in the work they do and to become comfortable with being uncomfortable are both part of the process.

### Exercise

1. Who am I? (Explore your background, class, race, gender, sexual orientation, and abilities.)
2. How has how I define myself changed over time?
3. How do my various identities change in different contexts?
4. What challenges and strengths do my own context and identity bring to my practicum placement?
5. What areas of privilege are important for me to explore in my placement?
6. Have I been placed in an area that is linked to my own experiences?
7. Am I focused on a particular field or client to meet my own needs?
8. What support do I require in my field seminar to create a safe space to engage in reflexive practice?

# Journals and Reflexive Writing

Many students of social work and human service come to appreciate the role that journalling plays in their education. The journal becomes a place for students to record what they are learning and to converse with faculty and field instructors about their challenges in ways that they might not in face-to-face communication. Journals provide a safe space to consider practice experiences encountered in field education and the values and assumptions that underlie choices. In this way, they link theory to action and help students and practitioners consider other perspectives. Journalling also encourages skills such as observation, recording, questioning, self-awareness, feeling and thought identification, and problem solving. Through the process of writing in a journal, students can critically reflect on the meaning of their experiences and articulate key questions about power, privilege, and the ethical challenges they encounter.

Key areas to explore in a journal include attitudes, values, conflicts, areas of new growth, and areas of challenge. Journalling should not only focus on the self of the practitioner, but also reflect on the practice of others and the agency where a student is placed. Students often encounter examples of practice in their field placement that challenge them, including black humour or discrimination against others. The journal is an important place to explore these concerns, which are often difficult to bring up in field supervision or field seminars. The journal is often the first place students articulate such concerns, and through dialogue with self and instructor, the critical examination of these issues can be furthered and encouraged.

Journalling is a key strategy in the development of the reflexive practitioner. It is also the site where self-reflection informs a reflexive practice. The journal can be used not only as a location for self-reflection, but also as a space for reflexivity, where field instructors and faculty can engage in dialogue with students, raising further questions and other perspectives for the student to consider.

# Counter-Storytelling

Counter-storytelling, or the sharing of stories from the point of view of those who have been silenced, is another tool of reflexive practice. Critical race theorist Richard Delgado (2000) describes counter-storytelling as the creation of narratives that can connect and create meaning and community, and that also "shatter complacency and challenge the status quo" (p. 61).

The power of storytelling in disrupting dominant narratives is well documented, and students' journals can be spaces where students begin this process (Dixon & Rousseau, 2005). For example, Proma Tagore (2006) describes how, for many Aboriginal students and students of colour, there is "a general silence around colonialism, racism, and racialised experiences ... and the absence of voices and histories that speak to the realities, knowledge, and needs of people of colour and Aboriginal people" (p. 8).

The use of a journal in reflexive practice creates a space where such stories can be told and new creative and critical ways of responding to these issues can be named, questioned, and framed. Rhonda Lee McIssac, in her chapter in Proma Tagore's book (2006), states that her act of choosing to write in her own language of Anishnawbenomin is "an act of resistance.... It becomes a way to make yourself different, or to take pride in one's differences from colonial norms" (p. 119).

In addition to journalling, sharing circles — such as talking circles and other forms of circle sharing — can also be an important tool for the telling of new and important stories that have been left out of classrooms and textbooks.

## Tips for Keeping a Reflexive Journal

- Keep your journal confidential. Do not identify names or reveal information about clients.

- Include only details that you are comfortable sharing; complete self-disclosure is not required. For example, you can share that you are encountering some challenges at home without sharing specific details.

- Ensure that you are engaged in a questioning process about your own experiences — you don't need to have "the answers," but you do need to be curious.

- Be creative. Include art, poetry, and narratives as a means of critical reflection.

- Know that the topics you might encounter difficulty in writing about usually relate to places of vulnerability, difference, and power or oppression (past and present).

- Include narratives of your own experience that tell stories that challenge dominant knowledge.

## Discussion Questions

1. When it comes to keeping your journal, what works? What doesn't work? What could you do differently?

2. What other options are available?

3. What theories or frameworks can guide interventions?

4. How does an intervention change when viewed from multiple perspectives (include diversity and the perspectives of others provided through seminars, staff meetings, case presentations, and supervision)?

5. What alternative stories exist about this experience? What stories have you encountered that resist previous teachings?

# An Intersectional Framework and Reflexive Practice: Power and Privilege

Social work and human service work are professions that invite students and practitioners to identify, or locate, themselves in relation to their evolving practice with children, youth, families, and communities. Professional identity is informed through the interconnection of identities. Social work and human service practitioners are continually answering the questions, "Who are you?" and "Why do you care?" Reflexivity is a daily activity that allows students to answer these questions and understand how their answers change over time as context changes. Each person has multiple social identities and places where they might hold privilege, and others where they might experience oppression; for example, in race, gender, sexual orientation, class, or ability. Students must explore how their thinking, knowing, and doing might vary as a result of racial, ethnic, class, and other cultural differences; different settings; and different times. Reflexivity encourages students not only to recognize their culture, privilege, and social location, but also to interrogate how these intersect — acknowledging the role that power and inequity play at such intersections. The Canadian Research Institute for the Advancement of Women, in a document titled *Intersectional Feminist Frameworks: An Emerging Vision* (2006), states that intersectional frameworks "have the potential to open new spaces for transformation by examining not only the complex factors operating in women's and men's lives that keep them marginalized, but also how they are often able to respond to those forces in creative and innovative ways" (p. 5).

Through an intersectional framework, students can engage in a creative and innovative, critical and reflexive practice that considers the power and influence they hold in various roles and the impact that gender, ethnicity, religious orientation, and social class have on their work. Students move beyond an awareness of knowledge, values, methods, and approaches to seeing these things as extensions of a cultural system that includes structures of power and oppression. In doing so, students learn to question these same systems in the classroom and in the field.

Students can begin the process of reflexivity by identifying who they are and questioning their own social locations and the complexity of their identities with respect to their field placements. Using tools of reflexivity, they can begin to analyze their own preconceptions and stereotypes about the culture, people, problems, and interventions they will be working with in their field placements.

## Discussion Questions

1. How do I define my community? What are my connections to the community where I live?

2. What impacts do age, race, gender, ethnicity, and sexual orientation have on the community where I live?

3. What is the role of the agency I have been placed at within the larger community context?

4. What communities do I "belong" to? What are the relationships among these communities?

5. What are the strengths and challenges of entering a community to which I already belong as a student? What are the strengths and challenges of entering a community as an outsider? (Questions adapted from Clark & Hunt, 2007)

## NOT WANTING TO LOOK IN THE MIRROR: THE CHALLEGE OF ENGAGING IN REFLEXIVE PRACTICE

At some point in their education, most students of social work and human services will feel challenged by the process of reflexivity that they are asked to engage in and will question how or why all this critical reflection is necessary. Implementing reflexive practice has its challenges: It is time-consuming and can create vulnerability in students. Vulnerability is often felt in reaction to discussions of oppression and the consideration of one's own power and privilege. The process of becoming a reflexive practitioner is really about learning to become comfortable with being uncomfortable — and, in fact, to invite and embrace this feeling.

Instructors of reflexivity in practice should encourage students to use their intuition. The acknowledgment of feelings of discomfort and other emotions can help students consider the grey areas they will encounter within the rules and prescriptive nature of ethics and professional values they are taught. An overreliance on rules and checklists does not allow for the messy reality of a change process that might involve "conflict, emotion, identity crises, and ethical dilemmas; and it may require that we confront racism, classism, sexism, ableism, 'professionalism,' and homophobia in ourselves and in others and in institutions as we struggle for wholeness" (Walter, 1997, p. 75).

Field instructors who share with students their own past experiences and uncomfortable moments create a positive environment in which students are encouraged to be curious and question themselves, rather than become fearful. bell hooks (1994) speaks of the importance of educators' willingness to engage in sharing, reflecting, and being vulnerable in the classroom. She says, "I do not expect students to take any risks that I would not take, to share in any way that I would not share" (p. 21). hooks criticizes instructors who ask students to share confessional stories but refrain from doing so themselves. Instead, she calls for instructors to take the first risk and, in doing so, to model the linking of reflexive and confessional narratives to professional theories and discourses. This, she argues, will illuminate how reflexivity in practice links theory with practice.

# Voices from the Field

In my teaching about values and boundaries in my field education seminar to first-year Human Service diploma students, I often tell them a story about a powerful learning experience I have had in relation to the topic and the role of reflective practice. One story that I use is of a young woman, Sarah, I was working with who was an Aboriginal young woman of 12 and who was in a relationship with an older male that was sexually exploitive. I was quite worried about her as she was not naming the relationship as such and I felt that she was at real risk. One day, driving her home after our weekly girls group, Sarah said to me that she really liked my hat. I proceeded without much thought to hand over my hat to her. It was only after I drove away that I really began to reflect on my actions: Why had I given her my hat? Not only was this out of context for me and something I had never done, but I was aware in that moment of the implications of my act not only on my relationship with Sarah, but with other girls in the group who would know that Sarah was wearing my hat when and if she wore it and would also reflect on the meaning of this. I began a process of internal critical reflection at this point: questioning my actions and the feelings that had resulted in this action and the dissonance between my professional values and my actions. The hat I had given her was in fact a gift from my own mother and something I valued. I wondered at the meaning of this in my behaviour. Had I behaved in a maternal way to Sarah in response to my worry and feelings about her risk at this time? My intuition said that this was the case and the metaphor of the hat my mother had given me to shelter me from Vancouver rain was not lost on me in this moment. I further questioned my values and intention as a non-Aboriginal woman who had worked hard to develop a relationship that was not built on colonizing histories and actions — about the meaning of the giving of the hat to our work. I then returned to work where in a circle of my colleagues I engaged in a process of critical reflection with others to further examine my behaviour and motives but also to query my actions or next steps, given what had transpired. Through both of these processes — internal and external — I was able to come to the realization that my worry for her had manifested in the giving of the hat and that I would explain this to her and why I needed to ask for the hat back. Through the telling of this story to my students, I am making visible a process whereby I crossed a boundary — and how I reflected on this internally and with others and my resulting actions. I then encourage them in their journals and in class to engage in a similar process of reflexivity. (Natalie Clark, faculty liaison)

# RESEARCH ON REFLEXIVE PRACTICE AND STUDENTS

Ching Man Lam and his colleagues (2007), in their research on the use of journalling in field education, suggest that field education curricula must be designed to assist students in moving from self-reflection to reflexivity. They found that students focused on the self in their reflective practice and did not move to reflexivity or critical reflection on the profession unless their values and attitudes were directly affected in the helping role. The authors propose that field instructors and faculty need to support and encourage students through providing space for moving from reflection to reflexivity. They argue that social work and human service education, through its increased focus on competence-based and evidence-based practice over the past 20 years, has created an environment not conducive to reflexivity.

Further, a study conducted by Ione Lewis and Natalie Bolzan (2007) at the University of Western Sydney in Australia found that students in first year are mostly concerned with direct practice skills and are not engaged in reflexivity about the field or the profession. Echoing these findings, D'Cruz and her colleagues (2007b), in their research on the meaning of reflexivity for practitioners working with children and families, found that participants all spoke of the difficulty in implementing reflexivity in their practice as contrasted with the easier system of following rules and procedures. In addition, it is noteworthy that the participants did not discuss the power that they had as practitioners with the children and families they worked with.

## Equity in Action: Challenges and Opportunities

The major finding of this research for students' learning of reflexivity is the importance of having both the time and the supportive space to move to reflexive practice. However, many students and practitioners are not provided with this time or support and, indeed, may not be safe if they do engage in it. Further, sharing in classes and field education seminars can often take the form of minority students being placed in the position of discussing their experiences as members of an oppressed group, which can be painful. For example, an Aboriginal student, in describing his experience of social work education, stated that he was called on in class again and again to share his life and describe stories of colonization and residential schooling (Bruyere, 1998). Students from minority groups are often placed in the position of educating students from dominant groups about oppression.

For students who are members of an oppressed group (e.g., because of their sexuality, their gender, a disability, their racial background, or a mental illness), a practicum can be a site that triggers fears, challenges, and ongoing reminders of past and current experiences (Razack, 2002b, p. 104). According to Narda Razack, "[r]acism and oppression are embedded in our structures.... People from racial minority groups have to face 'everyday' forms of racism and discrimination" (p. 107). Yet research has found that most field instructors avoid discussions related to race and professional identity; instead, most adopt a "colourblind" approach.

For students from racial minority groups and Aboriginal cultures, experiences of racism will be encountered in field education. In her research on the experience of racial minority students, Razack recommends that field education seminars and field supervisions be spaces where discussions about oppression can happen. Echoing Blackstock,

Razack (2002a) states that "social work values and ... [the] ideology of caring and empathy, allow social work practitioners to 'do good' by the students without delving into issues like imperialism, colonialism and other forces of oppression" (p. 226). This "colour-blind" approach hinders not only the process of supervision and the field seminar, but also students' own reflexive practice, as they are not able to fully ground themselves in their own experiences or reflect on the existence of race and racism in their practice. Field supervision must be a space where difficult and courageous conversations can occur.

Although being able to openly discuss such issues is ideal, it is not always safe to do so. For example, it is unrealistic for first-year students to challenge the policies or practices of the agency in which they are placed. Similar to hooks, Razack (2002a) questions the power dynamics present in the classroom and field educator role. She argues, "The classroom can be a colonizing space where power and dominance continue to be enacted" (p. 10). Instead, the focus should be on interrogating privilege and challenging dominant norms and ideologies. Field education seminars for students are one safe space where field instructors and educators can create a learning environment in which reflexive practice is supported through role modelling, their own sharing, and the challenging of privilege.

# REFLEXIVITY IN PRACTICE: LOOKING OUT AND LOOKING IN

## Self-Care and Wellness

Practicum, while an exciting time for most students, can also be a location of struggle and challenge. Some of the reasons for struggle can include life crises or traumatic events, reminders of one's own oppression, ethical crises, and conflicting time commitments. Further, the process of engaging in reflexive practice requires students to become comfortable with being uncomfortable, to challenge and interrogate their own privilege and oppressive behaviours and actions, and, ultimately, to question the very profession they have spent time and money to train in. As a result, practising self-care is a key component of reflexive practice for all students. A strong wellness plan is an essential tool for students in field education. They should create one and make it a living document, reviewing it and reflecting on the application of their goals as they move through their placements.

Key components of self-care include the following ABCs:

- **Awareness:** Know thyself and signs of stress. Our bodies let us know when we are under stress, and it is important to pay attention to the ways in which our body lets us know this. For example, increases in headaches and physical complaints, sleep disturbances, and emotional reactivity are some common ways our bodies demonstrate stress. Students should build supports for physical, emotional, mental, and spiritual wellness in whatever way has meaning for them.

- **Balance and boundaries:** Create boundaries in your practicum, at school, and in your own time. Students should consider scheduling time for family, friends, and the self just as they would schedule school or their field placements. They should allow for transition times between placement, school, and home to ensure that they are not bringing stress from one place to another. Students can seek support or mentoring from those around them who seem to do this well. Effective strategies are different for all individuals, and students must develop strategies that work for them.
- **Connection and consultation:** Seek out supervision and support. Consultation is an essential aspect of self-care and will assist students in making ethical and clear decisions. Students can use their field education seminar, field liaison, and field educator as resources.

## Exercise

Answer the following questions in your reflexive journal. Reflect on your own experience and feelings about practising in the field, and thoughts about areas where you may need support or self-care.

1. What personal issues have I experienced? What is my history of loss and trauma? What are my triggers?
2. What are my strengths and coping skills?
3. How much empathy do I have for myself?
4. What tools do I currently use to support self-awareness and self-care?
5. Who are my support systems? Who do I turn to?
6. What are my resources of spirituality? What is my culture and sense of belonging to something larger?
7. What are my hopes for my field placement?
8. What fears do I have about my field placement (feelings, thoughts)?
9. What behaviours might these fears result in?
10. What areas of support will I need as I go through my field practice?

## Sharing Power in Field Education Seminars and Supervision

An important part of engaging in reflexive practice is for students to see themselves as co-creators of social work and human service knowledge. As such, students have the ability to question not only their own practice and theory frameworks, but also those of others. Sharing power with students in field education seminars, practicum supervision, and evaluation processes are all key ways to challenge the oppressive nature of current professional education. As Noble (2001) states so eloquently, "Students on placements are in a privileged position of witnessing and participating in the 'doing' of social work" (p. 358). Valuing the student narratives that develop within these privileged positions is a means of "exploring how knowledge is constructed, taught and used" (p. 358) and "requires educators to move from the 'certainties' of expert to a more fragile, humble position of learning from students' attempts at practice" (p. 357).

## Voices from the Field

I ardently believe that teaching and learning are an intertwined process. "Tell me and I will forget. Show me and I will remember. Involve me, and I will understand" (Confucius, BC 450). Some of my most valuable learning has come to me from the teachings of the students I have had the privilege to co-learn with. I believe that an interactional, collaborative approach to teaching and learning is essential and allows the educator to position herself or himself as a co-learner working with the learner(s). This enables mutual respect between the educator and the learner, shared power, shared knowledge, shared knowledge, and shared action (Kaiser, 1997; Munson, 2002; Parsons & Durst, 1992). As a lifelong learner, the duality of teaching and learning allows me to perceive, conceptualize, devise, acknowledge, assess, and transform information with others, requiring me to constantly create and recreate myself both personally and professionally. Through my reflective practice of interactional learning, I believe in the concept of mutual respect and trust between educator and learner and I know that this is achieved through holistic, reciprocated, courageous, open conversation: communication based on deferential listening and dialogue. I believe this is fundamental to the supervisor/student relationship. My experience identifies the stronger the alliance in the fieldwork supervisor/student relationship, the greater the interactional learning (Fox, 1989; Kaiser, 1997; Munson, 2002; Parsons & Durst, 1992). In order to learn collectively, we, as fieldwork supervisor and student, must consider together what we teach, how we teach it, what we learn, and how we learn it at the onset of the field placement. This supportive, open, and mutual process inspires motivation and empowerment for the student and initiates a sense of balance, shared power, shared knowledge, shared meaning, shared action, honesty, and trust in the relationship. This valuable relationship allows both individuals to express difference in an open, safe environment that stimulates trust and facilitates voice, critical thinking, reflexivity, and learning; ultimately enabling construction, deconstruction, and co-construction in the ways both individuals connect and communicate with each other and with clients (Birkenmaier & Berg-Weger, 2007; Davys & Beddoe, 2000; Kaiser, 1997, Munson, 2002; Parsons & Durst, 1992).

Reflection allows me to step back and consider my holistic practice and my holistic being authentically and honestly. This can be both a comfortable and uncomfortable process of re-evaluation and truth. Reflective practice enables me to continually explore, challenge, and re-evaluate my understanding and application of shared power, shared knowledge, shared meaning, and shared action in my role as fieldwork supervisor; thereby, enhancing a stronger supervisor/student relationship and better practices in student and practitioner learning, and ultimately creating positive and better outcomes for the clients with whom we work. (Kathy McKinnon, field instructor)

## CASE SCENARIO

A teen has been referred to a child and youth care worker at a local community youth centre. The referral was initiated through the teen's sexual abuse counsellor and social worker. The goal is to connect the girl to services in the community and to provide positive activities for her daily life.

The child and youth care worker is a 28-year-old Caucasian female. She is married and has no children. She grew up in a rural setting and would describe herself as having a strong Christian upbringing. In fact, she attended a Christian school throughout high school and continues to attend church weekly. She comes from a two-parent family, has four siblings, and remains very connected to them. Her family is considered middle-class, and all the children have professional careers. She has no history of abuse. She enjoys music and dance and is currently involved in a community choir.

The teen is a 16-year-old Aboriginal female who is a permanent ward and currently living in foster-care. She is placed with her sister. She was apprehended at a young age from her family, who were living on a small reserve located near a small rural community. The family has since moved to the urban centre where the teen now resides with her sister. Both of the girl's grandparents attended residential school. She has an extensive history of childhood trauma, including sexual abuse by multiple offenders, including a previous foster parent. The youth was disconnected from her large extended family and community for a number of years while she was in foster care, but through her recent placement with her sister, she has been reconnecting with her community and has shown an interest in learning traditional singing and dancing. She was recently referred to mental health services because of concerns that she was dissociative — she had been hearing voices and having visions. She attended only one appointment at the mental health centre and refuses to go back. She recently dropped out of school.

## Questions

1. What power imbalances or barriers exist in this scenario? In what ways do these power imbalances or barriers intersect (e.g., barriers caused by race, gender, and age, and privilege based on class)? What are the intersections of power imbalances or barriers for the child and youth care worker? What power and privilege does the child and youth care worker need to consider? What impact will it have on their relationship? What impact will it have on the child and youth care worker's approach to helping?

2. What does the child and youth care worker need to consider when engaging in reflexive practice? What awareness might she need to gain? What knowledge? What skills or strategies might she use to accomplish this?

# CHAPTER SUMMARY

Reflective practice has been an essential element of social work and human service education and practice since the inception of these fields. Reflective practice is defined as the process of reflecting on one's feelings, thoughts, and actions to improve practice. Because of the influence of social theories that emerged from social movements, such as feminism, post-colonial theories, and postmodernism, the idea of reflection has evolved and been replaced by the concepts of reflexivity and critical reflection. Reflexivity can be defined as a critical reflection that includes awareness of the systems of power and oppression that have an impact on our identity, practice, and the very creation of the knowledge that guides our profession. Tools of reflexivity include grounding in one's experience, reflexive journalling, counter-storytelling, and instructional frameworks. Each of these tools assists students in moving from reflection to a critical reflexive practice whereby they not only examine the self, but also examine the field and the profession into which they are entering. The potential for transformation in our field and practice is found in reflexivity through the coming together of critical self-awareness, role awareness, interrogation of power and privilege as they affect our profession, and, finally, a questioning stance of "truths" and taken-for-granted assumptions that have formed our profession.

## Critical-Thinking Questions

1. Apply concepts of reflexivity to your goals for your field practicum. What elements of examining your profession and your own position with respect to power and privilege could be included here?

2. Which tools of reflexive practice do you currently engage in? Which new strategies could you use to further develop your reflexive practice?

3. What challenges exist for you in implementing reflexive practice? What strategies exist for addressing these challenges?

## Suggested Readings

Blackstock, C. (2005). "The occasional evil of angels: Learning from the experiences of Aboriginal peoples and social work [Special edition]." *International Indigenous Journal of Entrepreneurship, Advancement, Strategy and Education. I*(I). Retrieved from www.indigenousjournal.com/wipce2005.html.

Bruyere, G. (1998). "Living in another man's house: Supporting Aboriginal learners in social work education." *Canadian Social Work Review 15,* 169–176.

Clark, N. (2009). "'Who are you and why do you care?' Or how my new life as an academic is changing the answer to this question." In "Inside Out: Reflections on Personal and

Professional Intersections [Special issue]." *Reflections: Narratives of Professional Helping 15*(2), 5–14.

D'Cruz, H, Gillingham, P., & Melendez, S. (2007). "Reflexivity, its meanings and relevance for social work: A critical review of the literature." *British Journal of Social Work 37,* 73–90.

La Flamme, M. (2006). "An 'uppity' memoir and 'cheeky' tips: On what it is like for me to be a woman of colour at a university whose structure is still predominantly white and eurocentric in its focus." In P. Tagore (Ed.), In *Our own voices: Learning and teaching towards decolonizations* (pp. 121–132). Winnipeg, MB: Larkuma.

Margot, L., & McKenzie, L. (2006). *The wellness wheel: An Aboriginal contribution to social work.* Retrieved from the Dialog website: *www.reseaudialog.qc.ca/Docspdf/Loiselle McKenzie.pdf.*

Razack, N. (2002). *Transforming the field: Critical antiracist and anti-oppressive perspectives for the human services practicum.* Halifax, NS: Fernwood Publishing.

Schön, D. A. (1983). *The reflective practitioner: How professionals think in action.* New York, NY: Basic Books.

## Relevant Websites

### Critical Social Work

www.criticalsocialwork.com

This excellent open source journal from the University of Windsor focuses on issues of social justice and promotes dialogue on a wide range of topics to promote social justice.

### Relational Child and Youth Care Practice

www.cyc-net.org/Journals/rcycp.html

This open source journal deals with a wide range of practice issues important to reflexive practitioners in the area of child and youth care.

# Chapter 6

## Progressive Field Education: Social Justice, Human Rights, and Advocacy

Sandra deVink-Leblanc, Linda Turner, and Brian Carty

## Chapter Objectives

- Understand progressive field education.
- Define key concepts and theories related to progressive field education.
- Demonstrate how students can integrate human rights and social justice theory into practice.
- Demystify assumptions that may cause students to be hesitant about choosing field placements where social justice, human rights, and advocacy are primary components.
- Identify organizational and personal constraints and limitations of practice and provide strategies to overcome them.
- Describe the professional and personal benefits that students can gain through progressive field placements.

## SOCIAL JUSTICE AND SOCIAL CHANGE: DEFINITIONS AND THEORIES

Progressive field education provides experiences and knowledge that will enable social work and human service students to integrate a social justice orientation into their practice framework. Some of the key elements of progressive field education are social justice, human rights, inclusion, empowerment, and advocacy. The overall aim of progressive field education is to prepare students to acquire requisite knowledge and skill development that fosters a paradigm shift in how social work and human service work is conceptualized and practised. This shift is essentially about understanding the links between private troubles and public issues; viewing social problems as rooted in structural inequalities at the social, economic, and political level; and taking on problems such as classism, sexism, heterosexism, ageism, and ableism.

In progressive field education, field placements might be referred to as *social action* field placements because the focus of the placement is usually a project that is related to a social problem such as poverty, homelessness, violence against women, bullying in the workplace and in schools, racism, homophobia, discrimination, or inequality. As Martin (2007) explains, social action or activism is "action on behalf of a cause, action that goes beyond what is conventional or routine. The action might be door-to-door canvassing, alternative radio, public meetings, rallies, or fasting. The cause might be women's rights, opposition to a factory, or world peace." One of the ways a social action field placement differs from a traditional placement is that its focus on the social issue is broader and more structural than it would be in an individual-focused placement.

## Social Justice

The pursuit of social justice is a core value of both social work education and social work practice. Delaney (2005) states that "social work's commitment to social justice as the basis for a social transformation that can restore hope and possibility in an age of cynicism and despair reflects social work's role in a real world as well as its moral responsibility to influence that world based on the principles and knowledge that inform the profession" (p. 371).

In an interesting study about how social workers use social justice language, Hawkins, Fook, and Ryan (2001) did a search of social work literature and came up with the following list of terms associated with social justice: "rights/duties/obligations, equity/equality, access, participation, contracts, social change/activism, empowerment, advocacy, disadvantaged, oppression, social critique/critical consciousness, community development/organization/social development, politics, co-operation/co-ordination, feminist action-based, policy, critique, discriminatory" (p. 6). While the obligation of social justice and the upholding of human rights falls on the individual social and human service worker as a member of a profession that holds social justice as a core value, that individual social and human service worker cannot fulfill the obligation alone, but must work in concert with others, through organized bodies and as a member of an agency or a group whose purpose is to address a form of social injustice.

## Social Change

Social change has been a major preoccupation of sociological, political, and economic theorists through the centuries. Johnson, Schwartz, and Tate (1997) define *social change* as "an alteration, modification, or substitution in the institutions, structures, patterns of organizations, and exchanges and relationships between people in a given society" (cited in Rae & Nicholas-Wolosuk, 2003, p. 4). In a contemplative reflection about why social work and human service students should be educated for social change, Abramovitz (1993) challenges social work to "lead the way in making the fight for social justice an overriding professional goal" (p. 10). Shragge (2003) provides a valuable exploration of how people develop into activists who engage in social change and notes that passion for activism is often born during post-secondary education and travel experiences.

Within organizations, what factors affect the nature of change and the likelihood that it will occur? Detailed explorations of organizational theories can be found in texts providing a macro perspective (Netting, Knetter, & McMurtry, 1998; Kettner, Daley, & Nichols, 1985). Examples of familiar organizational theory clusters that help to articulate how organizations "tick" include organizational psychology, systems theory, theories about bureaucracy, management theories, and human relations theories (Wood, Zeffane, Fromholtz, Wiesner, & Creed, 2010). The climate of an organization and the cultural properties that characterize it are important backdrops to the theoretical analysis of how change is most likely to occur.

In their text *Changing Agency Policy: An Incremental Approach*, Rae and Nicholas-Wolosuk (2003) assert the following:

> In actual practice, in spite of their values and ethics, social workers are typically not involved in efforts to confront and transcend injustice and oppression and their roots in the fabric of society. They tend to consider their practice as politically neutral, and they separate it therefore, from their philosophical rejection of injustice and oppression. In reality, social work practice is ultimately connected to social welfare policy. (p. 124)

Given the direct connection between social welfare policy and social work practice, "policy practice," or engaging in efforts to bring about changes that respect human dignity and ensure equitable access to service, deserves significant attention. Rae and Nicholas-Wolusuk's (2003) Action-Strategy Model of Agency Policy Change, which is grounded in social systems theory, offers one strategy to bring about change to policy. Its authors describe it as "a professional, change-based intervention at the agency level … [that] includes a role for clients/consumers, incorporates critical thinking … and the values and Code of Ethics of social work" (p. 8). As well, anti-oppressive practice approaches demand commitment to transformative changes that facilitate enhanced respect and integrity for individuals and populations (Dominelli, 2006).

## SERVICE LEARNING AND PROGRESSIVE FIELD EDUCATION

"Academic service learning" has become an option for students in numerous professional programs and also in undergraduate courses, such as those exploring social inequality. *Service learning* refers to engaging with fellow citizens in a community setting in ways that "force students out of their comfort zones culturally, economically, and socially"

(Dicklitch, 2005, p. 128), while also being required to contemplate theory in the midst of experiencing "real life" processes and situations.

Eyler (2002b) points out that the term *service learning* is applied to what in reality represents a broad range of levels of engagement: "… the actual experiences of students range from intensive community experiences with close integration into academic study to brief 'add on' service activities largely unconnected to classroom discourse" (p. 518).

Progressive field education parallels what Eyler (2002b) purports to be the outcomes of service learning where engagement is concerned. She anticipates that service learning participants should develop "… positive attitudes towards community engagement … a sense of personal efficacy and commitment … deeper understanding of social issues (or other subject matter) … lifelong learning and problem solving skills … skills for community action and involvement … [and] post formal reasoning abilities necessary to deal with complex 'ill structured' social problems" (p. 519).

# STUDENT LEARNING IN PROGRESSIVE FIELD PLACEMENTS

It is the job of educators in conjunction with field placement agencies to assist social work and human service students in the process of learning the knowledge and skills they require in a step-by-step manner. Demystifying theory and concepts by describing what these things look like in action is one of the first steps in the process of learning. It takes time and several steps before one can integrate new concepts into practice skills. Three learning stages lead to integration: (1) the creation of cognitive maps (to understand concepts), (2) perception (to apply the concepts to real-life situations), and action (to integrate learning, our understanding of concepts is applied in some kind of action plan).

Cognitive maps have a multidisciplinary status and relevance and, as a result, are challenging to define. Kitchin (1994) has characterized cognitive maps as "advanced organizers that influence the impact of later direct experience of the environment" and points out that "we all have daily navigation decisions to make involving choice processes, for example, migration, shopping or recreation, which it is hypothesized are influenced by our ability to understand the everyday environment, i.e. cognitive maps" (p. 6).

To create cognitive maps, students need to acquire an understanding of the key concepts that are foundational in social action work, such as social justice, human rights, advocacy, awareness of structural inequalities, and empowerment. Using the example of advocacy, a social action–related concept that may be relatively unfamiliar to new students, the first step of learning would be to define the term by providing a cognitive map. Such a map could consist of examining explanations of advocacy from the literature, from stories and case studies of advocacy, and by comparing definitions. One author offers this straightforward characterization: "The skills of expressing your own view, even when it comes into conflict with other people's" (Doel & Shardlow, 1998, p. 69).

In the second phase of learning, *perception* refers to noticing and understanding the concepts in real-life situations: Once the concepts are at least tentatively understood through provision of cognitive maps, students need to perceive them in practice situations. That is, students will begin to connect theoretically derived understandings of a concept with what they are seeing and noticing in their field placements. Continuing with the example of advocacy, advocacy is not new or rare: Individuals and groups have always tried to influence people in power, in both their private lives and as part of their work. Advocacy is only one of several approaches to undertaking social justice work. However, it can make all the other approaches more effective by helping us gain the support of people in power and by changing the social environment in which we work. Almost all non-governmental organizations (NGOs) and community-based organizations (CBOs) already have experience with advocacy, even if they do not realize it or do not use the word *advocacy*.

The essential third phase that completes the learning process is *action*. To integrate learning, students' understanding of the concepts, initiated through cognitive maps and reinforced through perceiving the concepts in action, has to be applied in some kind of action plan to solidify the learning and ensure thorough integration. Entering the action phase of applying new skills always feels awkward at first, not unlike driving a car for the first time. With some time for critical reflection and feedback, the skills can be applied again. Students can continue the learning cycle with a view of gaining more confidence in applying this new knowledge in practice until there is a sense of full integration.

It's very easy for students to assume that they don't have the required knowledge and skills if they have never done any social action work before, and this can make the thought of participating in such a field placement overwhelming. However, with awareness and support, profound learning can take place in progressive field education environments.

We now turn to examining how constraints and challenges can be overcome through various strategies, both at the individual student level and at the organizational level within educational institutions and agencies.

## STRATEGIES TO ENGAGE IN PROGRESSIVE FIELD EDUCATION

It has been our experience as field education coordinators that when social work students begin to explore their field placement options and are confronted with the possibility of doing a "progressive field placement," many will express reservations and concerns, while a few will be excited, about this opportunity. The students who enter a social work and human service program with a strong social justice–related background and/or value base are often more interested in engaging in progressive field placements than traditional social service– or counselling–oriented field placements. Students need to clearly understand, prior to the decision-making process, what a progressive field placement is and how it differs from a traditional placement.

## Voices from the Field

Before I started the social work program I had never really considered social action as being a part of social work. Since completing the courses within the program I have begun to understand what it truly means to be a social worker … to work socially. I feel that through this placement I have become more appreciative of the role that social action has in social work and that there is no one way to be active in our role as a social worker. I never realized the amount of work that goes into preparing and proposing an issue and then taking action — it is not all about being a face in the community protesting or raising awareness. I feel energized and optimistic about the real change that I can make in my own community in my practice as a social worker … I want to take what I have learned in this placement and throughout the program and be an advocate for whatever clients I find myself working with in the future. (Kristin Zegers, student)

Students may make assumptions about social action field placements that reflect society's stereotypes about social activists being the "rebel type" who may engage in burning placards or in activities that lead to getting arrested. This view would obviously conflict with most students' goal of getting a job with a provincial or territorial government. The field education coordinator's job is to demystify progressive field education and clarify misconceptions that get in the way of students' ability to choose this type of placement. Students may raise or wish to explore the following common questions or preoccupations.

**Do I have the skills that are needed for this kind of placement?** Many skills used in social action field placement projects are already familiar to students. Often, students have organized a party or been part of an organizing committee for a social event that draws on organizational, time management, and planning skills. These are critical skills for all social action projects, although applied to a different type of activity. Many social work students come from a background where they have participated in church or in community activities for a good cause. The skills they learned in these activities, which perhaps addressed a problem on an individual basis, can be applied to social action projects, which look at issues from a broader context, with linkages made between local and global solutions. Students should understand that in social action placements they will rely on local experts to provide information rather than be experts on the issue. At the same time, in the process of organizing social action projects, students will become more educated on different issues and can bring this knowledge to future jobs.

## Voices from the Field

Both students gained a keen awareness of the need to tailor the group's message to the decision makers. They showed good organization skills to empower themselves and others to meet their social action objectives with our group. I believe they also gained an appreciation of the need to be patient, strategic, and committed for the long term when trying to effect social change. (Mark Darcy, field instructor)

**How can I benefit from a progressive field placement?** Many students are motivated by a career goal of offering counselling services to individuals in need and may question how a progressive field placement will be of benefit to their career goal. In our view, progressive field education enables students to make the links between the individual client's private problems and the related public issues that need a different kind of intervention for long-term solutions. By understanding these links, social work and human service practitioners can envision their work as being both inside the system (e.g., counselling individuals) and outside the system (e.g., volunteering at an antipoverty organization). The individuals who receive services will benefit from the practitioners' expanded knowledge of the issues and from their creative use of direct practice skills.

Many students have a strong desire to build a practice focused on the empowerment of clients. Through social action field placements, they can increase their ability to better understand the need for and use of skills that foster empowerment, such as universalizing (i.e., linking the client's situation or experiences with situations or experiences of others), providing support through normalizing, using consciousness-raising as a tool to conceptualize the client situation, and reframing the problem to enable growth and change.

**If I go to a non-profit agency, will I simply be an extra set of hands doing photocopying and making posters instead of being in an environment where my learning objectives will be respected and prioritized?** This concern is valid and it underscores the need for the educational team involved in a placement's initial development and the ensuing process to clearly communicate what the institution's objectives are with agency personnel. Students also need to assertively communicate with agency supervisors and their faculty liaisons if they recognize that the activities they are doing are steering away from learning appropriate to their educational program toward tasks that simply need to be done.

Host agencies in the non-profit sector usually have fewer paid staff and thus have a higher reliance on volunteers to deliver services, so having a student worker may be very appealing to them. It is also a reality that because community agencies are chronically underfunded, everyone from the executive directors through to the office staff often have to "pitch in" to prepare for various events, and this does, at times, mean that students could find themselves doing things they would not anticipate being asked to do in a governmental position. In terms of time spent engaged in such tasks, however, it should be the exception and not an ongoing expectation. When all members of the organization are required to be "on deck" to complete a project or contribute to an activity that will ultimately benefit service users, these activities often develop team spirit and collective pride in meeting needs and achieving goals — an added bonus.

**Will a social action field placement open doors to jobs with decent pay?** With the reality of high student debt loads, placements are sometimes seen as stepping stones to get a job with decent pay. Students recognize that non-profit salaries do not compare favourably with most positions in governmental bureaucracies. Two things may be helpful to consider in this regard. The first is how to market "transferable skills" gained in the non-profit sector placement upon graduation and when one is applying for jobs. Having been part of a non-profit governmental organization, students will have an ethic of productivity, resourcefulness, and flexibility, and a commitment to needs, teamwork, and goal-directed achievement: all qualities any supervisor will value when considering a job applicant. Secondly, in our experience, we have not seen a correlation between students whose field placements were with governmental agencies and the students who are eventually hired by governmental agencies. Likewise, students whose placements were with community organizations do not appear to have been hindered in their job searches. While this question may warrant an applied research study, we can think of several examples of students who cherish the learning provided through their experience of a progressive field placement yet today are in higher paying positions characteristic of government careers.

**Will this type of field placement be as valuable as others and serve my career goals?** Students prefer to see their placements as optimally in line with where they want to work in the future. Students often perceive that there will be a lack of client interaction in the social justice placements. Many express a need to build their comfort level with clients and fear missing the client aspect in social action. In addition, one of the fears that often goes unspoken is that government employers, depending on the setting, might view the prior experience of fighting for social justice as something negative. The question of whether this experience will hinder you when you graduate from the program is also worthy of reflection. The act of raising tough questions is, in fact, one of the skills required by those engaged in advocacy and social action work. Asking relevant and challenging questions is also an important skill in clinical practice. We suggest that if our career goal as social work and human service practitioners includes commitment to social justice, as the profession states, then participating in a field placement where we are closer to confronting issues and identifying the roots of problems, and where we are contributing to social change versus being focused on individual change, there is indeed congruency with our goal.

**Will internal problems of the organization cloud my field placement experience?** This question and concern likely is not unique to progressive field experiences. Again, clear communication with agency supervisors, and with the school faculty liaison, should lead to gaining the necessary support to negotiate the complicated internal dynamics that are sometimes inherent in an organization and not apparent until one becomes an "insider" in that organization.

**Will I know enough about social justice and global issues to be involved in such a field placement?** Students are often intimidated by a lack of confidence and a gap in knowledge and skill that they perceive is required to engage in social action work. It is easy to forget that the engaged activists in our communities were once students who experienced many of the same fears. So how did they go from being unsure students to engaged professionals? Students often have fears about being inadequate in either knowledge or skills to succeed in progressive field placements. This makes it far more challenging to take the step, because of feeling intimidated and not knowing where to start with a social justice placement. It can raise additional questions about whether there will be enough structure and role clarity. One strategy is to request a clear explanation from the field coordinator about what the differences are among field placements, and to explore specifics, such as "What will I be doing here?" Also, requesting a field placement where you can join an initiative that is on its way rather than having to initiate something on your own is wise.

## ORGANIZATIONAL STRATEGIES TO ENGAGE IN PROGRESSIVE FIELD EDUCATION

What are some of the constraints or challenges for professional schools that would like to see their students engaged more often in social justice–oriented field placements? One issue is the importance of students having ongoing access to supervision by a representative of their respective profession with the necessary qualifications. Sometimes social work programs have to rely on the faculty liaison to provide the supervision in field placements that don't have social workers on staff or for projects supported by groups or committees that are completely volunteer-run.

Another hurdle that may need to be overcome is broadening the mindset of some faculty who may be strongly attached to a vision of social work practice being "performed" in an individual, clinical model rather than a vision of structural social work whereby the root causes of the issues people face are seen as the targets for change: "Structural social workers seek to change the social system and not the individuals who receive, through no fault of their own, the results of defective social arrangements" (Mullaly, 1997, p. 133). Colleen Lundy (2004) further explains, "A structural approach to social work attempts to bridge the duality of the personal and the social, the individual and the community, and offers social workers an understanding of diverse populations in the context of social structures and social processes that generally support and reproduce social problems" (p. 119).

Schools of social work may need to more assertively and more regularly articulate the achievements of students who undertake what may be seen as non-traditional field placements to various audiences: to future employers of the program's graduates, to students themselves, and to the university community that may ponder, "But is that social work?" Many people simply do not associate the social work profession with its social justice mandate and, in this regard, sometimes members themselves can be their own worst enemy. Some social work and human service practitioners may need to refresh their knowledge of the powerful messages found in classic social work texts (Carniol, 1990; Fox, Piven, & Cloward, 1971) to be reminded that social workers "sign up" for a profession whose mandate is to identify where social change is needed and engage in actions, through advocacy or otherwise, that reflect a commitment to human rights and social inclusion.

## PROGRESSIVE FIELD AGENCIES

In this section, we provide four examples of agency settings where students have been able to participate in progressive or social action field placements.

### Making Waves/Vague par vague Inc.

Making Waves/Vague par vague Inc. (Waves) is a dating violence prevention program that was started in New Brunswick in 1995 by three women who had collectively spent many years working in the field of abuse and sexual assault — that is, at transition houses and sexual assault crisis centres. They had seen the "cycle of violence" repeat itself too often in New Brunswick. As a result, these women decided to develop a dating violence project to address the problem. The following text from the Partners for Youth website describes the program:

> Making Waves/Vague par vague (MW/Vpv) is an innovative and successful provincial relationship violence prevention program which has been in operation in New Brunswick since 1995. Guided by principles of equality, equity and diversity, we engage youth in a peer process to explore and raise awareness of relationship violence issues. Teens become active partners in creating a world in which violence is not tolerated.

### Hungry for Change

The mission of the Hungry for Change project is to connect with those who are living and struggling in the downtown area of Fredericton. The theology of this particular church encompasses the idea of abundance: that there are sufficient resources for all but distribution of those resources is the main problem. The project encourages and models generosity by challenging the structures that maintain poverty and want. Through creating projects with a focus on food security that will tie in local and global issues, students have been involved in a variety of activities, including working in a drop-in centre for persons with low incomes living in the downtown area, participating in bread distribution days, working on a peace education series, assisting with soup luncheons, assisting with a fair-trade café, writing letters for urgent action campaigns, and assisting with Christmas welcome hampers for refugee and immigrant families. As part of the placement, a major one-day event at the church included a men's breakfast, a food security workshop, breadmaking through workshop and discussion, a biblical survey, and a film followed by dinner and a discussion period with dialogue on issues related to food.

## Conservation Council of New Brunswick

The Conservation Council of New Brunswick describes itself as "A membership-based organization that has been at the forefront of environmental action in New Brunswick since 1969. The Conservation Council's campaigns to protect our air, land and water are run by a small, dedicated staff" (n.d.). It is an agency that maintains a high public profile in the province and has become involved in numerous issues of concern to most citizens.

## Voices from the Field

Social work students engaged in active lobbying to promote a green environment i.e.: banning pesticides from use in the city. They were able to hear the strong lobby from the industry that manufactures the pesticides and observe its impact on elected officials. Social work students wrote very clear and bold letters to the editor that engaged the community and sparked quite an active public debate. They were able to experience the power of engaging the community. I think it gave them a confidence that is otherwise hard to come by. (Gaila Friars, faculty field instructor)

## Doone St. Community Center Storefront

The Doone St. Community Center storefront was built in a public housing project as a strategy to empower the residents with low income and also to reduce incidents of crime in this small community located in Fredericton, New Brunswick. A police officer was seconded to work part-time as the coordinator of the community centre in the first four years of operation. This location was viewed as a great opportunity to develop a field placement that would provide students with a combination of community development, group work, and individual helping experiences in a grassroots context. Since there was no job description for the social work or human service students, they started by doing a needs assessment of residents that allowed them to go door to door to meet the community and gain information about their needs. This assessment was the basis for program development, such as a youth group, a women's group, and other community activities. The women's group, which was composed of single parents and some young adult women, met weekly for the duration of the first and second field placements at the storefront.

The women's group was co-facilitated by the female student and faculty liaison. Over the course of two years, the women became more engaged and active members of the community centre, taking on a variety of leadership roles. A few women chose to go to St. Thomas University and completed BA and BEd degrees as a result of the support their interest received by the social work and human service students, who arranged a special information session by St. Thomas University recruitment staff. Although encouraging university education was not an immediate goal of the project and the women's support group, this result does capture what is possible in a social action project that reflects an empowerment and strengths-based model of practice. These new credentials allowed the women to break the cycle of poverty.

## CASE SCENARIO

This case scenario is designed to engage participants in and create awareness about a social issue that presents a possible focus for an educational or awareness workshop. The scenario is an adaptation of an exercise described in *Team Challenges: 170 Group Activities to Build Cooperation, Communication and Creativity* (Bordessa, 2006). In the original example, the topic was family violence, and the exercise was used at the beginning of a workshop.

You are a young parent with a child in elementary school. You arrive for a school concert, and the parents are all mingling and chatting with one another. Suddenly, you notice a friend from high school, Jane, with whom you have lost contact. Excited about this chance meeting, you approach her to say hello and get reacquainted. Jane seems reluctant to engage in conversation and avoids eye contact. You are surprised by her reaction and disappointed in her lack of interest in reconnecting. Jane leaves abruptly, saying that she is late for an appointment.

The context of Jane's inner experience is that she has been in a difficult marriage for eight years, and, as a result, she has experienced physical, emotional, and sexual abuse. The pain and turmoil that she is carrying sound and feel like the statements below.

After you read each of the following statements, place a book in your backpack and lift it off the ground for a moment:

A. I'm becoming more and more isolated from my family and friends. I don't feel like calling anyone anymore.

B. He checks all my telephone calls because he wants to know everything I think or do.

C. I can't go shopping alone because he doesn't trust me with the money or because he will accuse me of running around and become abusive.

D. I have no control over or say about the money I make.

E. I have to be very careful about the clothes I wear or he'll become violent, accusing me of having an affair or being a slut.

F. I don't dare ask for anything that would make me look or feel nice.

G. My contacts with family and friends are superficial because I don't dare tell them the truth for fear of rocking the boat and making things worse.

H. I constantly worry about my kids and what the violence is doing to them.

**I.** I can't bring my problems to work because I'm scared of losing my job. I just do my work and keep to myself.

**J.** I make stupid mistakes at work because I can't concentrate or remember simple things.

**K.** I don't trust myself anymore because all my attempts to make things okay at home have failed and some even seem to provoke more violence.

**L.** He raped me again this weekend. Monday morning he sent some flowers to work.

**M.** I'm so scared! Scared to stay and afraid to go!

## Question

**1.** Now place your backpack full of books on your back. Describe your reactions to the experience of carrying the backpack now that it is filled with heavy books. How do you feel carrying that weight? Remember a time in your life when something bad happened, and recall what you did or said to feel safe and not powerless. Identify a step that can be taken to lighten Jane's load.

## CHAPTER SUMMARY

Students are sometimes timid to participate in a field placement with non-governmental agencies or groups where social justice and social action are the organization's cornerstones. In this chapter, we provide readers with a better understanding of social work's mandate to advocate and to facilitate empowerment. We also explore the critical process of reflection and its role in enhancing benefits to students. Scenarios and student voices are offered in an attempt to help the reader visualize the significance of progressive field placements and why increasing student access to engage in social justice activity is important. Stevenson (2004), while considering social and human service work's future, leaves us with fitting comments to ponder in relation to social justice: "Social work is an important ingredient in the implementation of social justice because it should, by definition, challenge social exclusion seeking to protect the vulnerable, and it is uniquely placed to pay attention to the element of creative justice in a fair society" (p. 246). Progressive field education provides concrete opportunities to inspire future practitioners to become preoccupied with the pursuit of "creative justice."

### Critical-Thinking Questions

**1.** Identify the social issue(s) that provide the theme of your field placement (e.g., unemployed youth, battered women, refugees, a physical disability).

**2.** What is it like to *live* this social issue?

**3.** What other services, agencies, or groups are concerned with this issue? How do they approach it? Visit them if possible.

## Suggested Readings

Carniol, B. (2000). *Case critical: Challenging social services in Canada.* Toronto, ON: Between the Lines.

Lee, B. (1997). *Pragmatics of community organization.* Toronto, ON: Commonact Press.

Leondar-Wright, B. (2005). *Class matters: Cross-class alliance building for middle-class activists.* Gabriola Island, BC: New Society.

Lundy, C. (2004). *Social work and social justice: A structural approach to practice.* Peterborough, ON: Broadview.

Mullaly, B. (2007). *The new structural social work* (3rd ed.) Don Mills, ON: Oxford University Press.

Radian, E. (2000). *Influences prompting the social action activities of Canadian BSW graduates.* Paper presented at the Joint Conference of the IFSW and the IASSW, Montreal, Quebec.

Shragge, E. (2003). *Activism and social change: Lessons for community and local organizing.* Toronto, ON: Broadview.

Thompson, N. (2001). *Anti-discriminatory practice.* New York, NY: Palgrave.

## Relevant Websites

### Canadian Centre for Policy Alternatives
www.policyalternatives.ca
The Canadian Centre for Policy Alternatives is an independent, non-partisan research institute concerned with issues of social, economic, and environmental justice. The Centre works on solutions to problems based on such principles as human dignity, freedom, environmental sustainability, and the public good. The organization sees itself as one of Canada's leading progressive voices in public policy debates.

### Canadian Council on Social Development
www.ccsd.ca
On its website, the Canadian Council on Social Development states that its mission is to "develop and promote progressive social policies inspired by social justice, equality and the empowerment of individuals and communities." On issues such as poverty, income security, and health, social work and human service students who are interested in affecting public policy change would find ample opportunity within the Council.

### Cooper Institute
www.cooperinstitute.ca
Cooper Institute is an example of a solid community organization with far-reaching accomplishments, within which social work and human service students could find themselves immersed in social justice activities connected to international as well as national and provincial projects. The organization's website describes the Institute as "an education and community development centre" whose primary program areas "are focused on livable income for all, food sovereignty and cultural diversity and inclusion."

# Chapter 7

## Improving Practice and Affecting Policy: Research in Diverse Contexts

Saara Greene

## Chapter Objectives

- Develop an understanding of the purpose, aims, and outcomes of agency-based research.
- Develop an understanding of the purpose, aims, and outcomes of community-based research.
- Develop an understanding of research and evaluation as practice.
- Understand the various roles that student practitioners have when conducting agency- and/or community-based research.
- Consider ethical issues for agency- and community-based researchers.

The effectiveness of social work and human service education depends on a number of factors; in particular, the skills and knowledge that students develop through engaging in a process of practice-based education and learning. Community-based organizations in Canada are generally non-profit agencies that often serve as field sites for placements in which students are offered a range of learning opportunities that include skill-building in community development work, advocacy, and direct practice. These skills can be enhanced through engagement in agency and community-based research placements in which students gain experience in the application of research methods that can advance an agency's overall effectiveness. Moreover, students can also learn to work alongside communities in the creation of new knowledge that can be applied to address specific community issues. Through collaborative work on community projects, front-line professionals, community-based researchers, and service users play a leading role in educating faculty and students about their lived experiences and needs through sharing alternate, but equally important, areas of expertise aimed at creating social change. Such collaborative approaches reflect the goals of community-based research as it attempts to create new knowledge that can be applied to address specific community issues. However, before discussing specific practice strategies for engaging in agency- and community-based research, it is first necessary to highlight the benefits of including community-based organizations, social work and human service workers, and service users in the research process.

## THE BENEFITS OF CITIZEN AND COMMUNITY PARTICIPATION

In a community development context, participation is "the inclusion of a diverse range of stakeholder contributions ... from identification of problem areas, to the development, implementation and management of strategic planning" (Schafft & Greenwood, 2003, p. 19). Similarly, agency- and community-based research reflects the spirit of community development with its emphasis on community involvement and empowerment. However, it is important to recognize that there are different degrees or levels of participation, which can range from mere tokenism to genuine sharing of power and citizen control. As Arnstien (1969) suggests, "[c]itizen participation is citizen power" (p. 216). Arnstien (1969) developed a "ladder of citizen participation" that highlights the degree or level of participation that communities can have in community-based initiatives. At the bottom of the ladder is non-participation of citizens; at the middle are degrees of tokenism through the involvement of communities in consultations and information sessions. At the top of the ladder are varying degrees of citizen power or community power, including citizen or community control and/or partnership. Arnstien and others recognized that participation taps the energies and resources of individual citizens, providing a source of special insight, information, knowledge, and experience that contribute to the soundness of community solutions. Today, citizen participation is viewed as an essential component in developing solutions that will ensure a more equitable distribution of resources for low-income communities; involving community members in the decision-making process may serve as a vehicle for empowerment (Gamble & Weil, 1995; Hardina, 2003). A commitment to citizen participation within the context of community empowerment is the grounding for participatory agency- and community-based research.

## AGENCY-BASED RESEARCH

Agency-based research is generally aimed at evaluating agency programs and researching the needs of the populations that the agency is committed to serving. For example, an agency that provides services for people with HIV would evaluate its success in being able to offer services and programs that reflect the needs of the HIV community. Community-based research and evaluation should be viewed as critical components of engaging in ethical practice because only by evaluating our ability to address the issues of the very people we are trying to serve will we know how effective our services are. In fact, the Council on Social Work Education (CSWE) in the United States identifies research as a required foundation curriculum content area in its Educational Policy and Accreditation Standards. Participating Canadian faculties and schools of social work and human service also use this CSWE document. The CSWE states, "Research knowledge is used by students to provide high-quality services; to initiate change; to improve practice, policy, and social service delivery; and to evaluate their own practice" (CSWE, 2004, p. 10). Hence, research from this perspective is viewed as an integral component of social work education that is deeply connected to developing and supporting ethical practices. This perspective can be integrated into the practice of human services workers as a component of research and evaluation because it is an ethical approach to building knowledge for practice (Shore & Richards, 2007).

Students commonly contribute to research in the form of conducting needs assessments or by developing and conducting program evaluations. Since this type of research is practice-based and therefore applied in its nature, most practitioners do not frame it as "research" but rather as an everyday part of their practice. Consequently, this kind of research is called *practice-based research*. Although there are many approaches to agency-based research, two of the most familiar and perhaps most useful are (1) needs assessment and (2) program evaluation.

## Needs Assessment

Needs assessments help social work and human service professionals develop an increased understanding and awareness of how to most effectively meet the needs of the service users that rely on their agency's services and programs. A needs assessment is probably the most popular form of agency-based research, and yet most practitioners do not see this work as "research," but rather as an integral part of their front-line responsibilities. The needs assessment is an applied form of research because it guides practice. For example, an agency that works primarily with young women may want to identify and prioritize the young women's current needs. The agency may also want to identify how these needs are currently being met in the community and how the agency can fill in any identified gaps.

Data can be gathered by doing individual interviews, focus groups, and surveys. Continuing our example of the agency that works primarily with young women, an interview will provide the researcher and an individual young woman with an opportunity to talk one-on-one in a confidential setting, whereas a focus group will bring a group of young women together to discuss their needs in a group setting. To reach a larger number of young women, the agency may use a survey, which usually takes the form of a questionnaire that the participants fill out either privately or in the presence of a researcher.

The information or data about the young women's needs could be gathered by agency-based professionals. They can collect the views of the young women in the community, other community-based professionals, school-based professionals, and other identified stakeholders. The feedback from the identified stakeholders can then be used to help to guide the future development of the agency's programs and services to ensure that they are relevant and reflect the young women's needs.

### Needs Assessment Case Study: Developing the Young Women's Health Group
Community workers representing a range of agencies and organizations that provided services for a socially and economically impoverished community in Ontario came together because of a shared belief that they were not adequately meeting the needs of the young women living in this community. After a brainstorming session, the community workers agreed that an in-depth needs assessment was necessary. This assessment would enable the community workers to develop services and programs that would best reflect the needs of the young women. The largest agency in the community offered to set aside time for two human service workers to develop and conduct the needs assessment on behalf of the wider community-based agencies.

The human service workers who were asked to do this work were also responsible for providing sexual health education to students in two local schools. Since this task provided them with direct access to young women, the human service workers requested and received permission from the schools to advertise a series of focus groups at their agency. The focus group would enable them to ask the young women questions about the kinds of services and programs they were currently accessing in the community: what they liked about those services, what they felt was missing from those services, the barriers and facilitators to accessing those services, and their opinions on what kinds of programs and services they felt were most important for young women living in the community. The young women were invited to participate in the focus groups and were asked to sign up for one of three focus group sessions. In addition to attending the focus group, the young women were asked to fill out a short survey that listed a range of issues that the various agencies could potentially address. They were asked to rate each issue as *not at all important*, *somewhat important*, *important*, or *very important*. Finally, the human service professionals also did a focus group with other social workers, human service professionals, and front-line workers in the community who engaged in direct work with young women. The participants of this focus group also shared their views, based on their professional experience, of what they believed were the most pressing issues.

During the focus groups, one of the human service workers facilitated the discussion while the other jotted down information on a flip chart that all the participants could see. This ensured that the note-taker was capturing all the information correctly and not missing out on important points that the participants were raising. The information collected from the focus groups with the young women and the service providers highlighted the need for programs and services that covered a range of physical, mental, and sexual issues for young women. The issues of most interest to the young women were related to relationships, body image, self-esteem, and safer sex. Based on information collected, the agency that conducted the needs assessment created the Young Women's Health Group, through which all the above issues would be attended to through weekly discussion groups, guest speakers, and activities. The group has been a success and is now in its seventh year.

# Program Evaluation

The purpose of a program evaluation is to find out if the aims and objectives of an agency-based service or program are effectively meeting the needs of the service users. If we go back to the example above, the needs assessment may have discovered that one of the priorities that emerged through the data collection process was a gap in service provision for young parents and the need to develop programs that would support them in attending high school. Once the group has been developed and the young parents are attending the program, it will be important to find out if the program is indeed supporting young parents in their desire to attend high school. This process can include the use of quantitative measures or statistics that tell us about the effectiveness of a program. In this instance, it may measure how many young parents attend a high school or high school equivalency program, how often young parents attend or miss classes, and how many young parents in the program stay in school until graduation. If the evaluation turns out positively, then the results can often be used to maintain funding or request additional funds to maintain, enhance, or expand the existing program. If the evaluation finds that the program is having little or no impact on increasing access to education for young parents, then the agency and service providers can use this information to make changes. Program evaluations can also qualitatively evaluate program aims and objectives by interviewing service users and other stakeholders such as teachers, youth workers, and agency staff about their views and experiences of the program. This qualitative information gathering is particularly important because it provides an opportunity for the front-line and personal experiences of individuals and communities to be heard and potentially used when designing programs and services.

## COMMUNITY-BASED RESEARCH

Social work and human service professionals can address community needs and concerns by conducting meaningful research that supports community-based organizations and community members by assessing their needs and evaluating their programs (Hyde & Myer, 2004). While on a community-based research placement, students can gain first-hand practical research skills through being exposed to the inner workings of community organizations and immersed in the daily issues faced by the community. Community-based research placements provide opportunities to work with and alongside communities in the creation of new knowledge that can be applied to address specific issues. Similar to agency-based research, community-based research can lead to the development and evaluation of relevant and necessary community-based services and programs. However, community-based research as a practice and as a philosophy demands that the expertise of a range of stakeholders, including community members, staff from community-based organizations, and, often, community-based or academic researchers, are equally valued and acknowledged within the research team. Community-based research takes place in community settings and involves community members in the design and implementation of research projects. Moreover, community-based research partnerships that position community voices, needs, and concerns at the centre of a research project will support and sustain equitable relationships at all points in the study. For example, making sure that the research team includes representatives from the community, including service providers and users, will ensure that the community's research priorities and interests are reflected in the questions that are being asked through the study.

## The Difference between Community-Based and Traditional Academic Research

Table 7.1 shows the distinction that the Edward Ginsberg Center for Community Service and Learning makes between community and academic research.

**Table 7.1** A Comparison of Community-Based and Traditional Academic Research

| Guiding Principles | Community-Based Research | Traditional Academic Research |
| --- | --- | --- |
| What is the purpose of the research? | To provide the community with the tools and information necessary to enact change | To contribute to the body of knowledge on a given topic |
| Who is the research intended to serve? | The local community and the academic community | The academic community |
| Whose knowledge counts? | That of both community members and academic experts | Academic experts |
| Who determines what topics are researched? | Members of the local community | Funders' interests, academic interests, professional interests, and personal interests |
| What is the rationale for choosing the research methodology? | Community empowerment and mutual learning | Academic conventions; the pursuit of "truth" and "objectivity" |
| Who controls the research process? | Community members and the researcher | Researcher |
| Who has ownership over the results of the research? | Community members and the researcher | Researcher |
| What aspect of research is emphasized? | Process | Outcomes |

Source: University of Michigan Edward Ginsberg Center for Community Service and Learning, (http://quod.lib.umich.edu/m/mjcsl).

# Principles of Community-Based Research

To achieve the goals of community-based research and ensure that the research process does not reflect traditional academic-based research, the following principles, prepared by the University of Washington, should guide the development of research projects that involve collaboration among community members, community-based organizations, and community and academic researchers:

- Community partners should be involved at the earliest stages of the project, helping to define research objectives and having input into how the project will be organized.
- Community partners should have real influence on project direction — that is, enough leverage to ensure that the participants adhere to the project's original goals, mission, and methods.
- Research processes and outcomes should benefit the community. Community members should be hired and trained whenever possible and appropriate, and the research should help to build and enhance community assets.
- Community members should be part of the analysis and interpretation of data and should have input into how the results are distributed. This point does not imply censorship of data or publication, but rather provides participants with the opportunity to clarify the community's views about the interpretation prior to final publication.
- Productive partnerships between researchers and community members should be encouraged to last beyond the life of the project. An extended relationship makes it more likely that research findings will be incorporated into ongoing community programs and, therefore, the research will provide the greatest possible benefit to the community.
- Community members should be empowered to initiate their own research projects which address needs they identify themselves. (University of Washington, School of Public Health and Community Medicine, n.d.)

# Peer Research Assistants

Some community-based research projects employ community members as peer research assistants (PRAs). A *PRA* is defined as someone who is affected by the issue being studied. For example, in Greene et al.'s (2009) study on the health and housing of people living with HIV/AIDS, PRAs were defined as "people living with HIV who have a history and understanding of the impact that housing instability has on the lives of people living with HIV/AIDS" (p. 362). There are a number of reasons why an agency- or community-based research team may want to employ PRAs. They are often recognized and trusted members of the community being researched and their reputations may make it easier to recruit research participants; hence, PRAs hold privileged access to the particular population group being studied. Employing PRAs also provides opportunity for community growth and empowerment through the process of learning and applying new skills and being employed in personally and politically relevant work (Elliot, Watson, & Harries, 2005; Greene et al., 2009; Marino, 2007). However, PRAs also require ongoing support, supervision, and peer debriefing opportunities, particularly if they are hearing troubling stories that reflect their own lived reality (Greene et al., 2009). Finally, researchers who employ PRAs should also consider how they can benefit from the skills and experiences of the PRAs without exploiting their labour, and researchers must also consider the extent to which others research participants, including other members of the community, are willing to accept the PRAs' role in the research (Price & Hawkins, 2002; Coupland & Maher, 2005; Elliot et al., 2005).

## Challenges of Community-Based Research

When conducting community-based research, significant time and effort is required to build trust and working relationships among partners because often the populations research groups are working with or researching come from vulnerable or marginalized communities that have experienced various forms of stigma and discrimination. In addition to getting to know the community, the following challenges need to be considered when working toward a research partnership:

- articulating and agreeing on a common purpose;
- seeking a balance between task and process/research and action;
- working together amid ethnic, cultural, social class, and organizational differences;
- balancing competing institutional demands;
- building up people's skills rather than only drawing on previous skills and experience;
- recognizing difference (e.g., in skills, ways of learning, or levels of participation); diverse needs must be supported in different ways; and
- capacity building (of less experienced community partners as well as more experienced researchers who may have to develop their knowledge of the community and the research priorities of that community).

Capacity building is a particularly important feature of community-based research partnerships, so we discuss it further in the next section.

**Capacity Building** There is no one definition of capacity building. Capacity building in the community-based research arena refers to a process that supports communities' increasing awareness about the issues that affect them (e.g., health, social, economic, and political issues) and develops or increases the community's ability to participate in addressing these issues via community-based initiatives, including research (Greene et al., 2009). An important function of the community-based researcher is to therefore provide capacity-building opportunities that will ensure that the community can actively participate as an equal partner in researching the very issues that affect its members. As addressed in the previous section, it can be a challenge to ensure that research partners who do not have any research expertise are provided with the opportunity to build their research knowledge for the purposes of ensuring equal participation in the research process. To provide effective capacity-building opportunities, community-based researchers should try to arrange to do the following:

- Ensure research processes and outcomes benefit the community and help build or enhance community assets.
- Provide opportunities for people to learn through experience — opportunities that would not otherwise be available to them.
- Involve people in the collective effort so they can gain confidence in their own abilities to influence decisions that affect them.
- Encourage and support community leadership.
- Provide opportunities for community members to sustain their newly developed skills so that they can transfer these skills to other community-based research projects or community-based practice.

## Students as Researchers

Most community-based organizations engage in some kind of research that will help them to more effectively address the needs of the individuals and communities that they serve. The research opportunities sometimes available to social work and human service students include developing and carrying out needs assessments, developing surveys and questionnaires, administering surveys to research participants, conducting face-to-face interviews, analyzing findings from surveys, and writing up the results of research in an agency-based or community report as part of the dissemination process. Research opportunities for students will depend on a number of factors, such as the level of research experience that the students have, the stage of the research project at the time the placement begins, and the length of time that students will be on their field placements.

Practicum students who are partaking in a diploma program and who have little or no research experience can expect to learn how to develop a needs assessment and will most likely have the opportunity to conduct their needs assessments with the larger community within a relatively short period of time. Similarly, students with little research knowledge could also be expected to learn how to evaluate a program, particularly if it is a program that they have been involved in as part of their practicum experience. However, because program evaluations can sometimes last longer than the time students are on placement, students may be involved in learning about different phases of program evaluation, such as developing the evaluation, facilitating the evaluation process (including gathering information), or analyzing the information that emerged from the evaluation itself.

Practicum students who are enrolled in an undergraduate program and who have had some exposure to research, either through a formalized course or through selected readings in other courses, will have increased opportunities to gain community-based research skills. Again, the opportunities will depend on the length of time that students are on placement and on the agency's research needs. Typically, undergraduate students could be involved in the same types of research activities as diploma students; however, in addition to possibly developing and engaging in needs assessments and program evaluations, students may also become highly involved in various aspects of larger and more formalized research projects. The case study on page 114 demonstrates the range of research opportunities that under-graduate students could experience. These technical experiences and skill development opportunities might include learning how to design structured and semi-structured interview schedules; learning how to conduct in-depth interviews with research participants; learning how to facilitate focus groups; and gaining some, albeit minimal, experience in analyzing in-depth interviews. Undergraduate students could also learn how to recruit participants and work collaboratively with community partners, including the community that will be most affected by the outcomes of the research and other community-based organizations. Finally, undergraduate students could learn how to write a community report that outlines the back-ground, purpose, process, and outcomes of a research study. It is important to state, however, that community-based research often takes much longer than the time students have on placement: Students may start their placements at the beginning, middle, or end of a research project. Consequently, undergraduate students may not develop skills in all the given areas; instead, they may become quite proficient in one or two research skills, such as interviewing or facilitating focus groups.

Finally, graduate students who engage in community-based research placements will have a range of opportunities to enhance and develop their research skills. The opportunities that these students will have available to them include all of the above research skills but may extend to developing their own research questions and projects. Some graduate students may use a research placement as a way to support them with a major research paper requirement or for a master's-level dissertation. Consequently, in graduate-level research placements, students can potentially go beyond working on pre-existing research projects to developing new projects that meet the needs and interests of the community, the agency, and themselves.

## Exercise

Students on community-based research placements will develop a learning plan that may reflect any of the following objectives:

- Become familiar with the current theories relating to community-based research.

- Become familiar with the literature about the topic of interest (e.g., homeless youth, single parents).

- Develop skills for communicating with service users and local community members, with professionals working in other community-based agencies and organizations, and with other researchers.

- Develop data collection skills, including individual and group interviewing skills.

- Develop skills for creating a needs assessment.

- Develop skills for creating an evaluation tool.

- Develop skills for creating a survey.
- Use supervision effectively as a forum for reflective practice.

**Question**

1. Choose one of the objectives listed above.
2. Create a plan for how you will meet this learning objective. Include the concrete steps that you will need to take to achieve your objective, as well as a section on how you will evaluate your success. In a third section, consider and write about how you will use supervision as a tool to ensure that you meet your learning goal.

# Pre-Research Planning

Before students begin a research project, they need to clarify the project's purpose and draft a plan for carrying it out. Answering the following questions will help them with clarification:

- What do you know? What do you want to know?
- What are you trying to measure?
- What will you do with the information collected?
- Who will be included in planning and conducting the research project?
- What are the roles and responsibilities of those involved in the research project?
- Where will the information come from?

**Identify the Target Population**  Who will be surveyed? All stakeholders should have an opportunity to provide input into recognition programs and activities. If conducting a research project for all the stakeholders is not feasible, it is important to ensure that the sample population be representative of the whole population.

**Determine the Information Collection Method**  Researchers can use a variety of methods, either alone or in combination, to collect information from participants. Time, resources, and knowledge of the various research methods will play a role in determining the information collection method. These methods will be discussed further below.

**Recruitment**  Participant recruitment is an essential component of any research project, including needs assessments, program evaluations, and community-based research studies. If an agency wants to conduct a needs assessment for the purpose of service or program development, then it will be important to recruit affected communities. For example, if the agency is considering increasing their youth-based programming, then it will be necessary to recruit youth for the needs assessment. Or, if the agency is doing an evaluation of an existing program, then it will be important to recruit current or past service users so that the agency can ensure that their experiences are reflected. The agency may also want to recruit other stakeholders affected by the research who would be able to evaluate the program, such as professionals from other community-based organizations. For a larger, issue-based, and more in-depth community-based research study, the agency will want to work in partnership with other agencies and community members to determine who the participants will be and how many people should be recruited for the study.

How agencies recruit participants varies depending on the purpose of their research. If they are conducting a needs assessment, then they may want to request the participation of other community professionals by email or phone. They may want to hold a community meeting for the purpose of sharing the research question and have a sign-up list at this meeting for potential participants. If agencies are doing program evaluations, they will not have to go far to recruit participants since they can request the participation of current program users and refer to contact lists of past service users who can contacted by email or post. Recruitment strategies for community-based research projects can also include putting up posters within the researching agency and in other community-based organizations that provide some details about the purpose of the study, the types of participants required, and the contact information of the research coordinator.

## Research Skills Development

For students who are interested in doing an agency- or community-based research practicum, the practicum will provide students with an opportunity to start developing the social work and human services professions' requisite research skills. These skills can be technical in nature, as is the case with literature searches and environmental scans. An environmental scan is one way of learning about programs and services that could benefit a particular community or population. Current program or service gaps can be found by developing a short questionnaire that other professionals in relevant organizations can fill out.

Students will need to develop skills in the areas of recruiting participants, developing research questions and methods, and collecting data. Skills in data analysis can also be developed and will include thematic analysis of interviews and focus group discussions as well as statistical analysis of surveys.

Agency- and community-based researchers require skills in communication, networking, partnership building, capacity building, and critical thinking. Of particular importance is the ability to understand how power imbalances have an impact on researcher–participant relationships and ethical issues, particularly as they relate to the effect that research has on marginalized individuals and communities. Finally, agency- and community-based researchers will need to be proficient at sharing or disseminating their research findings to people who will be able to use them in ways that will benefit the community.

## QUALITATIVE RESEARCH

Qualitative research is "an inquiry process of understanding based on distinct methodological traditions of inquiry that explore a social or human problem. The research builds a complex, holistic picture, analyzes words, reports detailed views of informants, and conducted the study in natural setting." (Denzin & Lincoln, 2000 p. 15). There are many ways to collect qualitative research data, including in-depth interviewing, focus groups, participant observation, and photography.

## In-Depth Interviews

The most common way of collecting qualitative research data is by interviewing research participants. According to Mischler (1986), qualitative research's particular features reflect the distinctive structure and aims of interviewing; namely, it is discourse shaped and organized by asking and answering questions. The purpose of the interview is to find out what views people hold, and the researcher must be careful not to affect these views with evaluative responses. The researcher should choose an interview environment and conditions in which the participants feel comfortable, secure, and at ease so they will speak openly about their points of view. Finally, an interview is a joint product of what interviewees and interviewers talk about together and how they talk with each other. Interviewers should avoid asking "yes" or "no" questions; instead, they should ask open-ended questions to collect as much detail as possible.

**Types of Interviews**  There are three types of in-depth individual interviews: unstructured, semi-structured, and structured. Unstructured interviews are open, adaptable, and conversational. The questions asked adapt to the interviewee and there are no predetermined questions. Semi-structured interviews provide general areas of focus but allow interviewers a degree of freedom in gathering information. Structured interviews include some closed questions, and all interviewees may be asked to choose answers from the same set of alternatives. When conducting semi-structured interviews, the researcher should consider to what degree the interview questioning can be recursive — that is, whether the interviewer can use what has been said in the interview to determine or define further questioning.

**Focus Groups**  Focus groups are group interviews. A focus group is similar to a group discussion except that is facilitated by a trained interviewer for the purposes of research. Focus group research involves an organized discussion with a selected group of individuals to gain information about their views and experiences on a topic. Focus group interviewing is particularly suited for obtaining several perspectives about the same topic. The benefits of focus group research include gaining insights into people's shared understandings of everyday life and the ways in which individuals are influenced by others in a group situation. Focus groups are a form of group interviewing, but it is important to distinguish between the two. Group interviewing involves interviewing a number of people at the same time, the emphasis being on questions and responses between the researcher and the participants. Focus groups, however, rely on interaction within the group based on topics that are supplied by the researcher (Morgan, 1997).

## Checklist for Conducting an Interview

☑ Choose a setting with minimal distractions.

☑ Explain the purpose of the interview.

☑ Explain the terms of confidentiality.

☑ Discuss the format of the interview, including how long it will take.

☑ Provide the interviewee with the interviewer's contact information.

☑ Allow the interviewee to ask questions about the interview prior to starting.

**Interviewing Techniques**  Effective interviewers pay attention to the following techniques: active listening, non-verbal communication, probes, and sensitive issues.

**Active Listening**  Active listening is a structured way of listening and responding to an interviewee to ensure that communication continues. Certain verbal skills are used in active listening to give feedback to the participants in order to acknowledge that the interviewer is listening to and understanding what they are saying. In addition, active listening encourages the interviewer to provide feedback to ensure that he or she *does* understand what the interviewees are sharing.

- Verbal and non-verbal signals or cues that interviewers use to let interviewees know that the interviewer is listening and understands:
    - verbal signals (e.g., "uhm hmm," "uh huh," "I see," "I understand," "I know what you mean")
    - intonation changes
    - non-verbal signals (e.g., maintaining eye contact, nodding head, smiling slightly)
- Verbal techniques that interviewers use to make sure that they have correctly heard and understood what interviewees have said:
    - repeating (e.g., "Did you say …")
    - paraphrasing (e.g., paraphrasing the interviewee's words by starting with "So you mean …" "In other words …" or "Okay, let me see if I've got it …"
    - summarizing briefly

**Non-Verbal Communication**  The non-verbal message interviewers present can speak louder than their verbal messages. Non-verbal messages can be transmitted via posture, eye contact, and attentiveness.

**Probes**  One of the key techniques in good interviewing is the use of probes. Patton (1990) identifies three types of probes:

- detail-oriented probes (e.g., "Can you tell me what it has been like to find housing for you and your family?")
- elaboration probes (e.g., "Can you give me an example?")
- clarification probes (e.g., "I'm sorry, but I don't quite get it. Could you tell me again?")

**Sensitive Issues**   Sometimes marginal or stigmatized groups can be reluctant to share revelations. To encourage sharing, interviewers follow these steps:

- Build trust before the interview (e.g., by being nonjudgmental).
- Be clear about the research's aims.
- Be clear about anonymity.
- Avoid interrogation.
- Do not probe beyond the point where the interviewee is uncomfortable.
- Be attentive and empathetic regarding the participant's display of emotions during interview.
- Prevent the interview from deviating too far away from the issues you want to explore and focus on.
- Understand that your role is not about giving advice but rather about listening and respecting the participant's experience.

# QUANTITATIVE RESEARCH

## Surveys

Surveys can be conducted via interviews or questionnaires. Most often, surveys are self-administered questionnaires that participants receive via post or email (which are then often completed in a person's home); however, they can also be administered within an agency or other community-based setting. Surveys can also be administered by a researcher, and these too can be completed in a person's home or at an agency or community-based organization.

Surveys can be administered to a large group of participants, who all answer the same questions. The questions can be based on levels of measurement, such as rating scales. For example, to find out levels of satisfaction with a particular service, researchers sometimes ask questions such as "On a scale of 1–5, with 1 being *never* and 5 being *always*, how happy are with the services you are using at this agency?" Surveys can also include questions that allow participants to provide more than one answer. For example, a survey might list all the programs offered at an agency and ask participants to check off those they attend or use. The answers to these types of questions are quantitative because they reveal the numbers of participants using particular services and the degree of satisfaction they have with these services.

# ETHICAL ISSUES

It is both necessary and required that research involving human participants adheres to certain ethical issues. Adhering to ethical standards protects research participants from undue harm. Some of the most pressing ethical issues are outlined in this section.

## Consent

Informed consent means that researchers inform participants about the overall purpose of the research, its main features, and the risks and benefits of participation. Participants can give consent in written format, or verbally, using an audio video recording.

Researchers must tell participants the following:
- the purpose of the research.
- the expectations the researchers have of the research participant, including the time required for participation.
- the expected risks and benefits of participation (e.g., psychological, social).
- that participation is voluntary and participants can withdraw at any time with no negative repercussions.
- how confidentiality will be protected.
- the contact information of the principal researcher, who can be contacted with questions or problems related to the research.
- the appropriate ethics board information about one's rights as a research participant (e.g., the contact information of a university's research ethics board representative).

## Confidentiality

Section 1.07(e) of the National Association of Social Workers' Code of Ethics (1996) highlights the social work and human service practitioner's responsibility to discuss both the nature and the limits of the right to confidentiality:

- Confidentiality in research means that all details of the client's business should be kept private by the researcher and not disclosed to any third party, except when legally obligated (e.g., where there's evidence of child abuse). Identifying information must be kept anonymous (e.g., numbers should identify participants rather than their names).
- Access to recordings and transcripts should be limited to investigators and research assistants.
- Identifying information (e.g., name, contact information) will not be linked with interview data.
- Recordings and transcripts will be kept in locked storage.
- Data to be destroyed two years after publication.

Ethical considerations for focus groups are the same as for most other methods of social research (Holman, 1991). For example, when selecting and involving research participants, the researcher must provide in writing and explain verbally full information about the purpose and uses of participants' contributions. Being honest; keeping participants informed about the expectations of the research, the individual or group interview, and the topic; and not pressuring participants to speak is good practice. A particular ethical issue to consider in the case of focus groups is the handling of sensitive material and confidentiality given that there will always be more than one participant in the group. At the outset, moderators need to clarify that each participant's contributions will be shared with the others in the group as well as with the moderator. Participants need to be encouraged to keep what they hear during the meeting confidential, and researchers have the responsibility of ensuring that group members are unidentifiable in research data.

The British Sociological Association's Statement of Ethical Practice (1999) states that its members should be aware that the research process may be a disturbing one for participants and that attempts should be made to minimize risks associated with sharing difficult and emotive experiences. In addition, section 5.02(j) of the National Association of Social Workers' Code of Ethics (1996) addresses the responsibility on the part of the researcher to "protect participants from unwanted physical or mental distress, harm, danger, or deprivation." In connection to the interview process, Goodman (2001) points out,

> in-depth interviews in social work research present unique human subjects issues. The intimate nature of the interview format means that sensitive material and, consequently, strong emotional responses may erupt, presenting special dilemmas for social research practitioners (p. 310).

In situations in which researchers will be interviewing participants about issues that may evoke strong emotions, they have certain ethical requirements. They must ensure that participants understand that the interview may cause them to experience uncomfortable feelings as a result of sharing personal details of their lives. Participants should understand that they may refuse to answer questions and may end the interview at any time and that their decision to do so will not negatively affect them in any way. Researchers should also ensure that participants have a resource list containing the names and phone numbers of relevant agencies and organizations, in case they require support in the future. Finally, researchers should also ensure that participants have access to a support person (e.g., a friend, a professional) following the interview in the event that they need to discuss their interview experience.

## Ethics Review Boards

Ethics review boards are situated in research institutions such as universities and hospitals to ensure that employees of the institution are carrying out research that is ethical and will not cause physical or emotional harm to research participants. Not all research requires an ethical review process. Agency-based research that is mainly concerned with research that does not involve human participants (e.g., literature reviews, needs assessments, or program evaluations that are for internal purposes only) do not usually require ethical review. However, when a practicum student is conducting this work, the student will often be required to sign a confidentiality agreement that will ensure that the student's knowledge of the service users' experiences are not shared outside of the agency setting. As such, the student has an ethical responsibility to ensure the privacy and confidentiality of the agency staff and service users. Research that involves humans and requires a more in-depth exploration of the issues that affect the agency's client base or the community more generally will require ethics approval. This type of research may also be shared outside the agency, such as at research conferences, in publications, or at other informal or formal venues.

## Ownership, Control, Access, and Possession: OCAP Principles

First Nations' Principles of OCAP stand for the right for Aboriginal communities to have ownership, control, access, and possession in research and is an expression of self-determination (Schnarch, 2004). In the context of research ethics, this means that in addition to the usual ethical guidelines that researchers must follow, they must also follow other ethical issues where Aboriginal communities are concerned. These ethical issues have emerged out of a long history of colonization as well as the harmful ways that research has had a negative impact on Aboriginal communities.

**Ownership** Ownership refers to the relationship of an Aboriginal community to its cultural knowledge, data, and information. The word implies that a community or group owns information collectively, in the same way that an individual owns his or her personal information. For example, in the past, when research was conducted in Aboriginal communities, the academic research partners kept, or "owned," the data, which meant that while the Aboriginal community may have had access to the data, they would have to go to the researchers for the information because it was kept on site at the research institution. Ownership in this context means that the community owns the data and thus keeps it in a safe and secure place designated by the community (e.g., at the lead community agency).

**Control** This word recognizes the aspirations and rights of Aboriginal peoples to maintain and regain control of all aspects of their lives and institutions, including their right to control the research process and the ways that information and data are managed and shared.

**Access** Aboriginal peoples must have access to information and data about themselves and their communities, regardless of where it is held. This term also refers to the right of Aboriginal communities and organizations to manage and make decisions regarding access to their collective information (Shnarch, 2004).

**Possession** Possession (of data) is a mechanism by which ownership can be asserted and protected. When data owned by one party is in the possession of another, there is a risk of breech or misuse. This issue is particularly important when trust is lacking between the owner and the possessor. To ensure that the data will not be misused, Aboriginal communities involved in research studies maintain their right to possess the data within the community.

# THE ROLE OF THE RESEARCHER

The role of the community-based researcher is to work with communities to identify issues, concerns, and goals that they have identified themselves and to facilitate a process of community inclusion and empowerment through this process. To achieve this, researchers need to consistently examine their own position throughout the research process and attend to issues of power and reflection.

## Power

It is very important that all researchers maintain an awareness of the amount of power they hold as researchers and the way in which this power can be experienced by service users and research participants alike. Regardless of how much power service clients, research participants, and other community members seem to have as a result of an agency's desire to support the community, researchers must be cognizant of the fact that they will always have considerably more power because they have the ability to affect the lives of the community through the programs and services their agencies deliver.

## Reflection

Issues of power can be attended to when the researcher engages in a process of reflexivity. Reflexivity is "a continued self-awareness about the ongoing relationship between a researcher and informants" (Wasserfall, 1997, p. 51). This process includes continually thinking about power differences and the implications they have on the research process. Reflection is a critical approach to professional practice that questions how knowledge is generated and, further, how relations of power influence the process of knowledge generation. Reflexive practitioners and researchers are aware of the assumptions that underlie how they make sense of practice situations and the cognitive process by which knowledge is created. What they know and how they know become the focus of scrutiny, along with an awareness of how relations of power are complicit in knowledge creation in social work and human service practice. Critical reflectivity is the practitioner's knowledge of self in relation to social structures for the purposes of creating social change (D'Cruz, Gillingham, & Melendez, 2007b).

# Dissemination

Dissemination of research findings is very important if the researchers and communities that work in partnership are committed to using the results for the purposes of creating change in practice and policy. In the current Canadian context, dissemination is often referred to as the process of knowledge translation and exchange (KTE). KTE strategies are important because they demand that researchers remain accountable to the communities they are researching to ensure that the information is relevant, useful, and accessible to the very people it seeks to support. Often times, communities find that research findings sit on a shelf and never make it into the hands of those who have the power to make change. Both agency- and community-based researchers are committed to developing creative and effective dissemination strategies that increase the opportunity for implementing research findings. Research data can be shared and disseminated in a number of ways. Needs assessments and program evaluations are usually shared with other agency staff or the leaders of an organization. Research data that emerges out of larger, ethics board–approved studies are often shared with a whole range of stakeholders, such as community members, other agency-based professionals, and academic researchers. This dissemination occurs in the form of community-based forums, at conferences, and in published articles in peer-reviewed publications and books.

## AGENCY-BASED AND COMMUNITY-BASED RESEARCH: EVALUATING THE HOMELESS OUTREACH PROGRAM

Fife House is an innovative, client-focused provider of secure and supportive affordable housing and services to people living with HIV/AIDS in the Greater Toronto Area. In my (the author's) position as the director of the Research and Evaluation Department, I was responsible for writing research funding proposals, leading and supporting community-based research studies, developing partnerships with other community-based AIDS services organizations and those providing allied health services, and evaluating on-site programs.

One of the programs requiring an evaluation was the Homeless Outreach Program (HOP). HOP is often the last resort for individuals and families living with HIV/AIDS who are living on the street or risking homelessness. HOP assists individuals and families by connecting them with private market landlords, not-for-profit housing programs, and Toronto's social housing sector. The social work placement student at Fife House was supervised in conducting a program evaluation to identify the barriers and challenges in accessing and maintaining housing and to identify housing needs and preferences of HOP clients. The overall purpose of this evaluation was to uncover which elements of HOP were operating effectively and which elements needed to be further developed.

To evaluate the program, a planned-out research process was developed. This included creating the research design, developing data collection methods, recruiting HOP clients to participate in the evaluation, developing consent forms for participants, analyzing the data, and writing an evaluation report that would be used as a guide to improve the quality of the program. The evaluation was not funded by an external body and relied on the internal resources of the organization. Consequently, the evaluation did not require ethics approval by an external review board; however, both the field instructor and the student followed the ethical guidelines necessary to ensure that the confidentiality, identities, and safety of the participants were protected. This is an important component of agency-based research that is aimed at evaluating and improving services, because in most cases the service users are still accessing the program, may need to access the program at some point in the future, and/or may want to access another program within the same agency. Services users may feel hesitant to participate or feel fearful of providing honest feedback if they feel that their access to the services or the agency more generally will be at risk. This is particularly important given that HOP service users represent a diverse group of marginalized communities that experience AIDS phobia, racism, sexism, homophobia, transphobia, and poverty.

Social work and human service professionals can use the program evaluation process as a tool for empowerment whereby service users are encouraged in voicing their feedback about the services that are meant to support them. When program evaluations include processes that protect the confidentiality of service users, the evaluation may lead to more meaningful outcomes that represent the needs and experiences of the community.

## Voices from the Field

I am a previous social work student, at York University in Toronto, Ontario. In addition to coursework, I had to fulfil two field placements in a human service agency. My first placement was at Fife House, which is a community-based HIV/AIDS supportive housing organization. Within Fife House, I was placed in the Research and Evaluation Department, under the supervision of the department director. This community-based research placement demonstrates what would typically be involved for undergraduate students.

The Research and Evaluation Department was scheduled to evaluate the HOP, which is offered to people living with HIV/AIDS who are seeking housing assistance. While working on the HOP evaluation, I had an opportunity to learn qualitative research design, focus group facilitation, qualitative data analysis, and evaluation report writing. While building knowledge about these research and evaluation activities, I relied on the use textbooks, peer-reviewed journals, a copy of an earlier HOP evaluation report, and a full-day workshop on focus group facilitation. But perhaps my most important learning came through my supervision time with my field instructor. Together, we discussed how to apply various types of disciplinary knowledge to create a research and evaluation plan.

As a student with very little research experience, it was important to apply concepts and theories learned in the classroom and relate it to practice. In the first year of my social work program, I was introduced to feminist, antiracist, and anti-oppressive theory, which was critical when engaging in the research and evaluation process. Given the extent of the diversity of HOP's clientele, we took the above theories into consideration during the research design phase. For example, having a focus group of only African and Caribbean women captured the unique housing experiences of woman of colour. I co-facilitated three focus groups, where I was able to practice facilitation skills within a group setting. Transcribing the focus group recordings allowed me to reflect on my strengths and weakness during the facilitation process, which enhanced my learning experience. I also engaged in qualitative data analysis to highlight the important themes related to the barriers and challenges of HOP service users. I also practised self-reflexivity to raise my awareness about how I was implicated in the generation, interpretation, and presentation of the data. I had to practise critically thinking about how to present the findings in a meaningful way. Creating a final evaluation report would assist Fife House and HOP staff to promote program modification to enhance program quality for people living with HIV/AIDS and experiencing challenges in housing. In addition to integrating theory into practice, I also practised my professional skills both within the agency as well as with outside agencies. While working on this evaluation, I made connections with other community-based AIDS service organizations. Building connections with organizations fostered a deeper learning about the types of agencies that serve people living with HIV/AIDS. (Paula K. Smith, student)

## CASE SCENARIO

The staff at a community-based organization that provides a range of services to people living with HIV are concerned that very few HIV-positive women are accessing the agency's services and programs. They are curious to know what barriers to their services women are experiencing and how they can address these barriers. The staff at the agency is busy engaging in front-line work. They agree that the staff member who is responsible for community development within the agency would be the best person to lead a small, community-based research project. The program developer has previous research experience in conducting needs assessments and program evaluations and, of equal importance, has already developed strong networks with other locally based agencies.

The community development worker has identified four important stages in this research process. The first stage will be focused on developing a community-based research team. This stage entails identifying key community stakeholders, developing stronger practice-based and research partnerships between the agency and other locally based organizations that serve women, developing stronger relationships with women living in the local community, and increasing the agency's visibility among women living in the community. This stage may also include building the research capacity of interested community members for the purposes of increasing their ability to participate as researchers at all stages of the study, including the identification of relevant research questions, data collection, analysis, and dissemination. The second stage of the community-based research process is aimed at addressing the research objectives. These include identifying barriers that prevent women from accessing the agency's services, identifying gaps in the agency's services that would reflect the needs of HIV-positive women, and identifying the ways in which the agency can more effectively reach out to and meet the needs of women living with HIV. The third stage will be to develop and implement the practice strategies that emerge out of the research findings. The final stage will be to evaluate the progress and success of the agency's strategy to increase the number of HIV-positive women who use their programs and services.

The community development worker is successful at recruiting interested community-based research partners from some local agencies. With the support of the community partners, the team also consists of a number of HIV-positive women who are open to sharing their knowledge and expertise of the unique issues facing HIV-positive women in this community, and who are interested in developing research skills. The team consists of the community development worker who initiated the study, a social worker who works with HIV-positive women at the local community health centre, a housing worker from a local women's shelter, a community worker from the local HIV/AIDS organization, a support worker from an agency that works with immigrants and refugees, a service user of the lead agency, and an HIV activist who is well known in the community for advocating on behalf of HIV-positive women like herself. The team has decided to recruit as many HIV-positive women as it can to participate in focus groups. As part of the capacity-building initiative, the two HIV-positive women on the team will be trained in focus group interviewing to co-facilitate the focus groups with the community development worker. It is hoped that they will recruit at least 30 women to conduct five focus groups of six participants. As the time gets closer to the focus group dates, only four women have signed up. The community development worker is concerned about the low numbers of participants and decides to call an emergency meeting to reconsider their research strategy.

## Questions

1. Why do you think few participants were interested in participating in the focus groups?

2. What else do you think the team needed to consider before recruiting participants and facilitating the focus groups?

# CHAPTER SUMMARY

This chapter has highlighted the values and skills necessary to engage in agency- and community-based research. The differences between agency and community-based research were also explored by providing concrete examples of the kinds of research that each form entails. This included thinking about the aims and objectives of the research, the goals of the research, and how the research findings will be used to interrogate and change existing practices and policies. Key points also included the research skills that are required to conduct agency- and community-based research projects. These included recruiting participants, collecting qualitative data (e.g., interviews, focus groups) and quantitative data (e.g., surveys, questionnaires), and developing communication skills. Ethical issues and concerns were highlighted as an important and necessary consideration when doing research on and with human participants. Through deeply considering the ethical responsibilities of the researcher, other important concepts such as power, reflection, and the dissemination of research findings were explored. When starting a research project that has the needs of individuals, groups, and communities at its centre, a well thought out research plan that includes all the above points is necessary. It is through engaging in the process of agency- and community-based research that we can experience the connection between research and practice.

## Critical-Thinking Questions

1. Reflect on the relationship between agency- and community-based research and social work and human service practice. Consider the ways that agency- and community-based research is practice.

2. Consider the ethical issues that researchers must attend to when doing research with human participants. What other ethical issues do practice-based researchers need to consider?

3. Communities are not homogenous and therefore there may be competing needs among members. How could agency- and community-based researchers work toward prioritizing a community's research needs?

## Suggested Readings

Israel, B., Schulz, A., Parker, E., Becker, A., Allen, A., & Guzman, J. R. (2003). "Critical issues in developing and following community-based participatory principles." In M. Minkler and N. Wallerstein (Eds.), *Community-based participatory research for health* (pp. 53–76). San Francisco, CA: Jossey-Bass/Wiley.

Keys, C., Horner-Johnson, A., Westlock, K., Hernandez B., & Vasiliauskas, L. (1999). "Learning science for social good: Dynamic tensions in developing undergraduate community researchers." *Journal of Prevention and Intervention in the Community, 18*(2), 141–156.

Maiter, S., Simich, L., Jacobson, N., & Wise, J. (2008). "Reciprocity: An ethic for community-based participatory action research." *Action Research, 6,* 305–325.

Reid, C., & Brief, E. (2009). "Confronting condescending ethics: How community-based research challenges traditional approaches to consent, confidentiality and capacity." *Journal of Academic Ethics, 7,* 75–85.

Rosner-Salazar (2003), "Multi-cultural service learning and community-based research as a model approach to social justice." *Social Justice, 30*(4), 64–76.

## Relevant Websites

### Community-Campus Partnerships for Health
http://depts.washington.edu/ccph/index.html
CCPH is a non-profit organization that promotes health through partnerships between communities and higher education institutions. They are committed to ensuring that community-driven social change is central to service learning and community-based research.

### The Ginsberg Center
http://ginsberg.umich.edu
The Ginsberg Center supports partnerships among students, faculty, and community through working together to meet community-based priorities. They do this by offering courses, workshops, and service learning and community-based research opportunities.

### Trent Centre for Community-Based Education
www.trentcentre.ca
The Trent Centre for Community-Based Education is an independent, non-profit organization that connects students and faculty with local organizations to create community-based research, service learning, and experiential education opportunities that enhance the social, environmental, cultural, and economic health of our communities.

### University of Victoria, Office of Community-Based Research
http://web.uvic.ca/ocbr
The Office of Community-Based Research at the University of Victoria is a community-university research partnership that supports community engagement and research to enhance the quality of life, economic well-being, and social well-being of communities.

### Wellesley Institute
www.wellesleyinstitute.com
The Wellesley Institute is a Toronto-based non-profit organization that brings together policy, capacity building, and community-based research to develop research and policy-based solutions that address urban health issues.

# Chapter 8

## Indigenous Field Education: Protocols and Practices

Shelly Johnson, Paul René Tamburro, and Natalie Clark

## Chapter Objectives

- Demonstrate an understanding of colonialism in Canada.
- Describe the history of Aboriginal social work and human service in Canada.
- Describe the importance of Indigenous knowledge and world view.
- Define cultural safety.
- Learn key components of Indigenous field education.
- Incorporate cultural practices into field education.

## ABORIGINAL AND INDIGENOUS PEOPLES IN CANADA

At the present time, when a person travels across Canada to visit Indigenous communities and events such as powwows, it may seem that most Aboriginal communities are much the same. It may also seem that knowing Native culture from one part of the country to another is rather simple. This perception, however, is only superficial: There is a general pan-Aboriginal culture on the surface that exists for many First Nations peoples when they are away from their communities, just as there is a general Canadian culture when Canadians travel overseas (Robbins, 1997).

Once people get past the general similarities among the groups of Aboriginal peoples of Canada, they find that a huge diversity exists in history, culture, and language. The archaeological record indicates that the Indigenous peoples of North America originated over 15 000 years ago (Dickason & McNab, 2009). There are approximately 53 independent Indigenous languages across Canada, with some regions having more diversity than similar-sized regions in other parts of the world (Dickason & McNab, 2009; Frideres & Gadacz, 2008). For example, the Aboriginal languages of British

Columbia contain more linguistic diversity than all of Europe, including five unrelated language families. This fact demonstrates a long-term occupation of place that has allowed for many languages to develop distinctive systems.

Today, under the Constitution, the Aboriginal peoples of Canada are defined as Inuit, Indian, and Métis. There is great diversity within each of these groups, as well as between them. The coastal peoples of the Atlantic, Arctic, and Pacific each have very different cultures, even though they are based in maritime environments. And the cultures that develop in these regions are very different from those of peoples of the plains, the eastern woodlands, and mountain or tundra regions. It is important for social work and human service students entering field placements to be aware of this diversity and the need to have specific knowledge about the peoples' histories, languages, and cultures in the area they are conducting their placements.

## History of Colonization

In spite of differences in culture and language, it is important to understand the similar experiences shared by all Indigenous peoples in North America as colonized peoples. The colonial history of Canada started 500 years ago and involved extensive contact with the Basque and with French, British, Russian, and other European colonial powers (Dickason & McNab, 2009; Frideres & Gadacz, 2008). These 500 years have seen numerous wars, alliances, diaspora, enslavements, land cessions or treaties, and confederacies among Canada's Aboriginal populations.

Over the past 200 years, Aboriginal peoples have been either forced off most of their lands or have experienced huge land concessions, so all Aboriginal peoples have experienced physical displacement in one form or another. In some cases, Aboriginal people are still living on the land of their ancestors, but the land base has been seriously reduced, as is the case on many small reserves. In other situations, people have been moved from one location to another over great distances. Over the past 150 years, especially since the passage of the *Indian Act* in 1876, there have been intense efforts on the part of the Canadian government to assimilate Aboriginal peoples by destroying their languages and cultures. The *Indian Act* forced children from their families for as many as seven generations; outlawed cultural ceremonies, including potlatches and dances; set up the status system, which removed Indian status from many women and some men; forbade Aboriginal peoples to travel without a pass; and limited their economic enterprise. Additionally, there has been a huge loss of life in many communities that can be directly attributed to disease, malnutrition, poor housing, and other consequences of extreme forced material poverty.

As a result, social work and human service students and their faculty liaisons must be extremely conscious of the concept of *multigenerational trauma* caused by many who tried to explain the aftereffects of what some have called the *Canadian Holocaust* (Annett, 2006). The effects of generations of cultural assault include the reality that many languages are near extinction. Much of the beautiful diversity in the art, music, dance, spirituality, family traditions, and other cultural forms of Canadian Aboriginal peoples has been seriously disrupted. It is extremely important to realize that many communities are working very hard to sustain, revive, and continue to grow their unique cultures.

## ABORIGINAL PEOPLES: A DEFINITION

Section 35(2) of the Canadian *Constitution Act* (1982) identifies the Aboriginal[1] peoples of Canada as Indian, Inuit, or Métis. First Nations people in Canada who have a legal definition as a "status Indian person" under the federal *Indian Act* may have in their possession one of four types of "status cards" issued to them by the federal government. People who identify as *Métis* may apply for a Métis citizenship card from the Métis National Council of Canada or a number of Métis provincial councils. Non-status Indian peoples may have identity cards issued to them by a number of urban Aboriginal organizations — for example, in British Columbia, by the United Native Nations, whose membership is open to anyone of Aboriginal ancestry living on or off reserves in urban, rural, or remote communities. The Inuit Tapiriit Kanatami (ITK) is the national Inuit organization in Canada, representing four Inuit regions — Nunatsiavut (Labrador), Nunavik (northern Quebec), Nunavut, and the Inuvialuit Settlement Region in the Northwest Territories.

## History of Social Work and Human Services with Indigenous Peoples

> Through very difficult lessons over many years, as Aboriginal people we have learned that it is not wise to believe that all people who are professionals will do things that we believe to be in our best interests. Usually they do things that are in their best interests. (First Nations Elder, personal communication, August 12, 2009)

Indigenous peoples living in Canada today are the descendants of peoples who have lived on this land since time immemorial. They represent diverse and complex societies that embrace different cultural, political, linguistic, social, economic, and spiritual traditional systems. Indigenous peoples have thrived with their unique world views and ways of knowing, being, caring and educating their children and families long before settler societies arrived approximately 500 years ago (Canada, 1996). Since the arrival of settlers, Aboriginal peoples in Canada have been subjected to, and, at times, legally

---

[1] *First Nations* and *Indian* refers to those persons identified and registered as "Indians" as defined in the federal *Indian Act*. Although the term *First Nations* is used primarily in this chapter, no legal definition of it exists. The terms *Aboriginal* and *indigenous* refer to one of three groups of people — First Nations, Inuit, or Métis — who have been recognized under the *Constitution Act*, 1982. All terms may be used interchangeably and depend on the specific context.

prevented from, resisting foreign ideologies, legislation, policies, and procedures (Blackstock, 2009; Sinclair, Hart, & Bruyere, 2009; Canada, 2006; Bird, Land, & MacAdam, 2002; York, 1999). For many Aboriginal communities, forced assimilation has resulted in profound loss and devastation of health and well-being in the physical, social, emotional, cultural, and spiritual spheres. Indeed, on socio-economic, educational, and health indicators of well-being, Aboriginal peoples in Canada are consistently found at the lowest levels (Reading, 2009).

The social work and human service professions, based in European Judeo-Christian values and beliefs, are relatively recent phenomena for Indigenous peoples in Canada (Sinclair, Hart, & Bruyere, 2009). According to the Canadian Association of Social Workers (CASW), human rights and social justice are the philosophical underpinnings of social work and human service practice, yet the history of the CASW (2005) shows that this level of practice or advocacy has not always been offered to Indigenous peoples by people in these professions.

In 1946, the CASW and the Canadian Welfare Council (CWC) issued a joint submission to the Special Joint Committee of the Senate and House of Commons that supported the idea that Aboriginal children should be assimilated into Canadian society and that Indian Residential Schools (IRS) had a place in the system of Indian education (Blackstock, 2009). According to the Royal Commission on Aboriginal Peoples (RCAP), social work and human service workers were active participants in the placement of Aboriginal children in IRSs up until the 1960s (RCAP, 1996). This participation occurred despite the fact that the CASW and CWC were presumably informed of public reports authored by Dr. P. H. Bryce, the Indian Affairs medical health officer, as to the deplorable health conditions of Aboriginal children in IRSs and estimates by the federal superintendant of Indian Affairs Duncan Campbell Scott of the death of an estimated 50 percent of Indian children in these schools from disease or maltreatment (Milloy, 1999).

The CASW and CWC advocated to the federal government to ensure that child welfare services could be provided to reserve communities by social work and human service workers. The section 88 amendment of the federal *Indian Act* in 1951 allowed the introduction of provincial child welfare social work and human services to reserve-based First Nations communities for the first time and gave the provinces the "legal capacity to administer provincial child and family services to people outside their constitutional jurisdiction" (Bennett, 2001, p. 1; Canada, 1996).

This change resulted in devastating consequences for Aboriginal populations that were reeling from the multiple and layered effects of generations of denial and suppression of their most basic human rights. They were dealing with issues related to residential school assimilation policies, poverty, lack of autonomy or representation, lack of community services, and the absence of a community capacity needed to address such issues as legalized theft and the profound abuses of their children by the churches and the state. According to Fournier and Crey (1997), living conditions in most reserve-based communities in Canada were appalling after decades of government manipulation and financial mismanagement.

While there is acknowledgment that some Indigenous peoples may not be alive today without the intervention and support of social and human service workers in terms of child safety needs, social work as a profession represents some of the most destructive practices in the psyche of First Nations peoples in Canada. The social work and human service professions embody a group of individuals that historically "stood by" government policies despite knowledge of the death and abuse of vulnerable children in IRSs (Blackstock, 2009). These professions, together with the judiciary and legislators, are responsible for the horrific effects on Indigenous child welfare of the "Sixties Scoop" (Johnston, 1983) and transracial adoption of Indigenous children into non-Indigenous families (Sinclair, 2009). Many Indigenous peoples believe that governments refused to provide adequate and required resources for programs and infrastructures that might have addressed the issues, believing that they instead allowed people in the social work profession to remove their children, thereby continuing to enforce their stated policy of assimilation (Fournier & Crey, 1997) and its newer incarnation of integration (Armitage, 1993).

Social work and human service students practicing with Indigenous individuals must have significant knowledge and understanding of these historical issues and present themselves as respectful, sensitive, and mature, with a clear vision of how they may be perceived in their role as representatives of the social work and human service professions. They can expect that relationship development may proceed in a measured way as trust is developed and Indigenous clients determine whether the student may be of any assistance to them. Depending on the type of social work or human service the student is learning to practice, some sound advice may be as follows:

- Wait to be invited into personal relationships with Indigenous families or communities.
- Be respectful and have a clear understanding of how the social work profession is perceived by the Indigenous peoples and communities with whom you will work.
- Take time to consider your actions and their implications.
- Adhere to community or Indigenous agency protocol and proceed when you are invited.

## Discussion Questions

1. How can child and youth care, human service, and social workers demonstrate an understanding of the history of social work and human service provision to Indigenous peoples?

2. How might you use your personal and professional power to create a better understanding of the history of social work and human service provision to Indigenous peoples?

# Residential Schools in Canada

Together with the federal *Indian Act* (1867), the Residential School Project (RSP) was a key assault weapon used by the Canadian government and Christian churches against Indigenous peoples in Canada. The goal of the RSP was to enforce colonial assimilation policies to socially re-engineer and forcibly separate over 150 000 First Nations, Métis, and Inuit children from their families, communities, and cultures as a means to indoctrinate them into the dominant Euro-Canadian Christian culture. In terms of post-traumatic stress disorders and intergenerational trauma, the legacy of the century-long RSP remains evident in our Aboriginal populations and continues to be so significant that Indigenous psychologist and professors Duran and Duran (1995) "fantasize that one day the DSM [Diagnostic and Statistical Manual of Mental Disorders] will have diagnostic criteria such as 'acute or chronic reaction to genocide and colonialism'" (p. 53).

For 120 years, between 1876 and 1996, the Government of Canada, through the Conservative and Liberal parties (and their predecessors), worked with Christian churches to develop and operate more than 132 IRSs in every Canadian province and territory except Prince Edward Island, Newfoundland, and New Brunswick (Frideres & Gadacz, 2008; Helin, 2006; Lawrence, 2004; Miller, 1997). While it is true that the Anglican, Presbyterian, and United churches contributed to the IRS project with the same assimilation goal as sought by the federal government — namely to "kill the Indian in the child"—the Roman Catholic church operated 70 percent of all IRSs in Canada with funding, land, per capita grants, and other material rewards from the federal government (Indian Residential Schools Survivors Society, n.d.). The Hawthorn Report (1967), a review of the RSP undertaken at the request of the federal government, pointed out:

> We note that the greater the educational resources possessed by a Church or the greater its investment in Indian education, the greater its anxiety to maintain the status quo. On the contrary, the faiths having the least material interest in Indian education are much more open to innovations. (p. 61)

Differential attendance by primarily male status First Nations students in IRSs in the years prior to 1884 created funding challenges for the religious orders and gave rise to criticism of the IRS system by both the government and First Nations communities. In 1884, the federal government amended the *Indian Act* to legally require all status First Nations children under the age of 16 to attend IRSs (Miller, 1997). This amendment effectively rendered First Nations, Métis, and Inuit parents helpless to oppose their children's removal from families, communities, and cultures. Federal Indian agents working in reserve-based communities, members of the Royal Canadian Mounted Police (RCMP; formerly the Northwest Mounted Police), politicians, judges, lawyers, social workers, and priests worked together to quell opposition from parents through new legislative powers to arrest, transport, and detain children at residential schools and to fine or imprison parents who refused to cooperate (Blackstock, 2009; Stout & Kipling,

2003). The full force of Canadian law and social control mechanisms supported these individuals to work within sanctioned political, legal, education, and social system contexts to maintain control and enforce assimilation policies over Aboriginal peoples. At the same time, these same systems ensured that *Indians,* as defined under the *Indian Act,* did not have the right to vote in federal elections until 1961, could not hire a lawyer, and continued to be relegated to the status of "wards" of the federal government. The trauma and terror inflicted on helpless First Nations, Métis, and Inuit children by those responsible for their care and education is well documented (Annett, 2006; Chrisjohn, Young, & Maraun, 2006; Stout & Kipling, 2003; Olsen, Morris, & Sam, 2001; Miller, 1997; Canada, 1996; Haig-Brown, 1988) and include numerous instances where Canadian society (i.e., the Christian churches, government officials, RCMP, social workers, and individuals) were well aware of IRS crimes yet did little to stop or intervene in the following actions against First Nations children:

- prolonged and repeated sexual, physical, emotional, and spiritual abuse (including rape that resulted in unwanted pregnancies; sodomy; murder; disfigurement; humiliation; assault; forcible removal from homes and confinement in institutions operated by people of a different race, far from the protection of families and communities; forcible separation of brothers from sisters and punishment for communicating with each other in residential institutions; bans of traditional spiritual practices)
- substandard health care (including the disregard for life through the introduction and spread of tuberculosis, pneumonia, smallpox, and other epidemic, infectious diseases into otherwise healthy residential school populations; poor dental, vision, speech, and hearing care)
- substandard and inadequate food, clothing, and shelter (resulting in poor nutritional care and lifelong health issues)
- prohibition of and severe punishment for the use of First Nations, Inuit, and Métis languages and cultural practices

This forced loss of identity and disconnection from nurturing families, communities, and cultures continues to be evident in Aboriginal communities today.

For the past 60 years, the racist actions and assimilation policies by the Canadian state are recognized as *genocide* under Article 2 of the United Nations (UN) Convention on the Prevention and Punishment of the Crime of Genocide. The UN Convention was adopted on December 9, 1948, when IRSs remained in full operation in Canada and the social work profession was aware of the deaths of children within the institutions (Blackstock, 2009). The Convention defines genocide as actions committed with the "intent to destroy, in whole or in part, a national, ethnical, racial or religious group, as such:

(a) Killing members of the group;

(b) Causing serious bodily or mental harm to members of the group;

(c) Deliberately inflicting on the group conditions of life calculated to bring about its physical destruction in whole or in part;

(d) Imposing measures intended to prevent births within the group;

(e) Forcibly transferring children of the group to another group" (United Nations, 1948).

It took the federal government 12 years from the time that the last IRS ceased operation in Saskatchewan, and 141 years (or approximately seven generations) since their inception, to make a public apology to IRS survivors for the government's role in developing and operating the IRS system. On June 11, 2008, Conservative prime minister Stephen Harper, Liberal Party leader Stéphane Dion, and New Democratic Party leader Jack Layton each made a Statement of Apology to former students of IRSs on behalf of the current and historical governments and major political parties of Canada. In part, the Statement of Apology delivered by Stephen Harper included the following text:

> Therefore, on behalf of the Government of Canada and all Canadians, I stand before you, in this Chamber so central to our life as a country, to apologize to Aboriginal peoples for Canada's role in the Indian Residential Schools system.
>
> To the approximately 80 000 living former students, and all family members and communities, the Government of Canada now recognizes that it was wrong to forcibly remove children from their homes and we apologize for having done this. We now recognize that it was wrong to separate children from rich and vibrant cultures and traditions that it created a void in many lives and communities, and we apologize for having done this. We now recognize that, in separating children from their families, we undermined the ability of many to adequately parent their own children and sowed the seeds for generations to follow, and we apologize for having done this. We now recognize that, far too often, these institutions gave rise to abuse or neglect and were inadequately controlled, and we apologize for failing to protect you. Not only did you suffer these abuses as children, but as you became parents, you were powerless to protect your own children from suffering the same experience, and for this we are sorry.
>
> The burden of this experience has been on your shoulders for far too long. The burden is properly ours as a Government, and as a country. There is no place in Canada for the attitudes that inspired the Indian Residential Schools system to ever prevail again. You have been working on recovering from this experience for a long time and in a very real sense, we are now joining you on this journey. The Government of Canada sincerely apologizes and asks the forgiveness of the Aboriginal peoples of this country for failing them so profoundly.
>
> Nous le regrettons. We are sorry. Nimitataynan. Niminchinowesamin. Mamiattugut. (Government of Canada, 2008)

While the apology was formally accepted by every First Nations, Métis, and Inuit political body in Canada, the road to reconciliation remains ongoing, both in terms of individual, family, and community healing and through the work of the Truth and Reconciliation Commission of Canada. Social work and human service students are advised to have a thorough understanding of, and the ability to demonstrate knowledge and sensitivity about, the IRS legacy, the IRS settlement process, the Truth and Reconciliation Commission process, various legal and advocacy options, and the healing initiatives or resources available to and in progress with the First Nations, Métis, and Inuit peoples they may be working with in their practica.

---

## Discussion Questions

1. How can child and youth care, human service, and social workers demonstrate a better understanding of the implications of the residential school project in their practice?

2. What can you do to use your personal and professional power to create healing relationships?

---

## Sixties Scoop, Millennium Scoop, and Current State of Aboriginal Child Welfare

> The road to hell was paved with good intentions and the child welfare system was the paving contractor. (RCAP, 1996, 3:29)

Patrick Johnston (1983) first coined the term *Sixties Scoop* to refer to the unprecedented rates of child welfare apprehension of Aboriginal children by social work and human service practitioners — sanctioned by the Canadian judicial system — between the 1960s and the mid-1980s. Apprehension statistics indicate that approximately 11 132 status Indian children were adopted between 1960 and 1990; because of inaccurate record management, the real number is thought to be much higher (Sinclair, 2009; Wharf, 2009; Walmsley, 2005). According to a report by Joyce Timpson, a social worker who completed a child welfare report for RCAP (Canada, 1996), this exponential increase in Aboriginal child welfare apprehension was due to the "federal government's willingness to pay child-in-care costs, along with federal and provincial governments' resistance to supporting prevention services, family counselling or rehabilitation" (p. 21). Both privately and publicly, many Indigenous peoples and academics (Armitage, 1993) identify the child welfare system as merely a replication of the IRS system — a continuation of the assimilation and integration policies of the federal government — and believe that foster parents and social and human service workers have replaced religious caretakers (Blackstock, 2009; Lawrence, 2004; York, 1999). However, at least in the IRSs, Aboriginal children had one another; in the child welfare system, frequent moves and adoptions meant that, at times, children in care have no siblings or connections to their Indigenous communities, cultures, or traditions (Fournier & Crey, 1997).

Frequently, Aboriginal academics comment that the "economy" of Aboriginal child welfare began in this era (Blackstock, 2009; Sinclair, 2009; Waldrum, 1997) and that the "big business" of Aboriginal child welfare and foster care (with money paid on behalf of Aboriginal children to caretakers, child care workers, social workers, the judiciary, and corrections and support services) has resulted in an economic system "that rests upon the Aboriginal child welfare system and has become firmly entrenched in the last half century" (Sinclair, 2009, p. 94).

Beginning in 1981, over 125 Aboriginal child and family agencies were developed in Canada to provide culturally sensitive delegated child welfare services to First Nations, Métis, urban-based, and reserve-based populations. Today, the removal of Aboriginal children based on imposed Euro-Canadian risk assessment criteria continues and the lack of available, preventative, culturally sensitive support services and equitable funding is the subject of a 2010 Canadian Human Rights Tribunal hearing (McCloskey & Andreae, 2010). The rates of Aboriginal children in care are now at three times the rate of Aboriginal children confined to IRSs at the height of their operation in the 1940s (McKenzie & Seidl, 1995); a situation called the *Millennium Scoop* by Dr. Lauri Gilchrist of Lakehead University (Sinclair, 2007). The situation today is so termed because Aboriginal children in care predominantly experience long-time frames of institutionalization rather than adoption (Sinclair, 2009), which contributes to what is known as "foster care drift," where children experience numerous foster care placements rather than a permanent placement until they are emancipated legally as adults.

Social work and human service students who work in collaboration with Indigenous communities must become familiar with protocols, delegation enabling agreements, and delegation confirming agreements between government representatives and Indigenous child welfare agency representatives regarding expected roles and responsibilities with respect to child protection and support services. In addition, the elected leadership in many First Nations communities expects that new agency social work or human service workers will make themselves known to a representative of the elected leadership prior to engaging with individuals in reserve communities. Finally, students should take personal responsibility to learn about historical and recent human rights advocacy efforts by Indigenous peoples and allies in the field of child welfare.

## Discussion Questions

1. How can child and youth care, human service, and social workers demonstrate a better understanding of the implications of the child welfare project in their practice?

2. How can you use your personal and professional power and advocacy skills to create healing relationships and change?

# THE IMPORTANCE OF INDIGENOUS KNOWLEDGE AND WORLD VIEWS

It is important for faculty helping with field education and students entering field practica to be aware of the importance Aboriginal communities place on the continuation and growth of their unique Indigenous ways. In many cases, communities may be involved in strong efforts to revive and restore cultural traditions and languages that have been seriously damaged, in part by past generations of social work and human service workers who thought they were doing *good* in the name of Canada's assimilationist agenda.

When visiting specific communities, the need for understanding the diversity among Aboriginal peoples becomes more apparent. Despite this, taken as a whole, Aboriginal peoples in Canada may have more in common with one another than they ever will with people who have moved here from other parts of the world. One fundamental reason for this is that all Aboriginal cultures emerged from and developed on this land over thousands of years, often in contact with other peoples in North America, which was referred to by many as Turtle Island.

Much of the histories, cultures, and languages of Aboriginal communities in Canada are not discussed in classroom texts. Indigenous faculty have also identified the concern that there is "a perceived lack of acceptance of the importance of Indigenous-based curricula and program delivery" (Sinclair, 2006, pp. 2005–2006). Therefore, it is important to recognize and use the knowledge that exists within the Aboriginal communities surrounding where students complete their field education. In colonial situations, the dominant culture does not privilege or foreground the knowledge of Indigenous communities in any part of its educational system. Therefore, this knowledge is kept and transferred through oral traditions and community-based interactions. Often this knowledge is transferred through Elders, the people who have spent the most time in communities and may have a memory of their own Elders, who had a connection to times when the dominant culture had less influence. Sometimes there may exist a younger generation of knowledgeable persons in the communities who have specifically sought out traditional teachings to bring them in touch with their heritage. This is often the case when, for generations, many potential Elders have died before they could transfer information to others or there was so much disruption and shame created in the community that people were not open to listening to those teachings. In any event, many Aboriginal communities across Canada are now going through a process of revalidating and valuing Indigenous knowledges.

The world views of the Indigenous peoples of the Americas, despite the great diversity among nations and languages, share many elements that make them similar to one another but very different than the overall world views of the various European nations. These differences include the varying perceptions of humans' relationship to land, to personal property, and to leadership; relations between children and adults and Elders; time; boundaries of personal space and material possessions; and concepts of generosity (Baskin, 2005; Cross, 1996; DuBray, 1994; Durst, 2000; Graveline, 1998;

Hart, 2001; Saulis, 2003; Waterfall, 2003; Yellow Bird, 2001). As educators and students become more familiar with Indigenous world views, they will no doubt be able to add to this list. Therefore, it is important for those involved in field education to move slowly and carefully and to take their time learning the world views of the communities they find themselves in as either students or practitioners. Social work as a profession, after all, developed as a way to solve problems created by what is known as Western civilization. Aboriginal social work and human service must not cause more damage and, instead, must assist in the restoration of Indigenous social systems that worked for thousands of years, giving them relevance in today's world.

## Integration of Indigenous Practices in Field Education: Understanding Indigenous Protocol and Practices across Canada

One way that social work and human service educators and students may gain some understanding of the Indigenous world view is by listening to storytellers and Elders engaged in various forms of oral tradition. Practitioners can also spend some time learning about ceremonies, songs, and dances. In one of the authors' projects with field students in Aboriginal community settings in Kamloops, British Columbia, traditional storytelling was used in field education research to help non-Aboriginal students and faculty better understand certain concepts, such as maintaining a *sense of humour* and the importance of *relationships*. In other parts of Canada, traditional Indigenous stories contain many different elements but usually involve a trickster character. The trickster often makes a fool of itself, but in doing so imparts wisdom and reveals many important truths about places. It is through these stories that names of places can be understood. For example, the meaning of Turtle Island, which for most Westerners and Europeans represents the continent of North America, is explained in Indigenous traditional stories. And with an understanding of place names comes the need to respect relationships. For example, if North America is actually a great turtle as the story tells, then there is a reason to treat the land much more respectfully and gently. This example is only one of many that illustrate the importance of world view and having a strong grounding in Indigenous knowledge before entering First Nations communities as part of field education.

Another important aspect of listening to stories and observing Elders is learning how to interact appropriately in First Nations communities. It is especially important to learn about family and extended clan relationships. The importance of family over the lifespan, including ceremonies related to birth, naming, marriage, puberty, and funerals is often a big surprise for non-Aboriginal service providers involved in field education. For example, in many Aboriginal communities, funeral ceremonies are not one-day events. There is an expectation that family members spend a significant amount of time involved with the various aspects of preparation, visiting, and finalizing the overall funeral ceremony, which is often much shorter in contemporary Western culture. It is frequently difficult for Aboriginal students in field placements to take the time they need away from their placements to be involved in funerals. It may also be difficult for non-Native students and faculty to understand the need for a student to change some of the roles they perform if they are placed in an Aboriginal community during a time of crisis, such as if several deaths occur. These events are often dealt with differently in Aboriginal communities than they are in the dominant culture. As another example, there is a need to understand the importance of including extended family in decision making regarding child placements or other important family decisions, which are often considered confidential and private in the Western social work and human service model. Learning which Elders, for example, should be present and/or consulted along with the biological parents during discussions about children is very important. Sometimes the needs and expectations of the members of an Aboriginal community may differ from the dominant culture's rules and policies, which are often used in social work and human service agencies. Having some understanding of how to deal with these potential conflicts is important in preparing for field education in Indigenous communities.

In many Aboriginal communities, it is very proper, and often expected, to serve food to visitors. And it is often considered rude to not accept food. The same may be said about gift-giving. There are certain times when gift-giving is considered very appropriate, such as the giveaway at a powwow or other cultural event. Social work and human service students who regularly refuse food or gifts because of school policies may create a perception that they are rude. Therefore, it is important for students to find out the expectations of community members.

Other communities may have expectations that social work or human service students work for the members of the community and not for an agency or a council. An example of this occurred in a community where a student was introducing herself to Elders at a gathering. One Elder asked, "Who are you here for?" The student replied, "I'm here with the permission of the Band Council and working for them." The Elder then said, "Well, if you're here for them, go over to their office and stop spending time with us Elders." The student's feelings were hurt, but the issue was resolved later when it was made clear that the Elder's comment was simply a lesson. In this particular community, the student needed to know that she was there for the people in general and not for any organization or agency, including the band council, even though it was the elected government. Students must understand that in Aboriginal communities, power exists within the members, not in an organization. Councils and other organizations exist to meet the needs of the people, and council members are often "corrected" by Elders, as was this student. Elders are the persons in the community who, as this example demonstrates, take on the task of educating students. This example also illustrates the importance of various community members, Elders, and the band government having acceptance for field education.

# INTEGRATION OF INDIGENOUS PERSPECTIVES INTO PRACTICE: EMERGING BEST PRACTICES

## Toward Decolonizing Field Education: A Research Study

The first research to examine Aboriginal field education and consider the process of decolonizing it was conducted in 2007 when author Natalie Clark, along with her colleagues, including Paul Tamburro, received a Social Sciences and Humanities Research Council (SSHRC) Aboriginal development grant to establish a research partnership among Thompson Rivers University in Kamloops, British Columbia, Nicola Valley Institute of Technology (NVIT) in Merritt, British Columbia, and the Interior Indian Friendship Society, also in Kamloops, to examine the process and practices toward decolonizing field education programs in interior British Columbia.[2] (See Clark et al. [2010] for a more detailed description of the team and the process of establishing this partnership.)

The following discussion questions address key issues that this study examined and that students should consider.

---

### Discussion Questions

1. What supports do Aboriginal students require in facilitating their learning (e.g., mentors, Elders, access to Aboriginal faculty, or learning resources and interventions)?

2. What is good practice for non-Indigenous social work and human service students who do their placements in First Nations settings? How can they "do no harm," given the history between social and human services workers and Aboriginal peoples?

---

## Cultural Safety

*Cultural safety* is a term that goes "beyond the concept of cultural sensitivity to analyzing power imbalances, institutional discrimination, colonization and relationships with colonizers" (National Aboriginal Health Organization [NAHO], 2006, p. 1).

---

[2] The team was recently awarded a three-year SSHRC research grant in partnership with other field education coordinators and faculty in universities across British Columbia to expand the research team. The goal is to administer a survey questionnaire that was developed during the pilot research project and to include qualitative and quantitative data from across British Columbia and from tribal communities in India. To extend culturally safe practices and commit to ongoing methods of collaborative research, the researchers will require other sites to adopt the practice of community advisory committees with gatekeeping Elders, and use the ethics practice principles as highlighted in Clark et al., 2010 (or see Jones, 2000).

The main themes of cultural safety are that we are all bearers of culture and that we need to be aware of and challenge unequal power relations at the level of individual, family, community, and society. Cultural safety draws our attention to the social, economic, and political position of certain groups within society, such as the Maori people in Australia/New Zealand or Aboriginal peoples in Canada. Cultural safety reminds us to reflect on the ways in which our health policies, research, education, and practices may recreate the traumas inflicted upon Aboriginal peoples. (University of Victoria, 2009)

For social work and human service students, cultural safety does not provide a how-to list or checklist of behaviours, nor does it focus on learning the rituals, customs, and practices of different cultural groups. Instead, cultural safety builds on the concept of reflexivity as explored in Chapter 5. Social work and human service students are required to engage not only in self-reflection about their own values and beliefs, but also in reflexivity with respect to social work and human service education and how it has and continues to contribute to colonization and harm for Aboriginal peoples in Canada. Culturally safe practice requires students to critically analyze their attitudes, values, and beliefs, and consider how the helping profession and their own practice may create conditions of "unsafety" for people who are not from the dominant culture.

For example, cultural safety helps us see how we influence the type of health care experience that people have in our various workplaces. We can learn to use our personal and our professional power to positively shape people's experiences of health and heath care and to create environments that support healing and protect the cultural identity of individuals. This might be through awareness of our tendencies to judge people, or through questioning organizational policies, rules, and practices that are based in only one view of health and healing and create restrictive practice environments for clients and their families.

Field education programs must work toward developing culturally safe practices for students in both post-secondary education and the community. Unlike the linked concepts of cultural sensitivity and cultural competence, which may contribute to a service recipient's experiences, cultural safety is an outcome that shifts the power to the service recipient, who then defines whether the relationship is culturally safe for them.

As this applies to students in field education, it is important to consider the role of power in the helping relationship, and to take into account how the person receiving services defines cultural safety. The process then shifts to rebuilding the relationship where it has been "historically harmful and broken, particularly by the professions of social work and education." In an educational setting, "first the educator must be culturally competent; and second, the student culturally safe in the learning relationship" (NAHO, 2006, p. 2). We should add one more note to our discussion of cultural safety: When Aboriginal field education students are from cultures other than the one with which they are working, cultural safety practices apply whenever they work from the base of their Aboriginal culture with clients from the local Aboriginal culture.

# The Decolonization of Field Education: One Research Study's Findings

One of the only studies examining best practices in Indigenous field education identified six areas of recommendation. Based on the analysis of data from interviews and focus groups, respondents identified several key factors regarding Aboriginal field education, best practices, and the experiences of non-Aboriginal students placed in Aboriginal field settings. The six areas of recommendations are (1) spirituality and ceremony within social work and human service programs, (2) Elders involved in all aspects of the students' education, (3) grief and loss honouring practices; (4) anti-oppressive education practices, (5) relational supports as strengths in education; and (6) the use of student wellness plans and self-care in practicum field placements. For a full discussion of these findings please see the article by author Natalie Clark and her colleagues in "Suggested Readings" (Clark et al., 2010).

Some of the recommendations emerging from each theme that have implications for Aboriginal field education include the following:

1.  **Including spirituality and ceremony in social work and human service field education programs**

    As noted earlier in the chapter, it is important that students understand that Aboriginal ceremonies and practices are not homogenous and that great diversity exists among First Nations communities in Canada. Further, it is important to consider when, and under what respectful conditions, non-Aboriginal students might participate in these practices.

2.  **Involving Elders in all aspects of the students' education**

    Students, field instructors, and Elders identified the need for Elders to be part of field education programs and practices. Recent literature has called for the inclusion of Elders in social work and human service programming (see Fire, 2006), and students clearly identified a need for support, care, advocacy, and protection provided by Elders. Some of the issues Aboriginal students need support for include personal crises, past trauma, and the impact on learning of feelings of belonging, the importance of "fitting in," large class sizes, and non-Aboriginal students as the majority. They identified the need to create communities for Aboriginal students and their allies, through both informal and formal supports, including potlucks, powwows on campus, or cultural retreats. Supports should be provided that reflect the needs of all Aboriginal students, including those who know their culture, those who are new to their culture, those who practice tradition, and those who were raised within the church.

> There is a need for counsellors, caring faculty, and Elders because Aboriginal students need support right through … someone they can trust — our people want the education but we need guidance — hand holding and it's important that the university accommodate Aboriginal students, they don't need to accommodate to it. (Clark, Drolet, Mathews et al, 2010)

One Elder, who is part of the Elders council at Nicola Valley Institute of Technology (NVIT), provided the following suggestion:

> Having Elders on campus is a culturally safe practice that assists to decolonize education and provide care, support and protection for Aboriginal students which means the integration of Elders in the university must be honoured through structural support to do so. (Clark, Drolet, Mathews, et al., 2010)

3. **Respecting grief and loss honouring practices in field education**

Almost all field education students and others involved in the practice through various roles (field education coordinators, instructors, and liaison) who participated in the study identified culturally unsafe practices tied to university policies related to grief and loss and recommended changes to policy in responding to Aboriginal students who experience grief and loss during their practicum.

> She's from a thousand kilometers away … some students will be gone for weeks to be away for a funeral. … Family, community and culture comes first … and there are some faculty who are just like nope they missed classes they are out. (Clark, Drolet, Mathews, et al., 2010)

4. **Applying anti-oppressive field education practices**

Field education programs need to consider the importance of viewing students as within an intersectional framework that meets their many needs. It must be understood that indigenity intersects with geography, social isolation, gender, poverty, age, ability, gender identity, and sexual orientation, and that this has an impact on the student and his or her needs and experiences within field education. As one student in our study shared:

> Well because I am an Aboriginal student, I'm a woman and person with disabilities. Honestly, there are no services on campus for persons with

disabilities other than audio-visual recording devises, someone to take notes, there are no disability services. (Clark, Drolet, Mathews, et al., 2010)

5. **Recognizing relational supports as strengths in field education**

Consistent across all participant responses was the recognition of relationships as a key support for students. This includes allowing the space and time to invest in these relationships among students, between students and Elders, and among students and field education supervisors and field education coordinators. As one student shared:

> She [faculty liaison] was always willing to give her time, even though I knew she was busy." She always assured me she was never too busy, that was comforting, because I felt bad … so that gave me a comfort level that that was okay. (Clark, Drolet, Mathews, et al., 2010).

6. **Using student wellness plans and self-care in practicum field placements**

Students and field instructors all strongly recommended the importance of developing and using wellness plans. Programs such as NVIT's use wellness plans as an essential component. As Fire (2006) states, "A healthy academic program would seek this balance holistically in its epistemology and its teachings, and encourage personal balance for faculty and students" (p. 4).

This exploratory research highlights that "all partners in field education including students, faculty, field education coordinators and field instructors need to interrogate the oppressive policies and practices that continue to perpetuate Eurocentric practices" (Clark, Drolet, Mathews, et al., 2010).

## FIELD EDUCATION IN ABORIGINAL AGENCIES AND COMMUNITIES: A CASE STUDY

Aboriginal agencies recognize that they are uniquely positioned to offer critical learning opportunities to Indigenous social work and human service students and, where possible, to non-Indigenous students. The specific capacity of the agency may dictate that Indigenous students will receive priority placement. The following is not meant to be an exhaustive list of key issues for placement consideration; rather, it is meant as a brief checklist to consider prior to and while engaging with Aboriginal agency personnel.

## Supporting the Aboriginal Agency

1. **Relationship with the student:** In the very best option, social work and human service students should be given an opportunity to meet in person with all staff of the entire agency (or as many staff members as possible) to formally discuss their

proposal to the agency. Students should consider and formulate their responses to the following questions:

- Why do I want to complete my practicum in the agency? What are my expectations of my role at the agency? Note: The answers to these questions are particularly important if the student being proposed to an Indigenous agency is not an Indigenous person.
- What knowledge, skills, and abilities can I bring to the agency?
- What knowledge do I have about pertinent issues in the mandate of the agency? For example, the IRS system, child welfare, adoption, health, addictions, and reconnection issues that different staff members or clients may experience in the course of either providing or receiving services.
- What knowledge, skills, and abilities do I hope to learn at the agency?

2. **Agency capacity:** It is important to remember that in smaller agencies, responsibilities for student learning may be assigned to a number of agency personnel; therefore, these employees should have an opportunity to assess their "fit" with proposed students. This may require more than one or two student visits to the agency. Students should be taught that these initial visits are an important part of relationship building, as they help to determine their "best fit" within the context of all that is happening in the agency.

3. **Involvement of Aboriginal community members in the decision making process:** At times, proposed students may be asked to meet with youth, Elders, boards, advisories, or community members who may also be responsible for helping the agency make a decision about their "fit." In many Aboriginal organizations, the contribution of Elders, youth, or community members is just as valued as that of the staff; in others, it may be valued more — or less. Students and faculty should understand that the decision may be a collective one, depending on the type of learning opportunities students are asking for or those the agency is offering.

4. **Agency needs and other obligations:** While the Aboriginal agency or organization may have interest, expertise, and desire to provide educational opportunities to students and recognize that this responsibility is key to developing potential future staff members, they need to be very clear that they can meet students' learning needs in the context of all their other obligations. It is important that the field placement coordinator develop a frank and open communication style with the agency leaders and be open to developing creative ways to meet the learning needs of students.

5. **Agency spiritual or cultural practices:** Many Aboriginal agencies practice traditional self-care techniques that are an integral part of healthy agency functioning. These may include collective or individual opportunities for drumming, singing, smudging, praying, learning Indigenous languages, sweating, feasting together, creating art projects, visiting with Elders, and so on. They may be informal

protocols or expectations that have been established by the agency and are understood by personnel. While opportunities may be provided, student and staff participation in spiritual or cultural practices is always voluntary. Different types of spiritual or cultural practices may not correspond with the values and beliefs of all students and should be discussed during the student interview.

6. **Community involvement expectations:** Working in an Indigenous agency as an Indigenous person means that students can expect to have multiple and overlapping relationships with community colleagues, clients, and co-workers. It can also mean that students may have dual accountabilities in their work and professional lives. Agencies need students who can work in an ethical way, can understand the absolute imperative of client confidentiality, and are open to the resolution of conflict in a timely and respectful manner. They must be open to cultural conflict resolution processes, learn or demonstrate that they know how to respectfully approach an Elder, and offer thanks for their help.

7. **Being a "community member" means being present and participating in functions and gatherings:** Students may be invited, usually informally, to participate in community functions and gatherings, much like an extended family member. Typically, the invitation comes in casual conversation to the entire group or is passed to people through the informal connections between specific members via email or a poster. Students should be advised that they may be expected to participate in any number of activities, from assisting Elders to be fed first to setting up chairs, tables, or food. In these community gatherings the titles of *executive director*, *social worker*, *faculty*, or *student* become irrelevant; as a community member, everyone is expected to work together, in the spirit of reciprocity, for the benefit of the entire group.

## Supporting the Indigenous Student

Certain considerations should be paramount when agencies are supporting Indigenous students.

1. **Indigenous identity of the student:** When Indigenous students begin a practicum opportunity at any agency, many find that they must make a conscious decision about how much of their Indigenous identity to bring with them into the agency. As one student explains, "In one Aboriginal practicum setting I needed all my cultural values, beliefs, medicines, and traditions to do the work that was expected of me; at another non-Aboriginal practicum setting, each day I decided to leave my bundle at the door in the morning and pick it up on my way home at night. It wasn't that the learning wasn't good, it's just a type of learning for which my bundle wasn't needed" (L. George, personal communication, March 12, 2010). Indigenous students need support to examine their "fit" within the practicum agency and to determine if the learning being offered is what they need at that time in their academic

development or if another agency would provide a better "fit" with their Indigenous identity.

2. **Family, community, spiritual, and cultural obligations and responsibilities of the student that may require flexibility and understanding:** The diversity in Indigenous nations in terms of cultural, spiritual, linguistic, social, political, and economic obligations can be a complex issue for Indigenous students to navigate in the practicum setting. Indigenous students might have important, specific, and reciprocal obligations that may require time away from their practicum and may require support to explain information to people from outside their families and communities. At times, because of cultural protocols, field experience students may not be able to share specific or sacred information with their practicum supervisors out of respect for specific teachings. To do so may cause conflict within their families and communities, so practicum supervisors must be sensitive to such issues. For example, the students may be expected to be involved in winter ceremonies on the West Coast, may have duties related to attending funerals in Saskatchewan that take four to five days to complete, or may have specific roles in caring for bereaved family members in Longhouse traditions. It may be helpful to ask Indigenous students at the beginning of their placements if they know of any cultural or family obligations that may occur during the practicum and how supervisors may respectfully address the issue.

3. **Respect for the Indigenous student:** In practicum settings, as in life, during the course of their duties, Indigenous students may experience racism, internalized racism, cutting remarks or inappropriate language, or bullying and silencing tactics. Depending on their knowledge, skills, or abilities to deal effectively with such incidents, Indigenous students may or may not want to bring the issues to the attention of their practicum supervisors. Fear of reprisal, fear of failure, and not knowing how to address these issues can often serve to silence Indigenous students and/or encourage them to leave their practicum setting. Through provision of practical legal information designed to address situations in a timely way; a supportive, mentoring relationship; and demonstration of respect for the Indigenous student's culture and rights, practicum supervisors can help students fulfill their duties and set an example that racism, bullying, or silencing tactics will not be tolerated in the workplace.

4. **Provision of relevant learning opportunities:** Many Indigenous students attend post-secondary institutions with a view to return to their home communities with knowledge, skills, or abilities that will enhance the well-being of their families and communities. Many Indigenous students have received messages from extended family members that their role in life is to be of service to others, and they are intent on fulfilling those community expectations. To that end, students should be integrally involved in decision-making processes and feel supported to engage in relevant learning opportunities that will help them make the most of their practicum

requirements. In many instances, Indigenous students will choose to complete their practicum in an Aboriginal agency setting, although others will choose non-Aboriginal agencies for specific opportunities.

# CHAPTER SUMMARY

This chapter aims to provide students in Indigenous field education with a better understanding of colonialism in Canada, the history and current reality of social work and human services provided to Aboriginal peoples in Canada, the importance of Indigenous knowledge and world view in service delivery, and a definition of the term *cultural safety*. It also offers a discussion about the key components of Indigenous field education and provides some examples of cultural practices in field education. It is intended to help students, faculty and agencies to begin and further important conversations to support learning about issues in Indigenous field education.

## Critical-Thinking Questions

1. What protocols, policies, or practices do an Indigenous agency and students explicitly or implicitly identify as important and respectful for their work with Indigenous peoples? How is this information communicated between the agency and social work and human service students?

2. What role do Elders, youth, and community members serve in supporting the learning needs of social work or human service students within an agency? Is there a reciprocal role for students?

3. How do Indigenous agency personnel and students demonstrate the concepts of respect, reciprocity, responsibility, and relevance in an Aboriginal agency?

## Suggested Readings

Clark, N. Drolet, J., Mathews, N., Walton, P., Tamburro, P., Derrick, J.,& Arnouse, M. (2010). "Decolonizing field education: Melq'ilwiye Coming together: An exploratory study in the interior of British Columbia." *Critical Social Work, 11*(1).

Dickason, O. P., & McNab, D. T. (2009). *Canada's First Nations: A history of founding peoples from earliest times* (4th ed.). Don Mills, ON: Oxford University Press.

Frideres, J., & Gadacz, R. (2008). *Aboriginal peoples in Canada*. Toronto, ON: Pearson Prentice Hall.

Loiselle, M., & Lauretta, M. (2006). *The wellness wheel: An Aboriginal contribution to social work*. Retrieved from: *www.reseaudialog.qc.ca/Docspdf/LoiselleMcKenzie.pdf*.

Meyst, S. (2005). "Learning how to be culturally safe." *Kai Tiaki Nursing New Zealand, 11*(6), 20–22.

National Aboriginal Health Organization (NAHO). (2006). *Cultural safety fact sheet*. Author. Retrieved from *www.naho.ca/english*.

Sinclair, R., Hart, M. A., & Bruyere, G. (Eds.). (2009). *Wicihitowin: Aboriginal social work in Canada.* Black Point, MB: Fernwood Publishing.

Tuhiwai Smith, L. (2001). *Decolonising methodologies: Research and indigenous peoples.* Dunedin, New Zealand: University of Otago Press.

## Relevant Websites

### Caring for First Nations Children Society

www.cfncs.com

This association provides professional development, research services, and liaison services for First Nations people who protect and promote the well-being of First Nations children and families by respecting and reaffirming traditional values and beliefs, encouraging innovative and quality child and family service delivery, and empowering the voices of First Nations peoples.

### Cultural Safety Modules: Peoples' Experiences of Colonization

http://web2.uvcs.uvic.ca/courses/csafety/mod1/index.htm

http://web2.uvcs.uvic.ca/courses/csafety/mod2/

http://web2.uvcs.uvic.ca/courses/csafety/mod3/

These excellent modules provide students with information on cultural safety and how it applies to social and human service work.

### First Nations Child and Family Caring Society of Canada

http://www.fncfcs.com

This society promotes and advocates for First Nations child welfare research, policy, networking, and professional development through an online journal, a website, conferences, and workshops.

### Indigenous Child Welfare Research Network

http://web.uvic.ca/icwr/home.htm

The creation and maintenance of the Indigenous Child Welfare Research Network is unique in North America and is a collaborative process among universities, agencies, and communities. The research and training agenda includes methods and analysis relevant to our diverse Indigenous traditional teachings, communities, and agencies.

# Chapter 9

## The Practice of Diversity in a Multicultural Society

Ransford Danso

## Chapter Objectives

- Critically analyze and respond appropriately to oppressive comments or situations.
- Discover strategies for combating racism, discrimination, and other forms of oppression.
- Apply theoretical concepts of diversity in practice.
- Explain the role of alliances and partnerships in social change.
- Create strategies for implementing fair agency policies.
- Explore strategies for practising diversity in social work and human service education and training.

## DIVERSITY: THEORY VERSUS PRACTICE

*Diversity*, a term frequently used in the helping professions, may be looked at from both a theory and a practice perspective. Many people are cognitively aware of differences between groups in terms of culture, ethnicity, language, race, religion, ancestry, or national origin. Diversity exists not only between and within groups, but also at the individual level. Individuals are made up of different characteristics that define their identity; for instance, gender, age, ethnicity, race, class, sexual orientation, abilities, ideologies, and political beliefs. Other dimensions of diversity include values, traditions, educational background, family status, language, appearance, group affiliation, and religion and spirituality. Every individual is a unique but complex diversity of characteristics. In sum, diversity encompasses the spectrum of observable and non-observable, tangible and intangible differences that shape or define personal and group experiences. Such conceptualization frames diversity as a social inclusion issue. Social inclusion entails the acceptance and validation of diversity as an integral part of society. Validating diversity helps to increase people's awareness of difference. In this chapter, the awareness that individuals, groups, and society have about the existence of differences is defined as the *theory of diversity*.

The theory of diversity focuses on the acknowledgment of differences that make a person or a group distinct and unique from another person or group. The theory entails the recognition of differences and similarities in the lived experiences, needs, concerns, and beliefs of people. "Diversity recognizes that there are similarities between persons that bind people together as part of our common humanity" (Lum, 2007, p. 44). Schriver (2001) has developed a fourfold typology that enhances understanding of the theory of diversity: (1) diversities and world views, (2) diversity within diversity, (3) multiple diversities, and (4) interrelatedness and interconnectedness of human beings.

According to Schriver (2001), diversities and world views represent the values and perspectives that shape the ideological beliefs and practices of an individual who is part of an ethnocultural group. Diversity within diversity refers to the shift from viewing the world in binary terms of Black and White people toward multiple racial realities of many diverse groups with diverse characteristics and qualities. According to this view, diversity exists within and between the ethnic groups and subgroups. The notion of multiple diversities suggests that individuals have multiple identities and may belong in multiple diverse groups simultaneously because of their ethnicity, gender, race, socioeconomic status, or sexual orientation. This interrelatedness and interconnectedness encourages a holistic approach that sees all elements of the environment. Diversity, by its very nature, calls for the inclusion of world views, mutual perspectives, interrelatedness, and interconnectedness (Schriver, 2001).

While the *theory* of diversity is fairly well known and is used in many different contexts, the *practice* of diversity has received only peripheral attention, particularly in social work, human services, and child and youth care training and education. There is little concrete information to guide the practice of diversity in multicultural societies such as Canada. This lack of attention is quite surprising in light of the identification of multiculturalism as the "fourth force" in the helping professions (Pedersen, 2000).

Pedersen (2000) and Shebib (2007) emphasize that multicultural practice is becoming increasingly important in counselling, alongside psychodynamic, humanistic, and behavioural perspectives. Multicultural practice has a profound impact on techniques used by social work, human service, and child care practitioners (Corey, Corey, & Corey, 2010). Increasing diversity in the twenty-first century challenges social work and human service students and practitioners to re-examine their methods of work and develop skills for delivering culturally responsive services (Fong, 2007; Shebib, 2007; Burnhill et al., 2009).

The paucity of scholarship on diversity practice suggests that not much exists in the way of guidelines for effective diversity practice. The absence of guidelines contributes to the inability of many students to translate the theoretical knowledge they discover about diversity into practice. How to practice diversity effectively in the field is the focus of this chapter. The chapter is organized around a number of themes, including the concepts of diversity, racism and discrimination, and antiracist and anti-oppressive practice. Other themes explored are the role of alliances in social change, equity policies, and the importance of student voices in diversity practice.

# DIVERSITY: A DEFINITION

The term *diversity* has evolved in social work and human services to convey the idea of difference among people on the basis of gender, ethnicity, race, culture, religion, language, sexual orientation, and other characteristics (Fong, 2007; Lum, 2007; Lee et al., 2009; Chappell, 2010). Diversity is a defining feature of all societies; there is hardly any society that can be described as completely homogeneous (Goldberg, 1994; Armit, 1997). For instance, there are about 50 different tribal, cultural, and linguistic groups with over 50 different languages among Aboriginal peoples in Canada (Chappell, 2010; Fleras, 2010). Similarly, differences exist in culture among Whites. Not all Black people share the same culture, either.

## Exercise

Create a list of what you believe to be the contributions of cultural diversity to Canada.

While diversity has always characterized human societies, contemporary society has witnessed it in complex forms, particularly in countries that have pursued active immigration policies as part of their nation-building projects (Danso, 2009). Canada, for instance, encompasses a rich complexity of diversity; there are over 200 different ethnocultural groups in Canada (Fleras, 2010). Today, the majority of immigrants admitted to Canada are "people of colour" — that is, immigrants from non-European countries. Perhaps, the single most important factor accounting for the sustained increase in ethnocultural diversity in Canada was the introduction of the Multiculturalism Policy in 1971. Canada accorded diversity official status with the promulgation of the *Multiculturalism Act* in 1988. Somehow, diversity constitutes a barometric measure for assessing the social health and viability of Canadian society. The mere mention of Canada commissions kaleidoscopic images of cultural diversity. Canada is, in fact, synonymous with diversity.

For many people, living and working in diverse communities is an enriching experience. However, there are others who perceive diversity negatively. Some people feel threatened or have difficulty interacting with individuals who are different from themselves (Appleby, Colon, & Hamilton, 2007). People who fear diversity see difference as a problem in itself as well as a source of social problems. Difference is not the problem, because there is nothing innate to difference that makes it a problem. Difference becomes a problem only when society construes it as such (Smith & Tudor, 2003). Construing diversity as a problem results in the oppression and exclusion of groups considered "outsiders" (Danso, 2009). Canadian social work and human service practitioners have an obligation to dispel misconceptions about diversity.

---

**Discussion Questions**

1. Defend the argument that diversity is not the cause of social problems in Canada.

2. What concrete steps can be taken to dispel myths and misconceptions about diversity in Canada?

---

# DIVERSITY AND THE SOCIAL WORK CODE OF ETHICS

Upholding diversity is among the core principles of social and human service work. The Code of Ethics of the Canadian Association of Social Workers encourages social workers to desist from discriminating against any person on the basis of her or his identity or membership in a social group (CASW, 2005a). Besides, social workers should demonstrate awareness and sensitivity to cultural differences in their practice. Diversity practice principles enshrined in the Code of Ethics challenge social workers to do the following:

- Strive to understand culture and its functions on human behaviour and society, recognizing the strengths that exist in all cultures.
- Acknowledge the diversity within and among individuals, communities, and cultures.
- Acknowledge and respect the impact that their heritage, values, beliefs, and preferences can have on their practice and on clients whose background and values are different from their own.
- Seek a working knowledge and understanding of clients' racial and cultural affiliations, identities, values, beliefs, and customs.
- Provide or secure, wherever possible, social work services in the language chosen by the client. If using an interpreter, social workers should, preferentially, secure an independent and qualified professional interpreter (CASW, 2005a).

Overall, the Code of Ethics encourages social workers to recognize and respect the diversity of Canadian society, taking into consideration the spectrum of differences that exist among individuals, families, groups, and communities (Shebib, 2007). These ethical guidelines highlight the need for social workers to actively engage in learning about other cultures to increase their sensitivity and awareness of how their values, beliefs, and ideologies affect their perceptions and their way of relating to others (CASW, 2005a).

# SOCIAL WORK AND HUMAN SERVICE THEORY IN DIVERSITY PRACTICE

Theory shapes the content and process of good social work and human work practice (Murphy & Dillon, 2008; Levitt & Bray, 2010). The integration of theory into practice is an indispensable aspect of effective diversity practice. Without this integration, students may find it difficult to comprehend the utility of the theories and methods learned in the classroom or how to apply them in professional practice (Bogo & Vayda, 1998; Dettlaff & Wallace, 2003). Effective practitioners "draw on research theory and experience as guides in determining which skills and procedures will best meet their clients' needs" (Shebib, 2007, p. 5). Yet strictly adhering to theory will most likely not help many ethnic-minority clients. In certain circumstances, effective use of judgment might produce better client outcomes than stubborn adherence to a particular theory (Pendry, Driscoll, & Field, 2007). Practitioners need to acknowledge that what works well in theory does not always work well in practice.

Traditional social work and human service theory is mostly White, male, Eurocentric, and middle class in origin and practice (Chang, Hays, & Shoffner, 2004; Shebib, 2007; Hays & Gray, 2010). Although social work and human service practice at any level is by definition cross-cultural (Pederson, 2001; Hays & Gray, 2010), many Western-trained social work and human service practitioners adopt one-size-fits-all approaches instead of approaches that respect cultural diversity. Western values may not be congruent for clients from different ethnoracial backgrounds (Hays & Gray, 2010). Social work and human service practitioners may be implementing techniques and interventions that conflict with clients' values and world views. Therefore, social work and human service practitioners must exercise caution when applying Western-based theories with racialized clients.

Culture "provides the essential context for understanding and responding to clients" (Shebib, 2007, p. 293). Understanding how cultural practices and values influence client behaviour and world view is therefore imperative. Some cultures hold fatalistic beliefs (Shebib, 2007; Samovar, Porter, & McDaniel, 2010). Clients with such beliefs usually attribute events in life to luck or fate; they believe that they do not have control over circumstances in their lives. Similarly, Western cultures emphasize the importance of eye contact in conversation. Many Western social workers use this theoretical technique in practice, and they expect clients from non-Western cultures to maintain eye contact. However, keeping eye contact is considered disrespectful in many non-Western cultures. Because of the Western emphasis on individualism and expression of feelings, and because of a lack of awareness of how diverse cultures influence behaviours, Western practice techniques may not be effective for most racialized clients (Neukrug, 2007; Hays & Gray, 2010).

Research shows that many traditional social work and human service practice approaches are not effective, and are sometimes even harmful, when used among racial-minority clients (Shebib, 2007). These approaches may create psychological harm and compel clients to terminate counselling more quickly than previously planned (Shebib, 2007; Hays & Gray, 2010). Research reported by Capuzzi and Gross (2001) found that racialized clients often avoid seeking help from mainstream counselling agencies unless it is unavoidable for them to do so. Moreover, they do not experience positive client outcomes if they perceive a counselling experience as "intrusive, objectifying, and dehumanizing" (Capuzzi & Gross, 2001, p. 417).

Just knowing what theoretical techniques to use in practice is not enough; when and how to use them are equally important in producing positive client outcomes. The decision or need to use a particular theoretical tool should be done with caution; it must take into consideration individual differences, since every individual represents diversity within her or his own cultural mix (Lum, 2007; Shebib, 2007).

## RACISM AND DISCRIMINATION

Racial differences and the salience of race must be acknowledged early in diversity practice to facilitate practitioners' ability to build trust (Shebib, 2007). Social work and human service practitioners have an ethical and professional responsibility to challenge acts of racial discrimination and social injustice any time they witness them. This responsibility requires practitioners to develop greater awareness of the manifestations of racism and discrimination in Canadian society. Awareness helps to develop skills for responding effectively to racist situations, and also creates conditions for educating people about the contribution of diversity to Canada. Awareness provides the tools diversity practitioners need for creating social change. Creating awareness about difference can help practitioners play two critical roles: initiators and catalysts.

*Initiators* are people who originate a change process; initiators can be individuals or a group (Danso, 2010). Practicum students can start a change process if they observe that a particular policy at their practicum agency is discriminatory against a client group. Similarly, students can initiate an advocacy process to implement a new program for a group not being served by the agencies within the community.

*Catalysts* are also agents of social change. However, unlike initiators, catalysts do not begin a change process; they accelerate the process. The term *catalyst* is not being used in the chemistry sense of a substance that precipitates an action without undergoing change itself. Rather, the term is used to denote the transformative role practitioners can play in the social change process. Change is a powerful dynamic, and agents of social transformation affect (change) and are affected by (changed) any change process (Danso, 2010). Without undergoing the change they seek to create, practitioners can contribute to entrenching the oppressive status quo; they become oppressors themselves. Failure to confront racism or discrimination can contribute to the perpetuation of social injustice and the oppression of racialized groups. Denying the existence or trivializing the impact of racism on racialized clients can cause further subjugation and instill a sense of suspicion.

**Discussion Question**

1. Some writers (e.g., Foster, 2005) claim that race is quickly losing its significance in Canada and that Canada has entered a "post-race" era where race does not matter anymore. Explain why you agree or disagree with this view. What evidence can you use to support your answer?

For many people, racism continues to be a major social problem in Canada that must be addressed. Supporters of this view argue that Canada is inherently racist in design, with a thin veneer of politeness and "tolerance that camouflages a pervasive white superiority complex" (Fleras, 2010, p. 51). Racial profiling, over-policing, unemployment, and poverty among people of colour, and the absence or under-representation of racialized bodies in elected positions, are examples of racial discrimination in Canada (Galabuzi, 2006; Tator & Henry, 2006; Curtis, Grabb, Perks, & Chui, 2009; Danso, 2009; Tanovich, 2009; Fleras, 2010; Henry & Tator, 2010). As far as racism is concerned, Canada still has some distance to go to eliminate the problem.

Racism can be tackled in many different ways. One approach is to take immediate steps to speak against acts of racial discrimination whenever they occur. To determine whether a comment or behaviour was racist, the context within which the event occurred should be carefully examined. Context is important because oftentimes what appears to be a racist situation may not actually be so. Since racism is a contentious and chameleonic issue, one needs to exercise care and tact when confronting, or when confronted with, racial bias. Critical thinking and sound situational assessment skills will help the diversity practitioner respond effectively to racism and discrimination. For instance, rather than reacting negatively or rashly to a racist behaviour, the practitioner could ask the individual involved for an explanation for her or his comments or action. Without being confrontational, the practitioner could tell the individual how the comment made her or him feel, or how it could affect members of racialized communities. Taking a proactive and constructive approach can diffuse a racially infused situation.

## CASE SCENARIO

A group of people are waiting for a public transit (TTC) bus at a subway station in Toronto. "No Smoking" signs are displayed at the station. Occasionally, an announcement will come over the public address system reminding patrons that "Smoking is not allowed anywhere on TTC property." Despite the reminders and the No Smoking signs, a White individual starts to smoke. The following exchange takes place between him and a Black individual.

*Black person:*     Sir, could you please put out the cigarette since the smoke is being blown in my direction? I am very allergic to smoke. The sign on the wall also says this is a no-smoking area.

*White person:*     Go back to your country!

## Questions

1. Assess the situation, and determine whether racism was manifested. Describe how you made your determination.

2. How would you have responded if you were the Black person?

# ANTIDISCRIMINATION AND ANTIRACIST PERSPECTIVES

Antidiscrimination and antiracist approaches focus on structural problems. The objectives of these approaches are not simply to eliminate racism or discrimination; they strive to create a new society based on respecting and embracing diversity as an indispensable part of human existence (Schimtz, Stakeman, & Sisneros, 2001). According to Fleras (2010), antidiscrimination and antiracist discourses seek to help people live with differences without sacrificing equality. Antiracist and antidiscrimination discourses emphasize the need to treat people fairly, including removing barriers to access to resources and opportunities for self-advancement. Because of differences in people's experiences, social status, education, and so forth, people cannot expect to be the same or equal. However, people can and must be treated fairly, for instance, by being given the opportunity to compete on merit. Diversity practitioners are obliged to advocate for social justice and inclusion through the implementation of equity policies.

Effective antidiscrimination and antiracist practice should link the personal, cultural, and structural levels of analysis of social issues (Payne, 2005; Thompson, 2006). At the personal level, practice interventions should focus on interpersonal relationships, and personal or psychological feelings, attitudes, and actions among people (Payne, 2005). Personal-level relationships happen within a cultural context, which influences and forms individual thought and action. Individuals are located within a cultural community that shares a set of beliefs, values, traditions, and practices that differentiate them from other groups.

The cultural context refers to how a collective generally thinks, feels, and acts, as well as the group's cultural norms. Socialization processes enable group members to learn, acquire, and internalize cultural values, norms, and traditions the group establishes.

The personal and cultural levels are embedded in a structural level, "which form an established social order and a set of accepted social divisions" (Payne, 2005, p. 279). The social order and the institutions a group establishes, alongside the cultural norms and assumptions and personal behaviour that result, come from acceptance of the social order and its divisions. Sound knowledge of how the personal, cultural, and structural levels interact and respond to one another is important for developing responsive intervention techniques for social change.

Antiracist and antidiscrimination frameworks are strongly recommended to diversity and social justice practitioners precisely because they hold great promise for retaining the focus of diversity practice. Antiracist and antidiscrimination frameworks help social and human service practitioners better understand social problems as an outgrowth of oppressive social structures, policies, and practices (Mullaly, 2007).

---

### Exercise

Develop a plan for a one-day antihomophobia workshop at a school campus.

1. Besides the theme, outline the specific topics to be covered in the workshop.
2. Describe how the workshop will be delivered. Who will be the facilitators, speakers, and participants?
3. Explain how the workshop will help students deal with homophobia at their school.

---

## Anti-Oppressive Practice

Structural problems require structural solutions. One structural framework for addressing social problems is anti-oppressive practice (AOP). AOP encompasses a variety of perspectives and models of social work and human service that emerged in the 1980s and 1990s (Healy, 2005; Payne, 2005). A key assumption of anti-oppressive theory is that oppression exists in multiple forms and no oppression is less or more important than another. Because oppression is structural in nature and exists in multiple forms, it is best addressed by using an integrated framework (Danso, 2010). A widowed senior denied access to employment may be facing ageism and sexism. When working with such a client, the strategies the practitioner adopts should be able to address the two forms of oppression simultaneously.

AOP frameworks are based on five core practice principles: (1) critical self-reflection; (2) critical assessment of clients' experiences with oppression; (3) empowering service users; (4) working in partnership, and (5) minimal intervention (Healy, 2005).

Critical self-reflection requires practitioners to conduct deep soul-searching to examine how their personal biographies and the "baggage of biases" they carry might influence their work with clients. Self-examination helps to reduce power imbalances between workers and clients.

Critical assessment encourages workers to identify the different kinds of oppression their clients are subjected to because of their identity (Healy, 2005). The AOP assessment process should draw practitioners' attention to a critical examination of how prevailing ideologies affect agency policies as well as the distribution of resources.

AOP seeks to empower clients to overcome the personal, systemic, and structural barriers that have control over their lives (Thompson, 2006). Empowering clients can be done at the interpersonal, institutional, and structural levels.

At the interpersonal level, practitioners should support clients to share their experiences with events or situations that disempower them. Practitioners should help clients understand how systemic and institutional injustices contribute to the oppression they face. As Mullaly (2007) suggests, social structures are often the source of social problems, which can worsen the issues facing individuals.

Empowerment at the institutional level typically involves changing the organization and delivery of social services to enhance AOP and client control. This change may entail introducing a new policy to ease or increase access to services for a particular client group. Similarly, it could mean changing an agency's hiring practices.

At the structural level, practitioners work toward transformative changes to existing socio-political structures such that they produce more just and equitable allocation of opportunities, resources, and social power (Healy, 2005; Payne, 2005). Social work and human service students can play an important role in this regard. Practicum students can encourage members of the community to write letters, organize demonstrations, or talk directly to their city councillors if the city decides to eliminate subsidies for daycare centres, for example. Students can help clients write the letters or, acting as a broker, direct the clients to resources within the community.

Working in partnership requires AOP workers to involve clients in decision-making processes. Clients know themselves and their presenting problem better than practitioners. In general, diversity practitioners rely on their skills, training, and experience to help clients deal with their problems, but that does not make them more knowledgeable about clients' issues than the clients themselves.

In partnering with clients, practitioners should avoid the trap of appropriating clients' contribution in the change process as if it was practitioners' original contribution or idea (Wilson & Beresford, 2000; Healy, 2005). Many helping professionals ignore the role clients play in the working relationship (Wilson & Beresford, 2000). Often, practitioners assume the expert position and may also use information provided by the client without acknowledging the client as the original source. Honesty and authenticity must be defining characteristics of the practitioner–client relationship. Valuing clients and their culture and choosing interventions that are similar to clients' cultural norms and values will promote meaningful partnerships (Danso, 2009).

The principle of minimal intervention requires service providers to adopt helping techniques that are the least intrusive or oppressive (Payne, 2005). Minimal intervention could be achieved in several ways. For instance, when working with teenage or first-time mothers, attention could be focused more on increasing their access to services, such as literacy and education services, to address long-term barriers to social and economic participation rather than honing in on parenting needs (Healy, 2005). Figure 9.1 outlines general guidelines for critical anti-oppressive social work and human service practice.

**Figure 9.1** Guidelines for Critical Anti-Oppressive Practice

1. Take appropriate steps to address an oppressive situation; for instance, do not let a homophobic comment go unchallenged.

2. Be proactive in challenging oppressive policies or service delivery methods. Ensure that policies that ought to be in place are implemented.

3. Acknowledge oppression as a complex, structural issue that interacts with other forms of oppression and manifests in different ways.

4. Address clients presenting issues holistically by situating them within a wider societal context to better understand the causes and manifestations of oppression.

5. Avoid falling into the "blame the victim" trap by attributing clients' problems to personal failures or deficiencies. Social problems have their roots in defective social structures and institutions, as well as social relations that marginalize and exclude subordinate groups.

6. Do not assume the expert role when working with clients. Respect that clients are more knowledgeable about their own issues than the worker.

7. Avoid perpetuating the oppressive status quo by actively pursuing social change. Be prepared to be personally affected by the change being sought.

8. Engage in social change as either an initiator or a facilitator; create change by starting or helping to accelerate the process. Do not always wait for consensus or unanimous decision to initiate change; act whenever there is a need to do so.

9. Create alliances and coalitions with both oppressed and privileged groups to bring about meaningful change. Allies are found on both sides of the oppression divide.

10. Use multicultural strategies to create social change, recognizing that every individual is a unique cultural mix.

11. Empower clients by acknowledging and privileging their voices and contributions to the change process. Work *with* rather than *for* clients.

12. Advocate for fair distribution and access to power, as all social relations are power relations. Inequities in access to power are the root cause of oppressions.

13. Gain a clearer understanding of the change being sought before acting. Specify the target of change, the resources needed, and strategies for achieving desired goals.

14. Develop a clear plan of action, including benchmarks and evaluation strategies, for the change process.

15. Acknowledge that the change process can be slow, challenging, and frustrating at times. However, determination, perseverance, and a clear sense of vision and purpose will produce positive outcomes.

16. Adapt strategies for change to suit the conditions or context within which the change is expected to occur. Change strategies should be self-sustaining and malleable to modification.

17. Ask whenever in doubt about a particular issue; assumptions can be wrong and negative in their consequences.

18. Use language that is inclusive and empowering; language is never politically neutral.

19. Promote attitudes, perceptions, relations, and practices that celebrate diversity instead of using difference as a basis for discrimination or exclusion.

20. Advocate for the incorporation and implementation of diversity courses and training programs at all levels of the educational system.

# ETHNICALLY SENSITIVE PRACTICE

Social work and human services work is committed to professional practice that is responsive to differences among people and is ethnically sensitive to clients' needs (Appleby et al., 2007). Sensitivity to and respect for cultural differences is foundational to effective diversity practice. Yet it is not always easy to practice diversity or deliver ethnically sensitive human services to clients (Lum, 2007). Challenges arise partly because people tend to have different cultural needs and perceptions about difference (Schmitz et al., 2001). Many people respond to diversity issues out of unquestioned beliefs, "received wisdom," or even anger or guilt.

For positive client outcomes, social work and human service practitioners must demonstrate cultural competence (Teasley, 2005; Weaver, 2005; Williams, 2006). Being culturally competent implies a commitment to diversity as well as recognition, respect, and affirmation of the value and worth of individuals, families, and communities (Gallegos, Tindall, & Gallegos, 2008). To emphasize the need for culturally competent practice, accredited social work and human service programs are mandated to incorporate standards regarding diversity, populations at risk, and social justice (Council on Social Work Education, 2006). As noted, the Code of Ethics of the Canadian Association of Social Workers encourages Canadian social workers to demonstrate commitment to diversity issues and culturally appropriate practice (CASW, 2005a).

## CASE SCENARIO

A White child-protection worker in Montreal investigated a case of child abuse and apprehended the three children in a family that had recently immigrated to Canada from Ghana. Neither parent speaks French or English well.

### Questions

1.  What factors should the worker have considered before apprehending the children? How will foster parenting affect the children? What skills or competencies did the worker demonstrate or fail to demonstrate in this case?
2.  If you were a diversity worker from Ghana, what suggestions would you give the child protection worker about working with immigrant clients from Ghana?

The importance of cultural competence in diversity practice cannot be overemphasized. However, practitioners must guard against seeing multicultural practice as something that is totally separate from "regular" practice. The concepts of cultural safety and intersectionality recognize social location from the perspective of the client or service user. Cultural safety is a useful framework and tool in working with diverse groups, including Indigenous and racialized groups in Canada. Suggested readings on cultural safety can be found in Chapter 8 of this book.

## Exercise

Develop a set of guidelines for ethnically sensitive practice for (a) health care providers at a community clinic, and (b) child and youth care workers in a group home serving diverse youth. Include specific steps for implementing each set of guidelines.

# ALLIES AND SOCIAL CHANGE

A primary goal of social work and human service training and education is to create change. Social work and human service practitioners should therefore engage people from different groups to work toward dismantling systems of oppression. Engaging groups can involve working with practitioners from other disciplines (Gibson, 2010). Allies are needed precisely because no one profession or discipline has all the tools to end social oppression or promote diversity by itself.

Hardiman, Jackson, and Griffin (2007) describe allies as members of an "advantaged group who act against the oppression(s) from which they derive their power, privilege, and acceptance" (p. 47). According to Hardiman and colleagues (2007), allies reject the dominant ideology and take action against oppression out of a conviction that eliminating social oppression benefits both advantaged and disadvantaged groups. Although allies may have different motivations for their actions, they play an important role as agents of social change, working with other privileged group members or in coalition with targeted group members to challenge systems of oppression. This role is an essential aspect of eliminating inequality and injustice. Being allies in the struggle to end oppression is one of the most important things members of both oppressor and oppressed groups can do (Kivel, 2007). According to Sisneros and colleagues (2008), coalitions and alliances are the bedrock of meaningful social change. Whether acting as initiators or catalysts, students can learn to be proactive in creating alliances with other helping professionals.

Learning and unlearning are crucial steps in becoming an effective ally in social change. *Learning* means acquiring new knowledge, skills, and tools to enhance one's level of cultural competence. The process of *unlearning* involves undertaking critical self-examination to rid oneself of biases, prejudices, and stereotypes against people from different cultures. Critical self-examination facilitates the acceptance of social diversity; it is an unending process for diversity practitioners and students. This component of the reflective process is identified by using the integration of theory and practice loop referenced in Chapter 1.

For many people, becoming an ally is a simple decision to make (Bishop, 2002). What often proves quite formidable is actually taking the steps to become an ally. Because of the difficulty and pain involved — for instance, in having to relinquish a privileged status — many members of advantaged groups resist or fail to take the critical first step toward ending oppression.

## Exercise

Identify a group of people with whom you could become an ally. Develop the steps you would need to take to become an ally. What would be your goals and challenges?

Many strategies exist for forming alliances, including building support, establishing networks, and working with already established groups. Alliances with different groups can develop strategies by drawing on energies, differential insights, and diverse avenues to power of coalition members (Bell, 2007). Another important strategy for building alliances is to use the stories and lived experiences of minority groups as a means of, for instance, assessing the role and impact of social policies and practices that reinforce systems of oppression. Listening to members of oppressed groups and reflecting on their experiences with oppression can help social work and human service practitioners support the actions oppressed people take (Kivel, 2007).

## Exercise

Outline steps that members of both minority and majority groups can take to become allies in creating meaningful social change in Canada.

Giving credence to and learning from the narratives, analyses, and experiences of minority groups can help members of dominant groups obtain a better understanding of how oppression works and can also suggest more imaginative alternatives for socially just relationships and institutional partnerships (Bell, 2007; Kivel, 2007). For members of oppressed groups, bonding with other people dealing with the same oppression creates a deep level of sympathy and understanding, as well as a growing pride in one's discovered identity. It acts as a satisfying sense of shared language (Bishop, 2002). Bonding enables oppressed groups to share their experience and collaborate to deal with their problems (Rogowski, 2008).

Certainly, there is strength in numbers and no one group can ever end social oppression by itself. However, in seeking to effect change, one does not always have to have unanimous decision before acting. Consensus is a necessary but not a sufficient condition for social change. Historically, many a spark for social change was lit by individuals with vision, dedication, and perseverance. One differently abled individual initiated a change process that eventually forced the Toronto Transit Commission (TTC) to provide an automated announcement service for its clients. After an 11-year fight and a ruling by a human rights tribunal, the TTC has now installed an automated system that announces every stop on bus, subway, and streetcar routes (Canada Broadcasting Corporation, 2007; Ontario Human Rights Commission, 2008). Collective action may start with one person's desire to improve a situation.

Diversity practitioners have a responsibility to lobby or advocate for changes in individual- or institutional-level practices that ignore the needs and concerns of vulnerable groups. Practitioners must not deny or belittle the impact of oppression on minority populations. As practitioners work with disadvantaged groups to effect social change, they should avoid the trap of "knowing what is good for the client" (Bishop, 2007; Kivel, 2007). Oppressed people can determine their own needs and what is good for them.

# EQUITY POLICIES

"Doing" diversity goes beyond improving interpersonal and intergroup relations to include changing discriminatory policies and practices. Policies are an integral part of the social and institutional landscape of Canadian society; therefore, they affect people in profound ways. The types of social services developed and the modes of delivery, the funding available for social programs, or whether someone can receive financial support to be able to pursue post-secondary education are all determined by policy. It is therefore important to ensure that policies are fair for all people, especially minority groups. The advocacy role of social work and human service becomes particularly important in changing oppressive and discriminatory policies.

## CASE SCENARIO

Maxine, a recent bachelor of social work graduate, has just been offered a good-paying job as the diversity manager at Agency X in Brampton, Ontario. Maxine wants to impress her supervisor so she will be kept on after her three-month probation. Agency X claims to be an equal-opportunity employer; it has a nondiscrimination policy. It also claims to value diversity. Upon starting work, Maxine notices that the agency does not have kitchen or washroom facilities that are accessible to employees or clients who use wheelchairs.

### Questions

1.  How should Maxine consider Agency X's nondiscrimination policy in terms of her observation? What concrete steps should she take to ensure Agency X is truly committed to diversity and that its staff's welfare and client service policies are more inclusive?

2. Suppose Maxine expressed concerns about her observation to management but her concerns were downplayed. Management argues that there is no money to redesign the kitchen or washroom. What should Maxine do about the situation?

Practitioners can advocate for change if an agency's service implementation policies use only Western-based models or practice techniques, especially if the clientele is multicultural. The curriculum development policies of an educational institution with a diverse student population that teaches only a Euro-Canadian curriculum or uses pedagogical techniques based on Eurocentric models also need to be changed. Such policies will have a negative impact on the learning and training of students, especially "students of colour" and those from non-European or non-White backgrounds. The above examples raise questions about the agency's and the educational institution's hiring policies and practices. In both cases, there is an obvious disconnection between the mission and vision of the agency and the school and their respective hiring policies. A social work or human service practitioner at such an agency or educational institution ought to first draw attention to the discrepancies and then initiate steps to change or replace the discriminatory policies.

## Exercise

Identify policies in Canada that have a disempowering impact on minority groups (e.g. immigrant communities, urban Aboriginals, First Nations peoples, and sexual minorities).

Policies are usually developed by people who are least likely to be affected by them. As Mullaly (2007) suggests, policies are made to serve the needs and interests of the dominant group and to maintain its power. Thus, one would be hard-pressed to find an individual on social assistance who is also a policy-maker that develops social welfare policy. Not surprisingly, many policy-makers couldn't care less about the impact that the policies they develop, or fail to change, have on vulnerable populations (see McKenzie & Wharf, 2010).

## CASE SCENARIO

A student has just started his field placement training at a multi-service agency. During his orientation, the week before he started the practicum, he observed that all the workers in managerial and supervisory positions at the agency are members of one particular dominant group (group x) while the majority of the front-line workers are from minority groups. Like his placement supervisor, the student is a member of group x.

## Questions

1. What should be the student's initial reaction to what he observed? What conversation should the student have with his supervisor about his observation?

2. The student's placement is with the Social Inclusion and Diversity Management Department of the agency, and his learning contract requires him to help develop policies for the agency. What specific policy or policies that relate to the observation he made should the student develop or recommend? Why?

Awareness of diversity practice issues can help practicum students assist agencies in developing equity and diversity policies. Equity policies are indispensable because Canadian social work and human service practitioners work in an environment characterized by increasing levels of cultural diversity. Like service providers, service users come from diverse cultural backgrounds. For these reasons, both practitioners and agencies must ensure that services are delivered in a manner that respects cultural, ethnic, religious, and linguistic diversity. Well-developed advocacy skills and strategies will help practitioners accomplish this goal. Advocacy is indispensable in social work practice; in fact, all social work is, inherently, advocacy work (Ezell, 2001; Haynes & Mickelson, 2006).

## Discussion Question

1. Explain how a diversity student can apply the principles of diversity practice discussed in this chapter to develop an equity policy for a human service agency. Who should the student consult?

2. What issues should the student consider in developing such a policy?

## Voices from the Field

I always give students different reading materials on diversity. I tend to be focused; for instance, if I find that some White students are not sensitized to cultural diversity issues, I give them readings around those issues. My goal is to raise awareness among students, not necessarily to make the learning experience social work–oriented. I might have something about a Black feminist talking about males, for example. To me, it is all related, because if students are able to analyze issues, it would help them develop critical thinking and transferable skills.

Last year, I used bell hooks; the Black students loved it but for the White students, it went over their heads, which I found very interesting. You know, bell hooks is quite "in your face, and right on." I consistently use one of her chapters that talks about White supremacy. That term, *White supremacy*, is a trigger; I look for articles like bell hooks's that trigger and get people angry. What happens is funny because the White students become angry and then the Black students often sit back and say, "Join the club." This year, I was very clear when I interviewed students, alerting them that this is a place where they would be challenged a lot and that the issue of racism is discussed a lot.

I have come to realize the importance of seeing every student as a unique individual. I assess their needs carefully to better understand their views and understanding of difference and diversity issues. When students come for practicum, I take time to structure things and understand their learning goals. I identify their strengths and areas they need to improve upon. I then structure supervision in such a way that it creates a learning environment that creates opportunities for students to discover new learning about diversity issues and how they can improve on areas where they lack knowledge. (Kim Kidder, field instructor)

# Voices from the Field

I did my field practicum at Agency Y (pseudonym), a multi-service agency in Brampton, Ontario. Agency Y provides services to clients from many different cultures and backgrounds. The clients I worked with were mostly people of colour. Agency Y's policies emphasize fairness and respect for diversity. Workers are required to act professionally and ethically with clients. This case study outlines experiences and learning I discovered about diversity practice during my field training at Agency Y.

Exactly two weeks into my practicum, I witnessed a situation that I considered detrimental to client welfare. Some workers were disrespectful to clients; they also used derogatory and offensive language, including racist jokes and slurs. Much as I was shocked to witness the situation, I could not do anything about it. I thought that being a practicum student I would not be taken seriously even if I expressed concerns and reported the incident to my supervisor. In fact, my supervisor had not motivated me to report unprofessional or unethical conduct I would encounter. This dilemma was crystallized for me when no action was taken on a case of inappropriate behaviour a colleague and a client reported to my supervisor. Reflecting on the experiences later, I acknowledged that I had allowed fear to prevent me from doing the right thing. I learned an important lesson and promised myself not to repeat the mistake. Therefore, when, a few days later, I overheard a worker make a racist joke, I approached the worker and told her/him how the behaviour contravened the agency's policies. I also explained the psycho-emotional harm the comments could cause clients.

My field training at Agency Y was a rich learning experience for me. Besides conducting intake and assessment, I also counselled clients and taught them employment and job search skills. I also worked with clients in the Ontario Works program. The practicum afforded me an opportunity to discover first-hand knowledge and skills about multicultural social work practice. Working one-to-one with clients helped me learn more about different cultural values, beliefs, traditions, and practices. The hypothetical case scenarios I had role-played at school became more realistic and meaningful as I worked with clients from diverse cultures and socio-economic backgrounds. I now demonstrate better understanding of the needs and concerns of different clients, especially racialized peoples and "immigrants of colour." The training helped me develop effective diversity practice skills and techniques, including the need to always seek the interest of the client first and avoiding attitudes or behaviour that can oppress clients. This conviction challenges me to speak up against injustices and oppression and take necessary steps to confront or change a situation, behaviour, or comment that excludes minority-group members. Moreover, I have learned to be more proactive and take initiative to advocate on behalf of clients. Above all, I am capable of integrating the theoretical concepts, skills, and techniques I learned in the classroom in practice. In general, my knowledge and understanding of diversity practice issues has expanded considerably as a result of my field training at Agency Y. (Francisca Hamilton, student)

## CHAPTER SUMMARY

Diversity requires Canadian social work and human service practitioners to demonstrate cultural competence. Social service providers' ability to understand that every individual is a unique cultural mix enables them to develop skills for culturally competent practice in multicultural Canada. Merely appreciating or celebrating diversity is not enough; greater attention should be paid to effective diversity practice.

Racism and discrimination are part of the sociocultural landscape within which Canadian diversity professionals practice their trade. Racial discrimination is also part of the lived realities of racialized groups. Traditions die hard; therefore, racial ideologies and ethnocentric attitudes often make the work of diversity practitioners more difficult. Although significant improvements have occurred in recent years in the fight to dismantle racial oppression in Canada, much work remains to be accomplished. Laws now criminalize many of the blatantly racist policies and practices that were socially endorsed only a few years ago. Many methodological frameworks and practice tools are available to diversity workers to end racialized relations and transform oppressive social structures, institutions, and relations into egalitarian and empowering ones. These approaches include antiracist, antidiscrimination, and anti-oppressive frameworks.

Effective diversity practice is facilitated by forming alliances and coalitions. The need for alliances derives from the fact that no one profession can create social change all by itself. Individuals and groups can initiate a change process or help to speed it up; however, the fact remains that there is strength in numbers. Much more can be accomplished by a group in a shorter time and with fewer resources than a single individual could achieve. Alliances with members of both dominant and minority groups are necessary for positive social change.

Diversity practice must stretch beyond improving interpersonal or intergroup relations to include changing practices and decision-making processes that result in discriminatory policies. Since policies affect people's lives in profound ways, they must be fair. Diversity practitioners should advocate for the replacement of oppressive policies with equitable ones. Excluding service users and minority groups from policy decision-making processes only maintains the oppressive status quo, but the status quo must be changed. There is also a need to privilege students' voices, since they can be strong allies and a rich resource base for promoting effective diversity practice.

## Critical-Thinking Questions

1. Why are awareness of and sensitivity to cultural differences indispensable to effective social work and human service practice in Canada?

2. Based on the material presented in this chapter, discuss how diversity can be translated from an abstract, theoretical concept into concrete practice principles in the social work and human service fields.

3. Select one social (systemic) problem in Canada. Explain why it is a systemic problem. Next, discuss how you can apply each of the five core AOP principles outlined in this chapter to address the problem.

## Suggested Readings

Al-Krenawi, A., & Graham, J. R. (Eds.) (2003). *Multicultural social work in Canada: Working with diverse ethno-racial communities.* Toronto, ON: Oxford University Press.

Angelini, P. U. (Ed.) (2007). *Our society: Human diversity in Canada* (3rd ed.). Toronto, ON: Nelson.

Baines, D. (Ed.) (2007). *Doing anti-oppressive practice: Building transformative politicized social work.* Halifax, NS: Fernwood Publishing.

Carniol, B. (2005). *Case critical: Social services & social justice in Canada* (5th ed.). Toronto, ON: Between the Lines.

Dei, G., & Calliste, A. (Eds.) (2000). *Power, knowledge and anti-racism education: A critical reader.* Halifax, NS: Fernwood Publishing.

Dei, G., Karumanchery, L., & Karumanchery-Luke, N. (2004). *Playing the race card: Exposing white power and privilege.* New York, NY: Peter Lang.

Diller, J. V. (2011). *Cultural diversity: A primer for the human services* (4th ed.). Belmont, CA: Brooks/Cole, CENGAGE Learning.

Dominelli, L. (2002). *Anti-oppressive social work theory and practice.* New York, NY: Palgrave Macmillan.

Dominelli, L. (2004). "Crossing international divides: Language and communication within international settings." *Social Work Education, 23*(5), 515–525.

Furuto, S. B. C. L. (2004). "Theoretical perspectives for culturally competent practice with immigrant children and families." In Fong, R. (Ed.), *Culturally Competent Practice with Immigrant and Refugee Children and Families* (pp. 19–38). New York, NY: Guilford Press.

Harrison, G. (2006). "Broadening the conceptual lens on language in social work: Difference, diversity and English as a global language." *British Journal of Social Work* 36, 401–418.

Hicks, S. (2006). *Social work in Canada: An introduction* (2nd ed.). Toronto, ON: Thompson Educational Publishing.

Hier, S. P., & Bolaria, B. S. (Eds.) (2007). *Race and racism in 21st-century Canada: Continuity, complexity, and change*. Peterborough, ON: Broadview Press.

Ingraham, C. L. (2000). "Consultation through a multicultural lens: Multicultural and cross-cultural consultation in schools." *School Psychology Review*, 29(3): 320–343.

James, C. E., & Shadd, A. (Eds.) (2001). *Talking about identity: Encounters in race, ethnicity, and language*. Toronto, ON: Between the Lines.

Kornbeck, J. (2001). "Language training for prospective and practising social workers: A neglected topic in social work literature." *British Journal of Social Work*, 31(2), 307–316.

Newman, P., Bogo, M., & Daley, A. (2008). "Self-disclosure of sexual orientation in social work field education: Field instructor and lesbian and gay student perspectives." *The Clinical Supervisor* 27(2), 215–237.

Razack, N. (2002). *Transforming the field: Critical anti-racism and anti-oppression perspectives for the human services practicum*. Halifax, NS: Fernwood Publishing.

Wallis, M. A., Sunseri, L., & Galabuzi, G-E. (Eds.). (2009). *Colonialism and racism in Canada: Historical traces and contemporary issues* (pp. 288–306). Toronto, ON: Nelson Education.

## Relevant Websites

### Canadian Centre on Disability Studies
www.disabilitystudies.ca
At this site, students can learn more about what this consumer-directed, university-affiliated centre is doing to create public awareness about disability issues through research, education, and information dissemination. Through its activities, the Centre promotes full and equal participation of people with disabilities in all aspects of society, locally, nationally, and internationally.

### Canadian Council for Refugees
www.ccrweb.ca
At this site, students can learn more about what this national human rights organization is doing to promote the rights and protection of refugees in Canada and around the world, and to help the settlement of refugees and immigrants in Canada.

### Canadian Heritage
www.pch.gc.ca
At this Government of Canada site, students can learn more about what this federal department is doing to foster cultural participation, active citizenship, and participation in Canada's civic life and to strengthen connections among Canadians. The department's Human Rights Program helps to promote the development, understanding, respect for, and enjoyment of human rights in Canada.

### Canadian Race Relations Foundation (CRRF)
www.crr.ca
At this site, students can learn more about what this federally created human rights organization is doing to foster racial harmony and cross-cultural understanding and help eliminate racism in Canada.

### Centre for Social Justice
www.socialjustice.org

At this site, students can learn more about what this advocacy-oriented organization is doing to strengthen movements for social justice in Toronto and globally. The Centre conducts research, education, and advocacy in pursuit of greater equality, democracy, and the enhancement of peace and human security.

## Child Care Advocacy Association of Canada

www.ccaac.ca

At this website, students can learn more about what this human rights organization is doing to ensure the right of all Canadian children to access a publicly funded, inclusive, quality, non-profit child care system.

## Council of Canadians with Disabilities (CCD)

www.ccdonline.ca

Students can learn more at this site about what this national human rights organization is doing to encourage accessibility and inclusivity in Canada. CCD seeks to achieve its mission through law reform, litigation, public education, and dialogue with key decision makers.

## DiversityWatch

www.diversitywatch.ryerson.ca

At this Ryerson University site, students can learn more about how online journalism is being used to increase awareness of the role ignorance plays in creating and perpetuating stereotypical coverage of racialized and religious communities in the Canadian media. The site offers practical help to assist journalists who want to achieve better coverage of diversity.

# Chapter 10

## International Field Placements: New Practices for the Twenty-First Century

Julie Drolet

## Chapter Objectives

- Describe connections and links between local and global levels of practice.
- Demonstrate self-awareness of personal values.
- State motivations for pursuing an international practicum.
- Describe international instruments and international organizations of relevance for international social development.
- Discuss critical issues and recent trends in international field placements.
- Describe the integrated and social development perspectives.

## CONTEXT OF GLOBALIZATION AND INTERNATIONALISM

In the twenty-first century, students have international practicum options in field agencies around the world. For this reason, it is increasingly important for social work and other human service professionals — whether involved in international or local activity — to equip themselves with knowledge of global events and processes and cross-cultural issues (Lyons, Manion, & Carlsen, 2006). Recent international events and the development of new technologies (such as the Internet and cellphones) have changed the way we communicate and share information. *Globalization* is a term used to describe the integration of economies through the exchange of goods and services, capital, people (labour), and knowledge (technology; Paredes et al., 2008). "The revolution in communications, the ability to travel readily to remote parts of the world, the increasing cultural diversity of national populations, enhanced global trade and economic activities as well as greater international political cooperation, have all fostered the globalization of the human experience (Midgley, 2001, p. 22). Beyond a doubt, globalization has facilitated the internationalization of social problems (Dominelli, 2004). Dominelli (2004) explains that globalization is a crucial contemporary context of practice. It has challenged the local nature of social and human service work and has encouraged practitioners to think about international dimensions in a more systematic and organized way (Dominelli, 2004).

It is hard to imagine a career in social work or human services that does not involve practice or problem situations with an international dimension. For example, climate change is now recognized as a significant environmental, social, cultural, and economic threat facing humankind. Rising sea levels, heat waves, and drought occurrences, as well as increased extreme precipitation events, have the potential to dramatically alter our quality of life. Preparing for practice means that we must acquire knowledge and understanding beyond what is currently required. Many social issues and conditions, such as environmental problems, global health, international migration, unemployment, food security, and poverty, require our immediate attention and action. Our international involvement is inevitable, and we face the challenge of how to make the world a better place. Whether working locally or internationally, it is imperative to have a broad understanding of the global context within which all practice occurs. We need to think beyond our borders. In the global context, students are increasingly demanding training and practice experience that prepares them to meet these conditions.

---

### Discussion Question

1.  How can you counteract the negative effects of globalization in your practicum?

---

Many schools offer opportunities for students to complete their practicum in international settings. Research on international field placements suggests they can be powerful learning tools that invite student learners to confront different views of human behaviour, to learn different systems of social welfare, and to see different ways to remediate social problems (Dominelli, 2003; Healy, 2001).

## Internationalism

For over a century, internationalism has been a prominent theme, and many pioneering social workers, such as Jane Addams in the United States, Alice Masaryk of Czechoslovakia, and Alice Salomon of Germany, have championed the causes of peace, war relief, human rights, and international avenues for dispute resolution (Hegar, 2008). Internationalism is also understood as an ideology that advocates greater international cooperation (Midgley, 2001). Many internationalists favour the replacement of national governments by some form of global governance that will enhance cooperation between peoples of different cultures and end international conflicts (Midgley, 2001).

Over a century ago, the social work and human service professions emerged in Western Europe and North America (i.e., the Global North) in response to the social problems of poverty and industrial capitalist development (Bradshaw & Graham, 2007). Formal social work education originated and developed as a full-fledged profession in the West. During the middle twentieth century, social work education expanded to other non-Western countries in an imperialistic fashion with the assumption that Western social work knowledge, mainly North American and British, was universal and transferable (Kreitzer, 2005). For example, social work and human service educational programs from the Global North spread to Hong Kong, India, and Egypt (i.e., the Global South) in the 1920s and 1930s (Bradshaw & Graham, 2007). The growth of the professions, particularly after World War II, is widely described as a post-colonial transmission of Northern (Western European and North American) approaches to practice, education, and research. Many countries adopted these practice approaches without cultural adaptation. Despite this development, practitioners, clients, and communities have tended to hold localized or Indigenous norms, values, and world views despite the prevailing Western origins of social work in the early twentieth century (Bradshaw & Graham, 2007). By and large, the Western education pattern remains in most parts of the world, though each country has added its own unique features to its education and practice models. There is a need to indigenize social work and human service education in accordance with varied country contexts (Cox & Piwar, 2006).

Not surprisingly, a number of debates related to the tensions between culturally based values versus universal approaches to social work and human service continue to engage the field of international social work and human service. Social workers engaged in international activities reflect more critically on the relevance of Western social work and human service to the cultural, economic, and social realities of other societies. Much of the discussion is focused on the developing countries of the Global South, which are characterized by a high degree of cultural diversity and by pressing problems of poverty and deprivation (Midgely, 2001).

## Post-Colonialism

*Post-colonialism* refers to the ways in which the domination of colonies by Western colonial countries did not disappear with the passing of European empires between 1950 and 1970 (Askeland & Payne, 2006). However, post-colonialism is not only limited to former colonies, but also describes identities, attitudes, and practices that affect a much broader area. For example, post-colonial practices manifest between powerful and powerless cultures and between majority and minority language groups everywhere (Askeland & Payne, 2006)

## Hegemony

Hegemony is the use of cultural and social relations to impose or maintain power (Askeland & Payne, 2006). Often, the hegemony of Western knowledge is shown to have influenced — and continues to influence — global knowledge production (Kreitzer, 2005). In this context, Indigenous knowledge, for the most part, is deemed primitive and unimportant (Kreitzer, 2005). This hegemony is seen in the historical domination of Western social work and human service knowledge worldwide and can be traced back to the colonial era.

## Localization

*Localization* and *indigenization* are terms that broadly refer to the process of making something relevant to the social realities of local contexts (Bradshaw & Graham, 2007). The localization of social work and human service education, research, and practice is a recognized area of interest that enjoys support from a number of social work and human service scholars and practitioners (Bradshaw & Graham, 2007). The need for, and development of, culturally localized responses to social problems is increasingly recognized as an imperative for social work and human service practice and scholarship (Healy, 2001). The words *indigenized* or *indigenization* are not to be confused with adaptations associated with Indigenous peoples; some authors apply the term *indigenize* to social work and human service work with non-Indigenous communities, while others use it to describe only work with Indigenous peoples (Bradshaw & Graham, 2007). For these reasons, many prefer the term *localization* (AI-Krenawi & Graham, 2003). Localization is considered to be the pattern of education, practice, research, and/or social service delivery that is adopted or adapted from one culture to another because of differing social or religious attitudes that affect the definition of social problems and their solutions (Walton & Abo-EI-Nasr, 1988).

## CRITICAL GLOBAL NORTH/GLOBAL SOUTH ISSUES

In Canada, most international placements are undertaken by Canadian students going to the "developing world," or Global South (Razack, 2002a; Alphonse, 2008). Power imbalances between nations and the one-way flow of students from North to South is an issue that is receiving critical examination. While greater attempts are being made to develop reciprocal or mutual student exchanges, there is a need to further explore the components of reciprocity in field education between post-secondary institutions and between field agencies.

---

### Discussion Question

1.  Considering the global context of international learning, what can you do as a practicum student to promote reciprocity?

---

How can an international practicum take into account North–South power relations characterized by a history of colonialism, imperialism, and Western hegemony? It is important to provide students with an opportunity to critically examine their motivations for undertaking an international field placement before they embark on their travels (Wehbi, 2009). Heron (2005) offers a critical discussion of international placements in sub-Saharan Africa by pointing to the need to integrate an analysis of globalization and colonialism in the debriefing sessions offered to returning students. A framework must be provided to allow students to make sense of their experiences upon return.

## CASE SCENARIO

Sarah is a fourth-year social work student interested in pursuing an international practicum. She advises her field education coordinator that she wants to go to a developing country to make a difference and help others. She says that she is a people person who has logged many hours of volunteer experience working at the local food bank. She wants to challenge herself by going overseas and having a life-changing experience. Sarah is concerned about the growing disparities in the world. She wants to experience a different lifestyle and share her knowledge and skills. Sarah hopes to learn to work and interact with groups that are culturally, ethnically, and racially different from her.

### Questions

1. Do you agree with Sarah's motivations for wanting to undertake an international practicum?

2. What are the critically important issues for Sarah to consider for her practicum?

Many international education initiatives are underway in Canada. Canadian organizations such as CIDA (Canadian International Development Agency) offer volunteer internship opportunities, including international field placements. Often international programs that bring Canadians to other countries do not discuss critical debates and issues that could result in professional exchanges (Razack, 2002a). Razack (2002a) states that international exchanges involving efforts to learn and glean from the "other" may be seen as a colonizing activity. Many students believe they are going overseas "to help others" as opposed to learning through their international placement experience about the Global North's role in perpetuating oppressive North–South relations. It is important for educators to understand students' reasons and motivations for wanting to participate in an international practicum in order to promote anti-imperialist values and principles.

### Exercise

Think about your personal and professional interests in pursuing an international practicum. Write a short paper on your motivations.

# An Integrated Perspective of Social Development

Cox and Pawar (2006) advocated for the use of an integrated perspective in international social work and human service. This perspective offers a comprehensive and useful approach for understanding global situations that adversely affect millions of people, incorporating global, human rights, ecological, and social development perspectives.

**Social Development Perspective** The goals of international social development are to promote people's well-being or quality of life, and to enable people to satisfy their aspirations and realize their potential. The values of practitioners and students adopting a social development perspective include respect for people and a belief in their capacity to grow and develop; a holistic understanding of human existence (physical, mental, emotional, and spiritual); acceptance of social and cultural pluralism, and the centrality of people's cultures and values; acknowledgment of the importance of ecological issues and people's links with nature and their environment; and acknowledgment that social relations are based on the right and obligation to participation, equality of opportunity, and social justice and human rights. Both a participatory process and an empowering process underpin the social development perspective.

---

## Discussion Question

1. What is the role of Canadian practicum students in promoting human rights and social justice during their field placements?

---

A number of strategies at the local, national, and international levels figure into the social development perspective, such as building the capacity of individuals, groups, and communities; encouraging local institutions and support for people's organizations; fostering self-reliance, creating an enabling environment within which all people can develop; participating in the development and functioning of social institutions; promoting the provision of adequate resources and services accessible to all; promoting a proactive role for the state in supporting participatory planning; engaging in the development and implementation of policies to enhance social development; coordinating development initiatives at all levels; and strengthening civil society in all its various aspects.

Practicum students working in social development can respond to broader and specific contexts by understanding the positive and negative roles of economic, political, social, and cultural development trends within a global and national context, particularly in terms of their impact on people and their well-being. Field agencies working from a social development perspective aim to understand people's needs in context, acknowledge aspirations and the barriers to their realization and working to understand people's culture and values and the nature of existing social institutions.

# International Conventions

The Universal Declaration of Human Rights adopted by the General Assembly of the United Nations asserts "recognition of the inherent dignity and of the equal and inalienable rights of all members of the human family is the foundation of freedom, justice and peace in the world." Human rights are the consequence of dialogue about what is important for all people in the world and what constitutes the important elements of our common humanity and global citizenship (Donelly, 1999). For this reason, human rights change over time and their expression varies from culture to culture. The role of practicum students in learning about human rights is to learn by listening, to work in solidarity with others, and to give voice to the disadvantaged (Ife, 2000).

International human rights declarations and conventions form common standards of achievement and recognize rights that are accepted by the global community.

According to the International Federation of Social Workers (IFSW), the following conventions are particularly relevant to practice and action:

- Universal Declaration of Human Rights
- The International Convention on Civil and Political Rights
- The International Convention on Economic, Social and Cultural Rights
- The Convention on the Elimination of All Forms of Racial Discrimination
- The Convention on the Elimination of All Forms of Discrimination Against Women
- The Convention on the Rights of the Child
- Indigenous and Tribal Peoples Convention

Human rights frameworks are used in many countries to guide practice, and students planning for an international practicum are encouraged to review those provisions in their pre-departure orientation work.

# INTERNATIONAL PRACTICUM PREPARATION

The planning process for an international practicum should begin at least four to six months prior to the anticipated start date. In Canada, some field education programs require that students begin planning up to one year in advance. It is important to have enough time to make all the necessary practicum arrangements, including the practical requirements for the host field agency and the post-secondary institution and related affiliation agreements.

While there have always been students interested in pursuing a practicum overseas, some field education programs remain hesitant to facilitate such opportunities. The reality is that there are a number of challenges in arranging such experiences. Canadian universities and colleges need to allocate sufficient resources to field education programs to meet the increasing need and demand for international opportunities. Planning for a successful international practicum requires attention to multiple issues: (1) building and sustaining international field partnerships; (2) developing mutually agreed upon learning arrangements, (3) supporting language acquisition and cultural preparation before departure, (4) monitoring the quality of field experiences, and (5) engaging in debriefing seminars on students' return. Additionally, the regularity and nature of faculty liaisons' contact with international practicum students while they are abroad is a crucial, though seldom documented, aspect of support.

Part of the preparation for an international practicum needs to happen from within. Students must become aware of their own locations and positions, and this will assist their professional development. Students must reflect on their social location and connection as a Canadian in the Global North (if undertaking a practicum in the Global South). *Social location* can include cultural background, gender, race, class, sexual orientation, and ability and how these factors intersect. Being from the Global North affects how practicum students are perceived and how they consider their relationships in the field placement. Developing an understanding of one's identity, subjugation, dominance, or marginalization is an important component of field discussions and learning during practicum through field seminars (Razack, 2002a). Field instructors need to learn how to initiate discussions of diversity and difference for students to integrate their knowledge and experience in practice (Razack, 2002a). International practicum students must be able to tolerate ambiguity and will often face struggles in learning cultural meanings throughout their experience. The process of adaptation and learning can be assisted by pre-placement preparation seminars, coursework, discussion, and directed studies.

Relevant coursework can be a valuable component of preparation for an international practicum. Courses in community development, international relations, history, economics, political science, Indigenous studies, and anthropology are recommended. Directed studies or independent study courses can allow students to prepare for the specificities of the region, population, or social welfare issue of focus for the field placement.

# Voices from the Field

Over the past 10 years I have worked with a number of international students from across the globe, students who come to India for placement. When a student arrives in India, our department provides a one-week orientation at the university. Lectures on social work practice in the Indian context highlight some of the complexities and problem-solving methods that are immersed in the culture. The familiar theories taught in Canada may not be congruent with the practice realities in India. It is a challenge for students to navigate the cultural differences that cannot be explained. Acknowledging this from the start of practicum is important because the differences can cause frustration for the student. When I reflect on my experiences, I realize that students need to consider certain important dimensions of practice in a different cultural setting.

1. It is imperative for students to have background knowledge of the practice field. For instance, the culture, the economic/political structure, and the country in the global scenario present issues. Students need to know in what area of interest they wish to gain experience while in India. This can be facilitated by providing reading material to students, projects and assignments pre-departure, and, very importantly, by meeting with faculty and students who have come to India for work/placement. In my experience, I have found that students who are prepared cope better. It also enables students to be prepared for the "realities of the placement."

2. Students need to consider different practice strategies. I have seen that many of the students coming to India have had experience in working only with individuals in a structured setting. This may not be so in an international placement. Students have to be prepared to work with groups and communities in very unstructured settings.

3. An open mind to learn and a deep sense of respect and sensitivity to another culture is a prerequisite. For example, willingness to wear culturally appropriate clothes for field work is very important. A student from Australia said, "Wearing a saree when I went to the community gave me an identity.... The acceptance and rapport building was easier." It certainly is not easy for a person to wrap a five-and-a-half-metre length of fabric around you, in the heat of Chennai!

4. Everything that one sees, feels, experiences, and eats can be overwhelming, and students need to consider their own abilities, mental health, and coping to deal with this.

5. Remember that an international placement should focus on "learning" rather than on "doing." I have found that students who say "I am not doing anything" get frustrated, find fault, and lose out on the experiences of reflection and learning in India.

## How does practice differ?

In my interviews with students, the following important practice differences were highlighted:

1. **Cultural differences in confidentiality:** As one student from Australia pointed out, the issue of collectivism versus individualism in the Indian context created a different understanding of confidentiality.

2. **Approach to work:** An international student reflected, "We have to go to the people. In my country, people come to us (social workers/agency). I think this has an important implication for practice — ability to take initiative becomes a very important skill."
3. **Time in India:** A student commented, "Time in India is so fluid!" The student also remarked that there is a spillover between the professional and personal. Students often find this very different from work in their own countries.
4. **Systems of practice:** There seems to be no structured system of practice, unlike the West. As one instructor put it to students, "You are the system!"

### What is challenging?

International students who complete their placements with us have to, to a very large extent, integrate with life here, and the challenges they have faced have been largely in the areas of communication (because most of the community people speak the local language), issues related to personal space, and unstructured work (they may be asked suddenly to attend a program or be given an appointment but their supervisor is not available). One of the important areas I have [witnessed] has been their ability to multitask (which is very different from our Indian students).

### What is valuable? What do students learn?

From my experience, I can boldly state that a cross-cultural social work experience certainly produces a new generation of social workers, who are trained in broader structural issues of social work of justice, equity, and rights perspectives. Students have stated that they are now equipped with skills to work in any setting, adjustable and accommodating ... a very valuable experience. [They have] learned that there are different ways to do the same thing, experienced rapport building with different types of people, and have gained a wider perspective of social work practice. (Miriam Samuel, field instructor)

Many practicum students are expected to develop a field education proposal to start the process of identifying and recruiting suitable field agencies for a practicum. The proposal can serve as a valuable tool to guide the placement process, identifying learning objectives, critically examining one's motivations and reasons for choosing an international practicum, and proposing focus points and/or contacts for the placement. Preparatory documents that can be useful in the placement process include a résumé, or curriculum vitae; a cover letter; and a brief descriptive essay on the country or region of interest.

Canadian study-abroad opportunities, and by extension international field placements, in some cases work best where there are ongoing agreements between institutions. It is very difficult to negotiate an international practicum when there are no previous agreements or contacts in the host field agency. Given the challenges associated with finding an appropriate supervisor or field instructor, as well as the practical realities of an international practicum, such as securing affordable and safe accommodation, it is best to go overseas with an experienced agency or organization. In Canada, non-governmental organizations offer Canadian students opportunities to plan for a practicum within their development programs and projects. Faculty can also play an important role in negotiating opportunities for practicum students.

International field placements can occur in large metropolitan urban centres or small, rural, and remote communities. The geographic location of your field agency and placement raises some considerations. For example, living in a small community often means that all members perform multiple roles, and rural practice brings together personal and professional lives in a different way. Rural social work and human service practitioners report challenges in managing professional and personal role boundaries as well as dual and multiple roles (Green, Gregory, & Mason, 2006). Rural workers negotiate availability and privacy on a daily basis (Green, Gregory, & Mason, 2006).

## CASE SCENARIO

As an undergraduate student living in the Greater Toronto Area, I faced a significant lifestyle change in my international rural practicum. During my practicum in northeast Brazil, I stayed with a family in a homestay program, and every night I set up my hammock on a hook in the living room — in the same room with five other family members. This was a challenging aspect of my practicum, adapting to living on a daily basis without my privacy and personal living space. The entire notion of privacy is very different in Brazil.

### Questions

1. What steps are necessary to plan for a significant change of lifestyle in your practicum?
2. What is your comfort level with the living arrangements mentioned above?

---

### Checklist for Reviewing the Student Practicum

In my university or college program, I have reviewed the information on international field placements and understand the following:

☑ number and types of practicum sites available

☑ specific requirements for completing the practicum (e.g., contact hours, scheduling, integrative practice field seminar requirements, and grading system)

☑ selection or placement process

☑ criteria used for selecting, approving, and training field instructors and practicum sites

☑ students are responsible for obtaining valid passports

---

# International Partnerships

Many post-secondary programs have agreements to facilitate international field placements and/or study-abroad exchanges. Building and sustaining international field partnerships is an important component for field education programs. These partnerships take many forms: between post-secondary institutions, agreements between international and local community agencies and with volunteer-sending organizations working in other countries. In Canada, several non-governmental organizations offer international opportunities, including practicum opportunities, for Canadian students. For example, World University Service of Canada (WUSC) offers Students Without Borders, a program that facilitates international field placements in Africa, Asia, and South America. These comprehensive educational programs are designed to meet a number of practical needs, including pre-departure orientation, arrival at the airport, transfers to your host community, accommodation, and supervision by qualified social work and human service professionals in the field.

Good international field placements require a sound philosophy and adequate preparation and participant debriefing. An international field placement can provide a professional development experience that has a profound impact. Faculty liaisons, field instructors, and students must all be prepared for the differences between an international field placement and a Canadian field placement.

## CASE SCENARIO

Lynne was a 24-year-old social work student determined to pursue an international practicum working with refugees in Africa. She had previously worked with sponsored refugee students on her university campus and was very interested in learning more about the situations faced by refugees in countries of asylum. More than eight months before starting her practicum, she prepared a letter of introduction to over a hundred international organizations and community groups to request a field placement. About two months later, she had received only three responses, none of which resulted in an offer. It was difficult because the post-secondary institution where she was studying did not have any contacts for international placements but was willing to support her search for an international practicum. Fortunately, Lynne was successful in obtaining a practicum through a Canadian non-governmental organization working in development projects.

### Questions

1. What challenges do students face in organizing an international practicum?

2. What resources are available to assist students planning for an international practicum?

3. How can students network and build relationships in Canada and overseas to coordinate an international practicum?

# Memorandum of Understanding

A memorandum of understanding (MOU) is a document that is signed by both a post-secondary institution and a field agency. It is an agreement that outlines each institution's roles and responsibilities in the field placement. A MOU can be a useful tool for facilitating international field placements in preparation for a practicum. It can clarify roles and responsibilities, establish timelines for field placements, and identify field instructor qualifications.

Post-secondary and field agency partnerships are beneficial to society because they

- provide service to the community;
- provide mutual benefit;
- engage in joint evaluation of student learning;
- increase the cross-cultural awareness and skills of students;
- enrich the educational environment; and
- can share learning resources (e.g., field education manual).

# Risk Management

Risk management issues are of concern for many post-secondary institutions involved in international field placements. There are risks associated with all field placements, and many of the liabilities covered by insurance for Canadian field placements do not apply out of the country. For this reason, it is necessary to plan for any risks students may face. Purchasing additional liability and medical insurance, taking precautions, being aware of safety issues and concerns, and developing contingency plans for theft and loss of property are important.

Some post-secondary institutions require students to sign waivers of liability and media consent forms, and attend pre-departure orientation sessions prior to their practica.

Most programs have a selection process that includes a written application and an interview. Increasingly, students are required to participate in university or college risk management seminars as part of their pre-departure orientation work. Find out if your program offers these sessions in advance.

# Costs

Students are responsible for covering all practicum costs, including tuition, travel, accommodation, and living expenses. Many students wonder if they can find sources of financial support to reduce the cost of an international practicum. For this reason, programs should provide students with information about potential sources of financial support for the costs of an international practicum. Many factors can affect the costs, and some of the factors are under students' control. For example, they can save by finding a cheap flight, sharing accommodation, choosing a placement in a rural area, and selecting a shorter placement. Costs for an international placement vary according to country. Estimated practicum costs for a three-month placement are provided in Table 10.1. The estimates include round-trip airfare, accommodation and living expenses, vaccines, health and travel insurance, and passport and visa fees. Some organizations require payment of a placement services fee, which is not included below. Further, the estimated costs do not include tuition fees paid to the university or college for credit courses.

**Table 10.1** Estimated Costs for an International Practicum

| | |
|---|---|
| Flight | $2200 |
| Accommodation and living expenses | 1500 |
| Vaccines | 250 |
| Health and travel insurance | 150 |
| Passport and visa fees | 150 |
| Total | $4250 |

Field education coordinators can find out if their university or college offers awards or bursaries for students who want to study overseas. The international office on campus may be able to provide some support.

## Pre-Departure Orientation

A pre-departure orientation is a necessary step before embarking on an international field placement. Becoming aware of the social, economic, and political realities through readings and coursework can provide valuable knowledge and information. Writing a reflective paper that includes student learning goals and objectives is a good first assignment.

---

### Checklist for Arranging a Practicum Location

I have inquired about the following:

☑ cost of living

☑ available and affordable student housing

☑ cultural opportunities

☑ recreation and social opportunities

☑ safety and security issues

☑ public and private transportation options

---

## International Health and Wellness

A travel insurance policy to cover theft, loss, and medical problems is a wise idea. There are a wide variety of policies, and prices and coverage vary considerably. In some health insurance policies, the insurance company pays doctors and hospitals directly. In others, students must pay immediately after receiving medical treatment and then submit claims to their insurance company later. If students opt for the latter, they must make sure to keep all documentation and receipts. Moreover, some insurance policies ask policy holders to call a centre in their home country where the insurance company makes an immediate assessment of the problem. Students should check whether the policy covers ambulances or an emergency flight home. Comprehensive international travel health insurance can be purchased with airplane tickets. Students should make sure the insurance is available for their entire stay in the country. In addition, some students travel within the country or region after completing their practicum requirements and should be sure to have health insurance beyond their practicum period.

## Exercise

Type a list of emergency contacts with names, telephone numbers, and email addresses. Provide your post-secondary institution and your international field setting agency with a copy.

Health and well-being is an important component of your practicum. Students should make sure they are physically healthy before they go abroad. Travel clinics throughout Canada provide advice on the health conditions in various countries, including required and recommended vaccinations and immunizations. Students with allergies should be familiar with the environmental and occupational health concerns that may arise in another country. For example, air quality may differ because of pollution. There are many unknowns in beginning a new practicum, and some students experience anxiety and stress in new situations.

It is important to develop a wellness plan for international practica, and students should recognize that they may not have access to the same supports or networks as in their home country. Many students face dramatically different living conditions during their practicum, and some feel isolated and lonely without their friends, family, and support networks. They can plan and be prepared for this change. Many bring books, music, and other leisure activities for their time spent outside of practicum. Bringing a notebook computer will provide students with access to writing projects and other interests in the evenings and on weekends. Students can also make new friends. Often, they will meet other international students who are interested in travelling on the weekends and sharing expenses.

Vaccinations provide protection against diseases students might encounter during their practicum. With few exceptions, students will be required to bring an International Health Certificate with a record of their vaccinations. Students can attain this certificate from their physician or health unit. Vaccinations should be planned well ahead of departure, since some require an initial shot followed by a booster and others should not be given together. Most Canadian students will have been immunized against various diseases during childhood, but their doctors may still recommend booster shots against measles or polio, diseases still prevalent in many regions. The period of protection offered by vaccinations differs widely.

Students should carry a small medical kit with them during their practica. They should also bring an adequate supply of all their essential medications and vitamins for the duration of their placements because particular medications or brand names may not be available locally.

---

## Checklist for Making a Medical Kit

☑  aspirin or panadol — for pain or fever

☑  antihistamine (e.g., Benadryl) — for use as a decongestant for colds and allergies, for easing the itch from insect bites or stings, or for preventing motion sickness

☑  antibiotics — for killing bacteria (useful if travelling in rural areas; however, they must be prescribed, so students should carry both the antibiotics and the prescription with them)

☑  kaolin preparation (e.g., Pepto-Bismol) — for mild stomach upset

☑  Imodium or Lomotil — for severe diarrhea

☑  rehydration mixture — for severe diarrhea

☑  antiseptic (e.g., Bacitracin, Mercurochrome, antibiotic powder, or similar dry spray) — for cuts and grazes

☑  calamine lotion — for easing irritation caused by bites or stings

☑  bandages— for minor injuries

☑  scissors

☑  tweezers

☑  thermometer

☑  insect repellent (with DEET)

☑  sunblock

☑  lip balm

☑  water purification tablets

☑  prescription medications (store in separate bags in case one is lost or stolen)

☑  personal care items (e.g., unscented soap, deodorant)

☑  spare pair of glasses and glasses prescription (if required)

---

Students can avoid many health problems by being careful. They should wash their hands frequently to prevent contamination of food. They should also clean their teeth with purified water rather than water from the tap, and should keep out of the sun when it is hot. Potential diseases can be avoided by dressing sensibly; students can avoid insect bites by covering their bare skin when insects are around or by using insect repellents.

They should consider the source of all drinking water, including ice cubes and frozen desserts (e.g., ice cream). It is important to eat hot food, which is cooked fresh, because it is healthier than eating lukewarm or cold items, which may not be fresh.

## Culture Shock

Many practicum students experience culture shock both on arrival and on return from their placement. The processes of adjustment and acculturation — to the food, the climate, modes of transportation, and living conditions — take place on a day-to-day basis. Spending three to four months at an international practicum means that students are not only obliged to master the tasks of daily living, but are also expected to learn and practice social work and human services with people whose lives are defined by different conditions. For example, a quarter of the world's population lives in severe poverty (UNDP, 1997). A number of geographic, cultural, economic, political, and socio-economic policy factors play roles in causing poverty. Its impact can be overwhelming to Canadian students.

## Personal Safety and Security

Every occupation has its own unique set of safety issues. The social work and human service professions require interaction with a variety of people, places, and situations, some of which pose risks or hazards (Brooks, 1998). The safety of students is of primary consideration in approving international placements. While living in foreign countries, students must adapt to the prevailing environment to stay safe. A proactive approach to safety in their practica requires students to be confident, knowledgeable, and sensitive to their surroundings and the people they meet (Brooks, 1998). Many field education programs provide suggestions or guidelines for general practice. Field agencies develop safety policies and practices that apply to practitioners, support staff, and practicum students, and also support safety committees. When students begin their practica, they should review these supports and discuss the findings with their field instructors and faculty liaisons.

---

### Tips for Staying Safe

- Be familiar with your neighbourhood at all times of the day.
- Select your travel and commuting routes accordingly.
- Learn where you can catch public transit.
- Trust your instincts, but be careful that cultural differences in your new country aren't manipulating your "gut" feeling.
- Talk to others about situations where you feel unsafe.
- Do not put yourself in a situation where you feel vulnerable because you are afraid of not acting professionally. (Adapted from Brooks, 1998)

---

If students become concerned about a personal or public safety issue during their practica, they should mention their concerns to their field instructors and faculty liaisons. Students should make copies of their student accident insurance, medical coverage, and vehicle insurance (if applicable), and provide a copy to their field education coordinator, faculty liaison, and field instructor. Students may find that their field agencies request that they restrict their movements, particularly in the evenings. Canadian men and women may find this a challenge. As students plan for their practica, they need to think about safety and some of the limitations they may experience. For example, Canadian women should consider fashions that are culturally appropriate.

---

### Discussion Questions

1. Does your agency have an employee safety manual? What about a safety committee or a safety orientation program for newcomers?

2. Is public transit accessible to your agency?

3. Have you discussed the safety of home visits and outreach activities with your field instructor?

4. Does your agency present any particular health risks?

---

By any standard, theft is a major problem in virtually all metropolitan cities around the world. Many thefts are due to lack of foresight. Students are less likely to be victims of theft if they leave their purses or wallets at home and instead hide their money in a small bag that they carry at all times, or they can wear clothing with lots of pockets that allow them carry what they need, leaving most of their money, their passport, their ID, their credit cards, and even watches at home.

## Sexual Harassment

Sexual harassment is defined as any unwelcome sexual advances, requests for sexual favours, or other verbal or physical conduct of a sexual nature by a person who knows or reasonably ought to know that the behaviour is unwanted or unwelcome (BSW Field Education, 2009). Most post-secondary programs in Canada have provisions for sexual harassment policies, but practicum students can be prone to sexual harassment during international practica. Different countries have important cultural and gender differences in what men and women can do. As stated by a field instructor in India, "Be alert; be sensible." Students should discuss situations that they feel might be harassment with their field instructors and faculty liaisons. If they experience harassment during their practicum, they should report the incident to their overseas field instructor and their faculty liaison in Canada. Changes in accommodations, staff reporting, and other duties may be necessary to ensure student safety and well-being. In some cases, depending on the severity of the situation, students may have to return home.

## Field Supervision

Social work and human service professions are defined differently depending on the country. Educational standards and content vary considerably. Theoretical frameworks and perspectives can present challenges for Canadian students who have developed advanced critical-thinking and analysis skills. Because practices vary, the tasks expected of practicum students will not always fit perfectly with those expected by Canadian educational programs. Arrangements for appropriate experiences and supervision require considerable preparatory work and must be built on relationships between sending and host programs or between faculty members in those programs. Educational programs with strict accreditation standards have to worry about comparability issues in order to meet other accreditation standards.

---

### Checklist for Assessing Field Instructors

My field instructor is fulfilling his or her role by

☑ creating and maintaining a learning environment

☑ providing an orientation to help me understand the agency system

☑ modelling skills as well as judgment and values in action

☑ providing educational supervision

☑ giving feedback and evaluation

☑ providing support

---

The student's own degree of comfort in the supervisory relationship is a factor in ensuring positive outcomes. In some agency settings, supervision functions are shared among a number of persons. Developing an understanding of the objectives and expectations in supervision will clarify roles for both students and field instructors. Feedback is the means by which systems improve functioning. Reporting to the field instructor (formally or informally) will enrich the process greatly for both participants, and will reinforce the field instructor's satisfaction in his or her supervisory role.

## Communication

In most cases, students and faculty keep in regular contact by email, blackboard postings, or WebCT; voice or video contact may also be possible, allowing for supplementary advising and support. New web-based video technologies, such as Skype, can facilitate international communication between international practicum students, faculty liaisons, and field instructors. Some international agencies offer blogs or other online discussion forums for practicum students to post their experiences. Students should determine how they will communicate with their program contacts before they leave.

## International Field Experience Sharing

Canadian students share their international practicum experiences with faculty and other students in field seminars. Field seminars are normally organized on a regular basis on campus during practicum. Students placed internationally can often participate by using a variety of online tools. Participating in field seminars can reduce students' feelings of isolation and promote student learning through discussion and exchange. Field seminars provide a structured setting for students to integrate their personal values and beliefs with the issues of class, race, gender, sexuality, and culture in ways that are professionally and personally meaningful for them.

Many post-secondary institutions provide venues for practicum students to feature their international experiences in newsletters, alumni features, and university newspapers. Many practicum students return to share their experiences with student clubs, community organizations, and professional associations. It is important for students to gather documentation and literature about their international practicum experiences. This information will assist them in preparing presentations, public talks, slide shows, and newspaper articles when they return.

## Voices from the Field

I've been in Botswana for approximately a month and a half now and in that time frame I've had so many new and different experiences. After my orientation in Gaborone, my WUSC officer and I were flown to Maun where I began my fourth-year social work practicum at Maun General Hospital. I've been placed with a family that consists of a Canadian wife and a Batswana husband and their two small children. They immediately welcomed me into their family and provided me with room/board and food. I believe my transition into Botswana life was made easier with the help and support from this family.

Working within the social work team at the hospital, who now consists of one head female social worker and two male social workers, my daily tasks consist mainly of pre- and post-HIV counselling, attending Pharmaceutical and Drug Adherence Counselling (PADAC) information sessions for patients whose CD4 counts are below 250 and who begin ARV therapy, general counselling, and making referrals to other community resources. I've recently worked on a multidisciplinary team, consisting of nurses and pharmacists, to co-develop an ARV adherence counselling focus group. The objective of these monthly groups will be to actively engage patients, who are defaulting from their ARV medicine, to participate in a short information session, discussion, and group problem solving. This was an exciting experience as all team members were motivated and creative in developing this group. I provided an evaluation form for feedback at the end of our trial group that was transcribed into Setswana and has provided a lot of insight for the delivery of future groups.

I've been dispatched to other community agencies as a way to learn about other services that are being offered in Maun. Women Against Rape (WAR) is a human rights organization that primarily supports abused women and children and that addresses the issues which contribute to their abuse. They also provide emergency shelter, educational programs, research, advocacy, and economic empowerment for women through skills training courses. Botswana Family Welfare Association (BOFWA) is a non-profit organization that primarily focuses on youth and individuals aged 10 to 29 and sexual reproduction information and informed decisions. They stem from the International Planned Parenthood Federation and are hugely involved with HIV testing and counselling. I've also participated in the social and community development sector of social welfare and helped to conduct assessments on referred households for the destitute program which provides qualified households with monthly food baskets among other financial aid.

Overall, I'm enjoying the orangey pink sunsets, the sweet smells of various vegetation, the beef and fat cakes, the elephants and giraffes, the music and dance, and the general camaraderie among Batswana folk. I'm finding the family connectedness a primary strength in Botswana culture, which I hope continues, especially through these more difficult times with the HIV/AIDS pandemic.

My time is nearing an end and I feel like I've only just begun settling in to both the lifestyle and work environment. I'm meeting many fascinating people, many who are Canadian females and working in the helping profession and environmental sector. This experience has been inspiring and has given me valuable insight into various areas for future work. (Jenny Turco, student)

# LEARNING OBJECTIVES

A major objective of international placements is to offer students opportunities to integrate their theoretical learning into international practice experiences. Noting differences and acknowledging the emotional impact of cultural variations are essential to personal and professional growth. Examples of journal writing, reflexive assignments, and informal ongoing discussions with others are key elements. Accordingly, the implications for supporting students in an international practicum are numerous and include the following:

- regular email contact that is responsive to students' questions and feelings
- acknowledgment of the emotional impact of the experience
- recognition that students educated in Western programs will likely feel conflicted about how to integrate practice principles overseas
- support and challenge for students who, when feeling overwhelmed, revert to ethnocentric criticism and judgment of the host culture
- articulation of student experiences through journal assignments

# Narrative of International Practicum

Student narratives dramatically highlight many of the realities, challenges, and opportunities students face while on placement. Writing about these experiences provides an opportunity to share workable responses to real and pressing issues. The power of reflection is in the images, remembrances, and situational immediacy that is conveyed in the writing. Field instructors and faculty get a glimpse of life as it is experienced from the students' perspective. Narratives can provide a window into the often contradictory and ambiguous nature of practice. For example, reflections on personal challenges can include instances when professional and personal boundaries are blurred; when feelings of personal inadequacy result from political decisions; when students face discriminatory practices; and the effects of feeling alienated and sometimes isolated on placement (Noble, 2001).

---

## Discussion Question

1. How will you share your international experiences and learning after you return to Canada?

---

Exercises such as reflective papers, journalling, practicum logs, and other writing assignments provide a means for sharing narratives during the practicum. In addition, emails and correspondence between faculty liaison, the student, and the field instructor can be reviewed and analyzed through e-supervision and e-learning practices.

# Diverse Cultural Practices

Canadian practicum students learn about culture, policy, practice, and community development abroad. Even though language and cultural barriers may preclude full involvement and participation, an international practicum has been found by Razack (2002a) to be a valuable learning experience. The benefits must be critically analyzed in terms of imperialism, socio-economic privilege, benevolence, and paternalism (Razack, 2002a). International practicum students need to be able to tolerate ambiguity and often face struggles to learn cultural meanings throughout their experiences.

## Exercise

Reflect on how diverse cultural practices affect the following areas: food, dress, religion, practices, and behaviour.

# Evaluation of International Practica

An essential aspect of field learning, which can be challenging in an international field placement, is evaluating students. Traditional skill-based evaluation criteria used by Canadian schools is often not transferable to international settings. To evaluate international practica, Canadian schools might assess students' ability to adapt to the work environments of their international field agency, their ability to collaboratively negotiate a learning agreement with field instructors that meet their learning goals, and their ability to remain responsive to the agency mandate. The ability to develop professional relationships with staff members who may be working from a different theoretical perspective is also a necessary component.

At the mid-term review, it is the student's responsibility to make samples of work available to the field instructor. The mid-term review is important for the student because it is an opportunity to receive specific feedback about performance that is tied to the work samples provided. A practicum student should schedule at least one or two hours for the evaluation. Students may wish to comment on what aspects of their practicum learning environment affect their practice. They can keep a journal or write reflective papers to record and monitor their cognitive and emotional responses in the field. Students' developing self-awareness and expressions of struggle should be encouraged while they come to an understanding about their tendency toward judgment and ethnocentrism. *Ethnocentrism* refers to the practice of viewing the world from a European perspective, with a belief in the pre-eminence of Western culture. It is important for students to understand how their values and beliefs support and impede their ability to function in the host culture and in the field setting. Students should be proactive with their learning and maintain ongoing relationships with their field instructor, bringing forward questions, engaging in regular discussion, and recording lessons learned.

## CHAPTER SUMMARY

In this chapter, an international practicum was discussed as a potentially powerful tool for international learning in social work and human service programs. International field placements allow students to become immersed in a cross-cultural learning experience and to confront different views of human behaviour and perspectives about how things operate (Healy, 2001). Increasingly, students are eager to complete an international field placement to gain international skills that will prepare them to incorporate international perspectives into local practice at home and, for some, to work in international settings. Many fields of practice seek practitioners who can make the connection between local and global realities, and some require previous international experience abroad. Students often return from international field placements and report that these were life-altering experiences (Healy, 2001).

This chapter introduced the context of globalization and internationalism, and highlighted the need to develop knowledge and skills in international contexts. Global North–Global South relations were discussed with a critical lens to examine student motivations and interests for pursuing international practica given the realities of Western imperialism, colonialism, and hegemony. The integrated perspective, incorporating a social development approach, provided a potentially useful framework for analyzing global issues in practicum, and international conventions demonstrated how these are enacted in practice.

The practicalities of preparing for an international practicum were discussed in detail.

Part of the preparation happens within students as they reflect on their location and connection to the Global North as a Canadian practicum student. The need for institutional partnerships that support international field placements were described in detail. An estimate for practicum costs and detailed checklists for practicum and health-related issues were provided to assist in the preparatory phase. Attention to personal safety and security is a concern for university and college programs, and this chapter provides some practical tips and questions that serve as a reference. Field supervision and communication practices with field instructors and faculty liaisons are important factors in international placements, and practical ways to stay connected were suggested. The evaluation of an international practicum as compared with a Canadian practicum was discussed to strengthen the way in which students are evaluated in international learning environments.

## Critical-Thinking Questions

1.  There are many debates and tensions in the field of international social work. How do the forces of globalization, Western imperialism, and post-colonialism have an impact on your learning in practicum?

2.  What values will guide your integration of theory into international practice? What will you do if these values conflict with those of your field setting?

3.  Do you believe in universal social work values or culturally based localized social work values? How will your position affect your practicum experience?

## Suggested Readings

Gray, M., & Fook, J. (2004). "The quest for a universal social work: Some issues and implications." *Social Work Education, 23*, 625–644.

Heron, B. (2005). "Changes and challenges: Preparing social work students for practicums in today's Sub-Saharan African context." *International Social Work, 48*, 782–793.

Razack, N. (2002). "A critical examination of international student exchanges." *International Social Work, 45*(2), 251–265.

Razack, N. (2009). "Decolonizing the pedagogy and practice of international social work." *International Social Work, 52*(9), 9–21.

Wehbi, S. (2009). *Deconstructing motivations: Challenging international social work placements. 52*(1), 48–59.

# Relevant Websites

**Amnesty International**

www.amnesty.org

Amnesty International is an activist movement that works to protect human rights worldwide.

**Canadian Association for the Study of International Development (CASID)**

www.casid-acedi.ca

The Canadian Association for the Study of International Development (CASID) is a national, bilingual, interdisciplinary, and pluralistic association devoted to the promotion of new knowledge in the broad field of international development.

**Human Rights Watch**

www.hrw.org

Human Rights Watch is an organization committed to the protection and preservation of international human rights.

**International Association of Schools of Social Work (IASSW)**

www.iassw-aiets.org

The International Association of Schools of Social Work (IASSW) is the worldwide association of schools of social work, other tertiary-level social work educational programs, and social work educators.

**International Consortium for Social Development (ICSD)**

www.iucisd.org

The International Consortium for Social Development (ICSD) is an organization of practitioners, scholars, and students in the human services.

**International Council on Social Welfare (ICSW)**

www.icsw.org

The International Council on Social Welfare (ICSW) is a non-governmental organization that represents national and local organizations in more than 70 countries worldwide.

**International Federation of Social Workers (IFSW)**

www.ifsw.org

The International Federation of Social Workers (IFSW) is a global organization striving for social justice, human rights, and social development.

**New Internationalist**

www.newint.org

New Internationalist is the world's leading independent publisher of magazines and books on global social justice and sustainable development.

**North-South Institute**

www.nsi-ins.ca

The North-South Institute is a Canadian-based non-profit institute conducting research relating to international development.

**Oxfam International**

www.oxfam.org

Oxfam International is a group of non-governmental organizations from three continents that works globally to fight poverty and injustice.

### United Nations (UN)

www.un.org

The United Nations (UN) is an international organization that was founded in 1945, after World War II, by 51 countries committed to maintaining international peace and security, developing friendly relations among nations, and promoting social progress, better living standards, and human rights.

### The UN Refugee Agency (UNHCR)

www.unhcr.ch

The United Nations High Commission for Refugees (UNHCR) is mandated to lead and coordinate international action to protect refugees and resolve refugee problems worldwide.

### The Universal Declaration of Human Rights (UDHR)

www.un.org/Overview/rights.html

The Universal Declaration of Human Rights (UDHR) is a declaration adopted by the United Nations in 1948. The Declaration arose directly from the experience of World War II and represents the first global expression of rights to which all human beings are entitled.

### World University Service of Canada (WUSC)

www.wusc.ca

World University Service of Canada (WUSC) is a network of individuals and post-secondary institutions that aim to foster human development and global understanding through education and training.

# Chapter 11

## Distance Field Education: New Technologies and Tools for Learning

Jessica Ayala, Myra Baynton, and Ellen Perrault

## Chapter Objectives

- Define distance education, and describe common technologies used in distance learning.
- Consider issues critical to completing practica or integrative field seminars at a distance.
- Understand how to be an effective distance learner.
- Identify and implement the steps involved in setting up a practicum at a distance.
- Learn how students, field instructors, and other key field education people can communicate effectively at a distance.
- Appreciate the learning potential of completing online integrative field seminars.

Distance education is learning in which the student and instructor are geographically separated and communication between them is facilitated by technology (Coe & Elliott, 1999). Students may have a variety of reasons for completing some of or all the components of their field education at a distance. For example, they may have moved to a different city or town during their program and thus need to complete the practicum in their new community. Or they may be completing an international placement. Students may also be enrolled in an online or blended program in which they complete a portion or the majority of their degree at a distance. Whatever the situation, this chapter will give students information and useful tips on successfully completing a distance practicum or distance integrative field seminar.

---

**Distance Education Terms**

**Online learning:** Educational opportunities that use the Internet as a platform for delivery (a.k.a. *e-learning, Internet-based learning, web-based learning*)

**Blended learning:** Courses or programs that purposefully combine online and face-to-face learning (a.k.a. *hybrid learning*)

**Asynchronous:** Time-delayed communication or tools, such as online discussion boards, which allow people to communicate with others and participate in courses on their own time

**Synchronous:** Communication or classes occurring in "real time," such as teleconferencing, video conferencing, or web conferencing

---

## CASE SCENARIO

Rachael started her BSW degree in an on-campus program. Partway through her degree, she became pregnant and had a daughter. In addition, she wanted to move back to her home province, so she explored the possibility of completing her degree via distance education. The social work program at Rachael's university had a distance BSW component, and she was able to transfer to that program to complete her degree. She moved home and completed her coursework and practicum there. In addition to allowing her to move home, Rachael found that completing her program via distance education was more convenient for her because she didn't have to be in classes during the day, which allowed her a more flexible schedule that facilitated her spending more daytime hours with her daughter.

### Questions

1. What issues or challenges may Rachael encounter while doing her practicum at a distance (and in a different province) from her university?

2. As she prepares for completing her distance practicum and online integrative field seminar, what can Rachael do to set herself up for success?

## PREPARING TO BE AN EFFECTIVE DISTANCE LEARNER

Completing distance courses or a distance practicum can be a challenging and can be an exciting and alternative way of learning. Increasingly, students are turning to distance education as a flexible and accessible alternative to traditional (face-to-face) education because it is a better fit for their busy lives. Researchers have shown that distance education, from a learning perspective, is as effective as traditional education (Phipps & Merisotis, 1999; Zhao, Lei, Yan, Lai, & Tan, 2005). Preparing to be distance learners is an important first step for students to take so they have successful, meaningful, and enjoyable practicum learning experiences.

## Distance Education Technologies

Rapid technological advances in recent years have resulted in many distance education tools and technologies, and new options and tools emerge every year. Here are some technologies that students may encounter in their distance field education experiences:

- **Teleconferencing and video conferencing:** *Teleconferencing* is a telephone meeting between people in two or more locations. *Video conferencing* transmits pictures in addition to voices. Students will often use these technologies to communicate with their instructors one-on-one and for practicum evaluation meetings.

- **Instant messaging and Internet phone services (e.g., MSN instant messaging, Skype):** This method of communication can facilitate synchronous text-based chats, voice conversations, and/or video conversations with one or more people.

- **e-Learning systems (e.g., Blackboard, Moodle):** This software creates a virtual classroom in which a range of educational tools is available, including document posting for sharing of course materials; asynchronous discussion forums; small-group areas to facilitate collaboration; external links to other websites; email; and online surveys and tests. Asynchronous discussion forums or boards, which allow instructors and students to post text-based questions or comments at their own convenience, and to which others in the class can respond at any time, are particularly popular. This software may be used for an online integrative field seminar.

- **Web conferencing (e.g., Elluminate, CentraOne):** This tool is used to conduct synchronous, or "live," presentations, meetings, or classes over the Internet. Students and the instructor meet in a virtual classroom, speak with one another over the Web, and can view presentations. Students may also work in small groups, visit websites, take surveys, and share applications.

- **Podcasts, online media, and recorded presentations:** Instructors may develop or use existing audio or video presentations (e.g., podcasts) or other local or online media files (e.g., YouTube videos) to deliver important information or course content. For example, Adobe Connect software allows instructors to add audio narration to their PowerPoint presentations, which students can listen to and view at their own convenience.

- **Blogs and wikis:** Blogs are online personal journals that are shared with others, and wikis are shared online documents or web pages that enable others to contribute to or modify their content (e.g., Wikipedia). Both tools can incorporate various types of media, such as pictures and videos.

- **Social networking sites (e.g., Facebook, MySpace):** Distance students or classes can use online communities to keep connected with one another, formally or informally.

First, students need access to the technical equipment required for their particular distance course or program. A computer, word-processing software (e.g., Microsoft Word), and an Internet connection are usually basic requirements. A high-speed Internet connection is ideal but may not always be available, particularly if students are living in an international, rural, or remote area. Most schools or programs will provide students with a website or information about the minimum technology requirements needed to complete a distance course or program. Schools may also have required software (including viewers, players, plug-ins, and antivirus software) available for downloading, and will perhaps even provide web tools to help students test or configure their computers for the necessary requirements. Students should make sure to ask about particular accounts or passwords they may need to access the school's distance education programs, platforms, or services. They will find that taking the time to prepare will be time well spent, as *not* having the right technology, software, or tools can result in much frustration and time spent dealing with technical problems rather than learning.

Next, students should ensure they have the technical knowledge and skills required to successfully participate in distance education. The necessary skills will vary depending on the technology used in the course or program. For example, online courses generally require that students have the ability to use the Internet and navigate online environments; to use email and send attachments; and to express concepts, ideas, and information in writing.

A number of checklists and assessment instruments can help students gauge their computer skills. Such tools can be found through a simple Internet search or perhaps even through their school or program (e.g., an information technology or e-learning website). Such tools will give students an idea of their technical readiness to engage in this type of learning and identify areas for improving their knowledge, comfort, or skills.

Finally, being an effective distance learner is different than being a face-to-face learner and requires particular skills. Being a distance learner usually calls for more self-direction, better organizational skills, and more self-motivation than a learner in a traditional (face-to-face) classroom requires. The traditional classroom has a teacher or instructor at the front of the room who is primarily responsible for passing on important content to students and for leading the students' learning. But in a distance education environment, the instructor tends to play more of a facilitator role and students are expected to take a more active role in guiding, completing, and being responsible for their own learning. This is what being *self-directed* means. For distance field education placements, this may also mean that students must take responsibility for finding their own placements.

Good organizational and time-management skills are also essential, and it is a good idea for students to commit particular times each day or week to participate in their distance course or to connect with their course or field instructor. Students should make note of important deadlines and plan ahead to successfully complete their practicum and course requirements while balancing other work and life responsibilities. Being self-motivated to engage in and participate in the distance course and complete the work is critical. Students should make it a goal to learn how to communicate with others effectively at a distance and take the initiative to seek out support (e.g., from their course instructor or field supervisor) when needed.

Distance education, and online learning in particular, can contribute to the creation of online learning communities, as well as promote critical thinking and reflection. Students in learning communities rely, collaborate with, and learn from one another with the guidance and support of their teacher (Tosey, 2002). Instructors may expect students to contribute to the creation of a learning community, which involves being open-minded about using and sharing personal experiences in the learning process, applying learning to personal experiences, and working with other students in the creation and sharing of knowledge (Palloff & Pratt, 2003). Students need to be prepared to be active participants in a variety of collaborative class activities, such as class discussions, small-group activities, and online web conferences. Learning communities may be particularly important in online integrative field seminars, which are addressed later in this chapter.

The ability to be reflective is another important quality of the successful distance student (Palloff & Pratt, 2003). Reflection is a purposeful framing and reframing process that involves "the ability to think critically about what one is thinking, to doubt what one knows, to question conventional and therefore comforting wisdom, and most of all, to balance what one knows and believes against real world experience" (Goldstein, 2001, p. 81). Asynchronous distance education in particular can provide the opportunity for students to reflect on content or discussions prior to participating or responding in class and, therefore, provides more time and space for reflection. Reflection is also critical to successful social work and human service practice, as reflecting on practice informs our problem solving, judgment, and actions as professionals (Merriam, Caffarella, & Baumgartner, 2006; Moon, 2004). In practicum, reflection is critical to the effective application and integration of theory and practice.

---

### Checklist for Determining If You Are Ready to Be a Distance Learner

- ☑ I have a computer that can access the Internet.
- ☑ I have basic word-processing skills.
- ☑ I know how to send and receive emails.
- ☑ I am comfortable navigating the Internet and finding information online.

☑ I am ready to take responsibility for my own learning.

☑ I have good organizational and time-management skills.

☑ I am self-motivated to learn.

☑ I have taken a distance course before.

The more "yes" answers you have to the above questions, the more ready you are to be a distance learner.

## Voices from the Field

To be an effective student online you have to be dedicated. You have to be a go-getter. If you're not the kind of person that can get yourself organized and give yourself a kick to get going, then it may not be the right kind of environment for you. You have to be more self-motivated and willing to go that extra mile. You have a lot more opportunity to, in your own time, do some extra research and make an extra comment when you're doing a course online. Some people really skipped out on the course by not posting to the discussion board much, and I think they really missed out on the learning. (Anonymous, student)

### Discussion Questions

1. What have been your past experiences (if any) with distance education? What were its advantages and benefits? What challenges did you encounter?

2. What strengths do you bring to the distance education environment that will aid you in being a successful distance learner?

3. What areas might you need to work on and improve before starting a distance education course or program? How do you plan to do this?

## SETTING UP THE PRACTICUM

Students who are completing a distance practicum may be required to find or develop their own practicum. On the positive side, this requirement is an opportunity for students to design a learning experience that is tailor-made for their particular learning needs. However, they may find that it takes extra time and effort, particularly in rural or remote communities, to secure a practicum that meets both their needs and the requirements set out by their school or program.

Students should familiarize themselves with the field practicum manual or other information provided by their school or program and aim to match these requirements with their own learning goals. Practicum coordinators, advisors, or faculty liaisons can also check students' ideas to ensure they are on the right track and meeting the school's expectations.

---

## Tips for Developing Your Own Practicum

When faced with developing or negotiating your own practicum, ask yourself:

- What do I want to learn in the field placement? What knowledge and skills do I want to develop or increase? What populations do I want to work with?
- What are my short-term and long-term career goals? How can this practicum contribute to these?
- What are the learning goals, expectations, or requirements of my school or program? What level of competency is expected of me?

---

## Contacting Potential Field Placements

Students will need to find potential agencies that can provide field placements that meet students' goals as well as those of their school. Personal networks can be used to identify potential contacts; students can ask co-workers, friends, classmates, instructors, and field coordinators for their ideas about potential agencies or specific contacts. Some programs allow students to explore placements within an organization at which they are already employed.

When students are contacting potential placements to discuss the possibility of doing a field placement, it is a good idea to provide each agency (in person or electronically) with an up-to-date résumé. The résumé will give the agency an idea of the applicant's past experience and will help to keep the applicant's name in front of the hirer if others are competing for the same placement. Some schools provide workshops to assist students in preparing concise and effective résumés. It is also a good idea for students to provide potential employers with a copy of their program's practicum manual or learning contract, as this will give the agency an idea of the expectations and learning goals associated with the practicum.

In some cases, students have to look for a practicum in a community with which they are not familiar. This can present its own challenges, as it may be harder for students to network and approach agencies in which they do not have a previous contact. (See "Tips for Finding a Placement in a New City or Town" on p. 216.)

If students need to contact an agency to investigate possible opportunities from a distance, they can do so first via email. They should try to find the contact for the person who is best positioned to make decisions regarding the availability of practicum opportunities. Large organizations (e.g., children's services, health regions) will tend to have a specific staff person that deals with student placements. In small organizations, a manager or director may be a good first contact. Students should send the contact person a letter, a brief résumé, and information about their program and field placement requirements. They should then follow-up with a phone call. Making arrangements for a synchronous (e.g., phone or in-person) meeting or interview increases the likelihood that students will be able to "sell" themselves to the agency and enhances the immediacy of the communication.

## Exercise

In this exercise, you will draft a letter to an agency or field instructor that you would like to approach for a field placement. Before you do so, make notes about the following:

1. To whom would you address this correspondence?

2. What will you tell him or her about yourself? (e.g., experience, interests)

3. What will you tell him or her about the expectations of the practicum?

4. What will you ask from him or her? (e.g., information, an opportunity to meet in person or by phone)

5. What role will distance education technology play? (e.g., in your interview or practicum)

## Tips for Finding a Placement in a New City or Town

- Use an Internet search engine to find the city or town where you want to find a placement. Then search for social service agencies or community services.

- Choose a few agencies that seem to fit with your area of interest.

- Search the agency websites to get an idea of the objectives, services, philosophies, and structures of the various organizations. Depending on your interests, you may want to search not-for-profit, health, and/or governmental agencies.

## Voices from the Field

I was moving into a new community near the end of my BSW program, and I had to find a practicum there. I found that picking up the phone and cold calling was the best way to network and find out what placement opportunities were available. I first searched on the Internet for different kinds of fields and local organizations that social work was involved in and that I was interested in. Then I called some of the places and found out who I needed to speak to. I ensured there was a registered social worker on site to supervise me, so that I wasn't wasting anyone's time. When you're searching for a placement, I think it's really important to not give up, but to keep trying. The first time I called the agency where

I did my placement, they told me that they wouldn't be taking any practicum students because they were just too busy. But I kept trying different departments, talking to different people and networking in that way, until I found someone willing to supervise me. So, it's important to make sure you're really talking to the people that are in charge of saying yes and no, and also to show that the placement is something you're really interested in, so they think "maybe this is someone I should really give a shot to." (Anonymous, student)

## Negotiating a Practicum

When students set up their own practica, their contact with potential placements often includes a process of negotiation, as they are in a position not only to request a field placement, but also to offer the agency some knowledge and skills. Discussing where there may be needs or gaps in the agency's services, programs, or policies may lead to an opportunity for students to meet their learning needs and for the agency to meet their needs through students' contributions.

Although it is important to treat the interview and negotiation process with the same attitude as one would a job, this situation is not the same, because the primary purpose of your field placement is to advance your learning. There are some similarities, however, so students should be professional, honest, and realistic about what they can offer the agency. Students should ensure that the agency will be able to offer them the time and support needed for learning and not just have them replace a staff position.

---

### Checklist for Exploring a Placement

When exploring or negotiating a placement with an organization, make sure to consider the following questions:

- ☑ To what extent does the placement fit with your own learning goals?
- ☑ Does the placement meet your school's requirements for practicum?
- ☑ What are the agency's expected outcomes for the work that you will be doing?
- ☑ Does someone at the agency have the time, expertise, and interest in sponsoring your practicum?
- ☑ Is there a qualified field instructor on staff, or will you need to find an external field instructor to supervise you?
- ☑ Will you need to communicate with your field instructor by distance? If so, what technologies are available to do so? Do you and your field instructors have the skills to use them?

---

## Addressing Administrative Requirements

Before students can start their practica, their school and field placement agency will likely require some form of affiliation agreement or contract. This agreement will spell out the commitments, roles, and responsibilities on the part of each organization. Because these affiliation agreements can range from short documents requiring signatures from agency and school administrators to longer documents prepared and vetted by legal departments in both organizations, it is advisable to check out early on what is required from both the agency's and the school's perspective. The latter will usually be indicated in the practicum manual prepared by your school or program and can usually be found on the school's website.

Because certain provinces require schools to cover workers' compensation (WCB) while other provinces do not, it is a good idea for students to look into what the practicum agency's WCB liability requirements are to see whether they will be covered. Because of lead times for reporting this information to the school's risk management departments or for having a contract reviewed by an organization or school's legal department, students would be wise to deal with this issue early so that the documentation is in place well in advance of the practicum start date. The various forms required for this process are most often contained in the school program's practicum manual or website.

Finally, students should check directly with their field placement agency to see whether the agency has additional requirements that students have to meet before starting the practicum (e.g., criminal or child welfare clearances, vaccinations, insurance). These requirements may take longer than usual to complete if students are arranging them at a distance.

## MANAGING THE PRACTICUM

If students are completing a distance field placement, the agency's field instructor and/or the school's faculty liaison and practicum coordinator may be at a distance. These people are integral to the success of a student's practicum. This section briefly outlines their roles, then focuses on how students can work effectively with them at a distance while completing their practica.

# Effectively Communicating with Field Instructors

A *field instructor* is the social work or human service practitioner who serves as an instructor and supervisor in the field placement, and is generally, but not always, an employee of the agency where students are completing their practicum. Field instructors play a key role in students' successful field education and field placement satisfaction as they prepare students for social work and human service practice by providing guidance, supervising work, evaluating performance and competence, teaching knowledge and practice skills, helping students make linkages between theory and practice, and serving as mentors and role models (Bogo, 2005; Bogo & Vayda, 1998).

The quality of the relationship between students and their field instructors is a critical factor in practicum success (Lazar & Mosek, 1993). Therefore, it is important that these relationships are open, positive, and supportive of student learning. However, building a relationship can be challenging when students and field instructors are at a distance from each other — for example, in a different agency, in a different community, or even in a different country. In these cases, both parties will have to be very purposeful in ensuring that they establish and maintain good communication, as this is a key part of developing and maintaining a good relationship.

In the initial phases of the student–field instructor relationship, it is a good idea to set out a workable schedule and plan communication sessions — for example, for supervision meetings. As described earlier in the chapter, there are a variety of technologies available that can facilitate communication between student and field instructor, from telephone, email, instant messaging, and Internet phone service with video to synchronous chat forums contained within e-learning systems such as Blackboard. The choice of which technologies to use depends on what best fits the communication styles of the student and the supervisor (e.g., access, comfort, skills).

Confidentiality is another major consideration when communicating at a distance about a practicum experience and student learning. When deciding which communication tools to use, students and faculty liaisons should make sure to consider security of information issues. When communicating via distance, steps can be taken to minimize the risk of breaching client or agency confidentiality. Students should not provide any confidential or specific client information in written communications. Such information should be removed before sending a message; to maintain confidentiality, initials can be used instead of full names or names can be changed. Or students could provide only general information in written communications and follow up with more detailed information in a phone call. Some agencies or schools may have software that will encrypt messages and thus reduce confidentiality concerns.

Students will find it useful to establish with their field instructor a schedule for regular communication. The field supervisor is often very busy, so they may need to take the lead in ensuring that communication and supervision take place at the regular or scheduled times.

There are many advantages to distance field supervision. A major benefit is that it is flexible and convenient, and so communication can be scheduled at a time that fits both the student's and the field liaison's schedules — even on evenings or weekends. The use of email and other technologies for communication also has the advantage of being learner-driven and allows students not to have to wait until they have a scheduled face-to-face meeting to deal with a question or a concern. Written messages allow time for reflection and may result in responses that are more thought out and helpful. Using technology for contacts and supervision sessions also reduces the need for travel, saving both time and money. Finally, some online technologies, such as email, chat, discussion boards, and web conferencing, can provide an ongoing record of student–field instructor communications, which students can review and use for targeted learning.

Keep in mind that there are also some challenges in distance field supervision. These include the lack of visual cues, verbal cues, and the physical presence of another person, which, depending on students' learning styles and experiences with distance learning and technologies, can take some time to get used to. Having to wait for a response from a field instructor can be frustrating, which is one reason why it is important that students and field instructors work out guidelines or explicit expectations regarding frequency and timing of responses. A guideline can be particularly important if students are dealing with crisis situations, time-sensitive issues, or certain kinds of clients. Because of the time lag, the supervision process can become out of sync with the therapeutic and learning process taking place in students' practica. If students find they need to work through something of critical importance with the field supervisors, then they may need to use synchronous technologies for all or specific parts of the supervision process.

As mentioned previously, technical difficulties can hamper the smooth functioning of communication and can lead to significant frustration, so both students and field instructors should ensure that they have the required equipment to facilitate any desired communication. They should also try to be patient and flexible when encountering technical glitches or difficulties.

Depending on the type of communication used (e.g., text-chat), space limitations may curtail message length. If this is the case, students may want to consider using another type of communication (e.g. a discussion board or email) or at least warn their recipient that their message may come in segments. When using a text-chat function, the few seconds that elapse between typed sentences may be interpreted as a correspondent who is not paying attention when, in fact, the other person may just be thinking through their response or typing. Students who discuss this issue with their field instructors circumvent this potential challenge.

A final caution about dealing with asynchronous or text-based communication is the occurrence of transference and projection. In transference within the supervisory relationship, the student can transfer previous relational expectations and patterns to the field instructor. Projection is a defense mechanism whereby the student or field instructor imagines that his or her own feelings are being expressed by the other person. Being aware that this can happen and questioning perceptions and assumptions is one way to reduce the negative impact of these phenomena.

# Tips for Communicating Effectively with Your Field Instructor

- Take the initiative to check in with your field instructor on a regular basis; don't always wait to be contacted. If you and your field instructor use email to communicate, make sure to check your email regularly so that you don't miss any messages.

- If possible, use a variety of available technology. Experiment with new ways to communicate with each other to see which methods work best for you.

- Take time to reflect on an email message or other asynchronous communication from your field instructor before responding. Keeping a journal as a learning tool can be an effective way to record what has happened since the last time you met with your instructor and can allow you to reflect on your learning.

- When composing a new email message about a continuing situation or idea, quote what was said in a previous email message. This will help you to build on earlier messages, decrease the possibility for misunderstandings, and keep communication clear.

- To enhance communication, consider using a webcam to provide visual cues that are missing in text messaging. Web cameras are relatively inexpensive and can be attached to your computer monitor, or may already be built into your computer. Video can add a more personal approach to your distance supervision session; however, it usually requires a high-speed Internet connection.

- Learning is an emotional as well as a social process; therefore, how you are feeling influences how you are learning. Include in your email or other communications some description of how you are feeling about your learning experience. With email and other types of text messaging, use emoticons or tags ☺ to help to express how you are feeling and provide the instructor with a greater understanding of your emotional state.

- The learning process is one of collaboration between you and your field instructor. This means that you need to be actively involved in identifying what you want to learn and communicating this to your field instructor. You need to mutually agree on the kinds of learning activities that best meet your learning goals so that there are no surprises and so that you both are clear as to what the expectations are. Clear expectations are an important foundation for good communication with your instructor.

- If you are involved in a supervision session while you are at home, ensure that your family knows you are in a scheduled supervision session so you won't be unnecessarily interrupted.

Select and research at least three possible synchronous or asynchronous technologies you could use for communicating with your field instructor. What are the strengths and limitations of each with regard to their potential for facilitating effective field supervision?

Set an agenda for the first supervision meeting with your field instructor. As you do so, think about the following:

- What are the most important items to be discussed?

- What are the key learning objectives you want to discuss?

- What are some of the organizational issues (e.g., scheduling, timelines, meeting dates) you need to talk about?

- What expectations need to be discussed?

- What relationship issues have to be addressed?

After your meeting, evaluate its effectiveness. Think about the following:

- Was I able to meet the goals of the session?

- Did the technology help or hinder our communication?

- What issues do I need to attend to next time we meet electronically?

- What can I do to enhance our communication at a distance?

# Resolving Problems with Distance Supervision

As with any communication, problems can develop with distance supervision. Difficulties can sometimes happen more easily in a distance environment because of the lack of visual cues and the time lags in between communication. It is important to catch any potential for miscommunication, conflict, or unhealthy interaction early on in the communication or supervision process so that it does not develop into something that could affect students' learning progress.

## Tips for Preventing or Minimizing Problems with Distance Supervision

- Set up some guiding principles for how you and your field instructor will work together in the supervision sessions (e.g., being honest, taking the time to clarify any possible misinterpretations, respecting each other's viewpoints). These principles are something you both develop and mutually agree on.

- Be aware of how you feel during and after a supervision session. Is this feeling okay? If not, then try to analyze what is going on in the session. Is it becoming unhealthy? If so, how?

- Name what you think is going on. Communicate with your field instructor in a language that demonstrates that you "own" your feelings about what is occurring. For example, use "I" messages to express how you are feeling and what you think is preventing you and your field instructor from dealing with it directly. Check out your perceptions with your field instructor.

- Problem solve the issue together, aiming to identify solutions and strategies to reach common interests and goals. Consider using a synchronous technology (e.g., phone, video conference) to allow you to express your emotions more fully.

- Set aside a separate session to deal with the supervisory relationship if there is not enough time in the regular supervision sessions to do so.

- If resolution cannot be achieved between you and your field instructor, you may need to contact the faculty liaison or the school's practicum coordinator to assist in the communication process. In such a case, consider using a synchronous technology to meet and facilitate clear communication.

## Voices from the Field

I had two field instructors for my placement. I found that during the first part of my placement, one of the instructors just didn't have time for me — I wasn't getting enough to do, and little direction or guidance. When you know something just isn't working out right, it's important to deal with it right away. If I hadn't said anything, I could have easily gone through an entire semester with significantly less learning and experience related to case management. It was a matter of not being afraid to assert myself. So, I took it upon myself to discuss this problem with my other field instructor and in doing so we were able to work together and make adjustments to my placement. These changes resulted in my ability to get a much more in-depth and involved practical experience. I found it important to be honest and straightforward about issues and not pretend everything was fine. It was really intimidating for me to say that my placement with one of my field instructors was not very beneficial for me, but ultimately it led to a better learning experience for me. (Anonymous, student)

## Working with Faculty Liaisons

The *faculty liaison* is usually a faculty member who is the teacher-of-record for a practicum course. The liaison is responsible for the coordination and linkage between the placement agency and the school. The liaison fulfils a collaborating and consulting role with the field instructor, agency, and student and is responsible for ensuring that administrative requirements (e.g., agency contract, student learning agreement) are in place and that practicum evaluations are completed. The liaison may also facilitate the integrative field seminars.

When students are not in the same town, city, or country as their faculty liaison, consultation and communication must take place via forms of distance communication. Many of the tips discussed above for facilitating effective communication between students and field instructors may also be useful for communicating with faculty liaisons.

Some educational institutions will set up a site in their e-learning system for students to ask questions and share experiences and resources related to setting up their practicum. Students should ask if their institution has such a resource.

Students must remember that because faculty liaisons may not be able to travel and visit them and their field instructors in person at their placements, they will need to be more proactive in keeping faculty liaisons informed of how things are going with their practicum.

---

## Tips for Working Effectively with Your Faculty Liaison

- Set up a means of regular communication with your liaison so that the liaison is aware and up-to-date about your plans, progress, and any issues that come up as you set up and complete the placement. Make sure to keep your faculty liaison informed about your plans for your practicum and your search and negotiation efforts.

- Check what the liaison needs from you in the way of documents, including how and when these need to be submitted to finalize the placement. Some schools will accept electronic documents (e.g., with electronic signatures), while others may require faxed or original copies.

- Be proactive in asking for any support you might need in either setting up your practicum or while in your placement. In particular, inform your liaison if there are any changes, concerns, or problems in your practicum. If the liaison doesn't hear from you, she or he may assume all is well, so it's important for you to take the initiative to inform your liaison if you are experiencing difficulties. In such a case, the liaison is a great resource because he or she will try to help you and will act as a mediator if required.

---

# Voices from the Field

Having a clear sense of the expectations and criteria for practicum was a really useful basis for clear communication with my faculty liaison. And having email and the telephone made it easy to communicate — you don't have to be in person to have a conversation or discuss things anymore. As trained social workers, I think that we have the skills and abilities to listen to one another and be open to hearing what another person has to say — whether it's in person or at a distance. Though sometimes I find there can be miscommunication by email. Your voice or tone can't always be recognized, so you have to be careful to express yourself a little further and more in-depth than you normally would to make sure you're getting your point across and are understood. (Anonymous, student)

# DEVELOPING THE LEARNING AGREEMENT

One of the most important documents students will be involved in developing in their practicum is the learning agreement. This document is usually completed shortly after the student starts the practicum, and it contains information such as the student's learning goals or objectives, the learning activities that the student will use to accomplish these objectives, the expected outcomes or ways to evaluate achievement of the objectives, and estimated timelines for attaining these goals. This document then becomes the framework or guideline for following and evaluating the student's learning progress throughout the field placement. It is intended to be a collaborative document between the student, field instructor, and faculty liaison, and should include goals that are clear, achievable, and measurable.

When completing learning agreements at a distance, students will want to keep in close communication with their field instructor and faculty liaison as they develop the document so that both are aware of and can have some input into the scope and content of the student's practicum learning goals and activities.

---

## Checklist for Completing the Learning Agreement

☑ I have completed as much of the learning agreement as I can, including my goals and my ideas for activities, outcomes, timelines, etc. (A typed copy may be preferable than a written one to facilitate sending it over distances [e.g., by email]).

☑ I have sent (e.g., via email, fax) the document to my field instructor for review.

☑ I have set up a time to discuss the contents with my field instructor. (A synchronous technology, such as phone or chat, is likely a good choice for this discussion.)

☑ I have revised the document, taking into account the discussion with and suggestions from my field instructor.

☑ I have sent (e.g., via email, fax) the revised draft to both my field instructor and my faculty liaison for final suggestions.

☑ I have incorporated their feedback into a final version.

☑ I have provided a copy of the finalized learning agreement to my field instructor and my field liaison. The faculty liaison will likely need a copy of the document with required signatures.

---

## Attending Evaluation Meetings

Students' performance in practica is usually assessed through mid-term and final evaluations. At these times, students, field instructors, and faculty liaisons get together and assess students' learning progress in their placements, using the learning agreement as a guide. These meetings give students a chance to consolidate their learning to date, receive verbal and/or written feedback, and articulate the learning goals for the next phase of the practicum or for future professional development.

As with other types of meetings discussed above, evaluation meetings can be facilitated over distances using a range of available synchronous technologies, such as teleconferencing, video conferencing, and Internet phone services with or without the use of a webcam. If the field instructor has access to the institution's e-learning system, then there may be a web conferencing system that can be used. Text chats or discussion boards can also work but can be a bit cumbersome unless the whole evaluation process is in written form. Combining a written and oral evaluation probably uses the best of both means of communication.

The educational institution will usually require some written documentation that the mid-term and final evaluations have taken place. This requirement may be contained within the learning agreement and may consist of completing a rating or checklist of the student's progress in achieving the practicum objectives, and perhaps some open-ended comments. As with the original learning agreement, faculty liaisons will likely need signed copies of these documents, which can be sent via email, fax, and/or mail depending on the school's requirements.

## Discussion Questions

1.  Which technologies do you think would work best for communicating on a regular basis with your field instructor for supervision? Why?

2.  Which technologies do you think would work best for communicating with your faculty liaison for consultation or evaluation meetings? Why?

## Voices from the Field

The evaluation meetings weren't as stressful as I thought they would be. They were actually a great time to touch base with my faculty liaison and field instructor. I found the telephone meetings worked well except sometimes it was hard to coordinate three different schedules: the faculty liaison's, the field instructor's, and mine. I prepared for the midterm and final term meetings by reviewing my learning contract and making sure that I had done what I said I was going to do. I also found that meeting with my field instructor before the meeting with the faculty liaison was useful as we were able to refresh our thoughts and go over any subject matter we thought might be relevant to discuss during the upcoming meeting. When the phone call came in, we took the time to go over my progress and how my field instructor thought that I was doing and where he thought I needed to improve. I found the mid-term and final meetings a great time to critically reflect on my experience, discuss constructive ways of improving my skills, refocus my learning perceptions and experiences, and further define upcoming learning goals. (Anonymous, student)

# PARTICIPATING IN INTEGRATIVE FIELD SEMINARS

The practicum course usually includes a series of integrative field seminars. These seminars have the purpose of engaging students in a collaborative learning process and developing their personal approach to practice. The major focus of these sessions is the integration of theory and practice, and the blending of conceptual, experiential, and value-based learning. In seminar, students usually present cases, share experiences and reflections from practicum, give and receive feedback, and actively discuss and debate professional and practice issues.

Students completing a distance practicum may be required to complete integrative field seminars that are offered face-to-face or via distance, or that use a blended approach — that is, distance sessions combined with face-to-face meetings. The type of seminar and the technologies used to facilitate it vary depending on the school, the instructor, and perhaps even the students. For example, where students are located (e.g., across a province or across the world) will have an effect on how the integrative field seminars take place. Some distance seminars may be facilitated via teleconferencing or video conferencing, but most seminars are now delivered at least in part through the Internet, using a range of synchronous or asynchronous technologies. Integrative field seminars may be facilitated by the instructor, the student, or a combination of both. This may depend on the philosophy and skills of the instructor, the experience of the student, and/or the focus of the content.

The use of e-learning systems such as Blackboard and Moodle and web-conferencing programs such as Elluminate and CentraOne are common. Integrative field seminars may also incorporate newer technologies, such as podcasting, online media and recorded presentations, blogs, wikis, and social networking sites such as Facebook and MySpace. Whatever technologies are used, schools or instructors will provide students with information about the required equipment (e.g., a headset with a microphone), the required software and plug-ins, and an orientation to the technology so that students can become comfortable and skilled in using it for the seminars.

The tips on preparing to be an effective distance learner presented at the beginning of this chapter will be particularly useful to students getting ready to participate in a distance integrative field seminar. Students can also prepare for their seminars by reflecting on their field experiences and on the knowledge, skills, and values learned from their practicum and social work and human service courses. Revisiting a learning journal or portfolio, if these were part of students' learning processes, can also provide rich material for reflection and discussion.

## Voices from the Field

I prepared for the integrative field seminar by reading the information the instructor provided about the course, reviewing the outline and expectations, surfing the Blackboard course site, and navigating the online resources that were posted for us. I found it was important to be professional online and respond appropriately and in a timely manner. The fact the responses were online and not just something that was said in class gave me the opportunity to really go over them and ponder what had been said — and in doing so, to create a more conscious, thoughtful and educated response. I could also support my assertions by adding links to websites that related to the topic at hand. (Anonymous, student)

---

## Tips for Successfully Completing an Online Integrative Field Seminar

- Go online frequently to help to manage the volume of emails or postings that you may need to deal with.

- Keep in touch with your instructor, particularly if you have any questions or concerns. For example, inform your instructor if you are experiencing technical problems and are unable to connect electronically for any length of time.

- When you respond to others in text-based discussions, provide examples from your own experiences to enrich the discussion.

- Be clear and concise in your written communication. Your classmates will appreciate your ability to not only make explicit your key points and meaningful reflections, but also to do so succinctly.

- Consider the text-based discussions an opportunity to refine your written communication skills, which are used often in social work and human service practice. A competent social work or human service practitioner requires good writing, recording, and reporting skills.

---

# Being Part of an Online Learning Community

Online integrative field seminars offer the potential to develop, participate in, and contribute to a community of learning in which students and the instructor play an active role in learning with and from one another. Because distance courses and programs can draw from a variety of geographic areas and can involve a mix of rural and urban practitioners and beginning and seasoned practitioners, the opportunity to learn from others and share different experiences is very rich.

As a member of a learning community, students need to do their part in creating an environment that is safe, cooperative, and conducive to learning. This includes being reflective, "open, flexible, honest, willing to take on the responsibility for community formation, and willing to work collaboratively with others" (Palloff & Pratt, 2003, p. 19). Students can also contribute to the development of this collaborative learning environment by being actively involved in providing information, personal comments, experiences, and feedback to others; directing responses to other students rather than always to the instructor; striving to achieve meaning through questioning and seeking agreement; sharing resources (e.g., books, articles, websites) with colleagues; and providing support and encouragement to colleagues (Palloff & Pratt, 2003).

## Exercise

To assess whether you are contributing to developing and maintaining a learning community, ask yourself the following questions:

1. Have I been actively involved in responding to the instructor and my colleagues?
2. Have I responded primarily to my colleagues by commenting on their postings?
3. Did I think about the responses of my colleagues and about my response before posting?
4. Have I raised some questions to seek further meaning on the issues discussed?
5. Have I added some personal experiences and comments to my postings?
6. Have I provided any resources, such as books, websites, or articles, that I think my colleagues would find useful?
7. Have I been encouraging and supportive of my colleagues' postings?
8. Did I keep my sense of humour when things seemed to go wrong?

Students will find that their efforts in creating a learning community will be rewarded through gaining deep knowledge and establishing meaningful relationships and networks with others.

## Voices from the Field

I found it was a lot easier to be more open about what I wanted to say in the online class. And you can join from the comfort of your own home rather than in a school setting — so it can take the pressure off in that way. It just made it more of a true discussion, taking that pressure off. At first it was a little intimidating, especially on Elluminate where everyone can hear what you're saying on their speakers. So you're thinking, "Oh my gosh, what am I saying? Am I rambling on? Am I making any sense?" But then you slowly get more comfortable having discussions with people in the class, hearing what they have to say and learning their stories. That was really awesome, because I didn't know what a lot of the other fields and social workers were dealing with — child and youth services, all these other services. And I wouldn't have learned about these fields without having this kind of in-depth learning experience in seminar. And we had people in different provinces and places — people up North were dealing with different populations there. And people in B.C. were dealing with different cutbacks than people in Alberta. So it gave you a more rounded perspective on what's going on across regions. (Anonymous, student)

# Working in Groups Online

Depending on the size of the seminar and how the instructor or faculty liaison designs it, students may be expected to work in small groups.

---

**Tips for Working in Small Groups Online**

- Set some guidelines regarding how you will work together (e.g., expectations for participation, respect, majority rules or consensus).

- Select a team leader, if appropriate.

- Determine the best way for the group to communicate (e.g., asynchronous, synchronous, a combination of both).

- Determine the division of labour. For example, decide who will take the lead to set up group meetings, who will remind others of deadlines, who will do each of the required group tasks, and who will take responsibility to post the group's work for the larger class.

- Be aware of the potential for conflict. Try to see conflict as part of the learning process and work it through with your colleagues. If, however, the team becomes stuck because of conflict, then you may need to involve the instructor to assist you in reaching a solution.

- Actively participate in the group's discussion or planning, raise questions, and share experiences and perspectives.

---

A successful distance online education experience requires that students be independent and active learners. The integrative field seminar completed at a distance can result in an opportunity for in-depth self-reflection about students' practica and practice.

# CHAPTER SUMMARY

This chapter contains information and tips on how to successfully set up and complete a practicum and integrative field seminar at a distance. Students must ensure that they are prepared to learn at a distance; this is an important first step in having a successful and enjoyable learning experience. To complete this step, students must ensure they have the required technical equipment and related technical knowledge and skills, as well as motivation and good organizational and time-management skills.

Since students may be required to set up their own practica, the steps involved in creating and implementing a practicum at a distance were provided. This includes how to contact potential field placements, negotiate a practicum, and address administrative requirements. Completing a distance field placement also requires that students communicate and work effectively at a distance with key field education people (e.g., field instructors, faculty liaisons). Working collaboratively to develop a plan for regular contact with each other is a good starting point for effective communication. Addressing misunderstandings, questions, and conflicts early in a direct, honest, and respectful manner will also help students prevent or minimize potential problems that may arise.

Finally, the purpose and potential structure of the integrative field seminar were described. The seminar engages students in a collaborative learning and reflective process as they develop their personal approach to practice, make linkages between theory and practice, and actively share, discuss, and debate professional and practice issues. Distance integrative field seminars may incorporate a range of distance technologies, tools, and approaches. Distance seminars may also provide opportunities to work collaboratively with other students through participating in online learning communities and group work. Being a successful participant in an online seminar requires students to be active learners: independent, engaged, and critically reflective.

## Critical-Thinking Questions

1. The purpose of any field education experience is to integrate social work and human service theory with practice. However, the process of setting up and completing a distance practicum may be different than a face-to-face practicum. What do you see as some of the major differences? What components or processes would remain the same?

2. What do you see as the benefits on an online integrative field seminar? What do you see as challenging?

3. What will you do to set yourself up for a successful distance learning experience (field placement or seminar)?

## Suggested Readings

Ganey, L. R., Christ, F. L., & Hurt, V. R. (2006). *Online student skills and strategies handbook.* New York, NY: Longman.

Mujtaba, B. G., & Salghur, S. (2005). "Essentials of cyberspace education for online students." *Journal of College Teaching and Learning, 2*(5), 1–16. Available online at www.cluteinstitute-onlinejournals.com/PDFs/200558.pdf.

Palloff, R. M., & Pratt, K. (2005). *Collaborating online: Learning together in community.* San Francisco, CA: Jossey-Bass.

## Relevant Websites

**Self-Evaluation for Potential Online Students**
www.ion.uillinois.edu/resources/tutorials/pedagogy/selfEval.asp

The Illinois Online Network has a variety of resources for online students and those considering becoming an online student. At this site, students can find a questionnaire to help them determine if an online program or course is right for them.

**How to Be a Successful Online Student**

www.elearners.com/guide/how-to-be-a-successful-online-student.pdf

This document provides helpful tips on being a successful online learner, including how to prepare for an online course and how to write good discussion postings.

# Chapter 12

## Rural and Remote Field Education: Practice Dynamics in Smaller Communities

Joanna Pierce and Glen Schmidt

## Chapter Objectives

- Understand rural field practice.
- Understand generalist practice in rural settings.
- Examine practice dynamics specific to small rural communities.
- Define collaborative practice skills in rural practice.
- Examine the complexities of confidentiality and ethics in rural practice.
- Understand the importance of relationship development in rural social work and human services.
- Examine the challenges of dual relationships in rural communities.
- Understand and define professional boundaries and socialization.

This chapter provides an overview of the practice concepts and dimensions of rural field placements. Rural field placements offer complex learning experiences and challenge the student to draw from several skill sets. Generalist practice skills have been acknowledged as beneficial in rural and remote practice (Collier, 2006). The generalist model in conjunction with rural community considerations assists the practitioner in appropriate case planning.

Many authors have written about the challenges of geography, isolation, industry, and the urbanized policy imposed on rural living in Canada. Students participating in rural placements should consider the practice shifts required in rural community practice. An awareness of the added complexities of rural practice and how these complexities influence service delivery must include an understanding of community.

This chapter offers rural practice experiences from northern Canada and guidelines for practitioners to consider in personal planning and travel for rural community practice. Thoughtful preparation prior to entering rural community practice will assist the student learner with the urban–rural transition.

## Voices from the Field

My first day in rural community practice began with a full day of travel just getting to the community. The scenery was nothing like I had ever seen before. As my day began, I was inundated with both welcoming gestures and requests for assistance. As I grappled with how to manage all the requests and how to approach each situation, I felt an overwhelming sense of being back in the house I grew up in.

Working in a small community is like the house you grew up in, it is filled with history, people you love, argue with, support, fight, and the most difficult component is you know all the stories of everyone who lives there. I quickly learned that community work would require a thoughtful approach, recognizing that everything was interdependent and connected. (Joanna Pierce, student)

## THE RURAL CONTEXT

The term *rural* can be defined in many ways and, in some instances, requires visual exposure to understand the context being described. In British Columbia, some professionals might define Prince George as a rural community, whereas practitioners from Prince George would define Fort St. James or the Hazeltons as truly rural. Those from the north know there is always a smaller community, each with its own unique presence. Varying definitions of *rural* portray it as country living, non-paved roads, small populations, and, in general, a close-knit lifestyle in which people know one another and come together interdependently. Statistics Canada (2007 defines *rural* as follows:

> The rural area of Canada is the area that remains after the delineation of urban areas which ... have been delineated using current census population data. Taken together, urban and rural areas cover all of Canada. Within rural areas, population densities and living conditions can vary greatly. Included in rural areas are: small towns, villages and other populated places with less than 1000 population according to the current census; rural fringes of census metropolitan areas and census agglomerations that may contain estate lots, [as well as] agricultural, undeveloped and non-developable lands; agricultural lands; remote and wilderness areas.

This definition has changed over time (see Appendix A in du Plessis et al., 2002). Typically, *rural* has referred to the population living outside settlements of 1000 or more inhabitants. The current definition states that census rural is the population living outside settlements with 1000 or more inhabitants with a population density of 400 or more per square kilometre (Statistics Canada, 2007).

Rural living factors include decreased service accessibility, year-round transportation challenges, economic disparities, and, depending on a community's geographic location, fewer available food sources. These factors are part of rural life and need to be carefully considered when taking on community practice.

The concept of "rural" represents one way of looking at what might be called *non-urban* or *non-metropolitan* social work and human service. In the United States, Josephine Brown's classic text *The Rural Community and Social Case Work* and Leon Ginsberg's *Rural Social Work* introduced rural social work practice as different from practice in urban environments. This view of rural social work was incorporated into the Canadian experience, but Zapf (1985) noted that the American concept of rural social work did not transfer well to northern and remote communities. For one thing, the population density was not comparable. Most rural areas in the United States have a high population density compared with those in Canada.

## Rural and Remote Practice in the Canadian North

Northern Canada can be seen as an enormous hinterland resting above a narrow southern heartland, a vast wilderness area that stretches the conventional rural characteristics of low population density beyond relevance. (Zapf, 1993, p.695)

Schmidt (2005) describes the enormity of the northern landscape as visually striking "whether one is driving through the mountains of northern British Columbia, flying over the muskeg of Manitoba and Ontario, or walking along the barren shores of the Hudson Bay, the sense of space is awe-inspiring" (p. 18). These descriptions help create an image of the potential practice implications for rural practitioners. There are many layers to rural field practice in northern Canada. In early social work and human service, urbanized delivery models were applied to rural settings, which, over time, proved to be inadequate. Researchers have studied this topic, but further research is required to document the rural and remote experience in order to contribute to the development of comprehensive resources for practitioners.

Differences related to latitude, climate, settlement patterns, the economy, and transportation contribute to the idea of remote and northern social work and human service practice as a variation of rural practice. The nature of the practice is heavily influenced by factors that might be grouped under the heading of geography.

Latitude has some obvious effects as one travels further north. The hours of sunlight vary greatly depending on the season, which influences resident populations as well as social work and human service students who have organized northern practica. For residents, sunlight governs seasonal activities and interaction within the community. During the long hours of daylight around the summer solstice, it is common to see young children playing outside around midnight. A student coming from an urban location might be troubled by this spectacle, but it is a normal part of life in northern and remote communities. During the winter, activity levels may diminish; the short days and lack of sunlight may prove troublesome for some people, including students unaccustomed to the limited hours of light.

The northern climate can be harsh and, depending on the location, it may be intensely cold during winter months. Hot days might be experienced during the summer, but in some places biting insects can be a ferocious challenge to outdoor activities.

Settlement patterns are also different in northern locations. Community populations can increase rapidly because of economic activity that has a seasonal basis. Construction and exploratory work may increase during the summer months, and a remote community can be inundated with "outsiders" who might import values and behaviours that aren't acceptable to long-term community residents. In First Nations communities, there may be seasonal migration from a town site to a fish camp or goose camp. Social work and human service practitioners may have more difficulty trying to locate people, given the seasonal nature of some settlement patterns.

The nature of the economy in the north also marks the location as somewhat different and unique. Some First Nations people and communities may be heavily dependent on traditional practices of hunting and gathering. In remote First Nations communities, few people are tied to a wage-based economy and the majority rely on gathering traditional foods. Social work and human service practitioners from outside the community are inclined to regard such people as desperately poor. While poverty is a significant factor for some First Nations people, those who have access to a healthy and thriving traditional economy may not need the same level of income as their urban counterparts.

Resource-based industries typify many far-flung northern communities, and the settlements have been referred to as "single industry towns" (Lucas, 1971). Single industry towns are characterized by a lack of economic diversification and the predominance of one major employer, often in the form of a mill or a mine. Canada's northern landscape is dotted with single industry towns, many of which were established after World War II. The communities depend on the demand of global markets for the specific commodity that they produce. When demand is high, the community usually experiences a boom characterized by high wages and population growth. People that move to single industry resource-based towns may not have large social networks of family and friends, and they may experience a degree of isolation. They also experience insecurity, as the global economy can be fickle and a "boom" can quickly turn to a "bust," with serious economic and social implications. Unlike urban areas or densely populated rural areas where alternative work might be found "next door," economic and employment collapse in a northern community often requires residents to relocate great distances at considerable cost.

Transportation emerges as a different challenge in the north. Transport is important for social work and human service practitioners and for the clients served by these workers. In urban areas and densely populated rural areas, public transport is available and is often fast and efficient. In remote northern locations, public transportation is not readily available and may be non-existent. More remote communities may require social work and human service practitioners and students to fly in on charter flights. The flights may land on water or ice, depending on the season and location. Weather conditions can affect transportation in and out of remote northern communities, and of course there is an added element of danger associated with ground transportation along icy snow-covered roads.

## The Benefits of Rural and Remote Placements

While it is clear that there are many challenges involved in rural and remote placements, these types of experiences are rich in opportunity. Many social work and human service students are hopeful of gaining employment following graduation, and a rural or remote placement can be of great assistance in this regard. The unfortunate reality of rural and northern remote social work and human service practice is that there is a high degree of turnover. People may view the north or a rural location as a place to gain experience before they move back to an urban centre. This turnover is one of the challenges for employing authorities and supervisors, but it does present opportunities for social work and human service students seeking employment. Jobs are available, and the quality of the experience gained in a rural or remote location is unique and full. The opportunities for creativity and innovative work are abundant, and students and new social work and human service practitioners can benefit greatly from this rich experience.

Work in rural or remote locations also means access to recreational opportunities that may not be available in an urban setting. Students who enjoy the outdoors and activities such as hiking, camping, fishing, hunting, canoeing, and skiing often find that the opportunities for these pursuits are readily available, easily accessible, and affordable.

Life in a small, isolated community can be rewarding in and of itself. The defined nature of the community contributes to a strong sense of place and a feeling of being part of something that can be seen, defined, and understood. Many communities exhibit a friendliness and openness that isn't as apparent in the relatively anonymous confines of an urban centre.

## Student Challenges and Rewards

Before practitioners can begin their work in rural settings, they need to be properly equipped to address issues of visibility, dual relationships, and "outsider" complexities. Student field placements provide the opportunity to examine how other professionals tackle these demands. Students who desire to work in the north will be faced with different challenges in practice delivery, which will be discussed later in the chapter. Issues of accessibility, geography, culture, and lack of available resources all contribute to the complexities of rural and remote practice.

Students in a rural community placement may find that they are faced with conditions they have not experienced or anticipated. It is important to acknowledge what perceptions are present and how to proceed. The practitioner might want to consider the anxiety most people experience when they access support services. Clients are vulnerable, unsure of the outcome, and perhaps fearful that the requested assistance may not produce the benefit they are seeking. A practitioner who is shifting from an urbanized office environment to a smaller community may experience similar anxieties, becoming vulnerable to the community's assessment of the practitioner's intent and skill. A student also faces the challenge of locating to a rural or remote northern community. Many of the social opportunities are bound to be different than what one might find in urban locations. There is a high degree of visibility, which means that one's behaviour outside the workplace is subject to a degree of scrutiny that isn't be experienced in an urban area. Rural and remote communities can exhibit a degree of localism, meaning that social rules and ways of being are defined from a local perspective and not from a perspective that might be considered more global in nature. Students need to develop an understanding of the local culture and particularly the unwritten rules governing behaviour and ways of being in the community.

In addition, students need to consider the dynamics of working in communities that have historically been impacted by colonization. Understanding the history of contact and colonization, and its unique impact on local Indigenous communities, is important. As described in Chapter 8, understanding protocols and practices before beginning placements in rural and Indigenous communities is crucial. Further, rural and northern communities have distinctive patterns and a history of immigration and migration within Canada that should be considered.

Students who are able to participate in rural placements are rewarded on several levels. They will experience practice from a generalist perspective that they may not experience in urban specialized agency settings. In addition, students often gain skills in negotiating partnerships and working creatively because of a lack of resources. In summary, students are far more likely to gain a broad practice experience and an increased level of exposure in many areas.

Students need to expand their thinking from individual, urbanized caseload management to include the community in decision-making approaches. Each practice decision made invites a set of responses the practitioner may not initially connect to the work at hand.

## Discussion Questions

1. What are the geographic implications of your role?

2. What services are available, if any?

3. Describe the community structure inherent in your place of practice? (e.g., with regard to culture, industry, values, history)

4. Whose Indigenous traditional territory will you be practising in? What is the historical and current impact of colonization within this community?

5. What is the pattern of immigration historically and currently in the community you will be practicing in?

6. What are the community's strengths?

7. What are the natural helping systems already in place, and how are they connected to the larger system?

8. What service demands will you face in your role?

9. Where will your initial challenges lie?

# GENERALIST PRACTITIONER

The generalist model is "an approach that chooses to use many foundations on many societal levels, rather than just few" (Collier, 2006, p. 37). The generalist approach is made up of a flexible skill set that can be adapted for many societal and structural issues. This approach is a practical fit for rural settings because of the lack of specialty sectors in service provision. Rural communities are often underserved and the lack of health and social services places community members at higher risk for things such as unemployment and health concerns. Smaller communities tend to structure themselves interdependently. There is an intrinsic dynamic to community structure, roles, and connections that must be understood by anyone who does not reside in the community. It is important that the generalist practitioner understand that there is a strong connection between the individual and their community. The generalist practitioner maintains knowledge of a variety of analytical models. Practitioners will often find themselves faced with the need to make immediate decisions, which demand an interdisciplinary approach.

The service requests received by a community generalist practitioner can range from specific, individualized supports to broad, community, system-based supports. For example, the practitioner should have knowledge in a variety of areas, such as addictions, child and youth care, parenting, abuse issues, mental health, and systems theories. Any of these examples may come forward because of an individual request, or the community might consider that one of these issues requires a collective, participatory response. The generalist practitioner will need to feel prepared to respond on both levels.

The demands for service in several social work or human service areas can overwhelm a student or a novice practitioner. It is important to recognize that, even with the generalist practice framework, practitioners will always need to gain further knowledge to address specific needs. Practitioners should be aware of their individual practice competency level and ensure that the delivery of all interventions is within their skill set. The practitioner should also be prepared to address any situations that fall outside of their defined level of competency.

Successful practice in rural settings tends to rely on informal connections and relationships. The generalist practitioner should gather as much insight as possible into the community's needs to prepare for service requests. The generalist practitioner should work carefully to establish community engagement, which is the basis for successful practice.

## Voices from the Field

I was about to assist my supervisor in providing an agency tour when the phone rang. When I answered the phone the voice on the other end asked to speak with my supervisor. I let the client know that she was unable to take the call and asked if I could take a message. The client said, "No, I am in jail and this is my only call," and then immediately began disclosing her situation to me on the phone. After listening to her disclosure, I realized the client needed assistance in finding addictions services, parenting supports, legal advice, and financial assistance. I didn't know where to begin. I wondered how I could support a client who was already in jail. Would it be possible to keep this family together with the primary caregiver in jail, and then heading off to rehab after her sentence was complete? (Jennifer Tkachuk, student)

### Discussion Questions

1. Put yourself in Jennifer's place. Given the situation above, where would you start?
2. Have you had a similar experience? If so, what were some of the dynamics?
3. Have you ever felt overwhelmed as a student learner during your practicum?

One of the most exciting characteristics of community generalist practice is the chance to facilitate creativity. Endless opportunities stem from successful community engagement and shared ideas. Through a generalist framework, new practice approaches, and the merging of mainstream practice with traditional community process, successful partnerships evolve.

This happens in part because of the lack of resources, and in particular, specialized resources. The lack of resources may be seen as a deficit and a disadvantage, but many rural and northern social work and human service practitioners regard this challenge in a positive way. Northern and rural practitioners are obligated to become creative in their practice, and the opportunity for creativity is supported and respected. In highly specialized urban environments that have a wide range of specific resources, there may not be the same need for creativity and initiative.

## PRACTICE DYNAMICS IN SMALLER COMMUNITIES

It is important to conceptualize the practice differences that occur between larger urban settings and smaller communities. The first challenge often presented in rural and remote community practice is travel. Is the community accessible by ground or restricted to air or water? Many times a combination of several methods may be required to get to a final destination. Personal reactions to float planes or flying in general, speed boats or small ferries, hours on dirt roads, and motion sickness are all important practice considerations for students. In addition, practitioners must learn if they will have access to technology while travelling: Once the plane is in flight or the car has exited the highway, will cellphone service end? Technology considerations can have a practical impact on the travel required for rural practice. For example, without cell service, practitioners on the road cannot contact CAA or emergency services. Moreover, a practitioner travelling alone may sometimes have to travel along unmarked roads. Practitioners may want to familiarize themselves with global positioning systems as a safety precaution. Winter survival may be a consideration in some remote locations. Isolated highways and winter roads require special precautions and necessitate the inclusion of survival gear on any trip.

In addition to travel dynamics, student practitioners need to be prepared to adapt to the differences in lifestyle once in the community. Depending on the community's location, the services available will vary greatly. The community may have a "professional building," where practitioners stay, or accommodations may be in a community member's home. More remote communities often have one store, in which supplies are limited and frequently become very slim while waiting for the next delivery to arrive. If a practitioner has dietary needs or reacts to changes in diet, it would be advisable to ensure that personal supplies include meal replacement items or trail mix, which are easily stored and stand up to travel.

## Checklist for Planning Travel to a Rural Community

☑  I know where the community is located.

☑  I know where the nearest essential services are (e.g., hospital, RCMP, place to find food).

☑  I know what communication system I will have access to (e.g., cellphone, land phone).

☑  I know which mode of transportation I will be taking (e.g., plane, car, boat).

☑  I know how I am travelling (e.g., with another person, with a local community member, by myself).

☑  I have packed the travel safety items that I need to bring with me.

☑  I have considered some of the hazards that I might face and thought out possible solutions (e.g., flat tire, delay in connection, animal presence).

## Checklist for Packing for Travel in Rural Communities

☑  I know what food supplies will be available to me in the community.

☑  I am aware of how I will satisfy my dietary needs.

☑  I have packed all the over-the-counter medicine I could need (e.g., Tylenol, Advil, motion sickness pills, bug repellent).

☑  I have enough of all my prescription medication (and extra, just in case travel is delayed).

☑  I have a small personal safety kit that is relevant to the area I am travelling to.

☑  I know whether the water where I am going is drinkable and have planned accordingly.

Students in larger, urban settings will likely acquire learning that is specific to their placement agencies and practice styles specific to their assigned supervisors. In the first week of learning, students are often asked to research their placement agencies and identify which referral agencies they should access for support services. Because of the larger populations in urban centres, it is possible to practice with less visibility and to conduct careers without experiencing or requiring a generalist knowledge base. Many practitioners in urban areas specialize early in their careers and devote their professional lives to developing their specialized knowledge.

Practice in smaller communities presents the opposite situation. Cheers (1999) states, "A community-embedded framework provides a different way of looking at rural practice — a new angle on where the practitioner, and practice, fit within a community" (p. 93). Wilkinson (1991) expands this notion, stating, "This process is perhaps more vivid in rural than urban communities for, in a rural locality, the limited pool of people produces a particular community through daily interaction across arenas — culture, social structure, economy, politics, religion and other natural environment" (p. 16).

Rural practice must consider community process and awareness of how each interaction has an impact on every position. The following practice example describes an urban practice environment and a rural practice environment. The Case Scenario illustrates key differences in approach, context, geography, and place, which influence a practitioner's approach.

## CASE SCENARIO

**A.**  As an urban mental health therapist, I practised in an office setting with appointments each hour. The appointments were a standard 50 minutes, with 10 minutes for file management, and all appointments occurred in the office space. Around those appointments, I did not see or interact with the clients in my caseload.

**B.**  As a community mental health therapist, the community knew when I arrived, who I was visiting, and where I was at any point in my day. My appointments rarely occurred in my assigned space; rather, they occurred in community homes, at a community park, during a long walk, or even on a fishing boat. Every social contact came with scrutiny, and every case required careful consideration focused on how the process would be viewed and received by the whole community.

## Questions

1. What are the main differences between examples A and B?
2. What do you think are important considerations for each setting?
3. How could you prepare yourself to work in each setting?

A rural community caseload defines the need for general practice knowledge and skill. As mentioned in previous sections, the practitioner's caseload may involve clients who require support with parenting, addictions, family violence, marital issues, identity issues, or youth behaviour, to name a few. Practice continuously presents challenges in boundaries and privacy. For example, in an urban setting, if a practitioner is working with a client and the client's family member requests service, then it is far easier to have a colleague take on the second request to address any conflict of interest issues that may arise. In a rural community, the practitioner may be the only service provider available. Practitioners will need to create a framework for addressing possible issues of conflict of interest in practice as part of their work.

Aside from their professional role, community practitioners may be asked to participate in community tasks such as organizing an event, selling tickets for a raffle, or participating in a potluck dinner. These requests should not be viewed as a poor use of professional time but as an important opportunity to gain creditability and strengthen relationships with community leaders. This participation is "community" practice. Participation in community-driven projects will result in an increase of trust and the lowering of resistance when planning around difficult issues.

# Community Engagement

It is important to be familiar with the community's process of change. Change is often a slow process requiring thought and consideration by community members on various levels. At first, the practitioner may consider gradual approaches, such as developing a community youth program or an after-school physical activity. This process will assist with facilitating community engagement and invite participation toward addressing more challenging topics. The practitioner must ensure all work facilitated is from the voice of the community and not what the practitioner deems as best.

To ensure the practitioner is prepared for successful practice, it is important that he or she research the community dynamics prior to arriving. If thought is devoted to preplanning, the practitioner will be able to begin effective work much more quickly once in the community.

# COLLABORATIVE PRACTICE SKILLS

Collaborative practice lends itself to rural community work. Guided by a generalist approach, collaborative work recognizes the need to work with the collective to address the identified issue. Both generalist and collaborative frameworks are flexible and offer the ability to be creative and to gather needed supports. The intervention goals can be applied individually or expanded to include several resources. The collaborative practice approach is a natural application in rural communities, which are collective and interdependent in nature.

Collaborative practice is a cooperative approach toward a defined outcome. The collaborative practice process can be facilitated on several levels. In rural community practice, collaborative practice can be the relationship established with an individual client or a relationship established at the community level. Delaney, Brownlee, and Zapf (2001) note, "Collaboration can be defined as a process and a commitment to work together, pool resources, mutually problem-solve, jointly act on decisions, and to share responsibility and authority. It is important for collaborative efforts to include all necessary stakeholders and for these stakeholders to share common principles and goals in striving for mutually agreed upon results" (p. 71).

When working with clients one-on-one, successful collaboration occurs when the client is equally involved in the helping process. Collaborative case planning requires the client to provide his or her thoughts on what the situation is, how the client wants things to look, and the steps that need to be taken to achieve the desired outcome. Case planning that engages clients facilitates ownership of the successful outcomes by the clients, and therefore they are better able to implement the learned skill into their daily lives.

Community collaboration involves working from the vision of the community. The practitioner provides a framework to assist the community in the process of achieving community-defined goals. This collaborative practice partnership creates the framework for each person involved to participate according to his or her individual strength to bring the collective vision forward. The process encourages dialogue, which leads to community decision making and collaborative efforts.

Rural and remote communities are close-knit and largely interdependent, which creates roles and structures. In rural community settings, collaborative practice can include community members who contribute traditional knowledge or healing practices that are core to the community's makeup. Collaborative work could also include natural leaders or community organizers identified by the community as vital to the community's structure. It is important to examine who the community defines as having leadership or helping roles. This model of practice is client and community centred and encourages solution-focused dialogue in case plan development.

Interdisciplinary collaborative practice models can also be applied to merge professional skill sets and increase the effectiveness of service provision. In cities, interdisciplinary collaborative approaches may include conferring, referral or inclusion of specialized services, or team approaches. In rural practice, collaborative practice can include other professionals working within the community, such as school teachers, nurses, or spiritual leaders. Interdisciplinary collaborative approaches are sometimes met with resistance because individuals are concerned about the crossing over of roles; in rural communities, this approach can strengthen and support the achievement of a larger vision. Community collaboration can be very complex and requires thoughtful planning. As a practitioner, it is important to recognize when collaborative practice approaches will encourage success and when they may cause disharmony.

Once a practitioner has established who in the community holds professional roles and who holds community leadership roles, conversation about collaborative practice options can take place. Workshops defining the benefits of collaborative practice may assist in answering questions and concerns brought forward by all stakeholders. A clear vision, possible benefits, and boundaries need to be established for all involved.

---

### Rural Collaborative Practice Role Terms

**Broker:** Guides client systems toward existing services, helping them negotiate the service system and/or linking components of the service system with one another

**Mobilizer:** Works with groups or committees to create resources that relate to existing problems

**Mediator:** Works with groups or individuals to resolve conflicts by mediating the interaction in an impartial manner

**Advocate:** Attempts to obtain services or rights for an individual or a group by fighting for those services or rights to overcome obstacles

**Clinician:** Works with individuals, families, or small groups to bring about specific change in their behaviour patterns, symptoms, or perceptions, including imparting information to develop various skills

**Data manager:** Collects, classifies, and analyzes data generated within the social welfare environment to aid the development of action plans

**Manger:** Manages a program, organization, or service unit

**Community organizer:** Works with large groups, organizations, or communities to help them increase their skills in solving social welfare problems (York, Denton, & Moran, 1989, p. 205)

---

## CONFIDENTIALITY AND ETHICS IN RURAL PLACEMENTS

Professional guidelines outline practitioners' professional obligation to have clients' best interests at the forefront of their practice. These codes of conduct are designed to provide professionals with a framework that guides ethical practice and assists with ethical decision making when necessary. The Canadian Association of Social Workers' (CASW) Code of Ethics (2005a) states, "Ethical behaviour comes from a social worker's individual commitment to engage in ethical practice" (p. 2).

## Core Social Work Values and Principles

The CASW Code of Ethics (2005a) outlines six core principles.

Value 1: Respect for Inherent Dignity and Worth of Persons
Value 2: Pursuit of Social Justice
Value 3: Service to Humanity
Value 4: Integrity of Professional Practice
Value 5: Confidentiality in Professional Practice
Value 6: Competence in Professional Practice (p. 4)

It is important that the definitions of ethical practice and confidentiality be explained to clients at the outset of the helping relationship. In some cases, this may be delayed, for example, in response to an immediate crisis situation. It is critical that as soon as possible after crisis management clients have an understanding of how the practitioner will manage their information and where the boundaries and limits are within the confidentiality guidelines. The CASW (2005a) defines confidentiality as follows:

A professional value that demands that professionally acquired information be kept private and not shared with third parties unless the client provides informed consent or a professional or legal obligation exists to share such information without client informed consent. (p. 10)

In some practice settings, confidentiality is limited to the client and practitioner relationship. In others, access to information may include support staff. In rural community settings, extending confidentiality to support staff adds complexity to maintaining privacy, as the support staff employee may be a client's family member, a relative, or a neighbour the client has known for several years. Thoughtful planning must be considered specific to each community setting and service centre.

The application of ethical practice is ultimately up to the practitioner. In rural community practice, the ethical practice implications become complex and require consideration of the urban–rural differences. This happens because of differences in space. The rural and remote social work and human service practitioner needs to become part of the community in order to be accepted and respected as someone able to contribute to the fabric of community life. The restricted and confined nature of space, especially in remote isolated communities, results in a situation where the professional and work aspect overlaps with the personal and private aspect of the social work and human service practitioner or student. In urban locations it is generally possible to establish a degree of anonymity and avoid overlap between the professional and private aspects of one's life. This is much more difficult in rural and remote practice. Efforts to construct rigid boundaries and put up barriers may be viewed negatively and may lead the social work or human service practitioner or student into a state of isolation or community rejection.

---

### Exercise

Consider the following examples and answer the questions below.

**A.** In rural community practice, it is not unheard of for a practitioner to walk clients home or visit their homes as part of the service provision. In urban settings, walking clients home would create concern.

**B.** In rural community practice, the clients on a practitioner's caseload may know intimate details of one another, may be related, or may be in conflict. In urban settings, a practitioner's clients will likely not know one another, and in a case where a connection may affect practice, it is easy to have a client assigned to another practitioner.

1. What challenges in rural practice might arise in examples A and B above?
2. Does either example raise concerns?
3. Would you feel confident in both the urban and the rural contexts mentioned in the examples?

---

# RELATIONSHIP DEVELOPMENT

Establishing relationships is foundational to successful practice outcomes. In larger centres, individuals seeking support can contact the appropriate agency and the relationship is constructed between the individual and the assigned practitioner. Rural practice requires that relationship development be structured from a community engagement perspective. The focus is establishing a relationship with the whole community to support community wellness.

Establishing relationships benefits all the parties involved. In rural community practice, practitioners should develop a plan for providing the community with the opportunity to get to know them. Communities want a sense of who the practitioners are, where they are from, and what their intentions are. A new community practitioner is like a stranger in a person's home, and the community's (home owner's) immediate reaction is to seek information that grounds the stranger in its world view. Once the community has established "who" the practitioner is, the process of "how" the practitioner becomes part of the existing system begins. The outcome is embedded in successful relationship development.

The practitioner might consider organizing an informal meet and greet, providing snacks and the opportunity for community members to stop by and ask questions. The practitioner may also consider attending community functions that are central to the community's socialization to gain insight into the community and show interest in participating at the community level.

## Voices from the Field

As a non-Aboriginal person I was very intimidated my first month of practicing in an Aboriginal agency. After learning about the historical impacts of non-Aboriginal people on Aboriginal people, I wondered if I would be accepted by the community at all. I had worked with other Aboriginal families, and my undergraduate degree was in First Nations studies, but would that help me at all? I knew I would have to work hard at building relationships and gaining trust within the community. How could I portray to the community who I really was and my purpose within the agency in a non-intimidating way? Would I be able to build strong relationships like my colleagues already had, or would I just be passed over? (Jennifer Tkachuk, student)

## Discussion Questions

1. Have you had a similar experience to the one Jennifer mentioned?
2. What concerns do you have when working cross-culturally?
3. How will you address your concerns?

## Dual Relationships

The concept of dual relationships speaks to the reality that practitioners have contact with clients and community members outside the traditional working relationship. Dual relationships occur when multiple roles take place between the helper and the client. The probability of dual relationships increases in smaller community practice settings.

Professional boundaries are important when working with dual relationships. For example, in a small community, visiting people in their homes, walking with clients, or working on multiple interventions violate the traditional "in office, by appointment" helping relationship.

When assessing roles and dual relationships, it is important to recognize that there are several contributing factors. Small, rural community dynamics often challenge the concept of dual relationships. A client's culture will affect what roles and boundaries are viewed as appropriate, and these boundaries may be different from the practitioner's. For example, over time, the professional may be invited to community events, a wedding, or a celebration for which attendance is viewed as significant by the community. Not attending may cause disharmony or barriers between the practitioner and the community.

The practitioner needs to be careful not to violate boundaries that will harm the client. Creating clear boundaries will assist the practitioner with facilitating a healthy working relationship. Examples of violations may include exploiting power, enmeshment, or actions resulting in the client not accessing support when needed in the future. The CASW Guidelines for Ethical Practice (2005b) outlines the following:

### 2.4 Dual and Multiple Relationships

Dual or multiple relationships occur when social workers relate to clients in more than one relationship, whether professional, social or business. Dual or multiple relationships can occur simultaneously or consecutively. While having contact with clients in different life situations is not inherently harmful, it is the responsibility of the social worker to evaluate the nature of the various contacts to determine whether the social worker is in a position of power and/or authority that may unduly and/or negatively affect the decisions and actions of their client.

2.4.1 Social workers take care to evaluate the nature of dual or multiple relationships to ensure that the needs and welfare of their clients are protected.

Corey, Corey, and Callanan (2007) suggest that, prior to entering into a dual relationship, practitioners should apply an ethical decision-making model to ensure all aspects have been appropriately considered. The authors quote Younggren and Gottlieb (2004), who offer the following questions as a guideline to decision making:

- Is entering in a relationship in addition to the professional one necessary, or should I avoid it?
- Can the dual relationship cause harm to the client?
- If harm seems unlikely, would the additional relationship prove beneficial?
- Is there a risk that the dual relationship could disrupt the therapeutic relationship?
- Can I evaluate the matter objectively? (p. 267)

It is important that practitioners be thoughtful in their assessments and clearly explain the implications to clients. Practitioners can also ask colleagues to consult on the case to ensure that their decision-making process was objective.

## Voices from the Field

A new client entered my office crying. I immediately recognized her as somebody who had taken many of the same undergraduate classes with me as a fellow grad student. I listened to her story and made a follow-up appointment the next week. I questioned whether or not it was ethical to have her as a client. During the next week, we saw each other in the halls, chatting occasionally. She even insisted I attend a presentation she was giving at the school. As a student counsellor, I wanted to build a strong, trusting relationship with this client, but at the same time, I needed to separate my role as a counsellor and my role as a fellow student. How could I do that without hurting our client–counsellor relationship and our budding new friendship? (Jennifer Tkachuk, student)

**Discussion Questions**

1.  Have you had a similar experience to the one Jennifer described?

2.  How would you manage this scenario?

3.  What are the implications of this kind of experience if you are the only counsellor in a small community?

4.  What concerns can you see with the situation described?

5.  What are the important considerations?

## PERSONAL BOUNDARIES AND SOCIALIZATION

A challenge faced by students and professionals in rural practice is socialization. Many students and practitioners leave their communities to seek training but hope to one day return home to assist their own communities. However, when practitioners return home, they find themselves overwhelmed by the demands. The community views the students or newly trained practitioners as the community members they have always known, and sometimes this can create upset when practice boundaries are introduced.

It is important that social work and human service practitioners educate community members about their new role and how their training can assist the community with its goals. This learning process may take time, and it may take a while for the practitioners to become part of the community structure; however, it is vital that practitioners maintain ongoing education around the value of their new role to the overall community.

Socializing can be a challenge because of lack of options and high visibility. Practitioners will likely see clients in restaurants, in grocery stores, at sports outings, and in schools, which may make it hard to maintain a private social life. Some community professionals recommend that practitioners create a social group with other professionals working in the community. Practitioners might also take frequent vacations from the community to address high visibility issues and to support personal wellness.

## CHAPTER SUMMARY

Rural community practice is both challenging and exciting work. Students who have an opportunity to participate in a rural field placement will experience a variety of learning. Rural practice requires a generalist approach, creating a rich learning experience that will advance a student's skills on many levels.

This chapter provides an overview of rural practice perspectives that must be viewed through a community lens. Student learners need to consider the differences in practice application. The additional complexities of travel, isolation, economy, and geography influence service delivery options and outcomes. Case management must include consideration of rural community living. The practitioner will be faced with challenges in privacy, dual relationships, and implications for ethical practice. It is important to examine how these concepts present from a community practice standpoint and what shifts in approaches to practice need to be understood.

Rural community practice provides the opportunity to practice creatively. Once the practitioner has established successful community engagement, he or she can begin goal planning. The process of working with the community to achieve a defined vision is a powerful collaborative experience.

## Critical-Thinking Questions

1. How do practice dynamics differ in urban and rural community practice?

2. `What ethical considerations can create challenges in rural practice?

3. How do practitioners create boundaries in rural practice?

4. As a student, what challenges to maintaining confidentiality in rural community practice might you face?

## Suggested Readings

Ban, P. (2005). "Aboriginal child placement principle and family group conferences." *Australian Social Work, 58*(4), 384–394.

Baskin, C. (2005). "Mino-yaa-daa: Healing together." In K. Bronwlee, & J. Graham (Eds.), *Violence in the family: Social work readings and research from rural Canada* (pp. 170–181). Toronto, ON: Canadian Scholars' Press.

Boone, M., Minore, B., Katt, M., & Kinch, P. (1997). "Strength through sharing: Interdisciplinary teamwork in providing social and health services to northern native communities." In K. Brownlee, R. Delaney, & J. Graham (Eds.), *Strategies for northern social work practice* (pp. 45–59). Thunder Bay, ON: Lakehead University Press.

Delaney, R., Brownlee, K., Sellick, M., & Tranter, D. (1997). "Ethical problems facing northern social workers." *The Social Worker, 65*(3), 55–65.

Faulkner, K., & Faulkner, T. (1997). "Managing multiple relationships in rural communities: Neutrality and boundary violations." *Clinical Psychology: Science and Practice, 4*(3), 225–234.

Larson, N., & Dearmont, M. (2002). "Strengths of farming communities in fostering resilience in children." *Child Welfare, 81*, 821–836.

Marais, L., & Marais, L. C. (2007). "Walking between worlds: An exploration of the interface between indigenous and first-world industrialized culture." *International Social Work, 50*, 809–820.

Morrissette, V., McKenzie, B., & Morrissette, L. (1993). "Towards an aboriginal model of social work practice. Cultural knowledge and traditional practices." *Canadian Social Work Review, 10*(1), 91-108.

Schmidt, G. (2005). "Geographic context and northern child welfare practice." In K. Brownlee & J. Graham (Eds.), *Violence in the family: Social work readings and research from northern and rural Canada* (pp. 16–29). Toronto, ON: Canadian Scholars' Press Inc.

Wonders, C. (Ed.). (2003). *Canada's changing north*. Montreal, QC, & Kingston, ON: McGill/Queen's University Press.

Wright, S. (1992). "Rural community development: What sort of social change?" *Journal of Rural Studies, 8*(1), 15–28.

Zapf, M. K. (2002). "Geography and Canadian social work practice." In F. Turner (Ed.), *Social work practice: A Canadian perspective* (2nd ed., pp. 69–83). Toronto, ON: Prentice Hall.

## Relevant Websites

### Canada's Rural Partnership

www.rural.gc.ca

This Government of Canada website examines population, economic, social, and health-services indicators in areas belonging to four different categories of rural. It describes the differences that exist not only between rural and urban areas, but also between different types of rural regions.

### The Rural Think Tank 2005—Understanding issues families face living in rural and remote communities

www.phac-aspc.gc.ca/dca-dea/pubs/rtt-grr-2005/2-eng.php

Canada has no official single definition of what is considered a rural or remote community. Several alternative definitions are used by Statistics Canada for policy analysis purposes. Each definition emphasizes different criteria (population size, commuting distance, etc.) and results in different thresholds.

### Making the Links Parts 1 and 2

www.youtube.com/watch?v=vLumuoFnJvc

www.youtube.com/watch?v=YVXRcCFC6Xw

The Making the Links program, offered by the College of Medicine at the University of Saskatchewan since 2005, is a unique service learning opportunity for health sciences students. Through the program, students gain an understanding of the diverse factors that contribute to health or illness, and partner with communities in their education. These complex themes are brought to the student through the stories and voices of real people who live in rural communities and are aware of the realities of doing so.

# Chapter 13

## Interprofessional Field Education: Reciprocal Learning for Collaborative Practice

Grant Charles, Shafik Dharamsi, and Carla Alexander

## Chapter Objectives

- Understand the dynamics of interprofessional interactions in practice environments.
- Explain how the values of the social work and health service disciplines, the concepts associated with mutuality, and interprofessional collaboration can improve the way practitioners interact with clients and colleagues.
- Recognize the influences that shape social work and health service practitioners as they begin to practice.
- Appreciate the importance of developing reciprocal relationships in daily interactions with colleagues.

## PROFESSIONAL IDENTITY

Placement is a time of change for students (Lamote & Engels, 2010). It is the time when they adopt their professional, or occupational, identities. Students often struggle with developing their sense of self as professionals (Ikiugu & Rosso, 2003).

## Voices from the Field

The worst thing about being a student for me was not knowing who I was. I wasn't the person I used to be. The stuff I had gone taken in class had made sure of that. The problem was I hadn't become who I thought I was going to be. I was kind of stuck in this kind of middle place. I felt lost in some ways. This changed as I came near to the end of my second placement. I had a better sense of being a practitioner. Not fully but enough that I could feel okay about it. Looking back, it had been a bit of a painful process for me. A good one but still hard. I hadn't even thought about how hard it was going to be. I thought I would learn a bunch of skills and then, I guess, just magically become a professional. I never realized the changes I would go through while at school. (Anonymous, student)

Students begin their training with a strong sense of their personal identities. They have an existing set of skills, values, attitudes, and knowledge. One of students' main tasks in their social work and human service training is to blend who they were when they began their program with their new professional identities. To a great extent, the practitioners that students will become is shaped by the interactions they have with people in their work environments, such as clients, colleagues, peers, and members of other disciplines. Students' relationships also have considerable influence on the quality of these interactions and how students interpret them. Those who build strong relationships with others and who are open to learning from and collaborating with members of their own discipline and members of other professions will become better practitioners.

## Discussion Questions

1. Identify three key influences that helped to shape your identity before you entered your current program.

2. Identify one of the core values about people that you have held for some time that influences how you interact with others.

3. Identify one of the core values that might have been different if you had grown up in another culture.

4. How do you think these factors will influence who you will become as a practitioner?

Professional identity can be defined as the group skills, values, attitudes, and knowledge that practitioners share with other people in their discipline (Adams, Hean, Sturgis, & MacLeod Clark, 2006). It is how social work and human service practitioners define themselves. Professional identity comes from how practitioners view their personal selves combined with what they perceive to be the context of their field or profession (Cohen-Scali, 2003; Ohlen & Sergesten, 1999). Students' sense of personal self comes from their families, cultures, friends, and all the other interactions they have in their lives (Garfat & Charles, 2007). Their sense of professional self comes from what they learn in class and their interactions with people in their profession and others in their work environments. For students to acquire professional identities, they must internalize the values and beliefs of the social work and human service professions and adapt their behaviour and self-views accordingly (Adams et al., 2006).

Professional identity is not fixed or finished (King & Ross, 2003). Rather, it is an ongoing process that changes and evolves as students interact with the world in which they work. Students' professional identities are constrained by the historical and contemporary perceptions of what it means to be a member of the social work and human service professions. These perceptions are a strong component of the socialization process that students undergo in their training. While students have some room to express their individuality and be different from other members of their profession, all members of the discipline are expected to have similar core values and beliefs.

When students begin their training, they often have a mental image of what they will be like when they graduate (Kaiser, 2002). Although classroom work modifies this notion, students often bring much of the original image of the discipline or profession into their field placements. Students' ideas of the professional self are further modified through their observations of others in the field. As they gain work experience in their placements, their sense of who they are as a member of their profession deepens and strengthens. They incorporate their original thoughts about the field, their classroom learning, and the interactions they experience in their placements and begin to compare and differentiate themselves from people in other professions or areas of work. Students gradually become members of their discipline or profession (Adams et al., 2006). During this process, they differentiate themselves from members of other professions and disciplines, although it is important to remember that the social work and human services professions or disciplines are not completely different from other areas of practice. All disciplines borrow from one another's realms of knowledge and practice wisdom.

It is important to note that students do not develop into their professional selves through the completion of a series of tasks during their placements. Instead, the transformation occurs through their interactions with others and their reflections on these interactions. As students develop into practitioners, they realize that their understanding of their role becomes clearer and more complex (Kyril, 1988).

Traditionally, as we have outlined, people have understood that they become professionals primarily through interactions with members of their own profession or discipline. Professional training emphasizes this as a part of socialization into any field of practice. However, researchers have recently realized that the socialization process is far more complex than traditionally thought. An understanding of the two-way or bidirectional nature of relationships is changing the traditional way of thinking (Alexander, 2008; Alexander & Charles, 2009). It appears that professional identities develop because of interactions with clients and *other* professions and disciplines. We are also beginning to appreciate that the other professions and disciplines can be complementary to the goals of our professions rather than seeing them as a potential threat. This new understanding is discussed later in this chapter. These changing beliefs may have a strong influence on what students do in their placements and who they eventually become as practitioners.

Discussion Questions

1. Identify three key influences that have helped to shape your professional identity since you entered your current program.
2. Identify one of the core values about people that you have acquired or strengthened since coming into your program that influences how you interact with others.
3. Identify a value that you previously held that has changed as result of your training.

## INTERPROFESSIONAL PRACTICE

Professions and disciplines have traditionally socialized their members to believe that they, of all professionals, are best able to serve their particular clients. This teaching has often led to major barriers among the various professions and disciplines, resulting in a lack of communication and collaboration (Charles, Bainbridge, Copeman-Stewart, Tiffin, & Kassam, 2006; Charles, Bainbridge, Copeman-Stewart, Kassam, & Tiffin, 2008; Salhani & Charles, 2007). The corresponding lack of communication and collaboration can cause serious, and often fatal, harm to clients. There are many examples of people being seriously harmed because various professions and disciplines didn't work well together (Kohn, Corrigan, & Donaldson, 2000).

## Voices from the Field

There was a point in my placement where I thought to become a member of my profession I had to reject the other professions. It seemed to me that they were almost the enemy. I know they weren't really but it seemed to me that I had to be loyal to my profession. I felt so loyal that it was hard for me to understand why anyone would want to be a member of any other profession. I also went through a period where I thought that the way my profession saw the world was the only right way to see the world. I didn't understand that different professions see the world differently. I didn't understand that rather than this being a threat that it could be a good thing. (Anonymous, student)

The barriers are often created as a result of turf protection and power differences among professions (Geva, Barsky, & Westernoff, 2000), of closed role boundaries (Miller, Freeman, & Ross, 2001), of role insecurity (Hornby & Atkins, 2000), and of the protection of "profession specific" knowledge (Miller et al., 2001). Other contributing factors include value and priority differences (Loxley, 1997; Miller et al., 2001) and a perceived threat to professional freedom (Loxley, 1997). These single or combined issues often create rigid barriers among the professions that set them apart from one another and the people they serve. These barriers exist within the post-secondary education system as well as in the practice community (Paul & Peterson, 2001).

In addition to these barriers, it is important to realize that practitioners hold stereotypes of people from other disciplines and professions (Carpenter, 1995). Some of them include "social workers are all bleeding hearts," "doctors are interested only in the medical model," and "child and youth care workers work only with children." These stereotypes have a great deal of influence on how social work and human service practitioners interact with others. Sometimes they are positive and may contribute to a helpful interaction, but most often stereotypes are negative and contribute to mistrust and poor communication, which often leads to negative outcomes for clients (Hind et al., 2003).

---

## Discussion Questions

1. Can you think of a time when you worked with a professional from another profession or discipline and you felt inferior? Describe how this perception affected your interactions with the person or with clients. Why do you think you felt this way?

2. Can you think of a time when you worked with a professional from another profession or discipline and you felt superior? Describe how this perception affected your interactions with the other person or with clients. Why do you think you felt this way?

---

Practitioners' assumptions of what they know about others' professional work are often mistaken. Their "knowing" is often based on their experiences prior to entry into the field, stereotypes of the "other," and their reactions to current interactions. Students must learn to treat all such views as suspect because few are based on seeing the world through the eyes of people from these other disciplines. It is only when students begin to "walk in their shoes" that they see that they can be driven by similar inaccuracies and misperceptions.

Placements can reinforce the barriers to interprofessional practice. In most instances and for most professions and disciplines, field education is uniprofessional (Charles et al., 2005; Charles et al., 2008, Charles, Bainbridge, & Gilbert, 2010). For example, social work students tend to do their field training with other social work students, while under the supervision of a social worker. Their interactions with members of other professions are often limited. Even when they occur, these interactions are often viewed through a lens that fosters interprofessional distance rather than collaboration. The issues of territoriality, ownership of expertise, value differences, and power imbalances that are often seen in the practice world are a part of the framework that students acquire during their field placements. The students come from the uniprofessional world of their classrooms to the uniprofessional world of their field placements. This experience almost guarantees that they will acquire the traditionally limited collaborative practices that cause so many difficulties for clients.

# Definitions of Types of Practice

**Unidisciplinary (Uniprofessional) Practice**   Members of a single profession working together. An example of this would be a child protection team in which all the professional staff members are social workers.

**Multidisciplinary (Multiprofessional) Practice**   When two or more professions work beside each other but not with each other. An example of this would be a counselling program where there are psychological therapists and family support workers with child and youth care training who are located in the same general space but have little professional contact with one another in the course of a day.

**Interdisciplinary Practice**   Work settings that use knowledge from a number of disciplines. An example of this would be a mental health clinic where a range of professions, such as medicine, nursing, psychology, child and youth care, and social work, operate within their own professions by using a shared practice framework developed from the knowledge of various disciplines.

**Interprofessional Practice**   When two or more professions intentionally interact to learn with, from, and about each other in order to improve effectiveness, collaboration, and the quality of service they provide to clients. An example of this would be a street outreach team made up of a nurse, a youth care worker, and a social worker. The team members have responsibilities specific to their discipline but also serve as assistants to one another. For this type of practice to work, each member must not only be an expert in his or her own area, but have an advanced understanding of the knowledge and skills of the other team members.

# A Cause of Interprofessional Conflict

An understanding of the way professionals develop is important to understanding interprofessional interactions (Charles et al., 2010). Throughout their classroom and placement training, students are surrounded by members of their discipline because they are generally taught and supervised by people from their profession. As mentioned earlier in the chapter, students' environments and the people they interact with greatly influence the type of practitioners students will become, so if they are surrounded by people from their own disciplines, they will acquire values and attitudes from those people. Students have traditionally learned from watching other members of their discipline model professional values, attitudes, and knowledge. As a result, as they progress through their training, they increasingly see the world through the eyes of the discipline. In many ways, this traditional method has served professions well. It is the easiest and most effective way for students to strengthen their sense of professional self.

The downside of this method of training is that the likelihood that students will see the world through the perspectives of other disciplines is decreased (Charles et al., 2010). This form of teaching subtly encourages students to see their discipline's perspective as the "correct" way of seeing the world. Once students have made the transition to perceiving the world in one way, there is an increased likelihood that there will be misunderstandings and miscommunications with members of other disciplines. If every profession is operating from the perspective that the way it views things is the "right" way, then it becomes easier to assume that the way others see the world is the "wrong" way. Given this, it becomes apparent why there can be so much suspicion and mistrust between professions, resulting in interprofessional conflict.

## Exercise

Think of three other disciplines or professions that work in the same professional area as you. What is your opinion of them? Do you see them as allies or enemies? What are the strengths of each of them? How are they supportive of your discipline and/or how are they a threat?

Interprofessional education seeks to change the relationships between how professionals and disciplines interact with one another as well as with the clients and communities that social work and human resources practitioners serve. This change requires moving from an expert-driven, top-down model to a model that acknowledges the expertise not only of other professions but also of clients. Clients' roles in identifying and dealing with their needs become more important in this framework. A recognition of the skills and strengths of others results in not only a more equitable system but also a stronger and more efficient one.

## Benefits of Interprofessional Practice

The following are benefits of interprofessional practice:

- enhanced work environments
- greater job satisfaction
- less stress and burn-out
- greater workplace efficiency and capacity
- higher staff retention rates
- fewer intervention errors
- enhanced quality of service

The authors believe that the only way to overcome the narrowing of perspective that comes from the traditional method of training students is to offer people the chance to interact in an organized way with members of other disciplines. Interprofessional education and collaboration does not mean just working side-by-side or being on a team together; instead, it involves occasions "when two or more professions learn with, from and about each other to improve collaboration and the quality of care" (Centre for the Advancement of Interprofessional Education [CAIPE], 2002). According to CAIPE (2002), effective collaboration involves working with other disciplines and professions to improve the quality of care for clients by pooling the strengths of a range of disciplines and recognizing that no single profession can do it all alone. Interprofessional collaboration serves to encourage people from different disciplines to respect the similar and unique contributions that other professions can make to the delivery of services to clients. It also places the needs of clients at the centre of all professional interactions and, as such, tries to engage those who use services to be actively involved in students' training.

All this means that we have to learn to put aside differences, stereotypes, rivalries, and negative views of other disciplines to learn together and work together. Students will benefit from working with practitioners from other professions. This interaction can take the form of taking some common classes with other students where there are the opportunities for everyone to discuss issues from the perspective of their individual professions. Students will also benefit from talking about their practice (i.e., what they do and why they do it the way they do). Opportunities to interact with practitioners of other disciplines will give students opportunities to argue and disagree with others in supportive and safe environments, to get past differences, to carefully listen to what people from other professions think and believe in order to understand them, and to get to a place where people from different disciplines can work together.

Another way students can begin to see the world through the eyes of other disciplines is to spend time with them during the placement. Some students may have the opportunity to use a block of time to shadow members of other professions. For example, a social work student who is doing a child protection placement might spend a shift or two with a youth care student who is doing their practicum in a group home. Seeing the youth care student's strengths and struggles as he or she works a shift with a houseful of adolescents will teach the social work student more about the youth care perspective than any isolated discussion with youth care workers could. There is a lot students can learn in these situations.

However, as mentioned, it is not enough to just be with the people from other disciplines. Students have to take time to reflect on the interactions because people don't change simply by having an experience (Merriam, 2004). Students need to let people from other disciplines correct them if they are misunderstanding what is being said or done. Students need time to think about what they are hearing and reflect on what it means to them. They need time to compare what they are seeing and being told with how their discipline does things. Students need to have time to critically reflect on the barriers that they may be building between themselves and other disciplines, as a member of a particular profession and as an individual. They must reflect on their stereotypes about others and how their training may reinforce them. Students need to learn new ways of interacting with others and to overcome the fact that they do things in their professions because the profession has always done them that way (Wackerhausen, 2009). In order to do all of these things, students need time to talk with others and reflect on others' words and their own actions (Merriam, 2004; Sockman & Sharma, 2007).

# Mutuality and Reciprocity: The Foundation of Interprofessional Practice

The foundation of interprofessional practice is the development of mutual and reciprocal relationships with members of other professions. As mentioned, professional identities develop, in part, through interactions with other professionals. The term *reciprocity* identifies the purposeful, responsive gestures of exchange within a relationship. Both reciprocity and absence of reciprocity provide information to relationship participants about their roles and the quality of the relationship. Gestures of reciprocity and mutuality, which are discussed later in this section, have an impact on the quality of the relationship. These interactions can also affect one's sense of identity as an effective or "good" professional.

Of course, the context of the interaction also informs how each participant interprets each gesture. In an interaction between members of two professions, if one person is anxious about his or her status as a beginning practitioner, the actions of the other person are likely to be more important. A perceived power imbalance between the two professionals can influence how the relationship develops, especially when they first meet. While the importance of the quality of the relationship varies depending on the nature of the task, a respectful working relationship is always core to the achievement of most goals. Practitioners are successful in their roles when they establish good relationships and work together toward the achievement of each contributor's goals.

Taking notice of reciprocal gestures is one of the ways practitioners report gauging the quality of relationships (Alexander & Charles, 2009). Sometimes reciprocal gestures are very subtle, such as smiles, inquiries about the practitioner's day, or even certain looks and glances. Gestures may also be more overt, such as direct statements of appreciation. Reciprocity includes respect, liking, and trust returned by others in response to the worker, and vice versa. Reciprocal practitioners report a sense of competence, value, and accomplishment in their work when they experience reciprocal gestures. In a reciprocal relationship, practitioners are willing to try to understand the views of another person even if they disagree with them. In addition, practitioners who participate in such relationships are committed to coming to an agreement on a course of action that takes into account both world views.

*Mutuality* is the phenomenon that describes a sense of shared relationship and joint investment for each participant. It may include "mutual empathy ... a two-way process that occurs when two people relate to one another in a context of interest in the other, emotional availability, responsiveness, and the intent to understand" (Jordan, 1986, p. 7). It involves the process of "bi-directional movement of feelings, thoughts and activities between persons in a relationship" (Genero, Miller, Surrey, & Baldwin, 1992, p. 36). Mutuality might be expressed through reciprocal gestures. These experiences of mutuality reinforce the shared human qualities of those in the relationship, whatever their professional affiliations (the same is true in practitioner–client relationships).

During the development of a professional role identity, an individual is likely to be particularly attuned to the responses of people from other professions and is looking carefully for signs of his or her own effectiveness. The quality of the relationship is a part of this evaluation, and indications of reciprocity and mutuality serve to indicate that both parties are engaged and willing to join with each other to achieve goals. All experiences working with others play a role in the development of a professional's identity. When professionals are oriented to noticing and acknowledging one another's expressions of mutuality and reciprocity, they receive strong reinforcement of their identities as effective practitioners and as caring human beings.

## Qualities of an Effective Interprofessional Practitioner

In their field placements, students are expected to develop the skills needed to become functioning and contributing members of their disciplines. In addition, they must ensure that they develop the skills they need to work effectively with members of other professions. Because interprofessional practice is a relatively new concept, there is not yet universal agreement on what these attitudes and skills are. However, we know enough about interprofessional collaboration to suggest that by the time students have completed their training, they should ideally be able to describe the roles and responsibilities of their own profession to other people. They also need to be able to take a critical view of their profession by identifying its strengths and limitations. Students should be able to recognize and acknowledge the roles and contributions of other professions, and should have the skills and attitudes required to resolve conflict with other professions and to lead interprofessional activities such as case conferences. One of these skills will be the ability to appreciate and tolerate differences in world views among the professions. Perhaps most importantly, students need to be able to enter into interdependent relationships with members of other professions to develop and implement intervention plans that serve clients' best interests. Interprofessional competencies include the ability to:

- describe one's roles and responsibilities clearly to members of other professions;
- recognize and observe the constraints of one's role, responsibilities, and competence, yet perceive the needs of clients in a wider framework;
- recognize and respect the roles, responsibilities, and competence of other professions in relation to one's own;

- work with members of other professions to effect change and resolve conflict in the provision of care and treatment;
- work with others to assess, plan, provide, and review care for individual clients;
- tolerate differences, misunderstandings, and shortcomings in members of other professions;
- facilitate interprofessional case conferences and team meetings; and
- enter into interdependent relationships with other professions (Barr, 1998).

## An Example of Interprofessional Practice

The Interprofessional Rural Program of British Columbia (IRPbc) was established in 2003 as a means of helping students in the health and human services to learn about other disciplines and to develop interprofessional skills during their field education experiences (Charles et al., 2006; Charles et al., 2008). Small teams of students from different professions are placed together in rural communities in British Columbia. While there, students fulfill the placement requirements for their own professional training while engaging in interprofessional activities with students from other professions. For example, students may spend time shadowing another team member while that person is performing a discipline-specific role. They may also develop interprofessional solutions to issues being experienced by members of the community in which they are placed. The program gives students a chance to talk together, disagree together, and learn together about other professions in an applied setting.

This program supports a positive process. While taking on the identity of a discipline helps us become professionals, its downside is that the process makes students more like the people in their own profession. This can distance them from the members of other professions who could enrich their practice, which can lead to communication problems and conflict. Indeed, these problems can cause serious harm to the people social work and human service practitioners serve. At the very least, the problems can lessen the likelihood that clients will receive the support they need at the level they should be able to expect. The IRPbc acts to improve interprofessional collaboration at the educational level and thus increase practitioners' acceptance of other world views.

## CHAPTER SUMMARY

In this chapter, we discussed the various influences that shape students in their training to become members of their particular disciplines. These influences have traditionally been the uniprofessional values, attitudes, beliefs, and behaviours that students are socialized to have through their classroom and placement interactions with other members of their discipline. These forces are extremely powerful and begin to shape students' world views in a particular way. While powerful, their influence can also be subtle so that the change that students go through often goes unnoticed. As a result, students become more like the members of their profession and less like those of other disciplines.

We suggest in this chapter that to become contributing members of their professions, while also retaining the ability to see and accept different world views, students should incorporate the concepts of mutuality, reciprocity, and interprofessional collaboration into their professional identities. We believe that students who incorporate these concepts into their ways of interacting with others will make their professions more effective, their lives more satisfying, and their interventions more creative.

## Critical-Thinking Questions

1. Think of a time when you were able to see the world through the eyes of someone else. What surprised you about your new knowledge of their situation? Can you think of how you might transfer this skill to another area and apply it to relationships with clients or members of other professions?

2. We obviously believe that the concepts we have presented in this chapter are critical for improving cooperation and collaboration with clients and colleagues. However, we also believe that every concept has two sides. What would be the downside to you, your profession, and your clients if you incorporated the concepts we have suggested into your daily practices?

3. Changing the way professions interact with the world means changing the professions, which can be a difficult process. What difficulties would you likely encounter if you tried to incorporate the concepts we have suggested into your practice?

## Suggested Readings

Alexander, C. (2007). "You are what you do." *Journal of Relational Child and Youth Care Practice, 20*(3), 17–21.

Alexander, C. & Charles, G. (2009). "Caring, mutuality and reciprocity in social worker–client relationships." *Journal of Social Work, 9*(1), 5–22.

Charles, G., Bainbridge, L., & Gilbert, J. (2010). "The UBC Model of interprofessional education." *Journal of Interprofessional Care, 24*(1), 9–18.

Garfat, T., & Charles, G. (2007). "How am I who I am? Self in child and youth care." *Relational Child and Youth Care Practice, 20*(6), 6–16.

Salhani, D., & Charles, G. (2007). "The dynamics of an interprofessional team: The interplay of child and youth care with other professions within a residential treatment milieu." *Relational Child and Youth Care Practice, 20*(4), 12–20.

## Relevant Websites

### College of Health Disciplines
www.chd.ubc.ca
This University of British Columbia website provides a framework of interprofessional competencies as well as a number of readings on interprofessional education.

### Centre for the Advancement of Interprofessional Education (CAIPE)
www.caipe.org.uk
This website provides a definition of interprofessional education and a number of related resources.

### Canadian Interprofessional Health Collaborative (CIHC)
www.cihc.ca
The CIHC website allows access to extensive list of readings, interprofessional project descriptions, and links to related websites.

# Chapter 14

## Transitioning from Student to Practitioner: Launching Your Career

Helen Szewello Allen and Jeannette Robertson

## Chapter Objectives

- Identify the steps for preparing an autonomous practice.
- Develop a lifelong learning plan.
- Understand the values shift from student to practitioner.
- Explore the role of lifelong learning and mentorship.
- Become a leader in one's field.

## PREPARING FOR THE FIRST PROFESSIONAL POSITION

The long-awaited goal of completing an educational program is a thrilling time. A great deal of learning has taken place, and students have a resulting sense of accomplishment. However, this poignant moment is often accompanied by anxiety about stepping out independently into the world of employment. This chapter will assist students in preparing a plan to transition from their educational program to finding their first job and starting the journey to success in a professional career.

Thinking about beginning employment is not dissimilar to the experience of planning for a first field placement. Many of the activities identified in Chapter 2 for preparing for a field placement also apply to finding a job. Students should thoroughly review this chapter as it will provide them with strategies for preparing for their initial practice experience. Graduating students have the experience of entering the field and knowing what that feels like. They have gained experience in entering a new organization; learning how an organization functions; providing clients with a service; and witnessing the variety of ways mentorship, guidance, and supervision are provided to assist a newcomer to an organization. Thinking about both the experiences that have been gained through field placements and the integration of learning that has taken place is an excellent starting point for entering employment. Reviewing Chapter 2 will not only remind students of the activities that are important when entering a new organization, but will also, on reflection, help them define the personal growth and development that has taken place over the course of their field placements and courses of study. Students in social work and human service fields acknowledge that they have learned a tremendous amount and gained insight into their own skills, their ability to work with people, their knowledge of the workings of an agency, and the pleasure of having an impact on the lives of people in very positive and meaningful ways. Students' confidence at this point in the career journey is strong, accompanied by a wonderful feeling of achievement. Beginning to look for a first job will be challenging, but with the strong foundation of an educational program and practicum experiences, students have a great deal to offer new employers. Students can choose from many employers and a variety of contexts to find a place where they can apply their social work and human service skills. The range available has been explored somewhat through the field placement experience. But students will find that the employment opportunities available to them are much broader and greater in scope than what was available to them for a field placement experience.

The next section will provide a detailed process for finding employment opportunities, preparing a résumé and letter of application, preparing for an interview, and negotiating for a position.

---

## Tips on How to Find Employment

- In the Wednesday and Saturday online editions of newspapers, search for employment in the region where you want to work.
- Using a web browser, search "social services," "health," "professional management careers," and "education."
- Keep the following sites bookmarked and check them regularly:

    - Public Service Commission of Canada, http://jobs-emplois.gc.ca
    - Workopolis via *The Globe and Mail* website, http://globecareers.workopolis.com/index.html
    - www.communityjobs.org
    - www.working.com
    - www.bcdirectory.com
    - www.jobhuntersbible.com
    - www.charityvillage.com

- You may want to create your own job. If so, write a grant proposal and present it to the organization you want to work for.

---

- While you wait to become employed, you may want to volunteer with the kind of organization you want to work for. Check out Vantage Point (www.thevantagepoint.ca), a website that matches volunteers with non-profit organizations.

# Preparing Job Search Documentation

Before students begin their job search, they need to update their résumé to include information about field experiences, committee participation, workshops and conferences attended, and any specific research undertaken during the course of the educational program. Figure 14.1 shows a sample résumé.

---

**Figure 14.1** Sample Résumé

Name
Address
Phone — home, work, cell
Email address

**Education**
2008 Bachelor of Social Work, University
2000 Child and Youth Care Diploma, University or College
1998 High School Diploma
[Note any other specialized certification]

Social Work/Child and Youth Care Field Practica
2003 Agency
Address
- Identify key area of responsibilities
- Identify the name of the supervisor

2002 North Kamloops High School
- Worked with at-risk youth, facilitated a group for girls with eating disorders, organized a parents forum on safe sex

**Employment [list chronologically, from most recent to oldest]**

**Employment in Social Services**
2000–2003 Position, Organization, City
- Describe responsibilities

---

**Other Employment**

1998–2000 Position, Business Name

1995–1997 Bartender at Johnny's

1994–1997 Babysitting

**Community Presentations Given**

- Spoke about poverty issues at the North Shore Community Association, 2006

- Workshop on bullying, Westsyde Elementary School. Presented two-hour session on bullying for Grade 5 students. Developed and provided a manual for the students to share with their parents, 2005

- Presentation on child and youth care program at new student orientation, 2000

**Community Service**

1999–present member of the Food Bank board of directors

- Identify the name of the supervisor

1997–1999 Chair of the subcommittee on street youth, Social Planning Council

- Supervised by Sally Fellows

1997–1998 Parent volunteer at Clayton Park Secondary School

- Supervised by Grant White

1996–1997 Fundraiser, Boys and Girls Club

- Supervised by Gil Talbot

**Professional Development**

- Participated in presentation by former premier Dave Barrett on Social Work in Public Life, January 2006

- Participated in the Invisible 10% Workshop for counselling gay and lesbian youth with Bill Ryan, McGill University, September 2002

**Awards**

Dean's List

2002 Name of Award

**Complementary Skills**

- Knowledge of Microsoft Word, Excel, Outlook, WebCT

- Languages spoken: English and French

- Languages written: English

- Driver's licence [Note: It is sometimes important that the applicant identifies that (1) he or she has a driver's licence, and (2) the type of driver's licence he or she has, as some positions require employees to transport clients.]

## Tips for Building a Résumé on an Ongoing Basis

- Update your résumé every year.
- Create a file called "Career" and collect notations that relate to your professional career, such as
    - thank-you notes received from clients or colleagues;
    - flyers for events attended;
    - invitations to participate on committees or projects;
    - emails noting or commenting appreciation for participation;
    - evaluations from supervisors; and
    - anything in writing that speaks to roles and responsibilities you have undertaken.

References need to be added to the résumé. Students should definitely ask their field instructors to be referees, as employers will want to receive information on students' performance during the field placement. Students should discuss with their instructors the details that the instructors will provide in a reference. Faculty members who know a student's work well and have expressed appreciation for student's classwork should also be approached to provide a reference. It is inappropriate to name a referee whose permission has not been sought. The references should be positive. Therefore, if students have had challenging relationships with a faculty member or a field instructor, they need to think carefully about the selection of referees.

## Tips for Identifying References

- Identify three references or the number asked for; follow the instructions in the advertisement for the position.
- Make sure the contact information is complete and correct for each referee.
- Seek permission to use each referee's name.
- Select references strategically, using the following exercise to assist in selecting the most appropriate referees.

### Exercise

1. Think about your work with your current field instructor. If the instructor were to provide a reference today, what would he or she say about your practice skills, values, accountability, interpersonal skills, and provision of service to clients? What unique contribution to your chosen field do you think your instructor will say you can make?

**2.** Think of one of your favourite professors. What would he or she say about your professional knowledge, your contributions to class discussion, the quality of your written work, and your ability to think critically? What unique contribution to your profession do you think your professor will say you can make?

---

## Tips for Preparing a Cover Letter

- Identify the job you are applying for and where you heard about it.

- Pull specific skills from your résumé and suggest how these will meet the expectations of the position.

- Prepare a new letter for each job that you apply for.

- Keep your letter to one page.

- Make sure there are no spelling mistakes or grammatical errors.

- Follow up. If you have not heard from the organization by about a week after the application deadline, call to make sure the agency received your application and ask when it will be making decisions about the position.

---

## Tips for Preparing for Your Interview

- Research the skill set required for the job.

- Research the content area of the job.

- Review an annual report from the organization.

- Look up the organization online.

- Find out who is on the board of directors: Do you know someone you can speak to about the job?

- Talk to people who work in this area to find out what the job might be like.

- Match your skill set and knowledge to the expected skill set and knowledge base of the job.

- Complete the following self-inventory to generate speaking notes about what you have to offer an employer.

---

### Exercise

Reflect on your values and think about what is most important to you. What excites you? What are you passionate about? How do you see yourself making a difference? What unique skills and characteristics do you bring to a new employer?

## Tips for Interviewing Successfully and Effectively

- Dress modestly and professionally. Don't overdress or underdress.

- Arrive with a notebook in hand.

- Be prepared to be interviewed by a panel.

- Don't babble, say *um* or *eh*, or use colloquial language. Sound like the college or university graduate you are!

- Don't say you don't know something. Reframe the question and say what you do know or that you are willing to learn in an area you are less familiar with.

- When sitting, lean forward with your hands on the table.

- Don't fidget.

- If you need to, practice the interview with some friends.

- Have your notebook open and write down questions during the interview.

- Come prepared to ask questions such as the following:

  - Tell me about the culture in this organization. What would employees say are the best things about working here?
  - What kind of supervision is provided for new employees?
  - What sorts of professional development opportunities are provided for employees?
  - What are the long-term goals for this organization?
  - Following the interview, send thank-you notes to anyone who has offered you an interview or been helpful to you in your job search. You will always be re-membered for your goodwill, especially the next time you apply at the same agency.

## Tips for Negotiating a First Job Offer

- Make sure you sign a contract before you begin working.

- Find out ahead of time whether the salary is negotiable. If necessary, *check with the union for what has been negotiated.*

- Determine whether you can negotiate for things such as benefits, professional development and training, flex days, and parking.

- Be clear about your start date and the time you will need to prepare to begin your new position. Arrangements may need to be made for child care or after-school care, or you may wish to take a brief holiday before you begin to work.

Finding a job should be viewed as full-time work. To get the position one wants, investment in research and attention to detail in the application process is vital. Knowing what is wanted and why ensures a successful job search and career launch.

## Values Shift from Student to Practitioner

In addition to taking the necessary steps toward securing a first professional position, it is important for social work and human service graduates to prepare for a value shift that will happen when moving from student to practitioner. The rite of passage to becoming a professional social work and human service practitioner is a developmental and transformational process. The education journey is a series of passages that must be bridged to fulfill our purposes as professional social work and human service practitioners. The journey begins with the commencement of the first course, and moves to the field placements and the succession of courses, and then to the final milestone of the graduation ceremony. With each passage from one stage of professional development to the next, students must evolve in unfamiliar ways.

The shift from the context of being a student under the direct supervision of field instructors and faculty members, where one was entrusted with another professional's caseload during field placements and somewhat insulated from the expectations that accompany professional practice, to the expectations that accompany becoming an independent autonomous practitioner calls for a shift of perspective. While shedding the security of the "student" identity is liberating for most, it also introduces new challenges. The transition from student to self-directed autonomous professional, where in the former the indicators of success and progress were received in the form of grades and ongoing structured feedback, to intermittent supervision and evaluation requires new skills, knowledge, and awareness. This process is part of developing a professional practice framework or approach to practice. New graduates can engage in a number of processes to assist them in developing their practice framework and to respond to these new professional expectations. Some of these processes include using supervision to enhance practice, building in peer or group supervision, locating a mentor, drawing on previous learning, continuing to enhance and maintain self-awareness, managing workplace and personal stress, engaging in ongoing professional development opportunities, staying current with research in the field, and acquiring membership(s) in professional associations. Once new social work and human service practitioners have developed professional competence, they will inevitably be called on to supervise new graduates who are making the transition from student to practitioner.

Supervision has a vital role to play in the development of professional practice competence and the promotion of a learning culture (Kadushin & Harkness, 2002; Tsui, 2005; Austin & Hopkins, 2004). In addition to many other considerations during the interview process, as noted earlier, it may also be helpful to inquire as to the availability, structure, and content of supervision for new practitioners. The "ultimate long-term objective of social work supervision is to provide efficient and effective services to clients" (Tsui, 2005, p. 15). Three components of supervision are identified in the literature: administrative, educational or clinical, and supportive supervision (National Association of Social Workers, 2003). According to Tsui (2005),

> In the short term, the objective of administrative supervision is to provide frontline social workers with a context that permits them to do their job effectively. Educational supervision aims to improve the staff's capacity to do the job effectively, by helping workers to develop professionally and maximizing their practice knowledge and skills. The goal of supportive supervision is to ensure that staff social workers feel good about their job. (p. 15)

Recognizing the importance of individual supervision, new professionals will want to seek effective supervision early on in their practice to develop relevant skills, insights, and support.

Each of these aspects of supervision is oriented to different functions. For example, administrative supervision is primarily oriented to ensuring that the work is performed in compliance with organizational or agency policy. Educational or clinical supervision is devoted to teaching knowledge, skills, and attitudes, and enhancing self-awareness, while developing therapeutic skills through a collegial supervisory relationship. Supportive supervision "is concerned with increasing job performance by decreasing job related stress that interferes with work performance" (National Association of Social Workers, 2003, p.1). Thus, it is necessary for new practitioners to seek specific feedback on matters of personal and professional development to enhance their professional competence and manage the challenges in human service organizations. In addition to individual supervision, new practitioners may also want to seek out opportunities for peer or group supervision. *Group supervision* is defined "as the use of a group setting to implement the responsibilities of supervision. In group supervision, the supervisor — given educational, administrative, and supportive responsibility for activities of a specific number of workers — meets with the group to discharge these responsibilities (Kudushin & Harkness, 2004, p. 390). It is also helpful to locate a mentor who can provide ongoing dialogue, insights, and support. The mentor role is different from that of a supervisor in that a mentor does not provide job supervision. Mentoring programs are available through professional associations such as the British Columbia Association of Social Workers (British Columbia Association of Social Workers, n.d.).

It is also critical to draw on previous learning. For example, it is helpful for graduates to reflect on the influence of their educational curriculum and field experiences by considering the following questions: What did they learn about practice in general, and about themselves, their strengths, and their limitations? Where might they struggle or shine? What practice areas do they feel they should avoid at the beginning of a career? What dimensions of learning from field placements were challenging or invigorating? Where might they need to seek specific feedback, knowledge, skills, or support? One of the most important cornerstones of practice is self-awareness. Without self-awareness one cannot develop sufficient insight into one's strengths and limitations in relation to practice. Self-awareness can be greatly enhanced through the various forms of supervision, mentorship, and reflection of previous learning. All these aspects are integral to managing workplace and personal stress.

## Voices from the Field

When I think of making the transition from university into the workforce, I feel a sense of anxiety because I feel like the expectations I have set for myself are very high; I should know what I am doing, after all I am a social worker now. I am expected to make decisions that will affect peoples' lives, after all isn't that why I have been in school for the last four years? I know that we all need to start somewhere in the workforce and that everyone has been the new person within individual work settings, but it doesn't make it any easier. But when I sit and I breathe I know I can do it. This is what I wanted to do, and this is what I am passionate about.

I found the transition between college to university very difficult and struggled my first semester. I started off with the Arts program for credits and I had one instructor who really supported me and I still appreciate it to this day. She did not let me give up and really encouraged and talked me though this process. When I finally reached the social work program I was ecstatic, it seemed as if I was seeing the light at the end of my very long journey. My practicum placements were great. I visited foster parents, interviewed potential foster parents, did some recruitment, and had many great experiences. After this practicum I knew I wanted to stay in child welfare and wanted to work with an Aboriginal agency for my fourth-year practicum. I also got to work with other case workers and got to see how they practiced. I really enjoyed this as I found that each case worker had their own way of doing things, while still following policy.

The majority of the learning I will take from the BSW program is from courses like the interviewing course that is so beneficial to social work. Policy and law classes also help us understand how Canadian policies and legislation works. It is surprising how many of us are clueless when it comes to politics. The First Nations classes help people who are not First Nations understand the reasons for why there are reserves and why there are so many problems on reserves. I enjoyed these classes, as the instructors would also look to the other First Nations students in the class to assist in answering questions. At first, I didn't understand why a lot of these classes were beneficial, but now that I have gone through the process I have seen the relevance, and how theory is also important. (Beverly Van der Weide, student)

## Voices from the Field

In the past few years, our interview process has changed from skills/knowledge interview to Behavioural Event Interview (BEI). We are using this interview structure to collect information about past behaviours of interview candidates. We know that having successfully completed the child welfare practicum, the applicants graduating with the Child Welfare Specialization have developed basic knowledge of the roles and duties of a Ministry for Children and Family Development social worker. The BEI questions help us to learn about the applicant's past performance in a key skill area (i.e., conflict resolution, developing relationships, teamwork, leadership, problem solving, diversity, knowing "self," and how one responds and expresses oneself in emotional and stressful situations).

The Public Service Agency [PSA] has developed a set of professional values. They are integrity, courage, teamwork, passion, accountability, service, and curiosity. These shared values define how staff do the work — regardless of their position or the level at which they work. Our annual staff evaluations are now based on those values and include a description on how we have or have not demonstrated those values in our work. So when we are hiring, we are looking to hire those who have the skills/knowledge base for the position plus share the same professional values of the PSA. One way an applicant can demonstrate they share the same values is through volunteer work/past experiences. I know when we are looking at prospective students, we look at their volunteer experience and the role they played as a volunteer. When interviewing prospective practicum students, we ask them BEI questions (i.e., Tell us about a time when you joined a new team: What worked for you? What did not work? Tell us about a time when you were required to solve a complex problem or issue. Please list the steps taken). Students often use their volunteer experience or a past practicum experience to answer the questions. They receive the question a week in advance and come well prepared to answer the question.

We are looking for staff who value diversity, are culturally sensitive, and can develop relationships with a wide range of people (children, youth, adults, seniors, team members, service providers, community professionals, and others). As we are a mandated service, the ability to develop and maintain relationships is very important in the work we do. We are looking for staff who are "lifelong learners" who are flexible and who value different viewpoints. (Twyla Russell, field instructor)

# Where the Real Meets the Ideal: Practising with Integrity

How do new practitioners maintain a commitment to social justice? This section explores how to practice with integrity, reflecting the values that underpin social work and human service practice, and distinguishes the link between values and actions. New social work and human service practitioners often enter the field with an enormous amount of enthusiasm and aspirations to change the world. They have been inspired by their field and faculty instructors and the educational curriculum to want to make a difference in the lives of the clients they serve through their practice. However, when the ideal meets the real in the practice world, this may often be followed by feelings of disillusionment at not being able to engage in the practice previously envisioned. Perhaps policies and procedures do not allow practitioners to provide needed resources in a timely fashion, or workload pressures and steep learning curves do not allow practitioners to develop the quality of relationships and attention to detail that they see as integral to their work. Before developing firm impressions of the strengths and limitations of the practice context, however, it is necessary to take the time to learn about the norms of the organizational culture and the possibilities for change that lie within it. It is important to pay attention to the subtleties that play out in the practice context, carefully interpreting office politics and dynamics, which includes the written and unwritten policies. It is necessary to stay aware and pay particular attention to office norms to fully understand the context before acting on these impressions.

Time should be spent during supervisory sessions grappling with the incongruities that often arise between the real aspects of practice and the ideal perceptions and assumptions that new practitioners are confronted with upon entering the profession. Affirming the professional value base may appear to be fraught with challenges. It is wise to use supervisors, peers, and mentors to dialogue about these challenges and to strategize around how to address policy and practice discrepancies. A continuum of responses will occur for new practitioners, including leaving the practice context to seek a better philosophical fit in another setting, adapting one's perceptions to complement the practice realities, or confronting the policies or practices that are incongruous with professional values. Mullaly (2007) provides practitioners with specific approaches to practice with respect to the latter responses that provide guidance for how new practitioners can affect the system through working within or outside of the system. Some of the options he suggests for working within the system are working with service users in progressive ways, affirming that the personal is political, and engaging in consciousness raising to highlight the connections between the social structures and human suffering. With respect to working outside the system, he emphasizes the importance of challenging and resisting the dominant order, and suggests working with professional associations and unions to carry out this mandate.

## Lifelong Learning

A post-secondary program provides a necessary foundation for professional practice. However, it does not provide all the knowledge and skills that will be required specific to the positions one will step into during a career. The habit of lifelong learning is necessary to stay current in one's field and develop specialization. There are many ways to continue to expand knowledge and enhance skills when stepping into the world of work.

**Reading** When students complete their college or university courses, they may have a strong desire to put their books aside. However, the textbooks will be useful again and again in a first job or even during future endeavours. For example, there may be a particular chapter that will provide the grounding of knowledge needed for working with a particular client or that will help practitioners understand a policy framework underpinning a particular social issue. Texts do contain a wealth of information (this is why they are selected for courses) and will maintain their relevance as practitioners encounter various challenges in new workplaces. Further, new practitioners who reference books that have been on the reading list may provide new knowledge to more established practitioners in their field who may not have had the opportunity to review the most current literature and research in a particular area.

As well, developing a culture of curiosity and nurturing it through reading will be stimulating. In the social work and human service fields, the stories of practice success teach many lessons. Reading about practice is encouraging and uplifting, and can provide the motivation to continue in contexts that can be quite draining. Reading also allows one to keep up to date on the latest research studies in the field, particularly evidence-based practice research. Knowing best practices as they evolve builds expertise. Most agencies have a resource library and may subscribe to journals relevant to their area of practice. It will be important to know what is available at the agency and to access these resources regularly. Maintaining a link to a college or a university as an alumnus often brings with it such privileges as the ability to have a library card. Joining a local community library is also good place to access local community information, research studies, and books on community leaders.

The social work and human service professions are challenging, requiring practitioners to confront people's pain and hardships on a daily basis. Reading the biographies of leaders in politics, community changers, or those who have made some kind of significant contribution to society can be very encouraging. Biographies and autobiographies are stories that inspire. They provide information about a career path, strategies for overcoming obstacles, and the components of career success. They are also fun and usually quick to read.

**Attending Conferences, Workshops, and Training Sessions** A new practitioner commencing a career will want to continue to hone and develop new skills. Attending events with other practitioners allows one to continue to learn and benefit from the practice experience of professional peers. This is invaluable. Again, it is the stories of practice that will reveal new approaches and strategies. How another agency solved a particular problem may be just the idea needed to address a problem being faced. Attending events also allows one to build personal networks of colleagues with whom the sharing of practice knowledge and ideas can continue long after the event. Most agencies have an ongoing professional development strategy and may have funding available to attend conferences or additional training. Some agencies may bring in speakers or workshop facilitators to teach about a new practice approach. Availing oneself of these opportunities will greatly strengthen practice. It is also imperative that practitioners continue to stay current with research in their field of practice. Engaging in ongoing professional development opportunities, such as conferences, workshops, or face-to-face or online courses, or the further progression from a certificate to a diploma or from an undergraduate to a graduate degree, are necessary considerations for enhancing and maintaining professional competence.

**Joining a Professional Association** Membership in professional associations, such as the provincial Association of Social Worker Child and Youth Care Association, or becoming a registered social worker with a regulatory body such as the Ontario College of Social Workers and Social Service Workers, also provides valuable opportunities for professional development and the process of adjusting to the demands of the new role as a social worker or human service practitioner. Professional associations are voluntary membership organizations that provide support and professional development services to their members. Professional associations hold annual conferences and ongoing professional development opportunities. Some provinces also have regulatory bodies that govern professional practice. Becoming a registered social worker or counsellor is another significant step in one's professional development. There are a number of requirements to becoming registered, such as providing references and successfully completing a clinical examination. Professional associations are provincially organized and represent specific professions. Provincial associations are often linked to a national association that takes action collectively on behalf of provincial requests and direction. For example, the Canadian Association of Social Workers will often comment on the federal budget and how this budget will affect the lives of members of society. This national perspective provides practitioners with an analysis of the context of service delivery, a summary of issues facing clients, and, for members, a voice with which to advocate on social policy issues.

Further, a professional association allows one to broaden professional relationships, access training opportunities, and contribute to the profession through collective advocacy. Professional associations are established to further the prominence and influence of the profession in society. Often this involves advocating for legislative changes or the promotion of knowledge about social issues. There may be times that a group of practitioners may wish to take action on an issue but cannot do so while working at a particular agency. As a member of a professional association, collective resources can assist in having an issue researched, analyzed, and a change strategy developed to advocate for, with the clout of all the members of the association. This venue provides practitioners with a way to have their say about issues they are passionate about. It also allows for the opportunity to find creative strategies to take action rather than becoming frustrated because of the limitations of a particular agency's mandate.

**Pursuing Further Education** Thinking about continuing their education is most likely the furthest thing from new graduates' minds when preparing for their first jobs. However, once in the field, they will discover there are many opportunities for moving from one position to another. After several years of working, new practitioners may wish to become a supervisor or manager, or even the executive director of an agency. Moving into positions of greater responsibility usually requires further education. If one has just completed a diploma, then the next step would be to complete an undergraduate degree to gain the possibility of greater job mobility and additional responsibility in the field. If one is completing an undergraduate degree, then a master's degree will allow one to compete for more senior positions in an organization or to teach in a college. A doctorate will provide a path to engaging in research or considering a teaching position at a university.

**Finding a Mentor and Becoming a Mentor** As noted earlier, preparing for a first job includes asking professors and field placement supervisors to be referees for employment. One can also consider them as future mentors. Mentoring can be formal or informal (Wellington & Spence, 2001). Touching base with former professors for coffee a year after graduation lets them know what one is doing and enables them to provide information that may direct one to the next step in a career. Intentional mentoring is organized through a formal relationship that identifies the time commitment to the relationship and the nature of the mentoring relationship. Mentoring is not supervision but an opportunity to explore professional and career advice. Some agencies may have a process of linking a senior staff member with a new employee to provide mentoring into a new field of practice. Mentoring is also intuitive. When beginning a new position, a practitioner will meet staff at various meetings and may find that a particular person is easy to communicate with, is knowledgeable, and could be helpful in providing direction in one's work and career. Approaching someone to be a mentor may be as simple as a suggestion for an occasional lunch or a coffee just to stay connected. Mentorship relationships can have significant life-directing and decision-making impacts and can result in lifetime friendships.

As one moves forward in a career, it is a time to think about becoming a mentor to students or practitioners just entering the field. Having gained professional experience, one will now have "insider" information to share. The process of expressing what is known is also a learning experience for a mentor, as it allows for an articulation of practice — a process of clarifying knowledge and practice skills. Being a mentor is also very personally enriching, as one has the privilege of watching someone else grow and develop professionally. Many professors and former field instructors continue to be friends and mentors after their encounters in a professional program at a college or university. Turning to someone who has observed one's professional development through the student years can assist in thinking through a career change or a practice dilemma. "Talking it through" with someone who has known the practitioner well for a long time can provide valuable insights. These reflections are grounded in intimate knowledge of the former student and observations of career accomplishments. And they can be impartial. Receiving honest feedback from someone who knows one well is most helpful.

**Networking** Valuable connections have been made in the classroom with peers. These relationships should be maintained after graduation. This is a practitioner's first network, and it may be the most lasting. Each student will be moving to a different agency and will have much to share about jobs, the opportunities of working with diverse client groups, and the culture of organizations.

One of the best strategies for networking is becoming a master at meeting people and finding out what they do. Obtaining and keeping business cards of individuals met at meetings or at conferences will build a file of valuable professional contacts for future reference. People in a network are a source of information on changes in social policy, funding available for programs, research on best practice, and new directions in practice. Networks are developed over the lifetime or a career and can be a practitioner's lifeline.

---

### Tips for Intentionally Building a Network

- Keep a file of notes on information gathered about someone's area of work.
- When changing positions, inform contacts on an email list and provide new contact information.
- Share information with others about conferences, a significant piece of research, or a good book to read.
- Watch how as you share, others will also share.

---

## Leading in the Field

Becoming a leader in one's field should be a goal for every practitioner. Leadership is an approach to work that values commitment, excellence, and contribution-making. While many see leadership as vested in senior positions, this does not have to be the case. Volunteering to research a specific social policy or a new counselling approach is providing leadership to the team by stepping forward and contributing new knowledge. Cashman, (2008) in his book *Leadership from the Inside Out,* suggests a few themes to assist people in mastering their leadership effectiveness:

- As a person grows, the leader grows.
- Leaders who learn to bring their purpose to conscious awareness experience dramatic, quantum increases in energy, effectiveness, and fulfillment.
- Leaders who work on achieving career-life balance are not only healthier, but more effective. (pp. 21–22)

The attention to ongoing personal self-development as noted above allows practitioners to maintain a reflective mindset that allows for continual examination of opportunities, choices, and intentionally planned activities that meet personal and professional goals.

## CHAPTER SUMMARY

Transitioning from school to work represents a significant achievement and pivotal turning point. The supportive and encouraging environment of the educational program may feel like it is coming to an end. A new world of autonomous practice needs to be found, new relationships established, and new goals identified to begin a successful career. This chapter has provided detailed steps for preparing for this transition through the careful preparation for a job search, application, and interview process and follow-up. Thinking about the transition to the first professional position examined the value shifts that will take place and the benefits and importance of using supervision to ensure that quality service is being provided in a new position.

Additionally, entering a profession is discussed in the chapter as a process of lifelong learning, with a variety of strategies provided to promote further success. Specifically, mentorship is identified as a key to having support and finding direction as one's career develops. Finally, seeing one's role as an opportunity for leadership will ensure that significant contributions are made through a successful career.

## Critical-Thinking Questions

1. What do you see yourself doing 10 years from now? What is the path you need to plan to be able to accomplish your goal in 10 years?

2. What strategies do you need to develop to maintain your integrity and values throughout your career?

3. What lessons have you learned through your educational process and how will these lessons affect your choice of a career direction?

## Suggested Readings

Cashman. K. (2008). *Leadership from the inside out: Becoming a leader for life* (2nd ed.). San Francisco, CA: Berrett-Koehler Publishers.

Krasna, H. (2010). *Jobs that matter: Find a stable, fulfilling career in the public service.* Indianapolis, IN: Jist Works.

Rath, T. (2007). *Strengths finder 2.0.* New York, NY: Gallup Press.

Wellington, S., & Spence. B. (2001). *Be your own mentor: Strategies from top women on the secrets of success.* New York, NY: Random House.

## Relevant Websites

### Preparing a Résumé and Cover Letter

www.students.ubc.ca/careers/students/get-career-guidance/job-search-skills/
www.tru.ca/careereducation/students/student_employment/resumes.html
www.ucalgary.ca/careers/studentsandalumni/resumescoverletterscvs
www.optimalresume.ca/aboutus.html
www.uregina.ca/cxc/index.php?id=38

These websites provide students with information on résumé building and writing effective cover letters.

# CODE OF ETHICS
## 2005

Association canadienne
des travailleuses
et travailleurs sociaux
Canadian Association
of Social Workers

ACTS
CASW

*Ce document est disponible en français.*

# Table of Contents

## Acknowledgements

The Canadian Association of Social Workers (CASW) acknowledges with thanks the National Association of Social Workers (NASW) for permission to use sections of the copyrighted NASW 1999 *Code of Ethics* in the development of the CASW 2005 *Code of Ethics* and CASW 2005 *Guidelines for Ethical Practice*.

The CASW also acknowledges that other codes of ethics and resources were used in the development of this *Code* and the *Guidelines for Ethical Practice*, in particular the *Code of Ethics* of the Australian Association of Social Workers (AASW). These resources can be found in the Reference section of each document.

Canadian Association of Social Workers (CASW) *Code of Ethics* © 2005

# Purpose of the CASW Code of Ethics

Ethical behaviour lies at the core of every profession. The Canadian Association of Social Workers (CASW) *Code of Ethics* sets forth values and principles to guide social workers' professional conduct. A code of ethics cannot guarantee ethical behaviour. Ethical behaviour comes from a social worker's individual commitment to engage in ethical practice. Both the spirit and the letter of this *Code of Ethics* will guide social workers as they act in good faith and with a genuine desire to make sound judgements.

This *Code of Ethics* is consistent with the International Federation of Social Workers (IFSW) *International Declaration of Ethical Principles of Social Work* (1994, 2004), which requires members of the CASW to uphold the values and principles established by both the CASW and the IFSW. Other individuals, organizations and bodies (such as regulatory boards, professional liability insurance providers, courts of law, boards of directors of organizations employing social workers and government agencies) may also choose to adopt this *Code of Ethics* or use it as a basis for evaluating professional conduct. In Canada, each province and territory is responsible for regulating the professional conduct of social workers to ensure the protection of the public. Social workers are advised to contact the regulatory body in their province or territory to determine whether it has adopted this *Code of Ethics*. [1]

## Recognition of Individual and Professional Diversity

The CASW *Code of Ethics* does not provide a set of rules that prescribe how social workers should act in all situations. Further, the *Code of Ethics* does not specify which values and principles are most important and which outweigh others in instances of conflict. Reasonable differences of opinion exist among social workers with respect to which values and principles should be given priority in a particular situation. Further, a social worker's personal values, culture, religious beliefs, practices and/or other important distinctions, such as age, ability, gender or sexual orientation can affect his/her ethical choices. Thus, social workers need to be aware of any conflicts between personal and professional values and deal with them responsibly.

---

[1] To find the IFSW declarations or information about your relevant regulatory body, visit the CASW web site: http://www.casw-acts.ca

### *Ethical Behaviour Requires Due Consideration of Issues and Judgement*

Social work is a multifaceted profession. As professionals, social workers are educated to exercise judgement in the face of complex and competing interests and claims. Ethical decision-making in a given situation will involve the informed judgement of the individual social worker. Instances may arise when social workers' ethical obligations conflict with agency policies, or relevant laws or regulations. When such conflicts occur, social workers shall make a responsible effort to resolve the conflicts in a manner that is consistent with the values and principles expressed in this *Code of Ethics*. If a reasonable resolution of the conflict does not appear possible, social workers shall seek appropriate consultation before making a decision. This may involve consultation with an ethics committee, a regulatory body, a knowledgeable colleague, supervisor or legal counsel.

## Preamble

The social work profession is dedicated to the welfare and self-realization of all people; the development and disciplined use of scientific and professional knowledge; the development of resources and skills to meet individual, group, national and international changing needs and aspirations; and the achievement of social justice for all. The profession has a particular interest in the needs and empowerment of people who are vulnerable, oppressed, and/or living in poverty. Social workers are committed to human rights as enshrined in Canadian law, as well as in international conventions on human rights created or supported by the United Nations.

As professionals in a country that upholds respect for diversity, and in keeping with democratic rights and freedoms, social workers respect the distinct systems of beliefs and lifestyles of individuals, families, groups, communities and nations without prejudice (United Nations Centre for Human Rights, 1992). Specifically, social workers do not tolerate discrimination[2] based on age, abilities, ethnic background, gender, language, marital status, national ancestry, political affiliation, race, religion, sexual orientation or socio-economic status.

---

[2] Throughout this document the term "discrimination" refers to treating people unfavourably or holding negative or prejudicial attitudes based on discernable differences or stereotypes. It does **not refer** to the positive intent behind programs, such as affirmative action, where one group may be given preferential treatment to address inequities created by discrimination.

# Core Social Work Values and Principles

Social workers uphold the following core social work values:

Value 1: Respect for Inherent Dignity and Worth of Persons

Value 2: Pursuit of Social Justice

Value 3: Service to Humanity

Value 4: Integrity of Professional Practice

Value 5: Confidentiality in Professional Practice

Value 6: Competence in Professional Practice

The following section describes each of these values and discusses their underlying principles.

### *Value 1: Respect for the Inherent Dignity and Worth of Persons*

Social work is founded on a long-standing commitment to respect the inherent dignity and individual worth of all persons. When required by law to override a client's wishes, social workers take care to use the minimum coercion required. Social workers recognize and respect the diversity of Canadian society, taking into account the breadth of differences that exist among individuals, families, groups and communities. Social workers uphold the human rights of individuals and groups as expressed in The *Canadian Charter of Rights and Freedoms* (1982) and the United Nations *Universal Declaration of Human Rights* (1948).

### *Principles:*

- Social workers respect the unique worth and inherent dignity of all people and uphold human rights.

- Social workers uphold each person's right to self-determination, consistent with that person's capacity and with the rights of others.

- Social workers respect the diversity among individuals in Canadian society and the right of individuals to their unique beliefs consistent with the rights of others.

- Social workers respect the client's right to make choices based on voluntary, informed consent.

Canadian Association of Social Workers (CASW) *Code of Ethics* © 2005

- Social workers who have children as clients determine the child's ability to consent and where appropriate, explain to the child and to the child's parents/guardians, the nature of the social worker's relationship to the child.

- Social workers uphold the right of society to impose limitations on the self-determination of individuals, when such limitations protect individuals from self-harm and from harming others.

- Social workers uphold the right of every person to be free from violence and threat of violence.

### Value 2: Pursuit of Social Justice

Social workers believe in the obligation of people, individually and collectively, to provide resources, services and opportunities for the overall benefit of humanity and to afford them protection from harm. Social workers promote social fairness and the equitable distribution of resources, and act to reduce barriers and expand choice for all persons, with special regard for those who are marginalized, disadvantaged, vulnerable, and/or have exceptional needs. Social workers oppose prejudice and discrimination against any person or group of persons, on any grounds, and specifically challenge views and actions that stereotype particular persons or groups.

### Principles:

- Social workers uphold the right of people to have access to resources to meet basic human needs.

- Social workers advocate for fair and equitable access to public services and benefits.

- Social workers advocate for equal treatment and protection under the law and challenge injustices, especially injustices that affect the vulnerable and disadvantaged.

- Social workers promote social development and environmental management in the interests of all people.

### Value 3: Service to Humanity

The social work profession upholds service in the interests of others, consistent with social justice, as a core professional objective. In professional practice, social workers balance individual needs, and rights and freedoms with collective interests in the service of humanity. When acting in a professional capacity, social workers place professional service before personal goals or advantage, and use their power and authority in disciplined and responsible ways that serve society. The social work profession contributes to knowledge and skills that assist in the management of conflicts and the wide-ranging consequences of conflict.

### Principles:

- Social workers place the needs of others above self-interest when acting in a professional capacity.

- Social workers strive to use the power and authority vested in them as professionals in responsible ways that serve the needs of clients and the promotion of social justice.

- Social workers promote individual development and pursuit of individual goals, as well as the development of a just society.

- Social workers use their knowledge and skills in bringing about fair resolutions to conflict and in assisting those affected by conflict.

### Value 4: Integrity in Professional Practice

Social workers demonstrate respect for the profession's purpose, values and ethical principles relevant to their field of practice. Social workers maintain a high level of professional conduct by acting honestly and responsibly, and promoting the values of the profession. Social workers strive for impartiality in their professional practice, and refrain from imposing their personal values, views and preferences on clients. It is the responsibility of social workers to establish the tenor of their professional relationship with clients, and others to whom they have a professional duty, and to maintain professional boundaries. As individuals, social workers take care in their actions to not bring the reputation of the profession into disrepute. An essential element of integrity in professional practice is ethical accountability based on this *Code of Ethics*, the IFSW *International Declaration of Ethical Principles of Social Work*, and other relevant provincial/territorial standards and guidelines. Where conflicts exist with respect to these sources of ethical guidance, social workers are encouraged to seek advice, including consultation with their regulatory body.

*Principles:*

- Social workers demonstrate and promote the qualities of honesty, reliability, impartiality and diligence in their professional practice.

- Social workers demonstrate adherence to the values and ethical principles of the profession and promote respect for the profession's values and principles in organizations where they work or with which they have a professional affiliation.

- Social workers establish appropriate boundaries in relationships with clients and ensure that the relationship serves the needs of clients.

- Social workers value openness and transparency in professional practice and avoid relationships where their integrity or impartiality may be compromised, ensuring that should a conflict of interest be unavoidable, the nature of the conflict is fully disclosed.

## Value 5: Confidentiality in Professional Practice

A cornerstone of professional social work relationships is confidentiality with respect to all matters associated with professional services to clients. Social workers demonstrate respect for the trust and confidence placed in them by clients, communities and other professionals by protecting the privacy of client information and respecting the client's right to control when or whether this information will be shared with third parties. Social workers only disclose confidential information to other parties (including family members) with the informed consent of clients, clients' legally authorized representatives or when required by law or court order. The general expectation that social workers will keep information confidential does not apply when disclosure is necessary to prevent serious, foreseeable and imminent harm to a client or others. In all instances, social workers disclose the least amount of confidential information necessary to achieve the desired purpose.

*Principles:*

- Social workers respect the importance of the trust and confidence placed in the professional relationship by clients and members of the public.

- Social workers respect the client's right to confidentiality of information shared in a professional context.

- Social workers only disclose confidential information with the informed consent of the client or permission of client's legal representative.

- Social workers may break confidentiality and communicate client information without permission when required or permitted by relevant laws, court order or this *Code*.

- Social workers demonstrate transparency with respect to limits to confidentiality that apply to their professional practice by clearly communicating these limitations to clients early in their relationship.

### Value 6: Competence in Professional Practice

Social workers respect a client's right to competent social worker services. Social workers analyze the nature of social needs and problems, and encourage innovative, effective strategies and techniques to meet both new and existing needs and, where possible, contribute to the knowledge base of the profession. Social workers have a responsibility to maintain professional proficiency, to continually strive to increase their professional knowledge and skills, and to apply new knowledge in practice commensurate with their level of professional education, skill and competency, seeking consultation and supervision as appropriate.

### Principles:

- Social workers uphold the right of clients to be offered the highest quality service possible.

- Social workers strive to maintain and increase their professional knowledge and skill.

- Social workers demonstrate due care for client's interests and safety by limiting professional practice to areas of demonstrated competence.

- Social workers contribute to the ongoing development of the profession and its ability to serve humanity, where possible, by participating in the development of current and future social workers and the development of new professional knowledge.

- Social workers who engage in research minimize risks to participants, ensure informed consent, maintain confidentiality and accurately report the results of their studies.

# Glossary

## *Capacity*

The ability to understand information relevant to a decision and to appreciate the reasonably foreseeable consequences of choosing to act or not to act. Capacity is specific to each decision and thus a person may be capable of deciding about a place of residence, for example, but not capable with respect to deciding about a treatment. Capacity can change over time (Etchells, Sharpe, Elliot and Singer, 1996).

Recent references in law point to the concept of "a mature minor," which Rozovsky and Rozovsky (1990) define as "…one with capacity to understand the nature and consequences of medical treatment. Such a person has the power to consent to medical treatment and parental consent is not necessary" (p. 55). They quote the comments by The Honorable Justice Lambert in *Van Mol v. Ashmore*, which help clarify common law with respect to a minor's capacity to consent. He states:

> At common law, without reference to statute law, a young person, still a minor, may give, on his or her own behalf, a fully informed consent to medical treatment if he or she has sufficient maturity, intelligence and capacity of understanding what is involved in making informed choices about the proposed medical treatment…once the capacity to consent has been achieved by the young person reaching sufficient maturity, intelligence and capability of understanding, the discussions about the nature of the treatment, its gravity, the material risks and any special and unusual risks, and the decisions about undergoing treatment, and about the form of the treatment, must all take place with and be made by the young person whose bodily integrity is to be invaded and whose life and health will be affected by the outcome.

## *Child*

The *Convention on the Rights of the Child* passed by the United Nations in 1959 and ratified by Canada in 1990, define a child as a person under the age of 18 years unless national law recognizes an earlier age of majority (Alberta Law Reform Institute, 1991). The age of majority differs in provinces and territories in Canada. Under the *Criminal Code of Canada*, the age of consent is held to be over the age of 14 years; age in the context of the criminal code frequently refers to capacity to consent to sexual relations. All jurisdictions in Canada have legislation regarding child protection, which defines the age of a child for the purposes of protection. In Canada, in the absence of provincial or territorial legislation, courts are governed by common law. Social workers are encouraged to maintain current knowledge with respect to legislation on the age of a child, as well as capacity and consent in their jurisdiction.

## Client

A person, family, group of persons, incorporated body, association or community on whose behalf a social worker provides or agrees to provide a service or to whom the social worker is legally obligated to provide a service. Examples of legal obligation to provide service include a legislated responsibility (such as in child welfare) or a valid court order. In the case of a valid court order, the judge/court is the client and the person(s) who is ordered by the court to participate in assessment is recognized as an involuntary client.

## Conduct Unbecoming

Behaviour or conduct that does not meet social work standard of care requirements and is, therefore, subject to discipline. In reaching a decision in Matthews and Board of Directors of Physiotherapy (1986) 54 O.R. (2d) 375, Saunders J. makes three important statements regarding standards of practice, and by implication, professional codes of ethics:

1. Standards of practice are inherent characteristics of any profession.
2. Standards of practice may be written or unwritten.
3. Some conduct is clearly regarded as misconduct and need not be written down, whereas other conduct may be the subject of dispute within a profession.
   (See "Standard of Practice.")

## Confidentiality

A professional value that demands that professionally acquired information be kept private and not shared with third parties unless the client provides informed consent or a professional or legal obligation exists to share such information without client informed consent.

## Discrimination

Treating people unfavourably or holding negative or prejudicial attitudes based on discernable differences or stereotypes (AASW, 1999).

## Informed Consent

Voluntary agreement reached by a capable client based on information about foreseeable risks and benefits associated with the agreement (e.g., participation in counselling or agreement to disclose social work report to a third party).

## Human Rights

The rights of an individual that are considered the basis for freedom and justice, and serve to protect people from discrimination and harassment. Social workers may refer to the *Canadian Charter of Rights and Freedoms* enacted as Schedule B to the *Canada Act* 1982 (U.K.) 1982, c. 11, which came into force on April 17, 1982, as well as the *Universal Declaration of Human Rights* (1948) proclaimed by the United Nations General Assembly December 10, 1948.

### Malpractice and Negligence

Behaviour that is included in "conduct unbecoming" and relates to social work practice behaviour within the parameters of the professional relationship that falls below the standard of practice and results in, or aggravation of, injury to a client. It includes behaviour that results in assault, deceit, fraudulent misrepresentations, defamation of character, breach of contract, violation of human rights, malicious prosecution, false imprisonment or criminal conviction.

### Self-Determination

A core social work value that refers to the right to self-direction and freedom of choice without interference from others. Self-determination is codified in practice through mechanisms of informed consent. Social workers may be obligated to limit self-determination when a client lacks capacity or in order to prevent harm (Regehr and Antle, 1997).

### Social Worker

A person who is duly registered to practice social work in a province or territory; or where mandatory registration does not exist, a person with social work education from an institution recognized by the Canadian Association of Schools of Social Work (CASSW) or an institution from outside of Canada that has been approved by the CASW, who is practising social work and who voluntarily agrees to be subject to this *Code of Ethics*. **Note:** Social workers living in Quebec and British Columbia, whose social work education was obtained outside of Canada, follow a separate approval process within their respective provinces.

### Standard of Practice

The standard of care ordinarily expected of a competent social worker. It means that the public is assured that a social worker has the training, the skill and the diligence to provide them with social work services. Social workers are urged to refer to standards of practice that have been set by their provincial or territorial regulatory body or relevant professional association (see "Conduct Unbecoming").

### Voluntary

"In the context of consent, 'voluntariness' refers to a patient's right to make treatment decisions free of any undue influence, such as ability of others to exert control over a patient by force, coercion or manipulation. ...The requirement for voluntariness does not imply that clinicians should refrain from persuading patients to accept advice. Persuasion involves appealing to the patient's reason in an attempt to convince him or her of the merits of a recommendation. In attempting to persuade the patient to follow a particular course of action, the clinician still leaves the patient free to accept or reject this advice." (Etchells, Sharpe, Dykeman, Meslin and Singer, 1996, p. 1083).

# References

AASW. (1999). *AASW code of ethics*. Kingston: Australian Association of Social Workers (AASW).

Alberta Law Reform Institute. (1991). *Status of the child: Revised report* (Report No. 60). Edmonton, Alberta: Law Reform Institute.

BASW. (2002). *BASW: A code of ethics for social workers*. British Association of Social Workers (BASW).

*Canadian Charter of Rights and Freedoms* Enacted as Schedule B to the *Canada Act* 1982, c.11 (1982). [http://laws.justice.gc.ca/en/charter/]

CASW. (1994). *Social Work Code of Ethics*. Ottawa: Canadian Association of Social Workers (CASW).

*Criminal Code*, R.S., c. C-34, s.1. (1985). [http://laws.justice.gc.ca/en/C-46/40670.html]

Etchells, E.; G. Sharpe; C. Elliott and P. Singer. (1996). Bioethics for clinicians: 3: Capacity. *Canadian Medical Association Journal, 155*, 657-661.

Etchells, E.; G. Sharpe; M.J. Dykeman and P. Singer. (1996). Bioethics for clinicians: 4: Voluntariness. *Canadian Medical Association Journal, 155*, 1083-1086.

IFSW. (1994). *The ethics of social work: Principles and standards*. Geneva, Switzerland: International Federation of Social Workers (IFSW).

(2004). *Ethics in social work: Statement of principles*. Geneva, Switzerland: International Federation of Social Workers (IFSW).

Lens, V. (2000). Protecting the confidentiality of the therapeutic relationship: Jaffe v. Redmond. *Social Work, 45*(3), 273-276.

Matthews and Board of Directors of Physiotherapy (1986) 54 O.R. (2d) 375.

NASW. (1999). *Code of Ethics*. Washington: National Association of Social Workers (NASW).

Regehr, C. and B.J. Antle. (1997). Coercive influences: Informed consent and court-mandated social work practice. *Social Work, 42*(3), 300-306.

Rozovsky, L.E. and F.A. Rozovsky. (1990). *The Canadian law of consent to treatment*. Toronto: Butterworths.

United Nations. (1948). *Universal Declaration of Human Rights*. New York: United Nations. [http://www.unhchr.ch/udhr/]

United Nations Centre for Human Rights. (1992). Teaching and learning about human rights: A manual for schools of social work and the social work profession (Developed in co-operation with International Federation of Social Workers and International Association of Schools of Social Workers). New York: United Nations.

383 Parkdale Avenue, Suite 402
Ottawa, Ontario, Canada
K1Y 4R4
Telephone: (613) 729-6668
Fax: (613) 729-9608
Email: casw@casw-acts.ca
Web Site: www.casw-acts.ca

# APPENDIX 2

## CODES OF ETHICS: CHILD AND YOUTH CARE

The Council of Canadian Child and Youth Care Associations is the national networking organization representing the child and youth care professions in Canada. Member associations are represented to the Council by representatives, and their members, in turn, are viewed as members of the Council.

Membership in the Council is made available through provincial child and youth care associations.

Please use the links provided to explore member association web sites, Council initiatives, and information pages, specifically codes of ethics for each child and youth care association.

Canada *www.cyccanada.ca* (click on Code of Ethics)

British Columbia *www.cycabc.com/index2.php#/info1/3*

Alberta *www.cycaa.com/pdfs/codeofethics.pdf*

Manitoba *http://cycwam.ca/index.php?page=cycwam-code-of-ethics*

Ontario *www.oacyc.org/index.php?m=15&page=14*

Quebec *www.garthgoodwin.info/QAE.htm*

Nova Scotia *www.garthgoodwin.info/NSCYCWA.htm*

# References

Abbott, A. A., & Lyter, S. C. (1998). "The use of constructive criticism in field supervision." *The Clinical Supervisor, 17*(2), 43–57.

Abramovitz, M. (1993). "Should all social work students be educated for social change?" *Pro. Journal of Social Work Education, 29,* 6–11.

Adams, K., Hean, S., Sturgis, P., & MacLeod Clark, J. (2006). "Investigating the factors influencing professional identity of first-year health and social care students." *Learning in Health and Social Care, 5*(2), 55–68.

Alberta Children and Youth Initiative (2007). *Information sharing for human service providers in the public sector.* Retrieved from Government of Alberta website: **http://justice.alberta.ca/programs_services/families /Documents/doc_ACYI__RedGreen.pdf.**

Alexander, C. (2008). "Accepting gifts from youth: Reciprocity makes a difference." *Relational Child and Youth Care Practice, 21*(2), 27–35.

Alexander, C., & Charles, G. (2009). "Caring, mutuality and reciprocity in social worker–client relationships." *Journal of Social Work, 9*(1), 5–22.

Al-Krenawi, A., & Graham, J. R. (2003). "Principles of social work practice in the Muslim Arab world." *Arab Studies Quarterly, 26*(4), 75–91.

Alphonse, M. (2008). "International social work practice: The exchange experience in India." *Canadian Social Work Review, 25* (2), 215–221.

Annett, K. (2006). "Unrepentant: Kevin Annett and Canada's genocide." Retrieved from The Hidden History: The Canadian Holocaust website: **www.hiddenfromhistory.org.**

Appleby, G. A., Colon, E., & Hamilton, J. (2007). *Diversity, Oppression and social functioning: Person-in-environment assessment and intervention* (2nd ed.). Boston, MA: Allyn and Bacon.

Armitage, A. (1983). "The policy and legislative context." In B. Wharf (Ed.), *Rethinking child welfare in Canada* (pp. 37–63). Toronto: McClelland and Stewart.

Armit, A. A. (1997). "Opening remarks to the Juliet Cuenco Annual Memorial Seminar." In A. Cardozo & L. Musto (Eds.), *The battle over multiculturalism: Does it help or hinder Canadian unity?* (Vol. 1, pp. 1–3). Ottawa, ON: Pearson-Shoyama Institute.

Arnstien, S. R. (1969). "A ladder of citizen participation." *Journal of the American Institute of Planners, 35,* 216–224.

Askeland, G., & Payne, M. (2006). "Social work education's cultural hegemony." *International Social Work, 49,* 731–743.

Austin, M., & Hopkins, K. (Eds). (2004). *Supervision as collaboration in the human services: Building a learning culture.* Thousand Oaks, CA: Sage Publications.

Barlow, C., & Hall, B. L. (2007). "'What about feelings?' A study of emotion and tension in social work field education." *Social Work Education, 26,* 399–413.

Barr, H. (1998). "Competent to collaborate: Towards a competency-based model for interprofessional education." *Journal of Interprofessional Care, 12*(2), 181–187.

Baskin, C. (2005). *Circles of inclusion: Aboriginal world views in social work education.* Toronto, ON: University of Toronto.

Bell, L. A. (2007). "Theoretical foundations for social justice education." In M. Adams, L. A. Bell, & P. Griffin (Eds.), *Teaching for Diversity and Social Justice* (2nd ed., pp. 1–14). New York, NY: Routledge Taylor & Francis Group.

Bennett, M. (n.d.). A general profile on First Nations child welfare in Canada (Fact sheet). Retrieved from the First Nations Child and Family Caring Society of Canada website: **www.fncfcs.com/docs/FirstNationsFS1. pdf**.

Bird, J., Land, L., & MacAdam, M. (Eds.). (2002). *Nation to nation: Aboriginal sovereignty and the future of Canada.* Toronto, ON: Public Justice Resource Centre.

Birkenmaier, J., & Berg-Weger, M. (2007). *The practicum companion for social work: Integrating class and field work* (2nd ed.). Boston, MA: Pearson Education.

Bishop, A. (2002). *Becoming an ally: Breaking the cycle of oppression in people* (2nd ed.). Halifax, NS: Fernwood Publishing.

Blackstock, C. (2005). "The occasional evil of angels: Learning from the experiences of Aboriginal peoples and social work [Special edition]." *International Aboriginal Journal of Entrepreneurship, Advancement, Strategy and Education, I*(I): WIPCE World Aboriginal People Congress on Education, Hamilton, New Zealand.

Blackstock, C. (2009). "The occasional evil of angels: Learning from the experiences of Aboriginal peoples and social work." *A Journal on Innovation and Best Practices in Aboriginal Child Welfare Administration, Research, Policy and Practice, 4*(1), 28–37.

Bogo, M. (2005). "Field instruction in social work: A review of the research literature." *The Clinical Supervisor, 24,* 163–193.

Bogo, M. (2006). *Social work practice: Concepts, processes, and interviewing.* New York, NY: Columbia University Press.

Bogo, M. (2010). *Achieving competence in social work through field education.* Toronto, ON: University of Toronto Press.

Bogo, M., & McKnight, K. (2005). "Clinical supervision in social work: A review of the research literature." *The Clinical Supervisor, 24*(1/2), 49–67.

Bogo, M., & Vayda, E. (1998). *The practice of field instruction in social work: Theory and process* (2nd ed.). New York, NY: Columbia University Press.

Bolzan, N., Heycox, K., & Hughes, L. (2001). "From pillar to post: Women and social work studies in the 21st century." *Australian Social Work, 54*(1), 67–79.

Bordessa, K. (2006). *Team challenges: 170 group activities to build cooperation, communication and creativity.* Chicago, IL: Chicago Review Press.

Bradshaw, C., & Graham, J. R. (2007). "Localization of social work practice, education, and research: A content analysis." *Social Development Issues, 29*(2), 92–111.

Briskman, L., & Flynn, M. (1999). *Community embedded rural social care practice.* Geelong, Australia: Deakin University Press.

British Columbia Association of Social Workers. (n.d.). "The BC Association of Social Workers mentoring program." Author. Retrieved from **www.bcasw.org/ Images/MemberServices** Sun **Life/About the BCASW Mentoring Program.pdf**.

British Sociological Association (1999). "BSA statement of ethical practice." Author. Retrieved from **www.britsoc.org.uk**.

Brooks, B. (1998). "A common-sense pro-active approach to increasing student awareness of safety issues" (Unpublished report). TRU Field Education Manual 2008–9.

Brown, J. (1933). *The rural community and social case work.* New York, NY: Family Welfare Association of America.

Brown, J., & Hannis, D. (2008). *Community development in Canada.* Toronto, ON: Pearson Education Canada.

Brown, L., Haddock, L., & Kovach, M. (2009). "Community control of child welfare: Two case studies of child welfare in First Nations communities." In B. Wharf (Ed.), *Community work approaches to child welfare* (pp. 131–151). Toronto, ON: University of Toronto Press.

Brown, R. (2001). "The wraparound process." In P. Lehmann & N. Coady (Eds.), *Theoretical perspectives in direct social work practice* (pp. 347–365). New York, NY: Springer Publishing Company.

Bruyere, G. (1998). "Living in another man's house: Supporting Aboriginal learners in social work education." *Canadian Social Work Review 15,* 169–176.

Bryce, G. K. (2005). "A counsellor's duty to warn foreseeable victims of a client with HIV/AIDS." *Insights 17*(2), 27–28.

BSW Field Education. (2009). *BSW Field Education Manual.* Kamloops, BC: School of Social Work and Human Service, Thompson Rivers University.

Burnhill, D. A., Butler, A. L., Hipolito-Delgado, C. P., Humphrey, M., Lee, C. C., Muñoz, O., & Shin, H. (2009). "Elements of culturally competent counselling in the 21st century." In C. C. Lee, D. A. Burnhill, A. L. Butler, C. P. Hipolito-Delgado, M. Humphrey, O. Muñoz, & H. Shin (Eds.), *Elements of culture in counselling* (pp. 245–247). Upper Saddle River, NJ: Pearson Education.

Canada Broadcasting Corporation. (2007). "Blind man wants to force TTC announce bus stops." Retrieved from **www.cbc.ca/canada/toronto/2007/04/26/ttc-challenge.html**.

Canada. (1996). *Royal Commission Report on Aboriginal Peoples.* Retrieved from **www.collectionscanada .gc.ca/webarchives/200711 5053257/http://www.ainc-inac.gc.ca/ch/rcap/sg/ sgmm_e.html**.

Canadian Association for Social Work Education. (2009). *CASWE Educational Policy Statements.* Ottawa, ON: Author.

Canadian Association of Social Workers. (2005a). "Code of Ethics." Author. Retrieved from **www.casw-acts.ca**

Canadian Association of Social Workers. (2005b). "Guidelines for Ethical Practice." Author. Retrieved from **www.casw-acts.ca/practice/guidelines_e.pdf**.

Canadian Research Institute for the Advancement of Women. (2006). *Intersectional feminist frameworks: An emerging vision.* Ottawa, ON: Author.

Capuzzi, D., & Gross, D. R. (2001). *Introduction to the counseling profession* (3rd ed.) Needham Heights, MA: Allyn & Bacon.

Carniol, B. (1990). *Case critical: Challenging social work in Canada.* Toronto, ON: Between the Lines.

Carpenter, J., (1995). "Doctors and nurses: Stereotypes and stereotype change in interprofessional education." *Journal of Interprofessional Education, 9*(2), 151–161.

Cashman. K. (2008). *Leadership from the inside out: Becoming a leader for life* (2nd ed.). San Francisco, CA: Berrett-Koehler Publishers.

Centre for the Advancement of Interprofessional Education (2002). "Defining IPE." Author. Retrieved from **www.caipe.org.uk/about-us/defining-ipe**.

Chang, C. Y., Hays, D. G., & Shoffner, M. F. (2004). "Cross-racial supervision: A developmental approach for white supervisors working with supervisees of color." *The Clinical Supervisor 22*(2), 121–138.

Chappell, R. (2010). *Social welfare in Canadian society* (4th ed.). Toronto, ON: Nelson Education.

Charles, G., Bainbridge, L., & Gilbert, J. (2010). "The UBC model of interprofessional education." *Journal of Interprofessional Care, 24*(1), 9–18.

Charles, G., Bainbridge, L., Copeman-Stewart, K., Kassam, R., & Tiffin, S. (2008). "The impact of an interprofessional rural health care practice education experience on students and communities." *Journal of Allied Health, 37,* 127–131.

Charles, G., Bainbridge, L., Copeman-Stewart, K., Tiffin, S., & Kassam, R. (2006). "The Interprofessional

Rural Program of British Columbia (IRPbc)." *Journal of Interprofessional Care, 20*(1), 40–50.

Cheers, B. (1992). "Rural social work and social welfare in Australian context." *Australian Social Work, 45*(2), 11–21.

Cheers, B. (1999). *Community-embedded rural social care practice.* Geelong, Australia: Deakin University Press.

Choy, B. K., Leung, A. Y., Tam, T. S. K., & Chu, C. H. (1998). "Roles and tasks of field instructors as perceived by Chinese social work students." *Journal of Teaching in Social Work, 16*(1/2), 115–132.

Chrisjohn, R., Young, S., & Maraun, M. (2006). *The circle game: Shadows and substance in the Indian residential school experience in Canada* (Rev. ed.). Penticton, BC: Theytus Books.

Clark, N., & Hunt, S. (2007). "The empress has no clothes: Exposing the truth of intersectional research with marginalized populations." Paper presented at the Invited Lecture Institute for Critical Studies in Gender and Health, Simon Fraser University, Vancouver, BC.

Clark, N., Drolet, J., Mathews, N., Walton, P., Tamburro, P., Derrick, J., … Arnouse, M. (2010). "Decolonizing field education: Melq'ilwiye coming together: An exploratory study in the interior of British Columbia." *Critical Social Work, 11*(1), pp. 6–25.

Coe, J. A. R., & Elliott, D. (1999). "An evaluation of teaching direct practice courses in a distance education program for rural settings." *Journal of Social Work Education, 35*(3), 353–365.

Cohen-Scali, V. (2003). "The influence of family, social, and work: Socialization of the construction of the professional identity of young adults." *Journal of Career Development, 29*(4), 237–249.

Collier, K., (2006). *Social work with rural peoples.* Vancouver, BC: New Star Books.

Confucius. (BC 450). Retrieved from the Wilderdom website: **http://wilderdom.com/experiential/elc/ExperientialLearningCycle.htm**.

Conservation Council of New Brunswick (n.d.). Retrieved from **www.conservationcouncil.ca**.

*Constitution Acts,* 1867 to 1982. Retrieved from Department of Justice Canada website: **www.justice. gc. ca**.

Corey, G., Schneider Corey, M., & Callanan, P. (2007). *Issues and ethics in the helping professions* (7th ed.). Pacific Grove, CA: Brooks Cole.

Corey, M. S., Corey, G., & Corey, C. (2010). *Groups: Process and practice* (8th ed.). Belmont, CA: Brooks/Cole.

Cottone, R. R., & Tarvydas, V. M. (2003). *Ethical and professional issues in counselling* (2nd ed.). Upper Saddle River, NJ: Merrill Prentice Hall.

Council on Social Work Education. (2004/2008). *Education policy and accreditation standards.* Alexandria, VI: Author.

Council on Social Work Education. (2006). Commission on accreditation handbook on accreditation standards and procedures (5th ed.). Arlington, VA: Author.

Coupland, H., & Maher, L. (2005). "Clients or colleagues? Reflections on the process of participatory action research with young injecting drug users." *International Journal of Drug Policy, 16*(3), 191–198.

Cox, D., & Pawar, M. (2006). *International social work: Issues, strategies and programs.* London, England: Sage Publications.

Creswell, J. (1994). *Research design: Qualitative and quantitative approaches.* London, England: Sage Publications.

Cross, T. L. (Ed.). (1996). *Cross-cultural skills in Indian child welfare: A guide for the non-Indian* (2nd ed.). Portland, OR: National Indian Child Welfare Association.

Curtis, J., Grabb, E., Perks, T., & Chui, T. (2009). "Political involvement, civic engagement, and social inequality." In E. Grabb & N. Guppy, (Eds.), *Social Inequality in Canada: Patterns, Problems, and Policies* (5th ed., pp. 409–428). Toronto, ON: Pearson Education Canada.

Danso, R. (2009). "Emancipating and empowering de-valued skilled immigrants: What hope does anti-oppressive social work practice offer?" *British Journal of Social Work 39*(3), 539–555.

Danso, R. (2010). "Undoing the toxic doings of race and racism in a 'post-race' North America." In J. K. Crennan (Ed.), *Race and ethnicity: Cultural roles, spiritual practices and social challenges* (pp. 1–59). Hauppauge, NY: Nova Science Publishers.

Davys, A., & Beddoe, L. (2000). "Supervision of students: A map and a model for the decade to come." *Social Work Education 19*(5), 437–449.

D'Cruz, H., & Jones, M. (2004). *Social work research: Ethical and political contexts.* Thousand Oaks, CA: Sage Publications.

D'Cruz, H., Gillingham, P., & Melendez, S. (2007a). "Reflexivity: A concept and its meanings for practitioners working with children and families." *Critical Social Work, 8*(1), 1–18.

D'Cruz, H., Gillingham, P., & Melendez, S. (2007b). "Reflexivity, its meaning and relevance for social work: A critical review of the literature." *British Journal of Social Work, 37,* 73–90.

Deal, K. H. (2000). "The usefulness of developmental stage models for clinical social work students: An exploratory study." *The Clinical Supervisor, 19*(1), 1–19.

Deal, K. H. (2002). "Modifying field instructors' supervisory approach using stage models of student development." *Journal of Teaching in Social Work, 22*(3/4), 121–137.

Delaney, R. (2005). "Social justice." In F. J. Turner (Ed.), *Encyclopedia of Canadian social work* (pp. 370–371). Waterloo, ON: Wilfrid Laurier University Press.

Delaney, R., & Brownlee, K. (1995). *Northern social work practice.* Thunder Bay, ON: Centre for Northern Studies, Lakehead University.

Delaney, R., Brownlee, K., & Zapf, M. K. (Eds.) (2001). *Issues in northern social work practice.* Thunder Bay, ON: Lakehead University Centre for Northern Studies.

Delgado, R., (2000). "Storytelling for oppositionists and other: A plea for narrative, in oppositionists and others: A plea for narrative." In R. Delgado & J. Stefancic (Eds.), *Critical race theory: The Cutting edge* (pp. 60–70). Philadelphia: Temple University Press.

Dettlaff, A. J., & Wallace, G. (2003). "Promoting integration of theory and practice in field education." *The Clinical Supervisor, 21*(2), 145–160.

Dewey, J. (1933). How we think. A restatement of the relation of reflective thinking to the educative process (rev. ed.). Boston, MD: D. C. Heath.

Dickason, O. P., & McNab, D. T. (2009). *Canada's First Nations: A history of founding peoples from earliest times* (4th ed.). Don Mills, ON: Oxford University Press.

Dicklitch, S. (2005). "Human rights — human wrongs: Making political science real through service-learning." In D. Butin (Ed.), *Service-learning in higher education* (pp. 127–138). New York, NY: Palgrave MacMillan.

Dixon, A., & Rousseau, C. (2005). "And we are still not saved: Critical race theory in education ten years later." *Race Ethnicity and Education, 8*(1), 7–27.

Doel, M., & Shardlow, S. (1998). *The new social work practice.* Aldershot, England: Ashgate Publishing.

Dolgoff, R., Loewenberg, F. M., & Harrington, D. (2009). *Ethical decisions for social work practice* (8th ed.). Belmont, CA: Thompson Education.

Dominelli, L. (2003). "Internationalising social work: Introducing issues of relevance." In L. Dominelli & W. T. Bernard (Eds.), *Broadening horizons: International exchanges in social work* (pp. 19–30). Hampshire, England: Ashgate Publishing.

Dominelli, L. (2004). Social work: Theory and practice for a changing profession. Cambridge, England: Polity Press.

Dominelli, L. (2006). Anti-oppressive social work theory and practice. London, England: Oxford.

Donelly, J. (1999). "The social construction of international human rights." In T. Dunne & N. Wheeler (Eds.), *Human rights in global politics* (pp. 71–102). Cambridge, England: Cambridge University Press.

Douglas, T. (1993). *A theory of groupwork practice.* Basingstoke, England: Macmillan.

DuBray, W. (1994). *Social work and American Indians/Alaska Natives: A model curriculum for CSWE* (Unpublished draft).

Duran, E., & Duran, B. (1995). *Native American postcolonial psychology.* New York, NY: State University of New York Press.

Durst, D. (2000). "Cultural Values." In D. Durst (Ed.), *It's not what but how! Social service issues affecting Aboriginal Peoples: A review of projects* (pp. 61–80). Regina, SK: Policy Research Unit, Social Work University of Regina.

E-ACFTS. (2008). *CASWE standards for accreditation.* Ottawa, ON: Canadian Association for Social Work Education.

Elliot, E., Watson, A., & Harries, U. (2005). "Harnessing expertise: Involving peer interviewers in qualitative research with hard-to-reach populations." *Health Expectations, 5*(2), 172–178.

Ellison, M. L. (1994). "Critical field instructor behaviors: Student and field instructor views." *Arete, 18*(2), 12–20.

Eyler, J. (2001). "Creating your reflection map." In M. Canada (Ed.), *Service-learning: Practical advice and models* (pp. 35–43). San Francisco, CA: Jossey-Bass.

Eyler, J. (2002a). "Reflecting on service: Helping nursing students get the most from service-learning." *Journal of Nursing Education, 41*(10), 453–456.

Eyler, J. (2002b). "Reflection: Linking service and learning — linking students and communities." *Journal of Social Issues, 58*(3), 517–534.

Ezell, M. (2001). *Advocacy in the human services.* Belmont, CA: Brooks/Cole.

Fire, A. (2006). "Recommendations to enhance the educational experience of Aboriginal social work students." *Critical Social Work, 7*(2), pp. 1–13.

Fleras, A. (2010). *Unequal relations: An introduction to race, ethnic, and aboriginal dynamics in Canada* (6th ed.). Toronto, ON: Pearson Canada.

Fong, R. (2007). "Cultural competence with Asian Americans." In D. Lum, (Ed.), *Culturally competent practice: A framework for understanding diverse groups and justice issues* (3rd ed., pp. 328–350). Belmont, CA: Thomson Brooks/Cole.

Fook, J. (2002). *Social work: Critical theory and practice.* London, England: Sage Publications.

Fortune, A. E. (2001). "Initial impressions and performance in field practica: Predictors of skills attainment and satisfaction among graduate students." *The Clinical Supervisor, 20*(2), 43–54.

Fortune, A. E., & Abramson, J. S. (1993). "Predictors of satisfaction with field practicum among social work students." *The Clinical Supervisor, 11*(1), 95–110.

Fortune, A. E., Feathers, C. E., Rook, S. R., Scrimenti, R. M., Smollen, P., Stemerman, P., … Tucker, E. L. (1985).: "Student satisfaction with field placement." *Journal of Social Work Education, 21*(3), 92–104.

Fortune, A. E., Lee, M., & Cavazos, A. (2007). "Does practice make perfect? Practicing professional skills and outcomes in social work field education." *The Clinical Supervisor, 26*(1/2), 239–263.

Fortune, A. E., McCarthy, M., & Abramson, J. S. (2001). "Student learning processes in field education: Relationship of learning activities to quality of field instruction, satisfaction, and performance among MSW students." *Journal of Social Work Education, 37*(1), 111–124.

Foster, C. (2005). *Where race does not matter: The new spirit of modernity.* Toronto, ON: Penguin.

Fournier, S., & Crey, E. (1997). *Stolen from our embrace: The abduction of First Nations children and the restoration of Aboriginal communities.* Vancouver, BC: Douglas and McIntyre Publishing.

Fox, R. (1989). "Relationships: The cornerstone of clinical supervision." *Social Casework: The Journal of Contemporary Social Work, 70*(3), 146–152.

Fox, R., Piven, F. & Cloward, R. (1971). *Regulating the poor: The functions of public welfare.* New York, NY: Pantheon.

Freeman, E. (1985). "The importance of feedback in clinical supervision: Implications for direct practice." *The Clinical Supervisor, 3*(1), 5–26.

Frideres, J., & Gadacz, R. (2008). *Aboriginal peoples in Canada.* Toronto, ON: Pearson Prentice Hall.

Galabuzi, G-E. (2006). *Canada's economic apartheid: The social exclusion of racialized groups in the new century.* Toronto, ON: Canadian Scholar's Press.

Gallegos, J. S., Tindall, C., & Gallegos, S. A. (2008). "The need for advancement in the conceptualization of cultural competence." *Advances in Social Work, 9*(1), 51–62.

Gamble, D. N., & Weil, M. O. (1995). "Citizen participation." In R. L. Edwards (Ed.), *Encyclopedia of social work* (19th ed., Vol. 1, pp. 483–494). Washington, DC: National Association of Social Workers/NASW Press.

Garfat, T., & Charles, G. (2007). "How am I who I am? Self in child and youth care." *Relational Child and Youth Care Practice, 20*(6), 6–16.

Genero, N., Miller, J., Surrey, J., & Baldwin, L. (1992). "Measuring perceived mutuality in close relationships: Validation of the mutual psychological development questionnaire." *Journal of Family Psychology, 6*(1), 36–48.

Geva, E., Barsky, A., & Westernoff, F. (2000). "Developing a framework for interprofessional and diversity informed practice.". In E. Geva, A. Barsky, & F. Westernoff (Eds.), *Interprofessional practice with diverse populations: Cases in point.* (pp. 1–28) Westport, CN: Auburn House.

Gibson, D. M. (2010). "Advocacy counseling: Being an effective agent of change for clients." In B. T. Erford (Ed.), *Orientation to the counseling profession: Advocacy, ethics, and essential professional foundations* (pp. 340–358). Boston, MA: Pearson Education.

Giddings, M. M., Vodde, R., & Cleveland, P. (2003). "Examining student-field instructor problems in practicum: Beyond student satisfaction measures." *The Clinical Supervisor, 22*(2), 191–214.

Ginsberg, H., (2005). "Social work in rural communities." *International Social Work, 43,* 337–349.

Goldberg, D. T. (Ed.) (1994). *Multiculturalism: A critical reader.* Malden, MA: Blackwell.

Goldstein, H. (2001). *Experiential learning: A foundation for social work education and practice.* Alexandria, VA: Council on Social Work Education.

Goodman, H. (2001) "In-Depth Interviews." In Bruce A. Thyer (Ed.) *The Handbook of Social Work Research Methods* (pp. 309–320). Thousand Oaks, CA: Sage.

Government of Canada (2008, June 11). Statement of apology to former students of Indian Residential Schools (Speech by Prime Minister Stephen Harper). Ottawa, ON. Retrieved from Indian and Northern Affairs Canada website: **www.ainc-inac.gc.ca/ai/ rqpi/apo/index-eng.asp**.

Graveline, F. J. (1998). *Circle works: Transforming eurocentric consciousness.* Winnipeg, MB: Fernwood Publishing.

Green, R., Gregory, R., & Mason, R. (2006). "Professional distance and social work: Stretching the elastic?" *Australian Social Work, 59,* 449–461.

Greene, S., Ahluwalia, A., Watson, J., Tucker, R., Rourke, S. B., Koornstra, J., … Byers, S. (2009). "Between scepticism and empowerment: The experiences of peer research assistants in HIV/AIDS, housing and homelessness community-based research." *International Journal of Social Research Methodology, 12*(4), 361–373.

Haig-Brown, C. (1998). *Resistance and renewal: Surviving the Indian residential school.* Vancouver, BC: Arsenal Pulp Press.

Hardiman, R., Jackson, B., & Griffin, P. (2007). "Conceptual foundations for social justice education." In M. Adams, L. A. Bell, & Griffin, P. (Eds.), *Teaching for diversity and social justice* (2nd ed., pp. 35–66). New York, NY: Routledge.

Hardina, D. (2003) "Linking citizen participation to empowerment practice: A historical overview." *Journal of Community Practice, 11*(4), 11–38.

Hart, M. (2002). Seeking mino-pimatisiwin: An Aboriginal approach to helping. Halifax, NS: Fernwood Publishing.

Hart, M. A. (2001). "An Aboriginal approach to social work practice." In T. Heinonen & L. Spearman (Eds.), *Social work practice: Problem solving and beyond* (pp. 231–256). Toronto, ON: Irwin.

Hawkins, L., Fook, J., & R. Martin (2001). "Social workers' use of the language of social justice." *British Journal of Social Work, 31,* 1–13.

Hawthorn, H. B. (1969). *A survey of the contemporary Indians of Canada: Economic, political, educational needs and policies.* (Vol. II). Indian Affairs Branch. Ottawa, ON. Retrieved from **www.collectionscanada. gc.ca/webarchives/20071126042509/http://www.ain c-inac.gc.ca/pr/pub/srvy/sci3_e.pdf**.

Haynes, K. S., & Mickelson, J. S. (2006). *Affecting change: Social workers in the political arena* (6th ed.). Boston, MA: Pearson Education.

Hays, D. G., & Gray, G. M. (2010). "Multicultural counseling." In B. T. Erford (Ed.), *Orientation to the* counseling profession: *Advocacy, ethics, and essential professional foundations* (pp. 163–192). Boston, MA: Pearson Education.

Healy, K. (2005). Social work theories in context — Creating frameworks for practice. New York, NY: Palgrave MacMillan.

Healy, L. (2001). *International social work: Professional action in an interdependent world.* New York, NY: Oxford University Press.

Hegar, R. (2008). "Transatlantic transfer in social work: Contributions of three pioneers." *British Journal of Social Work, 38*(4), 716–733.

Heinonen, T., & Spearman, L. (2001). *Social work practice — Problem solving and beyond.* Toronto, ON: Irwin Publishing.

Helin, C. (2006). *Dance with dependency: Indigenous success through self-reliance.* Vancouver, BC: Orca Spirit Publishing & Communications.

Henry, F., & Tator, C. (2010). *The colour of democracy: Racism in Canadian society* (4th ed.). Toronto, ON: Nelson Education.

Heron, B. (2005). "Changes and challenges: Preparing social work students for practicums in today's sub-Saharan African context." *International Social Work, 48*(6): 782–793.

Hind, M., Norman, I., Cooper, S., Gill, E., Hilton, R., Judd, P., & Jones, S.C. (2003). "Interprofessional perceptions of health care students." *Journal of Interprofessional Care, 17*(1), 21–34.

Holman, R. (1991) *Ethics in social research.* Harlow, United Kingdom: Longman.

hooks, b. (1994). Teaching to transgress: Education as the practice of freedom. London, England: Routledge.

Horejsi, C. R., & Garthwait, C. L. (2002). *The social work practicum: A guide and workbook for students* (2nd ed.). Boston, MA: Allyn and Bacon.

Hornby, S., & Atkins, J. (2000). *Collaborative dare: Interprofessional, interagency and interpersonal* (2nd ed.). Malden, MA: Blackwell Science.

Howe, D. (1994). "Modernity, postmodernity and social work." *British Journal of Social Work 24,* 513–532.

Hyde, C. A. & Meyer, M. (2004). "A collaborative approach to service, learning and scholarship: A community-based research course." *Journal of Community Practice 12*(1/2), 71–88.

Ife, J. (2000, July 31). "Local and global practice: relocating social work as a human rights profession in the new global order." IFSW/IASSW Biennial Conference, Montreal.

Ife, J. (2005). "What is critical social work today?" In S. Hicks, J. Fook, & R. Pozzuto (Eds.), *Social work a critical turn* (pp. 3–8). Toronto, ON: Thompson Educational Publishing.

Ife, J., & Tesoriero, F. (2006). *Community development* (3rd ed.). French Forest, Australia: Pearson Education.

Ikiugu, M. N., & Rosso, H. M. (2003). "Facilitating professional identity in occupational thereapy students." *Occupational Therapy International, 10*(3), 206–225.

Indian Residential Schools Survivors Society (n.d.). *The Roman Catholic Church ran more than 70 percent of the 130 Indian residential schools in Canada.* Author. Retrieved from **www.irsss.ca/history.html**.

Johnston, P. (1983). *Native children and the child welfare system.* Toronto, ON: James Lorimer in association with the Canadian Council on Social Development.

Jones, C. (2000). *The impacts of racism on health.* Department of Health and Social Behavior.

Jordan, J. (1986). "The meaning of mutuality." *Work in Progress, 23*(1), 1–11.

Kadushin, A. E. (1991). "Introduction." In D. Schneck, B. Grossman, & U. Glassman (Eds.), *Field education in social work: Contemporary issues and trends* (pp. 11–12). Dubuque, IA: Kendall/Hunt.

Kadushin, A., & Harkness, D. (2002). *Supervision in social work* (4th ed.). New York, NY: Columbia University Press.

Kaiser, R., (2002). "Fixing identity by denying uniqueness: An analysis of professional identity in medicine." *Journal of Medical Humanities, 23*(2), 95–105.

Kaiser, T. (1997). *Supervisory relationships: Exploring the human element.* Pacific Grove, CA: Brooks/Cole Publishing Company.

Karban, K., & Smith, S. (2009). "Developing Critical Reflection Within an Interprofessional Learning Programme." In H. Bradbury, N. Frost, S. Kilminster, & M. Zukas (Eds.), *Beyond reflective practice: New approaches to professional lifelong learning.* Routledge, London: Springer Publishing.

Kettner, P., Daley, J., & Nichols, A. (1985). *Initiating change in organizations and communities.* Monterey, CA: Brooks/Cole.

Kimmelman, J. E. C. (1985). No quiet place: Review committee on Indian and Métis adoption and placements. MB: Manitoba Community Services.

King, N., & Ross, A. (2003). "Professional identities and interprofessional relations: Evaluation of collaborative community schemes." *Social Work in Health Care, 38*(2), 51–71.

Kitchin, R. M. (1994). "Cognitive maps: What are they and why study them?" *Journal of Environmental Psychology 14,* 1–19.

Kivel, P. (2007). "What does an ally do?" In M. L. Andersen & P. C. Collins (Eds.), *Race, Class, & Gender: An Anthology* (6th ed., pp. 550–557). Belmont, CA: Thomson Wadsworth.

Knox, K., & Roberts, A. (2001). "The crisis intervention model." In P. Lehmann & N. Coady (Eds.), *Theoretical perspectives for direct social work practice* (pp. 183–202). New York, NY: Springer Publishing.

Kohn, L. T., Corrigan, J. M., & Donaldson, M.S. (2000). *To err is human: Building a better health system.* Washington D.C.: National Academy Press.

Kolb, D. A. (1984). Experiential learning: Experience as the source of learning and development. Englewood Cliffs, NJ: Prentice-Hall.

Kreitzer, L. (2005). "Indigenization of social work education and practice: A participatory action research project in Ghana (Dissertation abstracts)." *The Humanities and Social Sciences, 65*(12), pp. iii–iv.

Kyril, M. B. (1988). "Towards the emergence of professional identity." *Journal of Counselling and Development, 67,* 121.

Lager, P. B., & Robbins, V. C. (2004). "Field education: Exploring the future, expanding the vision." *Journal of Social Work Education, 40*(1), 3–11.

Lam, C. M., Wong, H., & Fong Leung, T. T. (2007). "An unfinished journey to reflexivity: Social work students' narratives of their placement experiences." *British Journal of Social Work, 37*(1), 91–105.

Lamote, C., & Engels, N. (2010). "The development of student teachers' professional identity." *European Journal of Teacher Education, 33*(1), 3–18.

Larson, G. (2008). "Anti-oppressive practice in mental health." *Journal of Progressive Human Services, 19*(1), 39–54.

Lawrence, B. (2004). "Real" Indians and others: Mixed-blood urban native peoples and indigenous nationhood. Vancouver, BC: UBC Press.

Lazar, A., & Mosek, A. (1993). "The influence of the field instructor-student relationship on evaluations of students' practice." *The Clinical Supervisor, 11*(1), 111–120.

Lee, C. C., Burnhill, D. A., Butler, A. L., Hipolito-Delgado, C. P., Humphrey, M., Mũnoz, O., & Shin, H. (2009). *Elements of culture in counseling.* Upper Saddle River, NJ: Pearson Education.

Lehmann, P., & Coady, N. (Eds.). (2001). *Theoretical perspectives for direct social work practice.* New York, NY: Springer Publishing Company.

Levitt, D. H., & Bray, A. (2010). "Theories of counseling." In B. T. Erford (Ed.). *Orientation to the counseling profession: Advocacy, ethics, and essential professional foundations* (pp. 95–123). Boston, MA: Pearson Education.

Lewis, I., & Bolzan, N. (2007). "Social work with a twist: Interweaving practice knowledge, student experience and academic theory." *Australian Social Work, 60*(2), 136–146.

Litvack, A. (2003). *Critical issues in field education: Developing field instructor competence* (Educational videotape and teaching guide). Toronto, ON: University of Toronto Press.

Litvack, A., Bogo, M., & Mishna, F. (in press). "Understanding the emotional impact of field experiences on MSW students." *Journal of Social Work Education.*

Loxley, A. (1997) *Collaboration in health and welfare: Working with difference.* London, England: Jessica Kingsley Publications.

Lucas, R. (1971). *Minetown, milltown, railtown.* Toronto, ON: University of Toronto Press.

Lum, D. (2007). "Social context." In D. Lum (Ed.), *Culturally competent practice: A framework for understanding diverse groups and justice issues* (3rd ed., pp. 42–72). Belmont, CA: Thomson Brooks/Cole.

Lundy, C. (2004). Social work and social justice: A structural approach to practice. Peterborough, ON: Broadview Press.

Lyons, K., Manion, K., & Carlsen, M. (2006). International perspectives on social work: Global conditions and local practice. New York, NY: Palgrave Macmillan.

McCloskey, G., & Andreae, D. (2010). "Bearing witness: A social worker's reflections on the Human Rights Tribunal hearing on the under-funding of child welfare services for First Nations children on reserves." *BC Association of Social Workers Perspectives, 32*(3), 18–19, 21.

McIsaac, R. L. (2006). "Anishnawbemowin dash bimadiziwin." In P. Tagore (Ed.), *In our own voices: Learning and teaching toward decolonization* (pp. 117–120). Winnipeg, MB: Larkuma.

McKenzi, B., & Seidl, E.. (1995). "Child welfare standards in First Nations." In J. Hudson & B. Galaway (Eds.), *Child welfare in Canada: Research and policy implications* (pp. 54–65). Toronto, ON: Thomson Educational Press.

Maidment, J. (2000). "Methods used to teach social work students in the field: a research report from New Zealand." *Social Work Education, 19*(2), 145–154.

Marino, P., Simoni, J. M., & Silverstein, L. B. (2007). "Peer support to promote medication adherence among people living with HIV/AIDS: The benefits to peers." *Social Work in Health Care, 45*(1), 67–80.

Martin, B. (2007). "Activism, social and political." *Encyclopedia of Activism and Social Justice.* Retrieved from Sage Reference Online website: **www.sage-ereference.com.ezproxy.une.edu.au/activism/ Article_n12.html**.

McKay, S. (1999). "Postmodernism, social well-being, and the mainstream/progressive debate." In F. Turner (Ed.), *Social work practice: A Canadian perspective* (pp. 10–20). Scarborough, ON: Prentice Hall Allyn and Bacon Canada.

McKenzie, B., & Wharf, B. (2010). *Connecting policy to practice in the human services* (3rd ed.). Toronto, ON: Oxford University Press.

Merriam, S. B. (2004). "The role of cognitive development in Mezirow's Transformational Learning Theory." *Adult Education Quarterly, 55*(1), 60–68.

Merriam, S. B., Caffarella, R. S., & Baumgartner. (2006). *Learning in adulthood: A comprehensive guide* (3rd ed.). San Francisco, CA: Jossey-Bass.

Merrill Education (2005). *A guide to ethical conduct for helping professionals.* Upper Saddle River, NJ: Pearson/Merrill Prentice Hall.

Midgley, J. (1981). Professional imperialism: Social work in the third world. London, England: Heinemann.

Midgley, J. (2001). "Issues in international social work: Resolving critical debates in the profession." *Journal of Social Work, 1*(1), 21–35.

Miller, C., Freeman, M., & Ross, N. (2001). Interprofessional practice in health and social care: Challenging the shared learning agenda. London, England: Arnold.

Miller, J. R. (1997). *Shingwauk's vision: A history of native residential schools.* Toronto, ON: University of Toronto Press.

Milloy, J. (1999). *A National Crime: The Canadian government and the residential school system 1879–1986.* Winnipeg, MB: University of Manitoba Press.

Mischler, E. G. (1986). *Research interviewing: context and narrative.* Cambridge, MA: Harvard University Press.

Moline, M. E., Williams, G. T., & Austin, K. M. (1998). *Documenting psychotherapy: Essentials for mental health practitioners.* Thousand Oaks, CA: Sage

Moon, J. A. (2004). A handbook of reflective and experiential learning: Theory and practice. New York, NY: Routledge Falmer.

Morgan, D. L. (1997). *Focus groups as qualitative research* (2nd ed.). London, England: Sage.

Mullaly, B. (1997) *Structural social work: Ideology, theory, and practice.* Toronto, ON: Oxford University Press.

Mullaly, B. (2007). *The new structural social work* (3rd ed.) Don Mills, ON: Oxford University Press.

Munson, C. (2002). *Handbook of clinical social work supervision.* (3rd ed.). Binghamton, NY: The Hawthorn Press.

Murphy, B. C., & Dillon, C. (2008). *Interviewing in action in a multicultural world* (3rd ed.). Belmont, CA: Thompson Brooks/Cole.

National Aboriginal Health Organization (NAHO). (2006). "Cultural safety fact sheet." Retrieved from **www.naho.ca/english**.

National Association of Social Workers. (2003). "Supervision and the clinical social worker." *Clinical social work: Practice update, 3*(2), 1–5. Retrieved from **www.naswdc.org/practice/clinical/csw0703b.pdf**.

Netting, F. E., Knetter, P., & McMurtry, S. L. (1998). *Macro social work practice* (2nd ed.). New York, NY: Longman.

Neukrug, E. S. (2007). *The world of the counselor: An introduction to the counseling profession* (3rd ed.). Belmont, CA: Brooks/Cole-Thomson Learning.

Noble, C. (2001). "Researching field practice in social work education: Integration of theory and practice through the use of narratives." *Journal of Social Work, 1*(3), 347–360.

Ohlen, J., & Segesten, K. (1998). "The professional identity of the nurse: Concept analysis and development." *Journal of Advanced Nursing, 28*(4), 720–727.

Oko, J. (2008). *Understanding and using theory in social work.* Exeter, England: Learning Matters.

Olsen, S., Morris, R., & Sam, A. (2001). *No time to say goodbye: Children's stories of Kuper Island Residential School.* Victoria, BC: Sono Nis Press.

Ontario Human Rights Commission. (2008). *Annual Report 2007/2008.* Retrieved from **www.ohrc.on.ca/en/resources/annualreports/ar0708?page=aren-Case.html**.

Palfrey, J., & Gasser, U. (2008). Born digital: Understanding the first generation of digital natives. New York, NY: Basic Books.

Palloff, R. M., & Pratt, K. (2003). The virtual student: A profile and guide to working with online learners. San Francisco, CA: Jossey-Bass.

Paredes, M., Mi Choi, K., Dipal, M., Edwards-Joseph, A., Ermakoy, N., Gouveia, A., … Benshoff, J. (2008). *International Journal for the Advancement of Counselling, 30*(3), 155–166.

Parsons, J., & Durst, D. (1992). "Learning contracts: Misunderstood and underutilized." *The Clinical Supervisor, 10*(1), 145–156.

Partners for Youth. "Projects." Author. Retrieved from **www.partnersforyouth.ca/projects.html**.

Parton, N. (2000) "Some thoughts on the relationship between theory and practice in and for social work." *British Journal of Social Work 30,* 449–463.

Patton, M. Q. (1990). *Qualitative evaluation and research methods* (2nd ed.). Newbury Park, CA: Sage Publications.

Paul, S., & Peterson, C.Q. (2001). "Interprofessional collaboration: Issues for practice and research." *Occupational Therapy, 15*(3/4), 1–12.

Payne, M. (2005). *Modern social work theory* (3rd ed.) Chicago, IL: Lyceum Book.

Pedersen, P. (2000). *A handbook for developing multicultural awareness* (3rd ed.). Alexandria, VA: American Counseling Association.

Pedersen, P. B. (2001). "Multiculturalism and the paradigm shift in counselling: Controversies and alternative futures." *Canadian Journal of Counselling, 35*(1), 15–25.

Pendry, L. F., Driscoll, D. M., & Field, S. C. T. (2007). "Diversity training: Putting theory into practice." *Journal of Occupational and Organizational Psychology, 80*(1), 27–50.

Phipps, R., & Merisotis, J. (1999). What's the difference? A review of contemporary research on the effectiveness of distance learning in higher education. Washington, D.C.: Institute for Higher Education Policy.

Power, R., & Bogo, M. (2002). "Educating field instructors and students to deal with challenges in their teaching relationships." *The Clinical Supervisor, 21*(1), 39–58.

Price N. L., & Hawkins, K. (2002) "Researching sexual and reproductive behaviour: A peer ethnographic approach." *Social Science & Medicine, 55,* 1327–1338.

Rae, A., & Nicholas-Wolosuk, W. (2003). *Changing agency policy: An incremental approach.* Boston, MA: Pearson.

Razack, N. (2002a). "Diversity and difference in the field education encounter: Racial minority students in the practicum." *Social Work Education, 20,* 219–228.

Razack, N. (2002b). Transforming the field: Antiracist and anti-oppressive perspectives for the human services practicum. Halifax, NS: Fernwood Publishers.

Reading, J. (2009). The crisis of chronic disease among the aboriginal peoples: A challenge for public health, population health and social policy. Victoria, BC: University of Victoria Centre for Aboriginal Health and Research.

Regehr, C., & Kanani, K. (2006). *Essential law for social work practice in Canada.* Don Mills, ON: Oxford University Press.

Richardson, C., & Seaborn, D. L. (2009). "Beyond audacity and aplomb: Understanding the Métis in social work practice." In R. Sinclair, M. A. Hart, & Brugere, G. (Eds.), *Wicihitowin: Aboriginal social work in Canada* (pp. 114–132). Black Point, MB: Fernwood Publishing.

Rogers, G., & McDonald, P. L. (1995). "Expedience over education: Teaching methods used by field instructors." *The Clinical Supervisor, 13*(2), 41–65.

Rogowski, S. (2008). "Social work with children and families: Towards a radical/critical practice." *Practice, 20*(1), 17–28.

Rothman, J. (1970). "Three models of community organization practice." In F. Cox, J. Erlich, J. Rothman, & J. Tropman (Eds.), *Strategies of community organization* (pp. 25–45). Itasca, IL: F.E. Peacock Publishers.

Royse, D. D. (2010). Field instruction: A guide for social work students. Boston, MA: Allyn & Bacon.

Saleebey, D. (Ed.). (1997). *The strengths perspective in social work practice* (2nd ed.). New York, NY: Longman.

Salhani, D., & Charles, G. (2007). "The dynamics of an interprofessional team: The interplay of child and youth care with other professions within a residential treatment milieu." *Relational Child and Youth Care Practice, 20*(4), 12–20.

Samovar, L. A., Porter, R. E., & McDaniel, E. R. (2010). *Communication between cultures* (7th ed.). Boston, MA: Wadsworth Publishing.

Saulis, M. (2003). "Program and policy development from a holistic Aboriginal perspective." In A. Westhues (Ed.), *Canadian social policy* (pp. 285–300). Waterloo, ON: Wilfrid Laurier University Press.

Schafft. K., & Greenwood, D. J. (2003). "Promises and dilemmas of participation: Action research, search conference methodology, and community development." *Journal of the Community Development Society, 34*(1), 18–35.

Schmidt, G. (2000), "Remote northern communities: Implications for social work practice." *International Social Work, 43,* 337–349.

Schmitz, C. L., Stakeman, C., & Sisneros, J. (2001). "Educating professionals for practice in a multicultural society: Understanding oppression and valuing diversity." *Families in Society, 82*(6), 612–622.

Schnarch, B. (2004). "Ownership, control, access, and possession (OCAP) or Self-Schriver, J. M. (2001)." *Human behavior and the social environment: Shifting paradigms in essential knowledge for social work practice.* Boston, MA: Allyn & Bacon.

Schön, D. (1987). *Educating the reflective practitioner.* San Francisco, CA: Jossey-Bass.

Shebib, B. (2007*). Choices: Interviewing and Counseling Skills for Canadians* (3rd ed.). Toronto, ON: Prentice-Hall.

Shore, N., & Richards, E. (2007). "Promoting ethical research." *Journal of Social Work Values and Ethics, 4*(3). Retrieved from **www.socialworker.com/jswve**.

*A Short History of Pan-Indianism.* (1997). Retrieved from the Hartford Web Publishing website: **www.hartford-hwp.com/archives/41/119.html**.

Shragge, E. (2003). Activism and social change: Lessons for community and local organizing. Peterborough, ON: Broadview.

Shulman, L. (1993). *Interactional supervision.* Washington, D.C.: NASW Press.

Shulman, L. S. (2005). "Signature pedagogies in the professions." *Daedalus, 134*(3), 52–59.

Sinclair, R. (2006). *Thunderbird nesting circle.* Paper presented at the Annual Program Meeting Canadian Association of Social Work Education, Toronto, Ontario.

Sinclair, R. (2009). "Identity or racism? Aboriginal transracal adoption." In R. Sinclair, M. A. Hart, & G. Brugere (Eds.), *Wicihitowin: Aboriginal social work in Canada* (pp. 89–113). Black Point, MB: Fernwood Publishing.

Sinclair, R., Hart, M. A., & Bruyere, G. (Eds.). (2009). *Wicihitowin: Aboriginal social work in Canada.* Black Point, MB: Fernwood Publishing.

Sisneros, J., Stakeman, C., Joyner, M. C., & Schmitz, C. L. (2008). *Critical multicultural social work.* Chicago, IL: Lyceum Books.

Smith, B., & Tudor, K. (2003). "Oppression and pedagogy: Anti-oppressive practice in the education of therapists." In C. Lago & B. Smith (Eds.), *Anti-discriminatory counselling practice* (pp. 135–150). London, England: Sage Publications.

Social Work Task Force (2010). *Building a safe and confident future: Implementing the recommendations of the social work task force.* London, England: HM Government.

Sockman, B. R., & Sharma, P. (2007). "Struggling towards a transformative model of instruction: It's not so easy." *Teaching and Education, 24,* 1070–1082.

Stalker, C. (2001). "Attachment theory." In P. Lehmann & N. Coady (Eds.), *Theoretical perspectives for direct social work practice* (pp. 109–127). New York, NY: Springer Publishing Company.

Statistics Canada. Retrieved from **www.statcan.gc.ca**.

Stevenson, O. (2004). "The future of social work." In M. Lymberry & S. Butler, (Eds.), *Social work ideals & practice realities* (pp. 225–247). New York, NY: Palgrave.

Stoltenberg, C. D. (2005). "Enhancing professional competence through developmental approaches to supervision." *American Psychologist, 60*(8), 857–864.

Stoltenberg, C. D., McNeill, B. W., & Delworth, U. (1998). *IDM supervision: An integrated developmental model for supervising counselors and therapists*. San Francisco, CA: Jossey-Bass.

Stout, M. D., & Kipling, G. (2003). *Aboriginal people, resilience and the residential school legacy*. Ottawa, ON: Aboriginal Healing Foundation.

Strozier, A. L., Barnett-Queen, T., & Bennett, C. K. (2000). "Supervision: Critical process and outcome variables." *The Clinical Supervisor, 19*(1), 21–39.

Sun, A. (1999). "Issues BSW interns experience in their first semester's practicum." *The Clinical Supervisor, 18*(1), 105–123.

Tagore, P. (Ed.). (2006). Our own voices: Learning and teaching toward decolonization. Winnipeg, MB: Larkuma.

Tanovich, D. M. (2009). "What is it?" In M. Wallis & A. Fleras (Eds.), *The politics of race in Canada: Readings in historical perspectives, contemporary realities, and future possibilities* (pp. 155–165). Don Mills, ON: Oxford University Press.

Tator, C., & Henry, F. (2006). *Racial profiling in Canada*. Toronto, ON: University of Toronto Press.

Teasley, M. L. (2005). "Perceived levels of cultural competence through social work education and professional development for urban school social workers." *Journal of Social Work Education, 41*(1), 85–98.

Thompson, N. (2006). *Anti-discriminatory practice* (4th ed.). Basingstoke: Palgrave Macmillan.

Tosey, P. (2002). "Experiential methods of teaching and learning." In P. Jarvis (Ed.), *The theory and practice of teaching* (pp. 108–122). London, England: Kogan Page.

Tsui, M. (2005). *Social work supervision: Contexts and concepts*. Thousand Oaks, CA: Sage Publications.

United Nations Development Programme. (1997). *Human development report*. New York, NY: Author.

United Nations. (1948). "Convention on the prevention and punishment of the crime of genocide." Author. Retrieved from the Human Rights Web website: **www.hrweb.org/legal/genocide.htm**.

University of British Columbia (n.d.). "School of Social Work." Retrieved from **www.socialwork.ubc.ca/program-information/bsw/field-education-year-3.html**.

University of Michigan Edward Ginsberg Center for Community Service and Learning. Retrieved from **http://quod.lib.umich.edu/m/mjcsl**.

University of Victoria. (2009). "Cultural safety: Module 1 people's experience of colonization." Retrieved from **http://web2.uvcs.uvic.ca/courses/csafety/mod1/glossary.htm#csa**.

University of Washington, Public Health and Community Medicine (n.d.). "Community-based research principles." Retrieved from **http://sphcm.washington.edu/research/community.asp**.

Urbanowski, M., & Dwyer, M. (1988). *Learning through field instruction: A guide for teachers and students*. Milwaukee, WI: Family Service Association.

Wackerhausen, S. (2009). "Collaboration, professional identity and reflection across boundaries." *Journal of Interprofessional Care, 23*(5), 455–473.

Waldram, J. B. (1997). The way of the pipe: Aboriginal spirituality and symbolic healing in Canadian prisons. Peterborough, ON: Broadview Press.

Walmsley, C. (2005). *Protecting Aboriginal children*. Vancouver, BC: UBC Press.

Walter, C. L. (1997). "Community building practice: A conceptual framework." In M. Minkler (Ed.), *Community Organizing and Community Building for Health.* (pp. 68–88). New Brunswick, NJ: Rutgers University Press.

Walton, R. G., & Abo-EI-Nasr, M. M. (1988). "Indigenization and authentization in terms of social work in Egypt." *International Social Work, 31*(2), 135–144.

Wasserfall, R. R. (1997). "Reflexivity, feminism, and difference." In R. Hertz (Ed.), *Reflexivity and voice.* (pp. 150–169). Thousand Oaks, CA: Sage Publications.

Waterfall, B. (2003). "Native peoples and the social work profession: A critical analysis of colonizing problematics and the development of decolonized thought." In A. Westhues (Ed.), *Canadian social policy: Issues and perspectives* (pp. 50–66). Waterloo, ON: Wilfrid Laurier University Press.

Weaver, H. N. (2005). *Explorations in cultural competence: Journeys to the four directions*. Belmont, CA: Thomson Brook/Cole.

Wehbi, S. (2009). "Deconstructing motivations: Challenging international social work placements." *International Social Work, 52* (1), 48–59.

Wellington, S., & Spence. B. (2001). *Be your own mentor: Strategies from top women on the secrets of success*. New York, NY: Random House.

West, L. (2009). "Really reflexive practice: Autobiographical research and struggles for a critical reflexivity." In H. Bradbury, N. Frost, S. Kilminster, & M. Zukas (Eds.), *Beyond reflective practice: New approaches to professional lifelong learning*. Routledge.

Wharf, B. (Ed.). (2009). *Community work approaches to child welfare*. Toronto, ON: University of Toronto Press.

White, S. (2001). "Auto-ethnography as reflexive enquiry: The research act as self-surveillance." In I. Shaw & N. Gould (Eds.), *Qualitative research and social work.* (pp. 100–115). London, England: Sage Publications.

Whitley, B. E., & Kite, M. E. (2010). *The psychology of prejudice and discrimination* (2nd ed.). Belmont, CA: Wadsworth.

Williams, C. C. (2006). "The epistemology of cultural competence." *Families in Society, 87*(2), 209–220.

Willkinson, K. P. (1991). *The community in rural america.* New York, NY: Greenwood.

Wilson, A., & Beresford, P. (2000). "Anti-oppressive practice: Emancipation or appropriation?" *British Journal of Social Work, 30*(5), 553–573.

Wood, J., Zeffane, R., Fromholtz, M., Wiesner, R., & Creed, A. (2010). *Organisational behaviour: Core concepts and applications* (2nd ed.). Milton, Australia: Wiley & Sons.

Yellow Bird, M. (2001). "Critical values in First Nations peoples." In R. Fong & S. Furuto (Eds.), *Culturally competent practice: Skills, interventions, and evaluations* (pp. 61–74). White Plains, NY: Longman Press.

Yogis, J. A., & Cotter, C. (2009). *Canadian law dictionary* (6th ed.). Hauppauge, NY: Barrons.

York, G. (1999). *The dispossessed: Life and death in native Canada.* Toronto, ON: McArthur & Company Publishing.

York, R. O., Denton, R. T., & Moran, J. R. (1989). "Rural and urban social work practice: Is there a difference?" *Social Casework, 70*(4), 201–209.

Younggren, J., & Gottlieb, M. C. (2004). "Managing risk when contemplating multiple relationships." *Professional Psychology: Research and Practice, 35*(3), 255–260.

Zapf, M. K. (1985). *Rural social work and its application to the Canadian North as a practice setting* (Working papers on Social Welfare in Canada Publications Series, #15). Toronto, ON: University of Toronto Faculty of Social Work.

Zapf, M. K. (1993). :Remote practice and culture shock: Social workers moving to isolated northern regions." *Social Work, 38*(6), 694–704.

Zapf, M. K. (2009). Social work and the environment: Understanding people and place. Toronto, ON: Canadian Scholars' Press.

Zhao, Y., Lei, J., Yan, B., Lai, C., & Tan, H. S. (2005). "What makes the difference? A practical analysis of research on the effectiveness of distance education." *Teachers College Record, 107,* 1836–1884.

# Index

# C

CAIPE. *See* Centre for the Advancement of Interprofessional Education (CAIPE)
Canadian Association for Social Work Education (CASWE), 4
  Code of Ethics, 246
  educational policy, 4
Canadian Association of Social Workers (CASW), 43, 140
  Code of Ethics of, 164, 172
Canadian Constitution Act (1982), 139
Canadian educational policy
  competencies, 5
  feature of, 4
Canadian Holocaust, 138
Canadian International Development Agency (CIDA), 187
Canadian legal system. *See* Legal system
Canadian Research Institute for the Advancement of Women, 87
Canadian Welfare Council (CWC), 140
Capacity building, in community-based research, 118–119
CASW. *See* Canadian Association of Social Workers (CASW)
CASW Code of Ethics, 49–50
CASWE. *See* Canadian Association for Social Work Education (CASWE)
Catalysts, 166
Centre for the Advancement of Interprofessional Education (CAIPE), 260
Change process, reflective practice and, 80
*Changing Agency Policy: An Incremental Approach,* 99
Checklist for Behaving Professionally, 33
Child protection legislation, 41
CIDA. *See* Canadian International Development Agency (CIDA)
Citizen participation, 112
Clarification probes, 125
Clark, Natalie, 150
Clients, student status and, 43
Climate, rural practice and, 236
Clinician, 245
CMC. *See* Computer-mediated communication (CMC)
Code of Ethics of CASW, 164, 172, 246
Codes of ethics, 45–46, 164
  purposes of, 46

Cognitive maps, 100
Collaboration, definition of, 244
Collaborative practice skills, 244–245
Colonization, 138–139
Common sense approach, 75
Communication
  asynchronous, in distance education, 210, 213, 220
  with field instructors, 219–221
  international practicum and, 201–202
  synchronous, in distance education, 210
Community-based research, 115–122. *See also* Research
  capacity building in, 118–119
  challenges of, 118–119
  collaborative approaches of, 111–112
  PRAs and, 117–118
  principles of, 117
  role of researcher in, 129–130
  students as researchers in, 119–120
  *vs.* traditional academic research, 116
Community development theories, 69–70
Community engagement, 243
Community organizer, 245
Community participation, 112
Computer-mediated communication (CMC), 55
Conferences, professional practice and, 279
Confidentiality, 49–52
  definition of, 246
  duty to warn and protect, 52
  informed consent, 52–53
  in research, 126–127
  rural field placements and, 246
Consent in research, 126
Conservation Council of New Brunswick, 107
Consultation, self-care and, 92
Contracts, 22
Control, research and, 128
Conventions, international, 189
Cost, international practicum and, 195–196
Council on Social Work Education (CSWE), 5
  research and, 112–113
Counter-storytelling, 85–86
Cover letter, 272
Crisis intervention theory, 66. *See also* Practice theories
Critical assessment, AOP and, 169
Critical reflection, and reflexivity, 82–83. *See also* Reflexive practice

Critical self-reflection, AOP and, 169
Critical theories, 67–68
Critical thinking, 59–60
CSWE. *See* Council on Social Work Education
     (CSWE)
Cultural practices, international
     practicum and, 204
Cultural safety, 150–151, 173
Culture shock, international practicum and, 199
CWC. *See* Canadian Welfare Council (CWC)

# D

Data collection in qualitative research, 123–125
     interview and, 123–125
Data manager, 245
Decolonization, Aboriginal field
     education, 150, 152–154
Detail-oriented probes, 125
Diagnostic and Statistical Manual of Mental
     Disorders (DSM), 142
"Digital natives," 55
Dion, Stéphane, 144
Discrimination, 166–167
     defined, 53
Dissemination, of research, 130
Distance education
     definition of, 209
     effective, 210–213
     evaluation meetings and, 225–226
     field instructor and. *See* Field instructor,
          distance
     integrative field seminars and, 227–230
     learning agreement and, 225
     online learning communities and, 213,
          228–229
     organizational skills and, 213
     practicum and. *See* Distance practicum
     reasons for, 209
     reflection and, 213
     technologies for, 211–212
     time-management and, 213
     *vs.* face-to-face education, 212
Distance practicum. *See also* Distance education
     administrative requirements for, 218
     communication with field instructors and,
          219–221
     faculty liaison and, 223–224
     field placements and, 215–216

integrative field seminars and, 227–230
management of, 218–224
placements and, 215–217
setting up, 214–218
supervision and, problems with, 222–223
Diversity
     Code of Ethics, social work, 164
     definition of, 163–164
     within diversity, 162
     practice. *See* Practice of diversity
     sensitivity to, 172–173
     theory, 162
     theory *vs.* practice, 161–163
Documentation, 54–55
     job search, 269–274
Doone St. Community Center storefront,
     107–108
Dress, for interviews, 26
Drop-in centres, 20
DSM. *See* Diagnostic and Statistical Manual of
     Mental Disorders (DSM)
Dual relationships, 248–249
Duty to warn and protect, 52

# E

Ecological systems theory, 66, 67
     adaptations of, 67
     criticizm, 67
Economy, rural practice and, 236
Education
     Indigenous peoples, 137–158
     professional practice and, 280–281
Elaboration probes, 125
Elders, involvement of
     Aboriginal field education and, 152–153
E-learning systems, in distance education, 211
Employment opportunities, 268–269
Empowerment, AOP and, 170
Equity policies, 175–177
Ethical decision making, 46–49
Ethical dilemma, 47
Ethics
     research and, 126–129
     review boards, 127–128
     rural field placements and, 246
Ethics review boards, 127–128
Ethnically sensitive practice, 172–173
Ethnocentrism, 205

Evaluation meetings, distance education and, 225–226
Evaluation of international practica, 205

# F

Face-to-face education, *vs.* distance education, 212
Faculty liaison
    definition of, 223
    working with, distance education, 223–224
Family law, 40
Feedback
    field instructor–student relationship, 10
    observing others and being observed with, 10–11
Feminist theory, 65. *See also* Grand theories
Field coordinator, 23, 24
Field education
    Aboriginal , decolonization of, 150, 152–154
    in Aboriginal agency, 154–158
    activities, 10–11
    components, 5–6
    contextualsocietal factor, defined, 12–13
    effects of, 2
    field instructor–student relationship, 6–10
    history and development, 3–5
    interactive factor, defined, 12
    organizational factor, defined, 12
    overview, 2–3
    psychosocial factor, defined, 12
    purpose, 3
    research, principles based on, 5–11
    as signature pedagogy of social work, 5
    terminological description, 3
Field education seminars, sharing power in, 92–93
Field experience, sharing of
    international practicum and, 202
Field instruction, 3
Field instructor, distance
    advantages to, 219–220
    challenges of, 220
    communication with, 219–221
    definition of, 219
    relationship with students, 219
Field instructor–student relationship
    balance between structure and autonomy, 7–10

developmental stage models, 8
    feedback, 10
    supportive field instruction, 6–7
Field placement, 23–37
    interview, preparation, 24–28
    professional behavior, 31–34
    résumé, 24–25
    social action, 101–105
    starting, 28–30
    suggesions ensuring preparation for, 29–30
    tools for, 36–37
Field supervision, 201
    international practicum and, 201
"Field work," 3
Fife House, 130
Focus groups, research and, 123
Formal theory, 63
"Foster care drift," 146

# G

Generalist model, definition of, 239
Generalist practitioner, rural communities and, 239–240
Genocide, 143–144
    definition of, 143–144
Gilchrist, Lauri, Dr., 146
Ginsberg, Leon, 235
Globalization, 183–184
Grand theories, 65–66
Groups online, integrative field seminars and, 230
Group work theories, 70

# H

Harassment, 53
Harper, Stephen, 144
Hawthorn Report, 142
Health, international practicum and, 196–199
Hegemony, 185–186
Homeless Outreach Program (HOP), 130–131
HOP. *See* Homeless Outreach Program (HOP)
Humanitarianism, 61
Human rights, 40
Human services
    in diversity practice, 165–166
    with indigenous peoples, 139–141
    students, 141, 146, 151
Hungry for Change, 106

# I

IFSW. *See* International Federation of Social Workers (IFSW)
Immigrants, 40
Indian Act, 138, 139
    Indians, definition of, 143
    Residential School Project, 142
    social work and human services, 140
Indian Affairs Duncan Campbell Scott, 140
Indian Residential Schools (IRS), 140
    crimes against First Nations children, 143
Indians, 138, 139
    definition of, 143
Indigenization, 186
Indigenize, 186
Indigenous people. *See also* Aboriginal peoples
    education, 137–158
    human services with, history of, 139–141
    knowledge, importance of, 147–148
    perspective into practice, integration of, 150
    practices, integration of, 148–149
    residential schools and, 142–145
    social work with, history of, 139–141
Indigenous stories, 148
Indigenous students
    Aboriginal agencies, support of, 156–158
    identity, 156–157
    learning opportunities, 157–158
    obligations and responsibilities, 157
    respect for, 157
Indigenous theories, 65
Individual change theories, 67
Informal theory, 63
Informed consent, 52–53
Initiators, 166
Instant messaging, in distance education, 211
Integration of theory and practice (ITP) loop model, 11–15
    exercises, 13–15
    linkage phase, 12, 13
    phase of taking action, 13
    reflections, 12, 13, 80–81
    retrieval and recall, 12, 13
Integrative field seminars
    distance education and, 227–230
    groups online and, 230
    online learning communities and, 228–229
    technologies and, 227
Interdisciplinary practice, definition of, 258

International Federation of Social Workers (IFSW), 189
International field partnerships, international practicum and, 194
International health, international practicum and, 196–199
International Health Certificate, international practicum and, 197
Internationalism, 184–185
International practicum, 186–187
    communication and, 201–202
    cost and, 195–196
    cultural practices and, 204
    culture shock and, 199
    evaluation of, 205
    field experience sharing and, 202
    field supervision and, 201
    health and, 196–199
    learning objectives of, 203–205
    memorandum of understanding and, 195
    narrative of, 204
    partnerships and, 194
    personal safety and, 199–200
    planning for, 190–202
    pre-departure orientation and, 196
    risk management and, 195
    sexual harassment and, 200–201
    wellness and, 196–199
Internet phone services, in distance education, 211
Interprofessional competencies, 262–263
Interprofessional practice, 256–263
    barriers to, 256, 257
    benefits of, 259–260
    cause of conflict, 258–259
    definition of, 258
    effective, qualities of, 262–263
    Interprofessional Rural Program of British Columbia (IRPbc) and, 263
    mutuality and, 261–262
    placements and, 257
    reciprocity and, 261, 262
    types of, 258
Interprofessional Rural Program of British Columbia (IRPbc), 263
*Intersectional Feminist Frameworks: An Emerging Vision,* 87
Intersectional framework, and reflexive practice, 87

## N

Narratives, of international practicum, 204
Needs assessments in research, 113–114
    Young Women's Health Group, 114
NGO. *See* Non-governmental organizations (NGO)
Non-governmental organizations (NGO), 101
Non-metropolitan social work, 235
Non-profit agency, 103
Non-urban social work, 235
Non-verbal communication, 124
Northern Canada
    rural practice in, 235–237

## O

Observation, 10–11
OCAP. *See* Ownership, control, access, and possession (OCAP) in research
"The Occasional Evil of Angels," 83
Occupational identity. *See* Professional identity
Online learning, 210
Online learning communities, distance education and, 213, 228–229
Online media, in distance education, 211
Organizational context, theories in, 72
Organizational skills, distance education and, 213
Ownership, control, access, and possession (OCAP) in research, 128–129
Ownership, research and, 128

## P

Participation
    citizen, 112
    community, 112
    definition of, 112
    level of, 112
Partnerships
    AOP and, 170
    international practicum and, 194
Peer research assistants (PRA)
    community-based research and, 117–118
    definition of, 117
Perception, as a learning phase, 101
Personal information disclosure, in interviews, 26
Placements
    distance practicum and, 215–216

interprofessional practice and, 257
    negotiation and, 217
Planning, for international practicum, 190–202
Podcasts, in distance education, 211
Possession, data, research and, 129
Post-colonialism, 185
Postmodern theories, 82
Power, of researcher, 129
PowerPoint presentations, in distance education, 211
Power sharing, with students, 92–93
Practice, defined, 64
Practice-based research, 113
Practice of diversity, 162–163
    human service in, 165–166
    multicultural, 161–177
    social work in, 165–166
Practice theories, 66. *See also* Theories
Practicum, international. *See* International practicum
PRAs. *See* Peer research assistants (PRA)
Praxis, defined, 64
Pre-departure orientation, 196
Pre-research planning, 121–122
    information collection method, 121
    recruitment, 121–122
    target population, identification of, 121
Privilege, defined, 50
Probes
    clarification, 125
    detail-oriented, 125
    elaboration, 125
Problem-solving approaches, 69
Professional associations, membership in professional practice and, 280
Professional identity, 253–255
    definition of, 254
    interactions and, 255
Professional liability. *See* Liability
Professional practice
    conferences and, 279
    education, pursuing, 280–281
    leadership and, 282
    lifelong learning and, 278–282
    mentoring and, 281
    preparation for, 267–282
    professional associations and, membership in, 280
    reading and, 278–279

relationship development and, 281–282
self-awareness and, 276
student to, value shift, 274–277
supervision and, 274–275
training sessions and, 279
values and, 277–278
workshops and, 279
Program evaluation in research, 115
Progressive field agencies, 106–108
Progressive field education
aim of, 97
field placements in, 98
organizational strategies for, 105–106
service learning and, 99–100
social justice, 98
strategies to engage in, 101–106
Progressive field placement. *See* Social action
field placement
Projection, definition of, 220
Purpose, defined, 60

# Q

Qualitative research, 122–125
data collection, 123–125
definition of, 122–123
Quantitative research, 125
surveys and, 125

# R

Racism, 166–167
approach to tackle, 167
Razack, Narda, 90
RCAP. *See* Royal Commission on Aboriginal
Peoples (RCAP)
RCMP. *See* Royal Canadian Mounted Police
(RCMP)
Reading, professional practice and, 278–279
Reciprocity
definition of, 261
interprofessional practice and, 261, 262
Recorded presentations, in distance
education, 211
Record keeping, 44, 54–55
References, in résumé, 271
Reflective journal, 36–37
Reflective practice
and change process, 80
concept, 79–80, 213

distance education and, 213
field education and, 80–81
ITP loop, 12, 13, 80–81
Reflective practitioners, 64–65
Reflexive practice, 81–82
challenges, 88
critical reflection and, 82–83
definition of, 129
instructors of, 88
intersectional framework, 87
journals in, 85, 86
power sharing, 92–93
researcher and, 129
research on, 89–91
in social work, 83–84
tools for, 84–86
Refugees, 40
Relationship development
dual relationships, 248–249
multiple rlationships, 249
professional practice and, 282
rural practice and, 247–249
Remote field placements. *See also* Rural field
placements
benefits of, 237
Research
agency-based research, 112–115
community-based research, 115–122
CSWE and, 112–113
ethical issues of, 126–129
needs assessments in, 113–114
OCAP principles, 128–129
practice-based research, 113
pre-research planning, 121–122. *See also*
Pre-research planning
program evaluation in, 115
qualitative research, 122–125
quantitative research, 125
skill development, 120, 122
Researcher
dissemination, research, 130
KTE strategies and, 129
power of, 129
reflexivity and, 129
role of, 129–130
student as, 119–120
Residential School Project (RSP), 142
goal of, 142
Residential schools, 142–145